Computer Science Workbench

Editor: Tosiyasu L. Kunii

Nadia Magnenat-Thalmann
Daniel Thalmann

Image Synthesis

Theory and Practice

With 223 Figures
80 of them in Color

Springer-Verlag
Tokyo Berlin Heidelberg New York
London Paris

Prof. Dr. NADIA MAGNENAT-THALMANN
Hautes Etudes Commerciales
Université de Montréal
Montréal H3T 1V6 Canada

Prof. Dr. DANIEL THALMANN
Département d'Informatique
et de Recherche Opérationnelle
Université de Montréal
Montréal H3C 3J7 Canada

Series Editor:
Prof. Dr. TOSIYASU L. KUNII
Kunii Laboratory of Computer Science
Department of Information Science
Faculty of Science
The University of Tokyo
Hongo, Bunkyo-ku, 113 Japan

ISBN 4-431-70023-4 Springer-Verlag Tokyo Berlin Heidelberg New York
ISBN 3-540-70023-4 Springer-Verlag Berlin Heidelberg New York Tokyo
ISBN 0-387-70023-4 Springer-Verlag New York Heidelberg Berlin Tokyo

Printed in Japan
Printing/Binding: Kowa Art Printing, Tokyo

Series Preface

Computer Science Workbench is a monograph series which will provide you with an in-depth working knowledge of current developments in computer technology. Every volume in this series will deal with a topic of importance in computer science and elaborate on how you yourself can build systems related to the main theme. You will be able to develop a variety of systems, including computer software tools, computer graphics, computer animation, database management systems, and computer-aided design and manufacturing systems. Computer Science Workbench represents an important new contribution in the field of practical computer technology.

Tosiyasu L. Kunii

To our three daughters, Mélanie, Vanessa, and Sabrina

Preface

Image Synthesis: Theory and Practice is the first book completely dedicated to the numerous techniques of image synthesis. As indicated in the title, both theoretical and practical aspects of the subject are treated in detail. Although numerous impressive computer-generated images are included in this book, the main purpose is to explain the most advanced techniques used to produce these images. The book contains a detailed description of the most important algorithms; other algorithms are summarized or simply listed. This volume is also a unique handbook of mathematical formulae for image synthesis. Algorithms are described using a pseudocode, which is something between PASCAL and structured English.

Before explaining the techniques of image rendering, four chapters survey the techniques of computer graphics which play an important role in the design of an image. In the first two chapters, the various geometric models, image and viewing transformations, and the role of virtual cameras and color systems are described. The next chapter presents the most important curves and surfaces, making a clear distinction between approximation and interpolation methods; among the most important techniques described in detail are Kochanek-Bartels interpolation splines, Bézier curves and surfaces, Coons surfaces, B-splines, and β-splines. Solid modeling techniques are also introduced in a specific chapter because of their importance in recent rendering algorithms, such as ray tracing; boundary models, constructive solid geometry and octrees are emphasized.

Each major topic in image synthesis is presented in a separate chapter. The first important problem is the detection and processing of visible surfaces; depth-buffer, scan-line, list-priority, and recursive subdivision techniques are explained in detail; several techniques specific to free-form surfaces and solids are also described. Two chapters are then dedicated to the central problem of light and illumination: In Chap. 6, basic algorithms such as Phong shading, Gouraud shading, and the Whitted illumination model are introduced; the processing of simple transparency surfaces is also described; in the next chapter, more complex models are presented: spotlights, complex light-source descriptions, complex refraction models, and interreflection models.

As aliasing is a major problem in image rendering, the most important antialiasing techniques are described in Chap. 8. As well as classic prefiltering and supersampling techniques, specific hidden-surface algorithms with antialiasing are explained. The motion blur problem is also presented in detail.

Chapter 9 is dedicated to the problem of shadows. The most common algorithms are presented: shadow volumes, the z-buffer approach, and the polygonal-clipping approach. Techniques for producing soft shadows and penumbrae are also emphasized.

In the last few years, image rendering has been strongly influenced by ray tracing techniques. For this reason, Chaps. 10 and 11 are dedicated to this important approach. After an introduction to the basic algorithm, ray tracing algorithms for specific objects are presented, including quadrics, implicit surfaces, parametric surfaces, and surfaces defined by sweeping. Optimization techniques are explained in detail: bounding volumes, ray coherence, cone tracing, beam tracing, and methods based on space division. The problems of antialiasing and the techniques of distributed ray tracing are also discussed.

Chapter 12 discusses texturing algorithms. Texture mapping, bump mapping and solid textures are the three major kinds of texture discussed in this chapter. Several algorithms are presented for each type of texture. Other types are also explained, including ray-traced textures, syntax-based textures, and textures based on a growth model. Textures based on recursive subdivision are presented in Chap. 13 because of their relation with fractals. Chapter 13 is completely dedicated to fractals from the formal Mandelbrot theory to the recursive subdivision approaches. Other approaches are presented such as iterated function systems and ray tracing of fractals.

Natural phenomena present a particularly difficult challenge in image synthesis. For this reason, we have chosen to devote a large portion of the book to this topic. In Chap. 14, we present the main theoretical approaches to the representation of fuzzy and soft objects. In particular, we explain in detail particle systems, the use of scalar fields, volume density scattering models, and cellular automata. Chapter 15 is more applied and describes various techniques for representing terrains, mountains, water, waves, sky, clouds, fog, fire, trees, and grass.

Techniques for combining images are also explained in Chap. 16; in particular, adaptive rendering, montage and composite methods are described.

The last chapter presents the MIRALab image synthesis software: the SABRINA image synthesis system is described in detail, because most of the techniques presented in this book are available in SABRINA. An informal presentation of the INTER-MIRA specification language, used to implement SABRINA, is also included in this chapter.

Finally, a very complete bibliography on image synthesis is provided at the end of the book.

NADIA MAGNENAT-THALMANN
DANIEL THALMANN

Acknowledgments

The authors are very grateful to Professor Tosiyasu L. Kunii, The University of Tokyo, who strongly encouraged the publication of this book. They would also like to thank all the individuals and organizations who provided illustrative material and/or comments and suggestions:

John Amanatides, University of Toronto
Bruno Arnaldi, IRISA, Rennes
Mike Bailey, Purdue CADLAB
Brian A. Barsky, University of California, Berkeley Computer
    Graphics Laboratory
J. Bloomenthal, Computer Graphics Lab, New York Institute of
    Technology
Dave Blunkett, Purdue CADLAB
Kadi Bouatouch, IRISA, Rennes
Christian Bouville, C.C.E.T.T., Cesson-Sévigné, France
Indranil Chakravarty, Schlumberger-Doll Research
H. Chiyokura, Ricoh Company Ltd.
Akira Fujimoto, Graphica Computer Co., Tokyo
Geoffrey Y. Gardner, Computer Graphics Lab, New York Institute
    of Technology
Andrew Glassner, University of North Carolina
Donald Greenberg, Cornell University
Ralph Guggenheim, PIXAR Corporation
Robert Marshall, Computer Graphics Research Group, The Ohio
    State University
Nelson Max, Lawrence Livermore Laboratory
T. Nishita, Hiroshima University
Monique Nahas, Université de Paris VII
E. Nakamae, Hiroshima University
Alan Norton, IBM Yorktown Heights Research Center
Michael Potmesil, AT&T
Darwin Peachey, University of Sakatchewan

Tom Porter, PIXAR Corporation
Thierry Priol, IRISA, Rennes
Alvy Ray Smith, PIXAR Corporation
Kenneth E. Torrance, Cornell University
J.J. van Wijk, Delft University of Technology
P. Wattenberg, Sandia National Laboratories
Turner Whitted, University of North Carolina
Lance Williams, Computer Graphics Lab, New York Institute of
    Technology
Roger Wilson, Computer Graphics Research Group, The Ohio
    State University
Brian Wyvill, University of Calgary

The authors are also indebted to the designers who have worked
on the production of images at MIRALab: Marie-Andrée Allaire,
Alain Caron, Dominique Guy, Rudy Lainé, Ross Racine, and
Daniel Robichaud. They also express their gratitude to all computer
scientists who participated in the development of the MIRALab
image synthesis software, in particular, Alain Brossard, Michel
Burgess, Luc Forest, Richard Laperrière, Nicolas Léonard, Eric
Primeau, and Denis Rambaud. They also would like to thank Ann
Laporte who revised the English text.

The authors express their gratitude to the "Service de la
Recherche des Hautes Etudes Commerciales de Montréal" which
partly sponsored the production of the illustrations.

Table of Contents

1 Modeling primitives

1.1 3D space

1.1.1 2D versus 3D

Human beings live in a 3D world, but when they draw they work with a 2D representation of the 3D world. There are two approaches to this:

1. Represent only planar faces of an object, e.g., the face of a house
2. Attempt to draw the scene using perspective laws

Since in computer graphics the graphics devices (screens) are 2D, both of these methods are used, each corresponding to a different approach to modeling, graphic systems, and applications.

A graphics system is said to be **2D** if the internal representation of the graphic information in the computer is 2D; a graphics system is **3D** when the computer has knowledge of 3D information. There is a fundamental difference between the two approaches. When an image of a house in perspective is displayed on a screen, it may not be possible to determine whether the image was produced with a 2D or a 3D system. The house may have been drawn in perspective and the projection entered into the computer using a 2D graphics system; in this case, the role of the system is simply to display the image. The house may also have been generated by a 3D graphics system using 3D data; in this case, the system calculated the projections before displaying the image. It is important to note that when we discuss 3D images in this book, we are referring to images based on 3D models stored by the computer and not 3D techniques like **stereoscopic views** (see Sect. 2.4.4) or **holography**.

It should be noted that 2D space can be viewed as a special case of 3D space, with the third dimension Z always zero. For this reason, we shall use a 3D system in such a way that the third dimension is simply added to the 2D system as shown in Fig. 1.1.

1.1.2 Modeling primitives, external and internal models

Typically, object representations may be classified into three levels:

- Wire-frame representations
- Surface representations
- Volume representations

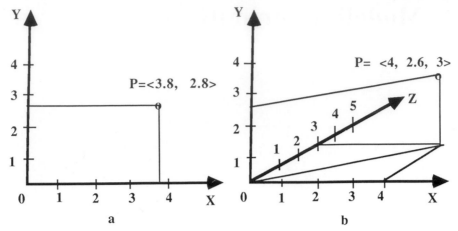

Fig. 1.1. Coordinate system.   **a** 2D;   **b** 3D

In a **wire-frame representation** (see Sect. 1.2.1), objects are merely represented by a set of segment lines, typically by vertices and edges, with no data on the surfaces and volumes. Such a representation is frequently too simple and cannot be used to achieve a high degree of realism.

In a **surface representation**, objects are represented by a set of primitive surfaces. Typically, three categories of description are used, depending on the object shape:

- Description by a set of polygons (see Sect. 1.2.2)
- Description by the equation of an algebraic surface (see Sect. 1.2.3 and Chap. 3)
- Description by patches (see Chap. 3)

In a **solid representation** (see Sect. 1.2.5 and Chap. 4), objects are essentially considered as a set of primitive volumes or as a bounded portion of the 3D space.

When a user builds an object, certain things have to be known about the model used to represent the object. This model, which requires some knowledge about the object, is called an **external model**. A high level external model is a **procedural model**, which is in fact a model based on data abstraction (see Sect. 1.4). In a procedural model, the object is not defined explicitly but is represented by a piece of code (a procedure or a high-level graphic type) to which parameters are passed. For example, a procedural model for a box (parallelepiped) may only require four vertices, as shown in Fig.1.2.

Then, the object is encoded according to an **internal model**. In our example, the cube may be defined:

- As a wire-frame: 12 segment lines (edges) defined by vertex coordinates
- As a surface: six polygonal facets defined by vertex coordinates
- As a volume: a solid defined by its boundary representation, a space subdivision, or as a volume primitive

Moreover, an object may be converted from a **geometric internal model** to a **display internal model**. For example, a parametric surface may be defined by a few coefficients, but converted into a polygonal planar facet internal model for the display step.

Image-synthesis systems often convert all external models into a unique internal representation, because this facilitates the manipulation and transformation of objects.

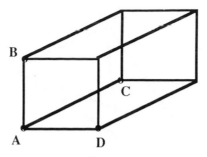

Fig. 1.2. A box

For example, the same deformation primitive cannot be easily applied to a cube and a sphere if the first is represented by planar facets and the second as a solid primitive.

Ideally, internal models should be hidden from the user. However, most existing image-synthesis systems and languages require the user to have considerable knowledge of the internal models used.

1.2 Wire-frame, surface, and volume representations

1.2.1 Wire-frame representation

The oldest and simplest type of 3D model is the **wire-frame representation**. This is composed of a list of points given by their coordinates or by a sequence of instructions of the type:

moveabs A	- move to a new location
lineabs B	- draw a line from the current location to a new location

where A and B are vectors defined as a set of three real numbers $<X,Y,Z>$

Consider, for example, the tetrahedron in Fig.1.3. This can be represented by:

```
moveabs  <<3,0,1>>
lineabs   <<5,0,1>>,<<6,0,5>>,<<3,0,1>>,<<4,3,6>>,<<6,0,5>>
moveabs  <<5,0,1>>
lineabs   <<4,3,6>>
```

1.2.2 Planar polygonal facet representation

The best known technique of this type involves describing an object by a **collection of polygons**. The definition of a polygon is not always very precise and varies among authors. We take a polygon to be a planar figure defined by a list of points (vertices) and linked by line segments (edges). All vertices are assumed to be different, edges cannot cross them, and an edge goes from the last vertex to the first. A polygon is **nonconvex** if there is at least one interior angle greater than 180°; otherwise it is **convex**.

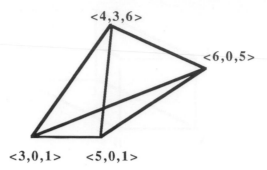

Fig.1.3. A tetrahedron

Although often expensive in terms of CPU time, polygonal models of 3D objects are the most common. In these models, all objects are decomposed into polygonal faces. For objects such as cubes or regular polyhedra, this decomposition is very effective. But for objects such as spheres or revolution surfaces, approximations are required. Unfortunately, large numbers of polygons are often needed to represent satisfactorily even comparatively simple shapes. Also, the essential character of some surfaces (e.g., spheres) is lost when they are approximated by collections of polygons.

To define an object using a polygon-based model, lists of vertices and polygons are specified, where each polygon is defined by its vertices, identified by their rank in the list of vertices. For example, the tetrahedron of Fig.1.3 can be defined by:

VERTICES <<3,0,1>>, <<5,0,1>>, <<6,0,5>>, <<4,3,6>>
POLYGON 1,2,4
POLYGON 2,4,3
POLYGON 1,4,3
POLYGON 1,3,2

1.2.3 Curvilinear surfaces

Most objects have curvature properties; as noted previously, it is possible to approximate them by flat polygons. It is also possible to represent them in the form of surface elements with polynomials of degree 3 or more. Moreover, objects may be described by nonplanar surfaces and then automatically converted into a polygonal-based representation for display purposes. Whatever the internal representation of such surfaces, they play a very important role. We may distinguish three types of surfaces:

1. **Ruled surfaces** such as cones, cylinders, parabolic cones, revolution surfaces, conoids. These may be constructed by sweeping techniques as described for solids in Sect. 4.3

2. **Parametric surfaces** given by their equations:

$$X=X(U,V) \quad Y=Y(U,V) \quad Z=Z(U,V) \tag{1.1}$$

3. **Free-form surfaces** can easily represent most complex curved objects; these surfaces are discussed in detail in Chap. 3; piecewise bicubic surfaces are the most used: e.g. Bézier surfaces, B-spline surfaces, and β-spline surfaces

1.2.4 Quadrics and superquadrics

Quadric surfaces provide a direct representation of curved surfaces and are suitable for representing a large class of geometric objects. However, quadric-based scenes are often stylized, being approximated by parts of spheres, ellipsoids, cones, cylinders, paraboloids and hyperboloids. The great advantage of quadrics is that specific manipulation and rendering methods may be developed. For example, human models have been designed using spheres (Badler et al. 1979), cylinders (Potter and Wilmert 1975), and ellipsoids (Herbison-Evans 1978). More details concerning these models are given in Badler et al. (1979) and Magnenat-Thalmann and Thalmann (1985b) (see Chap. 9). Quadrics have been generalized to superquadrics (Barr 1983) and are further discussed in Sect. 4.6.

1.2.5 Solids

Solids (or volumes) are important because real objects are solids. Their impact in image synthesis is mainly due to the following reasons:

1. Set operations on objects are very difficult to perform on nonsolid objects.
2. Methods for representing solids (e.g., octrees) are very useful in ray-tracing techniques (see Chaps. 10, 11)

There are several ways of representing solids. The most important are space decomposition, constructive solid geometry and boundary representation. These methods are presented in detail in Chap. 4, along with other methods and algorithms.

1.2.6 Automatic conversion of wire-frame models into surface models

Automatic conversion has been a research issue for some time (Idesawa 1973; Lafue 1976). Markowski and Wesley (1980) proposed an algorithm based on topology which needs explicit geometric information such as surface normals. This method handles ambiguous cases and holes but it is restricted to objects with straight edges and planar faces. Hanrahan (1982) and Dutton and Brigham (1983) use the technique of planar embedding in which the wire-frame is represented by a flat 2D edge-vertex graph in which none of the edges intersect except at vertices. The regions created represent the faces of the object. The technique works for objects with nonplanar faces and edges but fails for objects with ambiguities or holes. Ganter and Uiker (1983) propose a method which treats the objects as an edge-vertex graph which is examined to find a set of independent closed paths (cycles). Cycles are then combined in order to reduce their number until they correspond to faces. However, the faces still need to be oriented, so this algorithm requires interaction with the user. Courter and Brewer (1986) improve on this algorithm by changing the reduction process in which fundamental cycles yield faces. In particular, they add logic which automatically identifies and eliminates anomalies such as invalid faces. These anomalies are detected by the presence of edges belonging to more than two faces. Invalid faces are first deleted and then replaced with valid ones. After the deletion process, a set of edges of the object which belong to less than two faces remains; a graph is then formed containing these edges. This graph is broken down into a set of fundamental cycles, which are inserted into the cycle matrix of the object where the deleted faces used to be. The entire object is then fed back to the cycle reduction algorithm.

1.3 Creating the database

1.3.1 Techniques for creating a geometric model

Whatever the external or internal model, graphic data must be entered into the computer by the user. Several practical methods are available and have been surveyed by Smith (1983) and Greenberg et al. (1982).

The simplest, but most inconvenient way is by numerical input from a keyboard. Although this is probably the most accurate method, it is also the most time-consuming. Graphic input methods are more popular and more widely accepted. Various approaches are possible:

- Direct 3D digitizing (see Sect. 1.3.2)
- 2D digitizing and 3D reconstruction methods (see Sect. 1.3.2)
- Lofting methods (see Sect. 1.3.3)
- Extrusion and sweeping methods (see Sects. 3.8 and 4.3)
- Free-form surface generation methods (see Chap. 3)
- Methods based on procedural models (see Sect. 1.4)

1.3.2 Input scanning, digitizing and 3D reconstruction

The most direct 3D digitizing technique is simply to enter the 3D coordinates using a 3D digitizer. Three types of such devices are now available:

- Devices based on three orthogonal magnetic fields transmitted to a wand: the strengths of the fields are used to determine where the wand is located and establish a data point on the object's surface
- Devices based on three sound captors: the user digitizes 3D points, emitting a sound which is measured by the captors
- Devices based on laser light distance from the device to the object is determined by the laser

For example, an automatic 3D digitizing system has been developed by the laboratoire IMAGE of the Ecole Nationale Supérieure des Télécommunications (Schmitt et al. 1985). This microprocessor controlled video laser data acquisition system is capable of obtaining the coordinates of approximately 200 000 points/min.

A more common way of creating 3D objects is by 3D reconstruction from 2D information. Two techniques are possible:

1.3.2.1 3D reconstruction from 2D plans
Two or three orthogonal projections (plans) are entered and the computer is used to derive 3D coordinates. For example, consider the 3D input facility in the MIRALab image synthesis system (see Chap. 17). As shown in Fig.1.4, when the command is invoked, a grid corresponding to the XZ-plane appears; a Y-axis is also displayed on the right of the screen.

All points are entered by successively selecting a location on the XZ-plane and the Y-axis.

1.3.2.2 3D reconstruction from several photographs
1. Interesting points or grids are drawn onto the object
2. Several pictures (e.g., four orthogonal pictures) are taken of the object. It is important to maximize the distance between the object and the camera and to use a telephoto lens. The error caused by perspective is therefore partially corrected. In

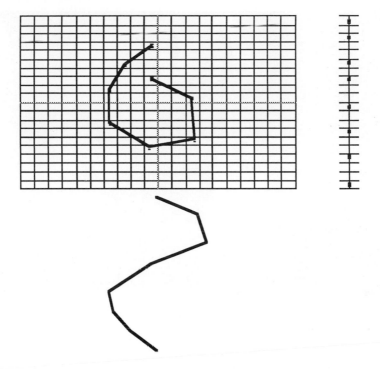

Fig.1.4. A 3D graphic input and the result curve

fact, the object is generally situated on a turntable that allows the angle of the object to be changed depending on the orientation of the camera
3. An appropriate coordinates system is drawn for each picture
4. Each point is identified by a number. Points have to be identified in at least two pictures to compute the X-, Y- and Z-coordinates of each point
5. After placing the pictures on the digitizer, the user marks points that determine the boundaries of the pictures and those that identify the coordinate systems
6. For each point, two different positions are successively marked
7. Connections between the points are identified by numbers: this defines the strokes of points in wire-frame models and grids in facet-based models

This technique was successively used to build the Statue of Liberty (see Fig. 1.5) in the film *Dream Flight* (Thalmann et al. 1982). A similar method was used by Information International to enter the data of actor Peter Fonda's head into their computers for the movie *Futureworld*. As reported by Smith (1983), the grid was projected onto the object (head) rather than drawn. Blum (1979) also describes a method using two photographs taken so that they both center on the same point of the object.

Figure 1.6 shows a volume reconstruction of the female pelvis.

1.3.3 Lofting methods

This popular method consists of reconstructing an object from a set of serial cross sections, like tracing the contours from a topographic map. Several reconstruction

Fig.1.5. Statue of Liberty in the film *Dream Flight*, by P.Bergeron, N.Magnenat-Thalmann, D.Thalmann © 1982 MIRALab, H.E.C. and University of Montreal

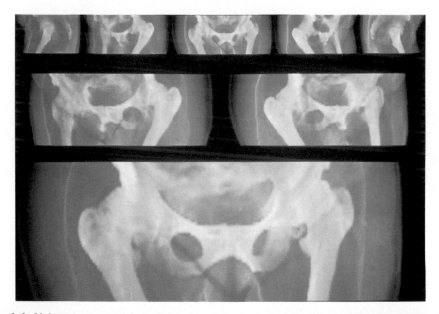

Fig.1.6. Volume reconstruction of female pelvis, by Robert Drebin © 1986 Pixar, all rights reserved. Forty nine computed tomography (CT) scans were used to generate the 3D reconstructions in this figure. The reconstruction algorithm, by Bob Drebin and Loren Carpenter, produces colored, antialiased views of image volumes. Each tissue may be assigned a different color and opacity. Here, bone is solid white, muscle and organs are semitransparent red, and fat is a very transparent green. The images were created on the Pixar Image Computer. The CT scans are courtesy of Elliot Fishman, M.D., John Hopkins Hospital.

Fig.1.7. Eglantine © 1986 MIRALab, H.E.C. and University of Montreal

algorithms are possible. The best known was introduced by Christiansen and Sederberg (1978). The algorithm converts complex contour line definitions into polygonal element mosaics. The algorithm works on pairs of contours as follows:

Map adjacent contours onto the same unit square
if contour loops branch into several loops
then create new nodes midway between the closest nodes on the branches
Connect nodes of one contour to their nearest neighbors in the other contour

Figure 1.7 shows a human model reconstructed from a set of serial cross sections.

1.4   Procedural models and data abstraction

1.4.1 The role of procedural models in geometric modeling

Procedural models (Newell 1975; Clark 1976) represent objects procedurally in an attempt to retain the essential information concerning the global coherence of the objects. Typically, a procedurally modeled object is entirely represented by its procedure and its parameters, and so a procedural model is changed by changing its parameters. For example, a sphere can be modeled as a call to a *sphere* procedure, with its radius and center parameters. A *tree* procedural model is defined by parameters such as height, width, and number of branches.

Procedural models also allow the implementation of geometric models to be hidden using the principle of data abstraction (Liskov and Zilles 1974). In particular, abstract graphic data types were first introduced by Thalmann and Magnenat-Thalmann (1979).

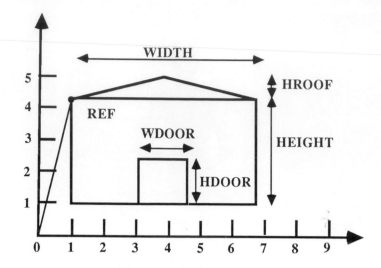

Fig.1.8. The parameters of a house

Time-dependent procedural models can also simulate behavior. Several kinds of such models have been proposed:

- Actor and camera data types (Magnenat and Thalmann 1983,1983a)
- Procedural models based on data flow (Hedelman 1984)
- Subactor data types (Magnenat-Thalmann and Thalmann 1985b, c)

In the latter case, subactors were used to hide the geometric implementation of objects based on sculptured surfaces such as Coons surfaces and ß-spline surfaces.

1.4.2 High-level graphical types

It is possible to build abstractions using very simple instructions as in a 2D wire-frame model. For example, a house may be parameterized and built as a high-level graphic type in the MIRA-2D language (Magnenat-Thalmann and Thalmann 1981).

Based on Fig.1.8, we obtain the following program:

```
type
  HOUSE=figure (REF:VECTOR; HEIGHT, WIDTH, HROOF,
               HDOOR, WDOOR:REAL);
     var HALF:REAL;
      begin
        HALF:=WIDTH/2;
         moveabs REF;
         linerel <<WIDTH,0>>,<<-HALF,HROOF>>,
                  <<-HALF,-HROOF>>, <<0,-HEIGHT>>,
                  <<WIDTH,0>>, <<0,HEIGHT>>;
          moverel <<-HALF-WDOOR/2,-HEIGHT>>;
          linerel <<0,HDOOR>>,<<WDOOR,0>>,<<0,-HDOOR>>
        end;
```

It is then easy to define two different houses:

> **var** H1,H2:HOUSE

and to create them with different dimensions:

> **create** H1 (<<1,4.3>>, 3.3, 5.8, 0.7, 1.5, 1.5);   {see Fig.1.8}
> **create** H2 (<<10,4>>, 4.5, 6, 2, 1.25, 1.75)

To build an object using a polygonal model, the principle is the same; but we use the statement **vertices** to defines the list of vertices, the statement **createface** to create the different faces, and the statement **faces** to define for each face the references to the vertices in the global list. To illustrate this model, take as an example a box (parallelepiped) defined by four vertices A, B, C, and D. The example is implemented in **MIRA-SHADING** (Magnenat-Thalmann et al. 1985) and corresponds to the box in Fig. 1.2.

```
type BOX=figure(A,B,C,D:VECTOR);
var CORI, BORI, DORI: VECTOR;
spec
  name 'BOX', shading CONSTANT,
  figure of 8 vertices, 6 faces;
begin
  CORI:=C-A;
  BORI:=B-A;
  DORI:=D-A;
  vertices:=A,C,B+CORI,B,D,C+DORI,D+BORI+CORI,D+BORI;
  createface 1 to 6 with 4 edges;
  face 1:=1,2,3,4;  face 2:=2,6,7,3;  face 3:=3,7,8,4;
  face 4:=5,1,4,8;  face 5:=1,5,6,2;  face 6:=6,5,8,7
end;
```

2 Transformations, cameras, and colors

2.1 Image transformations

2.1.1 Primitive transformations

Once 3D objects have been constructed (i.e., the database is ready to be used), object attributes must be manipulated and modified. Consider now these attributes. The most important ones are:

- Location
- Orientation
- Size
- Shape
- Color
- Transparency
- Reflectance
- Texture

Shape is an attribute which is strongly related to object modeling and construction, and its modification may become very complex. Color is discussed in Sect. 2.3. Other attributes are dependent on the display methods and will be presented in other chapters: transparency (Chaps. 6, 7, 10), reflectance (Chaps. 6, 7), texture (Chaps. 12, 13). A common feature of the first three attributes is that they may be modified by transformations called **primitive transformations**:

- Location is modified by **translation**
- Orientation is modified by **rotation**
- Size is modified by **scaling**

These transformations are also called **point transformations**, since they are applied on each point P of an object in order to obtain a new point P'. It is, therefore, possible to define each transformation by a relation between the original point $P = <P_x, P_y, P_z>$ and the transformed point $P' = <P'_x, P'_y, P'_z>$. Consequently, we have:

1. Translation of a vector $T = <T_x, T_y, T_z>$
   Components of T are added to the coordinates of P:

$$P' = P + T = <P_x+T_x,\ P_y+T_y,\ P_z+T_z> \qquad (2.1)$$

2. Rotation of an angle α about one axis
   The angle is possible about each axis:
   About the X-axis: $\mathbf{P'} = <P_x, P_y \cos \alpha - P_z \sin \alpha, P_y \sin \alpha + P_z \cos \alpha>$
   About the Y-axis: $\mathbf{P'} = <P_x \cos \alpha + P_z \sin \alpha, P_y, -P_x \sin \alpha + P_z \cos \alpha>$ (2.2)
   About the Z-axis: $\mathbf{P'} = <P_x \cos \alpha - P_y \sin \alpha, P_x \sin \alpha + P_y \cos \alpha, P_z>$

3. Scaling by a factor $\mathbf{S} = <<S_x, S_y, S_z>>$
   This transformation is used to scale dimensions in each coordinate direction separately :

$$\mathbf{P'} = <P_x S_x, P_y S_y, P_z S_z> \qquad (2.3)$$

Matrix notation is very often used instead of these equations. However, matrices of dimension 3 allow the definition of rotations and scalings but not translations. Therefore, it is essential to introduce homogeneous coordinates.

2.1.2 Homogeneous coordinates (4D)

With these coordinates, we work in a 4D space, in which each point $\mathbf{P}$ is defined as $\mathbf{P} = <P_x, P_y, P_z, 1>$, represented by the matrix $\mathcal{P} = [P_x \ P_y \ P_z \ 1]$. Conversely, each point $<x,y,z,w>$ in the 4D space represents the point $<\frac{x}{w}, \frac{y}{w}, \frac{z}{w}>$ in the 3D space. In this 4D representation, primitive transformations may be expressed by 4x4 matrices.

Translation of a vector $\mathbf{T}$:

$$\mathcal{T} = \begin{bmatrix} 1 & 0 & 0 & 0 \\ 0 & 1 & 0 & 0 \\ 0 & 0 & 1 & 0 \\ T_x & T_y & T_z & 1 \end{bmatrix} \qquad (2.4)$$

Rotation of an angle α about the x-axis:

$$\mathcal{R}_x = \begin{bmatrix} 1 & 0 & 0 & 0 \\ 0 & \cos \alpha & \sin \alpha & 0 \\ 0 & -\sin \alpha & \cos \alpha & 0 \\ 0 & 0 & 0 & 1 \end{bmatrix} \qquad (2.5)$$

Rotation of an angle β about the y-axis:

$$\mathcal{R}_y = \begin{bmatrix} \cos \beta & 0 & -\sin \beta & 0 \\ 0 & 1 & 0 & 0 \\ \sin \beta & 0 & \cos \beta & 0 \\ 0 & 0 & 0 & 1 \end{bmatrix} \qquad (2.6)$$

Rotation of an angle γ about the z-axis:

$$\mathcal{R}_z = \begin{bmatrix} \cos\gamma & \sin\gamma & 0 & 0 \\ -\sin\gamma & \cos\gamma & 0 & 0 \\ 0 & 0 & 1 & 0 \\ 0 & 0 & 0 & 1 \end{bmatrix} \qquad (2.7)$$

Scaling of a factor **S**:

$$\mathcal{S} = \begin{bmatrix} S_x & 0 & 0 & 0 \\ 0 & S_y & 0 & 0 \\ 0 & 0 & S_z & 0 \\ 0 & 0 & 0 & 1 \end{bmatrix} \qquad (2.8)$$

2.1.3 Transformation concatenation

Several point transformations may be sequentially performed by multiplying the matrices and applying the resulting matrix as a global matrix:

$$\mathcal{P}' = \mathcal{P}\,\mathcal{C}_1\,\mathcal{C}_2 = \mathcal{P}\,(\mathcal{C}_1\,\mathcal{C}_2) \qquad (2.9)$$

Consider, for example, the rotation of an angle γ about an arbitrary line d, given by a point **P** and a unit vector **N** (see Fig.2.1).

Processing steps are as follows:

1. Translation of -**P** to make d pass through the origin
2. Rotation of α about the Y-axis, then of β about the X-axis to transform the line d to the Z-axis. From Fig.2.1, we may write the following matrices:

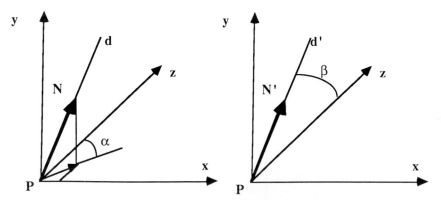

Fig. 2.1. Rotation to transform the line d to the Z-axis

$$\mathcal{R}_{y\alpha} = \begin{bmatrix} \dfrac{N_z}{N_{xz}} & 0 & -\dfrac{N_x}{N_{xz}} & 0 \\ 0 & 1 & 0 & 0 \\ \dfrac{N_x}{N_{xz}} & 0 & \dfrac{N_z}{N_{xz}} & 0 \\ 0 & 0 & 0 & 1 \end{bmatrix} \qquad (2.10)$$

$$\mathcal{R}_{x\beta} = \begin{bmatrix} N_{xz} & 0 & -N_y & 0 \\ 0 & 1 & 0 & 0 \\ N_y & 0 & N_{xz} & 0 \\ 0 & 0 & 0 & 1 \end{bmatrix} \qquad (2.11)$$

where N_{xz} is the projection of $\mathbf{N}$ on the XZ-plane.

3. Rotation of the angle γ about the Z-axis
4. Inverse rotation of $\mathcal{R}_{x\beta}$ and inverse rotation of $\mathcal{R}_{y\alpha}$
5. Translation of $-\mathbf{T}$

Note that inverse transformations may be easily expressed:

$$\mathcal{T}_P^{-1} = \mathcal{T}_{-P} \qquad (2.12)$$

$$\mathcal{R}_\alpha^{-1} = \mathcal{R}_{-\alpha} \qquad (2.13)$$

$$\mathcal{E}_S^{-1} = \mathcal{E}_{<1/S_x, 1/S_y, 1/S_z>} \qquad (2.14)$$

For the general rotation matrix, we obtain:

$$\mathcal{R}_C = \mathcal{T}_P \, \mathcal{R}_{y\alpha} \, \mathcal{R}_{x\beta} \, \mathcal{R}_{z\gamma} \, \mathcal{R}_{x(-\beta)} \, \mathcal{R}_{y(-\alpha)} \, \mathcal{T}_{-P} \qquad (2.15)$$

2.1.4 Other transformations

Among other point transformations, the most important ones are probably symmetries and homothesis.

Symmetries relative to the main planes are frequently used; in homogeneous coordinates, they may be expressed with the following matrices:

$$\mathcal{S}_{xy} = \begin{bmatrix} 1 & 0 & 0 & 0 \\ 0 & 1 & 0 & 0 \\ 0 & 0 & -1 & 0 \\ 0 & 0 & 0 & 1 \end{bmatrix} \qquad (2.16)$$

$$\mathcal{S}_{yz} = \begin{bmatrix} -1 & 0 & 0 & 0 \\ 0 & 1 & 0 & 0 \\ 0 & 0 & 1 & 0 \\ 0 & 0 & 0 & 1 \end{bmatrix} \qquad (2.17)$$

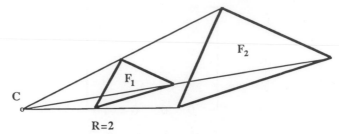

R=2

Fig. 2.2. An example of homothesis

$$
\mathcal{Y}_{xz} = \begin{bmatrix} 1 & 0 & 0 & 0 \\ 0 & -1 & 0 & 0 \\ 0 & 0 & 1 & 0 \\ 0 & 0 & 0 & 1 \end{bmatrix}
\tag{2.18}
$$

Homothesis is a well-known operation in geometrical optics which multiplies all distances by a factor R (the homothesis ratio) relative to a point (center of homothesis). Figure 2.2 shows an example. The homothesis matrix can be obtained by applying a translation -C, followed by a scaling operation of <R,R,R> and then a translation of C. Therefore

$$
\mathcal{H}_{RC} = \mathcal{C}_{-C}\ \mathcal{E}_{<R,R,R>}\ \mathcal{C}_{C}
\tag{2.19}
$$

2.2   Viewing system

2.2.1 Window and viewport

Given that we are able to model an object in the computer and to transform it, we still have to convert the object from the user space (generally 3D) to the screen space in order to view it. Not only is this space 2D, but terminal manufacturers have defined complex address spaces which differ from one terminal to another terminal. The purpose of viewing transforms is thus to convert objects from user space to the screen space.

We begin with a simple example of a 2D user space. Two concepts have to be defined—the **window** and the **viewport**.

In order to avoid problems with addresses for specific terminals, we shall consider the screen to be represented by a rectangle defined by the lower left vertex **VL** (often <0,0>) and the upper right vertex **VH** (often <1,1>). Then, any part of the screen which can be used is limited by vectors of components between 0 and 1. This part of the screen is called a **viewport**.

Our real world, assumed to be 2D, is of course unlimited and we have to specify which part of the real world we would like to represent. This part is a rectangle called a **window** and it is defined by its lower left vertex **WL** and its upper right vertex **WH**. The contents of the window will always be displayed in the viewport. In Fig.2.3, it can be seen that a point **P** in the window is transformed into a point **P'** in the viewport using Eqs. (2.20) and (2.21).

$$P'_x = \frac{(VH_x - VL_x)(P_x - WL_x)}{WH_x - WL_x} + VL_x \qquad (2.20)$$

$$P'_y = \frac{(VH_y - VL_y)(P_y - WL_y)}{WH_y - WL_y} + VL_y \qquad (2.21)$$

2.2.2 Planar projections

Consider now the 3D space; the first problem is to convert objects from three dimensions to only two. This requires projections of the objects onto a plane which is called the **viewplane**. Note that non-planar projections do exist. For example hemispheric projections have been used for several applications where a large field of vision is required.There are two kinds of planar projections—**parallel projections** (Fig.2.4a) and **perspectives** (Fig.2.4b).

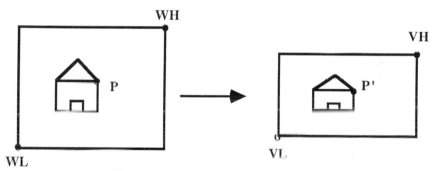

Fig. 2.3. From the window to the viewport

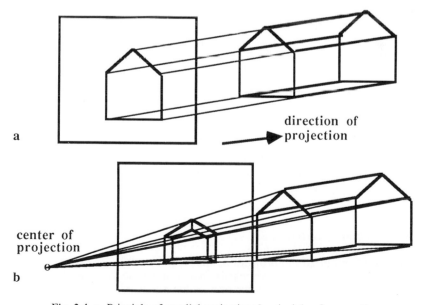

Fig. 2.4. **a** Principle of parallel projection; **b** principle of perspective

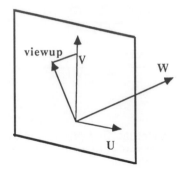

Fig. 2.5. Coordinate system of the window

In both cases, the object projection is obtained by tracing lines (called **projectors**) from the points of the object and by looking for the intersections of these projectors with the viewplane. In the case of a perspective, all projectors come from a single point—the **center of projection**. For a parallel projection, all projectors are parallel to the **direction of projection**. If the direction of projection is perpendicular to the viewplane, the projection is **orthographic**; otherwise it is **oblique**.

The window will be defined as the rectangle limiting what should be seen on the viewplane. The window is specified according to a coordinate system UVW where the V-axis is the projection on the viewplane of a special vector called the **viewup vector**. W is the normal to the viewplane and U is taken at 90^0 as shown in Fig.2.5.

We also define a view volume, which contains all objects which are projected. In the case of a perspective, the view volume is a semi-infinite pyramid with the main vertex as the center of projection; the window is a section of the pyramid. In the case of a parallel projection, the view volume is a parallelepiped.

We may now define the steps for processing a 3D scene.

2.2.3 Transformation pipe-line

From the list of objects composing the 3D scene to the physical screen coordinates, a series of transformations must be carried out:

1. Application of transformation matrices to geometric primitives in order to obtain a description in the world coordinate system
2. Transformation into a description of the objects as they are viewed (viewing geometric primitives)
3. Clipping according to the view volume
4. Projection on the window in the viewplane
5. Mapping from the window to the viewport
6. Mapping from the viewport to the screen

2.2.4 Projection matrices

We shall not explain all the projections matrices in detail. However, we shall show how to determine the perspective matrix in a simple case. Suppose that the center of projection **C** is placed in the negative part of the z-axis ($\mathbf{C} = <0, 0, C_z>$) and that the

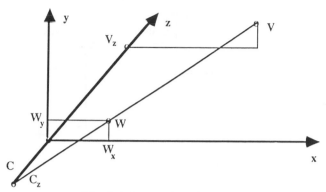

Fig. 2.6. Perspective of a point **V**

viewplane is the xy-plane. We can consider now a point $V=<V_x, V_y, V_z>$ and its projection $W = <W_x, W_y, 0>$ as shown in Fig. 2.6.

The following equations may be easily derived from Fig. 2.6:

$$W_x = \frac{V_x}{1-\frac{V_z}{C_z}} \quad \text{and} \quad W_y = \frac{V_y}{1-\frac{V_z}{C_z}} \tag{2.22}$$

If we now apply the following matrix:

$$\mathcal{M}_{per} = \begin{bmatrix} 1 & 0 & 0 & 0 \\ 0 & 1 & 0 & 0 \\ 0 & 0 & 0 & -\frac{1}{C_z} \\ 0 & 0 & 0 & 1 \end{bmatrix} \tag{2.23}$$

to the 4D vector $V=<V_x,V_y,V_z,1>$ we obtain $V' = <V_x,V_y,0,1-\frac{V_z}{C_z}>$. By reducing this vector to three dimensions, we have $<\frac{V_x}{1-\frac{V_z}{C_z}}, \frac{V_y}{1-\frac{V_z}{C_z}}, 0>$, which is **W**. We

conclude that $\mathcal{M}_{per}$ is the perspective matrix and we may affirm that any matrix in homogeneous coordinates (4x4) which has nonzero terms in the three first elements of the fourth column is a perspective matrix.

2.3 Colors

2.3.1 Role of color in image synthesis

In computer graphics, color plays an essential role for two main reasons. First, it allows different objects to be distinguished, and second it is required for any realistic

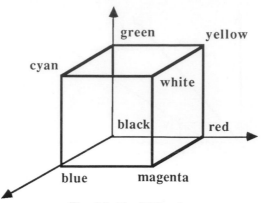

Fig. 2.7. The RGB cube

image. To distinguish between N different objects, N colors or often less are required; as it is very rare that many different objects are manipulated at the same time, a limited number of colors is generally sufficient. For realistic images, light plays an active role; when we consider, for example, a complex red object, many red tints may be required to represent the object. More generally, the production of realistic images with transparency, texture, and shadows requires a very large number of colors.

Note that depending on the type of application, colors are variables. Standard ways of specifying these colors are necessary. With a number limited to eight, we may use the usual color names; but for thousands or even millions of colors, numerical systems are essential.

Various numerical color systems have been defined: RGB, CMY, YIQ, HSV, and HLS. We shall present only the RGB and HLS systems and the color-naming system CNS.

2.3.2 RGB system

The RGB system is derived from the system defined in 1931 by the Commission Internationale de l'Eclairage (CIE). The CIE system defined a space based on three primary colors: **Red**, **Green**, and **Blue**. Every visible color is a linear combination of the three primary colors. The RGB system corresponds to the principle of TV monitors, where colors are created by red, green, and blue phosphors.

The RGB model generally uses a cube with unitary edges (length=1) as shown in Fig. 2.7.

Black is at the origin and white at the location<1,1,1>. The three primary colors are found along the three main axes. Finally, the colors cyan, magenta and yellow are located at the three last vertices of the cube. Each color may be expressed using a 3D vector with the components between 0 and 1. For example:

Red = <1,0,0>   Green = <0,1,0>   Blue=<0,0,1>
Yellow = <1,1,0>   Magenta = <1,0,1>   Cyan = <0,1,1>

Note also that along the main diagonal of the cube, there is a gray scale from black (<0,0,0>) to white (<1,1,1>).

It should be noted that the RGB system is based on additive color mixtures; artists are often more familiar with subtractive color mixtures, in which a combination of blue and yellow produces green.

2.3.3 HLS system

This system also specifies each color using three numbers; however these numbers have a different meaning. They are hue (H), lightness (L), and saturation (S).

Hues are sensations reported by observers exposed to various wavelengths. As stated by Murch (1986), hue is the basic component of color and the primary determinant of the specific color sensation. Therefore, hue is a psychological variable and wavelength is a physical one. For example the purest blue is at about 470 nm, pure green at 505 nm, and pure yellow at 575 nm. The hue H may be represented using a circle and the angle at the center of this circle. In degrees, the hue varies from 0° to 360° as shown in Fig. 2.8. With the three primary colors and the three complementary colors, a regular hexagon may be built.

Lightness (L) refers to the gamut of achromatic colors defined using a scale from 0 (black) to 1 (white) passing through all grays.

Saturation (S) is a measure of the number of wavelengths contributing to a color sensation. A value of 1 represents a pure or saturated color, corresponding to one wavelength; a value of 0 corresponds to a gray of the same lightness, which means a wide band of wavelengths.

The HLS system may be explained using a double hexacone (Fig.2.9). At the cone surface, all colors have a saturation of 1. Saturation is represented along the radius of a circular section of the cone. The hue is described by the angle at the center of the circle. Lightness is on the vertical axis.

It should be noted that hue is often expressed as a fraction of a revolution; this allows colors to be denoted by a vector of three numbers between 0 and 1: <H,L,S>, Primary and complementary colors may then be defined as follows:

Red = <0.33,0.5,1>	Green = <0.67,0.5,1>	Blue=<0,0.5,1>
Yellow = <0.5,0.5,1>	Magenta = <0.167,0.5,1>	Cyan =<0.833,0.5,1>

Figure 2.10 shows an example of graphic color interface.

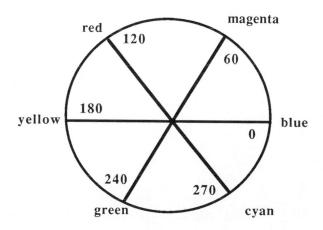

Fig. 2.8. The hue circle in the HLS system

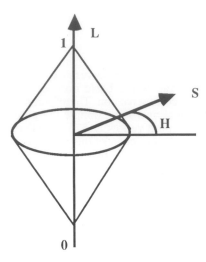

Fig. 2.9. The double HLS hexacone

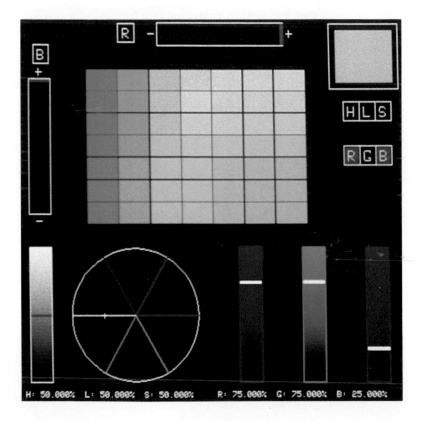

Fig.2.10. MIRALab Color interface

2.3.4 CNS system

Berk et al. (1982, 1982a) introduce an English-based color notation system called Color-Naming System (**CNS**). A total of 31 hue names are generated from seven chromatic hue names (red, orange, brown, yellow, green, blue and purple) and three achromatic terms (black, white, and gray). New names are generated using the following rules:

1. Two generic hues joined by a hyphen denote a hue exactly halfway between the two generic hues specified, e.g., green-blue, orange-yellow
2. If a color one-quarter of the way between two adjacent generic hues is desired, the farther hue is the modifier, appearing first with the suffix **-ish**, and the closer hue is modified, appearing second, e.g., reddish purple, reddish-orange

A complete syntax for this "color language" is described by Berk et al.

CNS is, in fact, a high level version of the HLS system. For artists, Kaufman (1986) proposes a new English-based color notation system called Artist's Color Naming System (**ACNS**), which allows the generation of several hundred color designations from a small number of English terms.

2.4 MIRALab virtual camera model

2.4.1 Introduction

One of the most impressive effects in computer-generated films (Magnenat-Thalmann 1986b) is the possibility of rotating around a 3D object or entering into any complex solid. Although people generally find these effects very spectacular, they are in fact quite easy to produce. Typically, these effects are obtained by simulating a camera, called a **virtual** or a **synthetic camera**, and by moving it. In fact, a single virtual camera consists only of a pair of vector characteristics known as the **eye** of the camera and the **interest point**. The model may be completed by a **zoom**. These features are very convenient for all wire-frame drawings and most shaded images. A more realistic camera model has been introduced by Potmesil and Chakravarty (1981) and will be described in Sect. 10.5; it approximates the effects of the lens and aperture function of a real camera. It allows the generation of synthetic images which have a depth of field and can be focused on an arbitrary plane.

The term "virtual camera" is frequently used by authors in computer graphics, but it is always an abstraction. A virtual camera is generally defined as kind of a procedural software responsible for the transformation from 3D space to a 2D projection, as described in Sect. 2.2. It may consist of a set of subprograms as defined in numerous graphics packages or it could be reduced to a few matrices which are applied to objects. The virtual camera is not considered an object which may be directed by a set of commands. At MIRALab, a virtual camera is a software entity that may be manipulated exactly in the same way as cameramen manipulate real cameras. For this reason, we have developed a virtual camera model which integrates such well-known functions as zoom, spin, viewport and clipping. Color filters and fog filters can be added to our cameras. The use of a stereoscopic virtual camera has also been introduced with a technique for the generation of shaded stereoscopic images on only one screen.

2.4.2 Integrated camera model

2.4.2.1 Eye and interest point

A virtual camera is a software entity that uses a few input parameters and displays a 2D view of a 3D scene. This means that the role of a virtual camera is to perform all geometric transformations needed to convert 3D points into points in the 2D image plane. Our basic virtual camera has a name and it is characterized by at least two parameters—the eye and the interest point. For example, we may define a camera called CAMERA_1 by:

$$\textbf{CAMERA } \text{CAMERA\_1 EYE INT}$$

The eye is a point (or vector) and it represents the location of the camera. The interest point is the point toward which the camera is directed.

2.4.2.2 Zoom

A zoom lens permits the cameraman to adjust quickly the size of the field being filmed by the camera. In a virtual camera, a zoom may be defined by changing the ratio between the dimensions in the image space and the display space. This generally consists of modifying the window. In our system, a zoom may be added to any camera, simply by specifying:

$$\textbf{ZOOM } \text{CAMERA\_1 ZOOMVALUE}$$

where ZOOMVALUE has been previously defined.

2.4.2.3 Spin

The eye and the interest point define a line and a direction on this line, which is in fact an axis. However, there is still one degree of freedom, i.e., the possibility of rotation by a given angle around the axis. This characteristic of a camera is called spin. Default spin corresponds to a zero angle. In our approach, a spin is associated with a camera by defining:

$$\textbf{SPIN } \text{CAMERA\_1 SPINVALUE}$$

2.4.2.4 Viewport and clipping

The term "viewport" has been introduced as a standard term in all graphics software and textbooks. It is generally defined as the portion of the graphics display corresponding to the window in the image space. In fact, we believe that a viewport should be defined as a characteristic of a camera and may be described as:

$$\textbf{VIEWPORT } \text{CAMERA\_1 VIEW1 VIEW2}$$

where VIEW1 is the lower-left point of the viewport and VIEW2 the upper-right point.

Clipping is also an essential camera characteristic. Generally, a clipping of all drawing outside the viewport is performed corresponding to a window clipping. However, it is often very useful to suppress this automatic clipping or to clip everything that is inside the viewport instead of outside. For example, we define:

$$\textbf{CLIPPING } \text{CAMERA\_1 INSIDE CLIP1 CLIP2}$$

or

$$\textbf{CLIPPING } \text{CAMERA\_1 OUTSIDE CLIP1 CLIP2}$$

to associate with a camera clipping inside or outside the rectangle defined by the lower-left point CLIP1 and the upper-right point CLIP2.

Figure 2.11 shows the use of three simultaneous virtual cameras.

2.4.3 Camera filters

2.4.3.1 Color filters

Filters for a real camera are glass lenses which are screwed into the front of the camera lens. In particular, color filters are used to correct colors or for special effects. In a virtual camera, color filters may be easily simulated by modifying colors during the display process. In our model, four kinds of color filter have been introduced:

1. Replacement color filters (**REPFILTER**): they replace one or several RGB component(s) by a new value, e.g.:
   REPFILTER CAMERA_1 <1,-1,1>, with this magenta filter, the image has the components R and B replaced by 1; component G is not modified (a negative value signifies no change)
2. Additive color filters (**ADDFILTER**): they add constant values to one or several RGB components
3. Subtractive color filters (**SUBFILTER**): they subtract constant values from one or several RGB components, e.g.:
   SUBFILTER CAMERA_1 <0.3,0.3,0.3>, this filter subtracts 0.3 from all components; the result is a dark image
4. Limit color filters (**LIMFILTER**): they are characterized by two vectors $<R_1,G_1,B_1>$ and $<R_2,G_2,B_2>$ which define a range; any component RGB outside the range is replaced by the limit value. For example, if the component R is less than R_1; it is replaced by R_1, e.g.:
   LIMFILTER CAMERA_1 <0.4,0.4,0.4>,<0.6,0.6,0.6>, this filter makes all colors with components in the range 0.4 to 0.6; the result is an image which tends to be gray (<0.5,0.5,0.5> in RGB)

2.4.3.2 Fog filter

A fog filter may be simulated by combining an image with the background color. The fog is deeper when the distance between the point considered and the eye is greater; this means that a fog may be considered a characteristic of the camera. We define a fog filter for a camera CAMERA_1 by the command:

FOG CAMERA_1 DIST

where DIST is the distance to the point where the color is 50% mixed with the background color.

Figure 2.12 shows the effect of a fog filter. Other techniques of fog simulation are described in Sect. 15.7.3.

2.4.4 Stereoscopic display

2.4.4.1 Stereoscopic cameras

Images produced on a terminal using a single virtual camera model have a defect because only one eye is simulated. In reality, the brain receives two pictures, one from each eye. As the eyes are not exactly at the same location, this gives a depth perception. With only one eye, depth perception is suppressed and this is especially

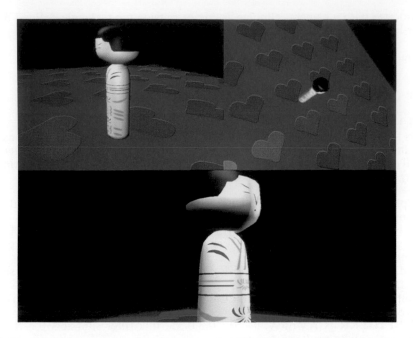

Fig.2.11. Three simulatenous virtual cameras. © 1986 MIRALab, H.E.C. and University of Montreal

Fig.2.12. Effect of a fog filter © 1986 MIRALab, H.E.C. and University of Montreal

limitative for wire-frame drawings. One way of solving this problem is by the introduction of stereoscopic virtual cameras. Such cameras are defined in the same way as other cameras, but they are declared as stereoscopic by for example:

STEREOSCOPIC CAMERA_1 12

This means that the camera CAMERA_1 will have two eyes separated by 12 units. The two eyes are located on either side of the location of the eye as defined in the camera. Now, for any scene that is viewed with such a camera, two views are produced, one for each eye. The first view corresponds to the left eye and the second view represents the view from the right eye. In fact, to view this stereoscopically it is necessary to wear special glasses in which the left glass does not allow the right image to be seen and the right glass blocks the left image.

2.4.4.2 Generation of shaded stereoscopic images on the same screen

One technique for generating stereoscopic views is by using color separation. The usual way is the production of two different images, one for each eye. Both images are then superimposed or projected on two different screens. At MIRALab, left and right images are produced on the same screen by the scan-line algorithm (see Sect.5.4).

For each scan-line, two scan-line z-buffers are computed, one for the left eye and one for the right eye. One z-buffer is obtained using a cyan color filter and the other one using a red color filter. Both scan-line z-buffers are then added to obtain the final z-buffer, which is then displayed.

Other techniques involving special hardware are described by Hodges and McAllister (1985, 1985a).

3 Free-form curves and surfaces

3.1 Introduction to curves and surfaces

3.1.1 Curves and surfaces

The design of curves and surfaces plays an essential role in the construction of 3D objects for image synthesis. Although many objects may be constructed by assembling geometric shapes like cubes, spheres, or pyramids, most objects have a free-form shape, e.g., human faces, car bodies, airplanes, shoes, clothes, clouds, mountains.

As the primitive way of entering the data of a three-dimensional object by digitizing is fastidious, designers need methods for developing free-form surfaces easily from a limited set of data. Many objects can be generated using ruled surfaces and surfaces generated by sweeping methods (see Sect. 4.3). But these surfaces require one or several free-form curves as input. Methods for creating these free-form curves are, therefore, essential. In addition, most free-form surfaces are constructed as a tensor product of curves (see Sect. 3.1.4).

More details on curves and surfaces may be found in the survey by Böhm et al. (1984) and the indexed bibliography by Barsky (1981). Free-form surfaces which are not the tensor product of curves are not described in the present volume. However, interesting algorithms are described by Barnhill (1983) and Chiyokura and Kimura (1984). An example of the application of very specific surfaces is described in Sect. 3.1.3.

3.1.2 Interpolations and approximations

A curve or a surface is generally given by a set of 3D points. Methods for generating the curve or the surface are numerous and may be classified into two categories—**interpolations** and **approximations**. An approximation curve (or surface) is a curve (or surface) which passes near but not necessarily through the given points, while an interpolation is guaranteed to pass through them. The advantage of an approximation is that it generally preserves second-order continuity. Interpolated curves and surfaces may have undesirable kinks.

Approximation methods are sometimes separated into **control point methods** and **fits**. A fit is a method which tends to minimize the distances between the given points and the generated curve (or surface). A typical example of a fit method is the **least squares fit method**, which minimizes the sum of the squares of the distances between the given points and the corresponding points (in X) on the curve to be generated. This type of method is not very useful in computer graphics and where control point methods are much more preferable because they allow the user to control easily the shape of the curve or surface generated. The definition of the **convex hull** of a set of control points should be noted: it is the convex polygon obtained by connecting the control points.

In this chapter, we describe the most important interpolation and approximation techniques.

Interpolation methods:

For curves: -Linear interpolation
                               -Parabolic blending
                               -Akima local interpolation
                               -v-spline interpolation
                               -Catmull-Rom spline interpolation
                               -Kochanek-Bartels spline interpolation
For surfaces: -Coons interpolation

Approximation methods:

For curves and surfaces: -Bézier approximations
                               -B-spline approximations
                               -ß-spline approximations
                               -ß2-spline approximations

A comparison between approximating and interpolating methods is shown in Fig.3.1.

We also present the **propagation control graph** (PCG) technique for aiding the design of control points for surfaces generated by approximations.

3.1.3 Specific approximation technique for cloth representation

Weil (1986) presents a solution for the following specific problem: a piece of cloth exists in three dimensions and its location is fixed at chosen constraint points. The piece of cloth is to be represented with all its folds as it hangs from these constraint points. The cloth is assumed to be rectangular and is represented by a grid. There are two stages in the method.

3.1.3.1 Approximation to the surface within the convex hull of the constraint points

This stage consists of tracing curves from every constraint point to each other constraint point. Weil derived the curve equation from the two end points and the length of the thread hanging between. This curve is called the **catenary** and is of the form:

$$y = A + B \cosh\left(\frac{x-b}{a}\right) \tag{3.1}$$

As constraint points are connected by tracing catenaries between them, the grid points which lie along the lines between the constraint points can be positioned and triangles are created. This series of triangles can then be used for the approximation of the surface. Each triangle is repeatedly subdivided until each grid point in its interior has been positioned.

3.1.3.2 Iterative relaxation process

This relaxation of points is iterated over the surface until the maximum displacement of the points during one pass falls below a predetermined tolerance.

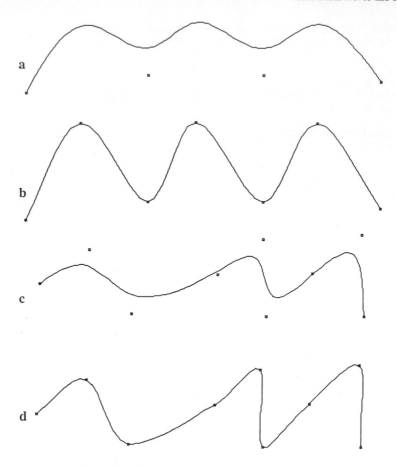

Fig.3.1 a-d. A comparison between approximation and interpolation methods. **a** Approximating spline (B-spline); **b** corresponding interpolating spline (Catmull-Rom spline); **c** another approximating spline (B-spline); **d** corresponding interpolating spline (Catmull-Rom spline)

3.1.4 Basis functions and tensor products

A curve $C(u)$ is often expressed linearly in terms of basis functions $F_i(u)$:

$$C(u) = \sum_{i=0}^{n} c_i F_i(u) \qquad (3.2)$$

where c_i are coefficients.

Suppose now that each c_i traces out a curve $c_i(v)$ which is also expressed linearly in terms of basis functions $G_k(v)$:

$$c_i(v) = \sum_{k=0}^{m} a_{ik} G_k(v) \qquad (3.3)$$

Substituting for c_i in (3.2), we obtain the resulting surface $S(u,v)$ which is a **tensor product surface**:

$$S(u,v) = \sum_{i=0}^{n} \sum_{k=0}^{m} a_{ik} F_i(u) G_k(v) \tag{3.4}$$

Curves and surfaces are often cut into small pieces or segments, which are separately processed. Typically, a curve $C(u)$ is segmented into parts corresponding to a partition of its domain by values of u called **breakpoints** (or **knots**): $u_1 < u_2 < u_3 ,... < u_p$. The points of $C(u)$ correponding to the breakpoints are called **knot points**. Each interval $[u_j, u_{j+1}]$ is called a **span**. Similarly a surface may be segmented using a partition of the domain corresponding to **knotlines** defined by the breakpoints: $u_1 < u_2 < u_3 ,... < u_p$ and $v_1 < v_2 < v_3 ,... < v_q$.

3.1.5 Linear and polynomial interpolation

The problem of interpolation may be summarized as follows: given $N+1$ data points, P_i, $i=0$ to N, find a curve $Q(t)$ passing through these points. We assume that the value of the parameter t is given by the knots t_i of $Q(t)$. Two extreme cases are possible:

1. Join independently the pairs of points $\{P_i, P_{i+1}\}$
2. Find a unique curve passing through all the P_i

The first case corresponds to **linear interpolation**. It is the simplest method, and consists of joining the P_i by straight lines. If we consider a local parameter t varying between 0 and 1, the linear interpolant between P_i and P_{i+1} is given by:

$$Q(t) = P_i (1-t) + P_{i+1} t \tag{3.5}$$

The second case may be solved by finding a polynomial $Q(t)$ of degree N. A solution is obtained using **Lagrange polynomials**:

$$Q(t) = \sum_i P_i L_{iN}(t) \quad \text{NOTE:} \tag{3.6}$$

$$\nwarrow t{-}t_i \text{ missing}$$

with

$$L_{iN}(t) = \frac{(t-t_0)...(t-t_{i-1})\,(t-t_{i+1})\,...(t-t_N)}{(t_i-t_0)...(t_i-t_{i-1})\,(t_i-t_{i+1})\,...(t_i-t_N)} \tag{3.7}$$

$$\nwarrow t_i{-}t_i \text{ missing}$$

Since the degree of these functions is directly related to the number of points P_i, the interpolating curve tends to oscillate with large values of N. Moreover, it could be computationally very expensive.

Between the two extreme cases, there is a better approach—piecewise continuous interpolation of the curve. The interpolating curve must be continuous at the knots only up to a certain order m of its derivatives, i.e., it should be C^m continuous. For example, a piecewise third-degree polynomial can be constructed to achieve C^2 continuity (second derivative continuity) at the knots.

3.2 Smooth interpolation by piecewise cubics

3.2.1 Concept of spline

The term **spline** comes from a familiar drafting tool used in several industries. It is a thin and elastic lath used to draw a smooth curve through a set of given points as in interpolation. Splines can be described mathematically as piecewise approximations of cubic polynomial functions. Schoenberg (1946) noted that a certain class of functions corresponded to the Bernouilli-Euler elasticity equation. He called them **spline functions**, because they allowed the simulation of spline drafting tools. Consider now the Bernouilli-Euler equation:

$$M(x) = \frac{E \; I}{R(x)} \tag{3.8}$$

where $M(x)$ is the flexion momentum, E is the Young modulus, I the inertia momentum, and $R(x)$ the radius of curvature. For a small radius of curvature, $R(x)$ may be replaced by $1/y''$. As $M(x)$ is a linear function, we may write:

$$y''(x) = \frac{d^2 y(x)}{dx^2} = \frac{a \; x + b}{E \; I} \tag{3.9}$$

The solution of this differential equation has the following form:

$$y(x) = a_3 x^3 + a_2 x^2 + a_1 x + a_0 \tag{3.10}$$

which corresponds to the cubic spline function. Moreover, this type of cubic spline function has the property of minimal curvature, since it minimizes the integral:

$$\int_a^b |f(x)|^2 \; dx \tag{3.11}$$

in the space of the functions $f(x)$.

Two kinds of splines are very popular: interpolating splines with C^1 continuity at knots, and approximating splines with C^2 continuity at knots. Typical interpolating splines are v-splines, cardinal splines, Catmull-Rom splines, and Kochanek-Bartels splines. Examples of approximating splines are B-splines and ß-splines.

Assume $N+1$ points P_i, i=0 to N, with their knots given by t_i. It is possible to find an interpolating piecewise polynomial $C(t)$ for $[t_0, t_N]$ so that the function in each span is a parametric cubic function and $C(t)$ is C^2 continuous at the knots. However, such an interpolated curve may have unwanted oscillations and any change made locally will be propagated over the entire curve. Because of these drawbacks, this kind of interpolation, called **global cubic-spline interpolation** requires very high-quality input data and, therefore, is not very useful in image synthesis. **Local interpolation** methods are much more popular, because they allow better interactive input with the possibility of correcting input errors.

The principle of local cubic interpolation is very simple, and various methods have been proposed: parabolic blending (Overhauser 1968), Akima (1970) local interpolation, cardinal spline and Catmull-Rom spline. These methods are considered to be local interpolation methods, because the curve at anyone knot is dependent on at most five points, two ahead and two behind.

3.2.2 Parabolic blending and Akima local interpolation

3.2.2.1 Overhauser parabolic blending

Parabolic blending was first proposed by Overhauser (1968). Consider four points P_i, i=0 to 3, as shown in Fig. 3.2.

The idea is to find the equation $C(t)$ for the center span P_1P_2, by blending two parabolas $K_1(r)$ and $K_2(s)$ defined respectively by the points P_0,P_1,P_2 and P_1,P_2,P_3. $C(t)$ is calculated as a weighted sum of $K_1(r)$ and $K_2(s)$:

$$C(t) = K_1(r) \left(1 - \frac{t}{|P_2 - P_1|}\right) + \frac{K_2(s)\, t}{|P_2 - P_1|} \qquad (3.12)$$

By changing the coordinate system (from r to t and s to t) and substituting the parabola equations into Eq. (3.12), we obtain the complete equation for the curve $C(t)$. This is a cubic function of t, because K_1 and K_2 are multiplied by a linear term.

3.2.2.2 Akima local interpolation

The second method is basically a 2D method and was proposed by Akima (1970). The method consists of finding a portion of a cubic curve between two points in such a way that the curve passes through the points and that the tangent at each of the two points is determined only by the point, the two previous points and the two following points. With this method, Akima proved that the slope M of the tangent at a point P_3 (see Fig.3.3) may be calculated as a function of the slopes m_1, m_2, m_3, and m_4 only, where m_i is defined as:

$$m_i = \frac{y_{i+1} - y_i}{x_{i+1} - x_i} \qquad (3.13)$$

with $P_i = <x_i, y_i>$ and i = 1 to 4

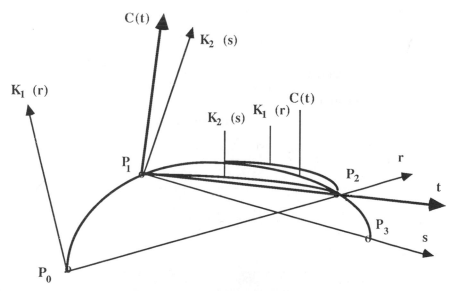

Fig.3.2. Principle of parabolic blending

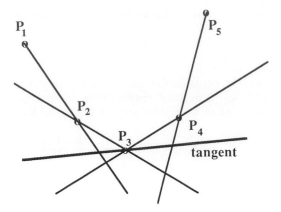

Fig.3.3. Representation of the points necessary to calculate the tangent at P_3

The slope of the tangent is obtained as follows:

$$M = \frac{m_2\sqrt{|(m_3-m_1)(m_4-m_3)|} + m_3\sqrt{|(m_2-m_1)(m_4-m_2)|}}{\sqrt{|(m_3-m_1)(m_4-m_3)|} + \sqrt{|(m_2-m_1)(m_4-m_2)|}}$$

(3.14)

To determine the cubic polynomial between two points P_1 and P_2, Akima uses the following equation:

$$y = \Omega_0 + \Omega_1 (x-x_1) + \Omega_2 (x-x_1)^2 + \Omega_3 (x-x_1)^3$$

(3.15)

with the four conditions:

$$x=x_1 \Rightarrow y = y_1$$
$$x=x_1 \Rightarrow \frac{dy}{dx} = M_1$$
$$x=x_2 \Rightarrow y = y_2$$
$$x=x_2 \Rightarrow \frac{dy}{dx} = M_2$$

(3.16)

Using Eqs. (3.15) and (3.16), the four real coefficients Ω_i may be found:

$$\Omega_0 = y_1$$
$$\Omega_1 = M_1$$
$$\Omega_2 = \frac{-m_2-2m_1}{\beta} + \frac{3\,(y_2-y_1)}{\beta^2}$$
$$\Omega_3 = \frac{m_1+m_2}{\beta^2} - \frac{2\,(y_2-y_1)}{\beta^3}$$

(3.17)

with $\beta = x_2-x_1$.

For the first two and the last two points of the curve, Akima proposes calculating two extra points at each end using a quadratic function.

3.2.3 Splines in tension and v-splines

Schweikert (1966) and Cline (1974) first showed the utility of tension parameters that allow the user to tighten the spline curve. Such a spline is called a **spline in tension** and is defined by the following properties:

Let t_i be the knots and f_i the corresponding ordinate data, i= 1 to n.

1. T_Ω has the form $a + bt + c \sinh(\Omega t) + d \cos(\Omega t)$ on each subinterval $[t_i, t_{i+1}]$
2. $T_\Omega(t_i) = f_i$
3. $\dfrac{dT_\Omega}{dt}$ and $\dfrac{d^2T_\Omega}{dt^2}$ are continuous on $[t_i, t_{i+1}]$
4. $\dfrac{d^2T_\Omega(t_1)}{dt^2} = \dfrac{d^2T_\Omega(t_n)}{dt^2} = 0$

There are two interesting asymptotic properties:

1. When the tension $\Omega \to 0$, the spline in tension is reduced to a cubic spline
2. When the tension $\Omega \to \infty$, the limiting interpolant is the polygonal line joining the control points

Nielson (1974) described polynomial alternatives to splines in tension, called v-splines. These curves $C(t)$ are comprised of piecewise cubic polynomials such that:

1. $C(t) = P_i$ i=1 to n
2. $\dfrac{dC(t)}{dt}$ is continuous on the subinterval $[t_i, t_{i+1}]$
3. $\dfrac{d^2C(t_1+)}{dt^2} - \dfrac{d^2C(t_1-)}{dt^2} = v_i \dfrac{dC(t)}{dt}$

Under these conditions, the v-spline curves are defined as:

$$C(t) = a + bt + \sum_{i=1}^{n-1} \alpha_i (t-t_i)^3 + \sum_{i=1}^{n-1} \beta_i (t-t_i)^2 \qquad (3.18)$$

with $C(t_i) = y_i$ and $\beta_i = v_i \dfrac{C(t_i)}{2}$ $i = 2, \dots n-1$

The v_i are tension parameters which permit additional control over the shape of the curve. Advantages of the v-spline compared with the spline in tension are that the tension v_i can be applied at each control point.

An extension of v-spline curves to surfaces has been recently developed by Nielson (1986) and is called **rectangular v-splines**. The concept of tension has been largely used in other splines including Kochanek-Bartels interpolating splines (see Sect. 3.2.5), ß-splines, and ß2-splines (see Sect. 3.6).

3.2.4 Cardinal and Catmull-Rom spline interpolation

Consider again a list of points P_i and the parameter t along the spline. A new point V is obtained from each value of t from the four nearest given points along the curve (two behind, two ahead) by:

$$V = \boldsymbol{\mathcal{C M P}}^T \qquad (3.19)$$

where $\mathcal{T}$ is the matrix $[t^3\ t^2\ t\ 1]$, $\mathcal{M}$ is the spline matrix, and $\mathcal{P}$ is the matrix $[\mathbf{P}_{k-1},$ $\mathbf{P}_k, \mathbf{P}_{k+1}, \mathbf{P}_{k+2}]$.

With this approach, the spline matrix $\mathcal{M}$ is used to generate, for each four consecutive points $\mathbf{P}_{k-1}, \mathbf{P}_k, \mathbf{P}_{k+1}$ and $\mathbf{P}_{k+2}$, the portion of the spline curve between the two middle points $\mathbf{P}_k, \mathbf{P}_{k+1}$.

Several spline matrices have been proposed. The simplest is the **Catmull-Rom spline** matrix:

$$\mathcal{M}_{RC} = 0.5 \begin{bmatrix} -1 & 3 & -3 & 1 \\ 2 & -5 & 4 & -1 \\ -1 & 0 & 1 & 0 \\ 0 & 2 & 0 & 0 \end{bmatrix} \tag{3.20}$$

A more general case is the **cardinal spline** matrix:

$$\mathcal{M}_{CA} = \begin{bmatrix} -A & 2-A & A-2 & A \\ 2A & A-3 & 3-2A & -A \\ -A & 0 & A & 0 \\ 0 & 1 & 0 & 0 \end{bmatrix} \tag{3.21}$$

The parameter A, called the **tension**, causes the spline to bend more sharply; it increases the magnitude of the tangent vector at the knots.

3.2.5 Hermite interpolation and Kochanek-Bartels spline interpolation

Kochanek and Bartels (1984) propose a method of interpolating splines with three parameters for local control—tension, continuity, and bias. The method was designed for generating in-betweens in keyframe animation (Magnenat-Thalmann and Thalmann 1985b); however, it is also a very powerful tool for generating ordinary curves from a set of points. Consider again a list of points $\mathbf{P}_i$ and the parameter t along the spline to be determined. What is new is that a point $\mathbf{V}$ is obtained from each value of t from only the two nearest given points along the curve (one behind $\mathbf{P}_i$, one in front of $\mathbf{P}_{i+1}$). But, the tangent vectors $\mathbf{D}_i$ and $\mathbf{D}_{i+1}$ at these two points are also necessary. This means that, we have:

$$V = \mathcal{T}\mathcal{H}\mathcal{C}^T \tag{3.22}$$

where $\mathcal{T}$ is the matrix $[t^3\ t^2\ t\ 1]$, $\mathcal{H}$ is the Hermite matrix, and $\mathcal{C}$ is the matrix $[\mathbf{P}_i,$ $\mathbf{P}_{i+1}, \mathbf{D}_i, \mathbf{D}_{i+1}]$. The Hermite matrix is given by:

$$\mathcal{H} = \begin{bmatrix} 2 & -2 & 1 & 1 \\ -3 & 3 & -2 & -1 \\ 0 & 0 & 1 & 0 \\ 1 & 0 & 0 & 0 \end{bmatrix} \tag{3.23}$$

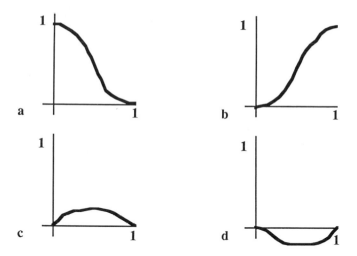

Fig.3.4 a-d Hermite interpolation basis functions **a** $H_1(t) = 2t^3 - 3t^2 + 1$; **b** $H_2(t) = -2t^3 + 3t^2$; **c** $H_3(t) = t^3 - 2t^2 + t$; **d** $H_4(t) = t^3 - t^2$

This matrix corresponds to the four functions $H_1(t)$, $H_2(t)$, $H_3(t)$, and $H_4(t)$ represented in Fig.3.4. These functions are often used as basis functions for the cubic polynomial because of the following properties:

$$
\begin{aligned}
&H_1(0) = 1 \\
&H_2(0) = H_3(0) = H_4(0) = 0 \\
&H_2(1) = 1 \\
&H_1(1) = H_3(1) = H_4(1) = 0 \\
&\frac{dH_3(0)}{dt} = 1 \\
&\frac{dH_1(0)}{dt} = \frac{dH_2(0)}{dt} = \frac{dH_4(0)}{dt} = 0 \\
&\frac{dH_4(1)}{dt} = 1 \\
&\frac{dH_1(1)}{dt} = \frac{dH_2(1)}{dt} = \frac{dH_3(1)}{dt} = 0
\end{aligned} \tag{3.24}
$$

Kochanek and Bartels formulate the cardinal spline using Eq. (3.22) by defining the tangent vector $\mathbf{D_i}$ at $\mathbf{P_i}$ by:

$$\mathbf{D_i} = a\ (\mathbf{P_{i+1}} - \mathbf{P_{i-1}}) \tag{3.25}$$

The Catmull-Rom spline is then obtained for a=0.5:

$$\mathbf{D_i} = 0.5\ (\mathbf{P_{i+1}} - \mathbf{P_{i-1}}) = 0.5\ [(\mathbf{P_{i+1}} - \mathbf{P_i}) + (\mathbf{P_i} - \mathbf{P_{i-1}})] \tag{3.26}$$

This equation shows that the tangent vector is the average of the source chord $\mathbf{P_i} - \mathbf{P_{i-1}}$ and the destination chord $\mathbf{P_{i+1}} - \mathbf{P_i}$. Similarly, the source derivative (tangent vector) $\mathbf{DS_i}$ and the destination derivative (tangent vector) $\mathbf{DD_i}$ may be considered at any point $\mathbf{P_i}$.

Using these derivatives, Kochanek and Bartels propose the use of three parameters to control the splines—**tension, continuity,** and **bias.**

The tension parameter t controls how sharply the curve bends at a point P_i using the equation:

$$DS_i = DD_i = 0.5 \ (1-t) \ (P_{i+1}-P_{i-1}) \tag{3.27}$$

The continuity c of the spline at a point P_i is controlled using the following equations:

$$DS_i = \ \ 0.5 \ [(1+c) \ (P_{i+1}-P_i) + (1-c) \ (P_i-P_{i-1})] \tag{3.28}$$
$$DD_i = \ \ 0.5 \ [(1-c) \ (P_{i+1}-P_i) + (1+c) \ (P_i-P_{i-1})] \tag{3.29}$$

The direction of the path as it passes through a point P_i is controlled by the bias parameter b according to the following equation:

$$DS_i = DD_i = \ \ 0.5 \ [(1-b) \ (P_{i+1}-P_i) + (1+b) \ (P_i-P_{i-1})] \tag{3.30}$$

Equations combining the three parameters may be obtained:

$$DS_i = \ \ 0.5 \ [(1-t)(1+c)(1-b) \ (P_{i+1}-P_i) + (1-t)(1-c)(1+b) \ (P_i-P_{i-1})] \tag{3.31}$$
$$DD_i = \ \ 0.5 \ [(1-t)(1-c)(1-b) \ (P_{i+1}-P_i) + (1-t)(1+c)(1+b) \ (P_i-P_{i-1})] \tag{3.32}$$

A spline is then generated using Eq. (3.22) with DD_i and DS_{i+1} instead of D_i and D_{i+1}.

Figure 3.5 shows the impact of the three parameters on a typical spline curve.

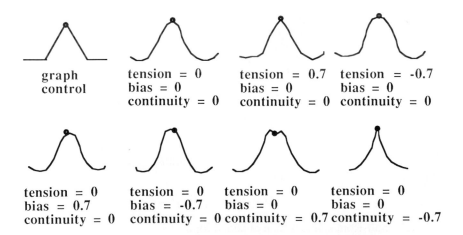

Fig.3.5. Impact of the parameters tension, continuity, and bias

3.3 Coons surfaces

3.3.1 Definition of a Coons surface

With this method (Coons 1964), a parametric surface $S(u,v)$ is constructed from four curves $P(u,0)$, $P(u,1)$, $P(0,v)$, and $P(1,v)$ (see Fig. 3.6) using Eq. (3.33).

$$S(u, v) = \sum_{i=0}^{1} F_i(u)\, P(i,v) + \sum_{j=0}^{1} F_j(v)\, P(u,j) - \sum_{i=0}^{1}\sum_{j=0}^{1} F_i(u)\, F_j(v)\, P(i,j) \qquad (3.33)$$

where $P(0,0)$ is the intersection point of $P(u,0)$ and $P(0,v)$, $P(0,1)$ is the intersection point of $P(u,1)$ and $P(0,v)$, $P(1,0)$ is the intersection point of $P(u,0)$ and $P(1,v)$, and $P(1,1)$ is the intersection point of $P(u,1)$ and $P(1,v)$. F_i are functions which have to be adequately chosen. The only condition is that the $F_i(j)$ must satisfy the Kronecker symbol δ_{ij}. The simplest F_i are:

$$F_0(u) = 1\text{-}u \quad \text{and} \quad F_1(u) = u \qquad (3.34)$$

but other forms may be used as, for example:

$$F_0(u) = \cos^2(\pi/2 * u) \quad \text{and} \quad F_1(u) = \sin^2(\pi/2 * u) \qquad (3.35)$$

According to Coons, a point of the surface is a weighted average of the corresponding points (with the same parameters) of the four border points. The four last terms in Eq. (3.33) ensure that the intersections between the curves are not taken into account twice.

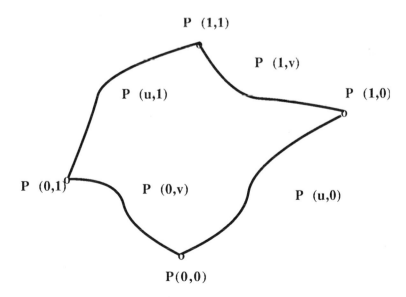

P (1,1)

P (1,v)

P (u,1)

P (1,0)

P (0,1)

P (0,v)

P (u,0)

P(0,0)

Fig. 3.6. Coons surface

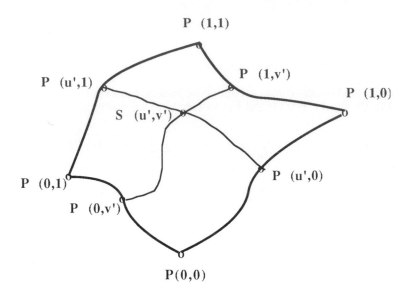

Fig.3.7. Dependence of a point S(u',v')

3.3.2 Advantages and disadvantages of Coons surfaces

From a continuity point of view, the interpolation function ensures the continuity of the surface but not the continuity of the first derivative. This means that when several Coons patches are linked together, there is no continuity of the first derivative at the border curves. It is possible to introduce interpolation of the derivatives. However, this implies a large amount of CPU time and limits interactive control. It can be shown that to ensure the continuity of the normal, Hermit cubic polynomes can be used. The surface is then defined as:

$$S(u, v) = \sum_{i=0}^{1} \sum_{j=0}^{1} \sum_{k=0}^{1} \sum_{l=0}^{1} g_{ki}(u) \, g_{lj}(v) \, [\partial^{k+l} P(u, v) / \partial u^k \partial v^l]_{u=i, v=j} \quad (3.36)$$

where the g_{ij} functions are the Hermite functions defined in Fig.3.4 with the correspondances $g_{00}=H_1$, $g_{01}=H_2$, $g_{10}=H_3$ and $g_{11}=H_4$.

Coons surfaces are the simplest surfaces in geometric modeling; they are very different from other surfaces like Bézier surfaces, B-spline surfaces, and ß-spline surfaces. Because Coons surfaces pass through the original curves, they should be classified as interpolation surfaces.

The advantage of Coons surfaces is their simplicity; because they pass through the curves and they are interpolations of these curves, their shape may be easily predicted. Disadvantages are the lack of first derivative continuity in the primitive form and their dependence on the original curves. However, note that as shown in Fig.3.7, a point S(u',v') of the surface is only dependent on the four points **P**(0,v'), **P**(u',0), **P**(u',1), and **P**(1,v').

3.4 Bézier curves and surfaces

3.4.1 Bézier surfaces

Bézier surfaces were first used in the UNISURF system at the "Régie Renault" in France. They were introduced by Bézier (1972).

Bézier surfaces are parametric surfaces $S(u, v)$, calculated from a grid of M*N control points (called a **control graph**), using the following equation:

$$S(u, v) = \sum_{i=0}^{N} \sum_{j=0}^{M} P_{ij} \, B_{iN}(u) \, B_{jM}(v) \qquad (3.37)$$

where u and v are defined between 0 and 1 and the B_{ik} are Bernstein polynomials:

$$B_{ik}(w) = \frac{k!}{i! \, (k-i)!} \, w^i \, (1-w)^{k-i} \qquad (3.38)$$

Note that $B_{ik}(w)$ is the discrete Bernouilli probability distribution. This means that we may write:

$$\sum_{i=1}^{k} B_{ik}(w) = 1 \qquad (3.39)$$

$$B_{ik}(w) \geq 0 \qquad (3.40)$$

$$\forall \, i,k > 0 \text{ and } \forall \, w \in [0,1]$$

The condition in Eq. (3.39) means that the surface is independent of the coordinate system and the condition in Eq. (3.40) ensures that the surface is inside the convex grid of the control polygons.

The surface is then controlled by the P_{ij}. Unfortunately a modification of a single control point changes the whole surface and the degree of the polynomials is strongly linked to the number of control points. This greatly increases the complexity of calculations as the number of control points becomes large.

As a Bézier surface is a tensor product of Bézier curves, we may explain some properties of the surfaces by examining the curves.

3.4.2 Bézier curves

A 3D Bézier curve is defined by a control polygon of N+1 vertices, denoted by P_0, P_1...P_N. A point of the curve is then given by the equation:

$$C(t) = \sum_{i=0}^{N} P_i \, B_{iN}(t) \qquad (3.41)$$

To generate the curve, the parameter has to vary from 0 to 1. $B_{iN}(t)$ are defined as

$$B_{iN}(t) = C_i^N \, t^i \, (1-t)^{N-i} \qquad (3.42)$$

with $C_i^N = \dfrac{N!}{(N-i)! \, i!}$

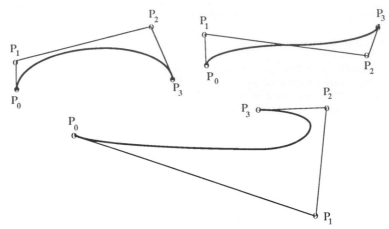

Fig.3.8. Examples of Bézier curves for N=3

For example, consider the curve defined by four control points $\mathbf{P_0}$, $\mathbf{P_1}$, $\mathbf{P_2}$, and $\mathbf{P_3}$. The four Bernstein polynomials are:

$$B_{0,3}(t) = -t^3 + 3t^2 - 3t + 1 \qquad\qquad (3.43)$$
$$B_{1,3}(t) = 3t^3 - 6t^2 + 3t$$
$$B_{2,3}(t) = -3t^3 + 3t^2$$
$$B_{3,3}(t) = t^3$$

The curve is then :

$$\mathbf{C}(t) = (1-t)^3\mathbf{P_0} + 3t(1-t)^2\mathbf{P_1} + 3t^2(1-t)\mathbf{P_2} + t^3\mathbf{P_3} \qquad\qquad (3.44)$$

Note that:

$$\mathbf{C}(0) = \mathbf{P_0} \text{ and } \mathbf{C}(1) = \mathbf{P_3} \qquad\qquad (3.45)$$

This means that the first and last points of the curve correspond to the first and last control points, as shown in the examples of Fig.3.8.

For the derivatives, we may write:

$$\frac{d\mathbf{C}(0)}{dt} = 3 \,(\mathbf{P_1} - \mathbf{P_0}) \quad \text{and} \quad \frac{d\mathbf{C}(1)}{dt} = 3 \,(\mathbf{P_3} - \mathbf{P_2}) \qquad\qquad (3.46)$$

These equations mean that the Bezier curve is tangential to the control polygon at the first and the last points. This property is very important for linking together Bézier curves and also Bézier surfaces.

3.4.3 Advantages, drawbacks, and applications of Bézier curves and surfaces

Bézier surfaces and curves do not pass through the control vertices. However, an important property of Bezier curves is that they are guaranteed to remain within the **convex hull** of the control vertices. Similarly, a Bézier surface lies inside the convex hull of its control graph. Bézier curves also have the **variation diminishing property**, which means that the number of intersection points of any straight line with the curve is less than that with the control polygon. It is also essential to note that Bézier surfaces and curves do not have **local control**. This means that while control points have greatest impact closest to them, they also have an influence anywhere on the surface or the curve. The movement of a single vertex affects the entire surface or curve.

The most important drawback of Bézier surfaces (and curves) is their dependence on the number of control vertices. A series of N control points generates a Bézier curve of degree N-1.

Schmitt et al. (1986) describe a top down method for the problem of surface fitting from sampled data. Their method is based on an adaptive subdivision approach. It begins with a roughly approximated surface and progressively refines it in successive steps, adjusting the regions where the data are poorly approximated. The method constructs a parametric piecewise Bézier surface representation possessing G^1 continuity (i.e., the surface possesses a continuous tangent plane in addition to a continuous position). The surface is adjusted with respect to the sampled data by generating and exploiting new degrees of freedom. Each patch is tested and is accepted without further processing when a certain criterion is satisfied. This criterion involves a tolerance level specified by the user. Otherwise, the adaptive subdivision phase subdivides the patch into four sub-patches, creating new vertices which are then positioned so as to achieve a closer approximation of the underlying data. The method provides a hierachical representation of the surface as a quadtreelike structure (see Sect. 4.2.3).

3.5 B-spline curves and surfaces

3.5.1 B-spline curves

B-spline curves and surfaces provide partial solutions to two problems with Bézier curves and surfaces: nonlocalness and the fact that the degree is dependent on the number of control points. Their formulation is not very different from that of Bézier curves and surfaces.

Consider a control polygon of N+1 vertices P_i with corresponding knots t_i. A B-spline curve is defined by the following equation:

$$C_k(t) - \sum_{i=0}^{N} P_i N_{i,k}(t) \qquad (3.47)$$

$N_{i,k}$ are **basic B-spline functions of order k**; they are recursively defined as:

$$N_{i,1}(t) = 1 \text{ if } t_i \le t \le t_{i+1} \qquad (3.48)$$
$$0 \text{ otherwise}$$

$$N_{i,k}(t) = \frac{(t-t_i) N_{i,k-1}(t)}{t_{i+k-1} - t_i} + \frac{(t_{i+k}-t) N_{i+1,k-1}(t)}{t_{i+k} - t_{i+1}} \qquad (3.49)$$

The basis function $N_{i,k}(t)$ is a polynomial of degree k-1 which guarantees C^{k-2} continuity for the whole curve. In other terms, a B-spline of order k may be mathematically defined as a piecewise polynomial of degree k-1 that guarantees continuity of the first k-2 derivatives. A B-spline of order k for a span i may also be considered as weighted average of the B-splines of order k-1 on the spans i and i+1. As shown in Eq. (3.49), each weight is obtained by the ratio of the distance between the parameter t and the end knot to the length of the k-1 spans. It is important to note that the calculation of $N_{i,k}(t)$ only involves knots t_i to t_{i+k}. This means that local control is possible; the modification of a single control point does not change the whole curve but only a limited portion. A knot may be repeated several times to increase the effect of the corresponding control point, as shown in Fig.3.9.

The order of the B-splines is controlled by k, which means that for the same control vertices, it is possible to obtain a curve which is more or less close to the control vertices, as shown in Fig.3.10.

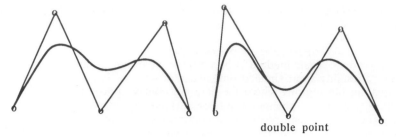

double point

Fig.3.9. Effect of a double point

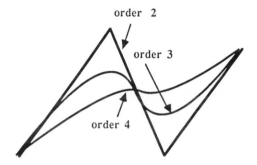

Fig.3.10. Effect of the order in B-spline curves

A useful case of B-spline curves is based on a uniform knot spacing with the first and last knot value each repeated k times. Knots are then chosen as:

$$
\begin{aligned}
t_i &= 0 \text{ if } i < k \\
t_i &= i-k+1 \text{ if } k \le i \le N \\
t_i &= N-k+2 \text{ if } i > N
\end{aligned}
\tag{3.50}
$$

3.5.2 B-spline surfaces

A B-spline surface is defined by the following tensor product:

$$
\mathbf{S_{k,l}}(u,v) = \sum_{i=0}^{N} \sum_{j=0}^{M} \mathbf{P_{ij}}\, N_{i,k}(u)\, N_{j,l}(v)
\tag{3.51}
$$

where k and l are the B-spline surface orders.

Lines of constant u are B-spline curves with control vertices

$$
\mathbf{Q_i}(v) = \sum_{i=0}^{1} \mathbf{P_{ij}}\, N_{j,1}(v)
\tag{3.52}
$$

3.5.3 Properties, advantages, and drawbacks of B-spline curves and surfaces

B-spline curves and surfaces preserve the advantages of the Bézier method (control polygons, convex hull property, variation diminishing property). The B-spline method has the great advantage of **localness**. This means that changing the position of a control vertex only modifies the curve or surface shape in a defined section. This feature is quite interesting for the development of interactive graphics systems. The order of continuity of a B-spline surface is controlled by the orders k and l, as shown for a curve in Fig.3.10. This order is independent of the number of control vertices. Unfortunately, when k or l is increased, calculations become much more complex. Moreover, as k and l are orders, they are integers and continuous variation, which may be required in animation, is quite impossible.

3.5.4 Localized surface modulation and the Oslo algorithm

Huitric and Nahas (1985) show that B-splines can be used to model shapes (see Fig.3.11) in the same way as a sculptor models clay or plasticine, because of the **Oslo algorithm** (Cohen et al. 1980).

The surface can be modulated by varying control points according to a modulation function T_{ij}:

$$P_{ij} = P_{ij} + T_{ij} \tag{3.53}$$

T_{ij} may be a mathematical function, an array defined by a set of control values, or a random variation.

The Oslo algorithm is very useful because it permits control points to be added to any region of the surface without changing its form. This is important since the density of control points is directly related to the possible modulations. The extent of the influence of a control point is dependent on the density of the environment.

The Oslo algorithm simultaneously inserts r new knots which, together with the old ones, form a refined partition $\{\tau_j\}$. The n-1 old control points $P_{s-n+1},...,P_{s-1}$ have to be replaced by the n-1+r new control points $P_{1,s-n+1},...P_{r,s-}$

Fig.3.11. High-pass Fourier filtering of control points, from the film *Un jeu d'enfant* . Courtesy of M.Nahas, Université de Paris VII

$_{n+r},...,\mathbf{P}_{r,s},...\mathbf{P}_{1,s}$. Every new control point $\mathbf{Q}_j$ corresponding to the knot t_j of the refined partition is computed by the de Boor algorithm: if $t_j \in [t_k,t_{k+1}]$, x is replaced row by row by $\tau_{j+n+1-k}$. Starting with $\mathbf{P}_{0,s-n}=\mathbf{P}_{s-n},...,\mathbf{P}_{0,s} = \mathbf{P}_s$ again $\mathbf{Q}_j$ will be computed instead of $\mathbf{P}_{n,s}$.

3.6 ß-spline curves and surfaces

3.6.1 ß-spline curves

ß-spline curves (Barsky 1984) are also produced from a control polygon, but they have the great advantage of being based on geometric considerations. To introduce ß-spline curves, Barsky and Beatty (1983) developed a new formulation of the i-th segment of a uniform cubic B-spline curve based on N+1 control points as:

$$\mathbf{C}_i (t) = \sum_{r=-2}^{1} \mathbf{P}_{i+r} \, b_r(t) \tag{3.54}$$

where $0 \le t \le 1$ and $i = 2$ to N-1.

Based on the following continuity conditions at the joints:

$$\mathbf{C}_{i-1} (t_i) = \mathbf{C}_i (t_i)$$

$$\frac{d\mathbf{C}_{i-1} (t_i)}{dt} = \frac{d\mathbf{C}_i (t_i)}{dt} \tag{3.55}$$

$$\frac{d^2\mathbf{C}_{i-1} (t_i)}{dt^2} = \frac{d^2\mathbf{C}_i (t_i)}{dt^2}$$

we may express the basis B-spline functions:

$$b_1(t) = \frac{t^3}{6}$$

$$b_0(t) = \frac{1 + 3t + 3t^2 - 3t^3}{6} \tag{3.56}$$

$$b_{-1}(t) = \frac{4 - 6t^2 + 3t^3}{6}$$

$$b_{-2}(t) = \frac{1 - 3t + 3t^2 - t^3}{6}$$

Similarly, the i-th segment of a ß-spline curve based on N+1 control points may be expressed as:

$$\mathbf{C}_i (t) = \sum_{r=-2}^{1} \mathbf{P}_{i+r} \, b_r(ß_1,ß_2,t) \tag{3.57}$$

where b_r (r=-2 to 1) is a cubic polynomial called the r-th basic ß-spline function.

Barsky and Beatty introduce less restrictive continuity conditions:

$$\mathbf{C}_{i-1} (t_i) = \mathbf{C}_i (t_i)$$
$$ß_1 \frac{d\mathbf{C}_{i-1} (t_i)}{dt} = \frac{d\mathbf{C}_i (t_i)}{dt} \tag{3.58}$$
$$ß_1^2 \frac{d^2\mathbf{C}_{i-1} (t_i)}{dt^2} + ß_2 \frac{d\mathbf{C}_{i-1} (t_i)}{dt} = \frac{d^2\mathbf{C}_i (t_i)}{dt^2}$$

The second condition corresponds to the continuity of the unitary tangent vector and the last condition expresses the continuity of the radius of curvature.

Using these conditions, the following basis functions are found:

$$b_1(\beta_1,\beta_2,t) = 2\,\frac{t^3}{\mu}$$

$$b_0(\beta_1,\beta_2,t) = \frac{2\beta_1^2\,t^2\,(-t+3)+2\beta_1\,t\,(-t^2+3)+\beta_2\,t^2\,(-2t+3)+2\,(-t^3+1)}{\mu}$$

$$b_{-1}(\beta_1,\beta_2,t) = \frac{2\beta_1^3\,t\,(t^2-3t+3)+2\beta_1^2\,(t^3-3t^2+2)+2\beta_1(t^3-3t+2)+\beta_2(2t^3-3t^2+1)}{\mu}$$

$$b_{-2}(\beta_1,\beta_2,t) = \frac{2\,\beta_1^3\,(1-t)^3}{\mu} \tag{3.59}$$

with $\mu = 2\,\beta_1^3 + 4\,\beta_1^2 + 4\,\beta_1 + \beta_2 + 2$

3.6.2 Bias and tension

In the basis ß-spline functions of Eq. (3.59), β_1 and β_2 are two parameters called **bias** and **tension**. The bias β_1 provides control over the symmetry of the curve generated from the control polygon, and the tension β_2 controls the degree of adherance of the curve to the control polygon. When β_1 is increased, the curve begins to skew to one side and approach the control polygon in an asymptotic fashion. When β_2 is increased, the curve flattens and uniformly approaches the control polygon.

We may summarize the effect of both parameters as follows:

$\beta_1 = 1$	$\Rightarrow$	the curve is said to be unbiased
$\beta_1 = V,\ V \geq 1$	$\Rightarrow$	the curve is skewed to one side
$\beta_1 = \frac{1}{V},\ V \geq 1$	$\Rightarrow$	the curve is skewed an equal amount to the other side
$\beta_2 = 0$	$\Rightarrow$	the curve is said to be untensed
$\beta_2 > 0$	$\Rightarrow$	the curve tends to flatten when β_2 is increased

Figure 3.12 shows the effect of these parameters in the case of a curve.

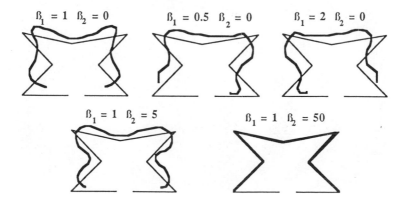

Fig. 3.12. Effect of bias (β_1) and tension (β_2) in a ß-spline curve

When we substitute $ß_1=1$ and $ß_2=0$ into Eq. (3.59) we obtain Eq. (3.56), which means that the ß-spline basis functions are reduced to the uniform cubic B-spline basis functions.

A theoretical analysis of geometric continuity in ß-spline curves has been presented by Goodman and Unsworth (1986). Goldman (1986) has also proposed urn models to gain some insight into the properties of ß-splines.

Continuously shaped ß-spline curves are ß-spline curves with shape parameters $ß_1$ and $ß_2$ (denoted by $ß_k$) that vary along the curve. Each parameter $ß_{k,i}$ (k=1,2) may be obtained by a function of t. For example, Barsky and Beatty have shown that the following function is suitable:

$$ß_{k,i}(t) = \Omega_{k,i-1} + (\Omega_{k,i} - \Omega_{k,i-1})(10t^3 - 15t^4 + 6t^5) \tag{3.60}$$

where $\Omega_{k,i}$ is the value of $ß_k$ associated with the joint between $C_{i-1}(t)$ and $C_i(t)$.

3.6.3 ß-spline surfaces

A ß-spline surface is described by a control graph in 3D space and is defined by the following tensor product:

$$S_{i,j}(u, v) = \sum_{r=-2}^{1} \sum_{s=-2}^{1} P_{i+r,j+s} \, b_r(ß_1,ß_2,u) \, b_s(ß_1,ß_2,v) \tag{3.61}$$

where $0 \le u \le 1$ and $0 \le v \le 1$, i = 2 to m-1 and j = 2 to n-1.

Continuously shaped ß-spline surfaces may also be defined similarly to continuously shaped ß-spline curves.

Figure 3.13 shows examples of ß-spline surfaces.

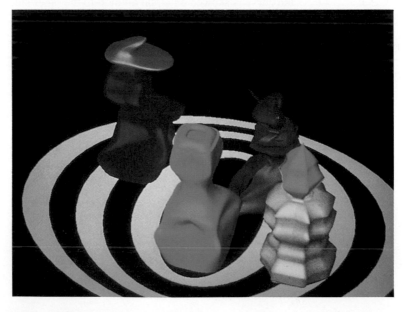

Fig. 3.13. ß-spline-based bottles © 1984 MIRALab, H.E.C. and University of Montreal

3.6.4   Properties, advantages, and drawbacks of ß-spline curves and surfaces

ß-spline curves and surfaces may be easily used in an interactive environment because they are flexible and based on geometric relations. The method for transforming these curves and surfaces is more natural than other methods based on algebraic considerations. The shape parameters may continuously vary since they are real numbers.

As the degree of ß-spline curves and surfaces is constant (3 for curves, 6 for surfaces), the CPU time is the same for any value of the shape parameters.

The main drawback of ß-spline curves and surfaces is that they do not pass through any of the control vertices, not even the first and the last. This means that two fictitious control points may, if necessary, have to be added to circumvent the problem.

3.6.5   ß2-spline curves and surfaces

Barsky and DeRose (1985) developed a special type of ß-spline curve called the ß2-spline. The shape of a ß2-spline is controlled by only one parameter, corresponding to the tension parameter β_2. Similar to Eq. (3.54), the i-th segment of a ß2-spline curve based on N+1 control points may be expressed as:

$$C_i(t) = \sum_{r=-2}^{1} P_{i+r} \, b_r(\beta_2, t) \tag{3.62}$$

where b_r (r=-2 to 1) is a cubic polynomial called the **r-th basic ß2-spline function**.

This approach is simpler than the ß-spline method and computationally more efficient. In the case of the ß2-spline, the requirement of continuity of the unit tangent is replaced with that of the first derivative vector. Curvature vector continuity is still used instead of the second derivative vector. The new continuity conditions are as follows:

$$C_{i-1}(t_i) = C_i(t_i)$$

$$\frac{dC_{i-1}(t_i)}{dt} = \frac{dC_i(t_i)}{dt} \tag{3.63}$$

$$\frac{d^2C_{i-1}(t_i)}{dt^2} + \beta_2 \frac{dC_{i-1}(t_i)}{dt} = \frac{d^2C_i(t_i)}{dt^2}$$

This implies the following basis functions:

$$
\begin{aligned}
b_1(\beta_2, t) &= 2\,\Omega\, t^3 \\
b_0(\beta_2, t) &= \Omega\,[2 + t\,(6 + t\,(3\,(\beta_2 + 2) - 2t\,(\beta_2 + 3)))] \\
b_{-1}(\beta_2, t) &= \Omega\,[\beta_2 + 8 + t^2\,(-3\,(\beta_2 + 4) + 2t\,(\beta_2 + 3))] \\
b_{-2}(\beta_2, t) &= 2\,\Omega\,(1-t)^3
\end{aligned}
\tag{3.64}
$$

with $\Omega = \dfrac{1}{\beta_2 + 12}$

Similarly, ß2-spline surfaces may be defined as the tensor product of ß2-spline curves.

Barsky and DeRose describe detailed algorithms for the evaluation of the ß2-spline basis functions and the approximation of ß2-spline curves and surfaces via subdivision. The subdivision algorithm approximates a ß2-spline by transforming it into an equivalent Bézier curve or surface. It then approximates the Bézier spline using recursive subdivision.

3.7 Propagation control graphs

3.7.1 Definition of a propagation control graph

Bézier, B-spline, and ß-spline surfaces have proved to be powerful ways of building 3D free-form objects. Usually, control graphs are created and only a few control points are then modified. ß-spline surfaces are controlled by geometric parameters called bias and tension. In computer animation, there is a great need for tools to generate these kinds of surface; however, designers are generally unable to create complex graph controls to generate surfaces.

One important class of control graph can be generated by moving (or propagating) a polygon along a path. We call this type of control graph a **propagation control graph** (Magnenat-Thalmann and Thalmann 1986). A propagation control graph (PCG) is defined by the following elements:

1. A path which may be either a polygonal line or a 3D curve
2. A polygonal specification which consists of one, two, or a set of polygons
3. Several evolution functions

The PCG is obtained by propagating the polygon(s) along the path according to evolution functions as shown in Fig.3.14.

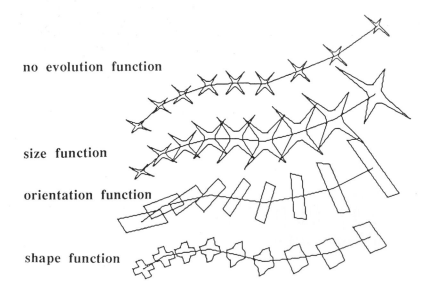

no evolution function

size function

orientation function

shape function

Fig.3.14. Evolution functions

We observe that the definition of a PCG corresponds to the definition of an object defined by a sweeping operation (see Sect. 4.3). However, it should be noted that the PCG is only one step toward producing a surface like a Bézier surface; or a ß-spline surface. The PCG is not a surface but a collection of polygons propagated along a path.

The PCG approach has the great advantage that the user may easily change the path and even animate it and regenerate the control graph and then the surface. This may be considered an analog to the interactive skeleton approach introduced in 2D keyframe animation. The idea behind the skeleton technique (Burtnik and Wein 1976) is that skeletons of the figures, rather than the figures themselves, can be used as a basis for in-betweening. A skeleton or stick figure is a simple image composed of only a few points, describing only the form of movement required. This allows the animator to create many keyframes consisting only of skeletons.

3.7.2 Evolution functions

Evolution functions provide an effective way of generating many control graphs for a given path and a given polygonal specification. Typically, we have size, orientation, and shape functions.

3.7.2.1 Scale functions
The purpose of such functions is to control the size of the polygons that are propagated. In fact, a scale function is a vectorial function scale (L), where L is defined as the current length on the path. Examples of commonly used scale functions are linear, acceleration, deceleration, sinusoidal, and random (see Fig.3.15).

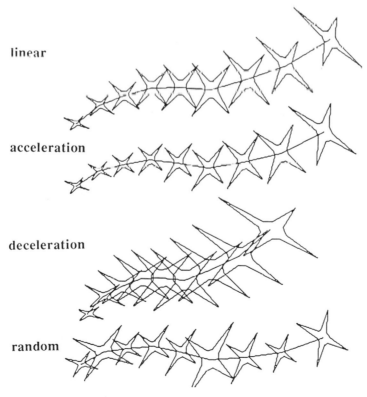

linear

acceleration

deceleration

random

Fig.3.15. Scale functions

3.7.2.2 Orientation functions

Once the instances of polygons have been positioned and scaled, they may be oriented in various ways. By default, we may choose the normal to the plane or the polygon to be tangential to the path. A standard orientation of the polygon in its plane must also be defined. For example we may assume an original rotation of 90^0 around the y-axis and a rotation of 90^0 around the z-axis. Now, an orientation function is used to define the variation in orientation relative to the current length L on the path. Several possibilities should be considered: the normal to the polygons may be defined in an absolute way or relative to the tangent to the path. The orientation of the polygon in its plane may also be varied along the path. This feature creates a torsion effect.

3.7.2.3 Shape functions

The shape of the instances of the polygons may also change along the path. Although it is possible to define a series of polygons, this is generally a laborious process and requires the same number of vertices for each polygon. However, we may apply the keyframe interpolation technique to this problem. A starting polygon and a final polygon may be provided and in-between polygons may be computed using an interpolation technique. Typically an interpolation law has to be provided such as one of the four basic animation laws. A more complex example involving several evolution functions is displayed in Fig.8.4.

3.7.3 Implementation of a PCG

Basically, the algorithm for generating a PCG works as follows:

Compute the path length and the initial direction of the normal
for each vertex (or each step on the curve)
    Compute the current distance on the path relative to the total length
    Compute the orientation of the normal to the polygon to position
    Determine the rotation matrix to be applied to the previous normal by transforming
        both normals in spherical coordinates (R,θ,ϕ)
    Apply an orientation function if required
    if there is no interpolation
    then
        Rotate the polygon using the rotation matrix
    else
        Apply the rotation matrix to both keyframe polygons
    Compute the in-between according to the interpolation law
    Compute the scale factor to avoid undesirable distorsion when the angle between
        two normals is large; apply the scale function if required
    Rotate the scale factor (which is a vector) according to the rotation matrix
    Apply the scale operation
    Translate the polygon to the correct position

4 Solid modeling

4.1 Representation of solid objects

4.1.1 Role of solids in image synthesis

The generation of 3D solid objects and more generally solid geometric modeling is very important in computer-aided design (CAD) and computer-aided engineering (CAE). In CAD and CAE, solid modeling (an important branch of geometric modeling) is used to create and communicate shape information. Typically, two main types of representation scheme are mainly used—constructive solid geometry (CSG) and boundary models. In CSG, objects are described in terms of half-spaces or boundary primitive solids. Each object is represented by a binary tree of Boolean operations. With boundary models, solids are described in terms of their spatial boundaries; they are represented as unions of faces, bound by edges, which are bound by vertices.

In image synthesis and 3D computer animation, there is also an important need to include some means of representing 3D objects. However, there is a fundamental difference between the use of 3D objects in CAD and in image synthesis: in the former, the main purpose is to generate objects to study them; in image synthesis, objects are created to be displayed in an esthetic way. For this reason, methods like CSG which truly model a solid are less useful here than in CAD and most interactive systems are based on faceted models, which may be considered a limited form of boundary representation.

However, several concepts introduced in solid modeling now play a fundamental role in current image synthesis. For example:

-Set theoretic operations on 3D objects like union, intersection and, difference are only possible using solid representations.
-Storage of complex objects may be based on techniques like CSG
-Sweep representations used in solid modeling are very common techniques of generating surfaces
-Octree encoding is very useful for the optimization of ray-tracing algorithms

An interesting example of the use of solid modeling systems for image synthesis is the case of MAGI Synthavision (Goldstein and Malin 1979), which has produced some of the most beautiful computer-generated images and animation sequences using the Synthavision solid modeling system.

4.1.2 r-Sets

According to Requicha (1980), models of solids should have certain properties. A solid must have an invariant configuration and shape (rigidity) and an interior. It must occupy a finite portion of space. Rigid motions and certain Boolean operations applied to solids must provide solids. Solids should be described using a finite number of elements (e.g., number of faces, vertices). The boundary of a solid must determine unambiguously what is inside and outside. Requicha argued that suitable models for solids are subsets of the 3D Euclidean space that are bounded, closed, regular, and semianalytic; he terms them **r-sets**. For readers unfamiliar with these concepts of set theory, we briefly introduce them here. A **bounded** set is a set that occupies a finite portion of space. A **closed** set is a set that contains its boundary. A set is a **regular** set if it equals the closure of its interior. A set is **semianalytic** if it may be expressed as a finite Boolean combination (using set theory operators) of sets of the form:

$$\{ <x,y,z> \mid F_i\,(x,y,z) \leq 0 \} \tag{4.1}$$

where F_i are analytic functions.

r-Sets are topological polyhedra which may have holes through them and need not be connected. They are not closed under the normal set theory operators but only under the regularized set operators. A regular set operator **OP*** is defined by the following equation:

$$A\ OP^*\ B = CI\ (A\ OP\ B) \tag{4.2}$$

where $CI(X)$ signifies the closure of the interior of X and OP is one of the operators $\cap, \cup, -, \neg$.

4.1.3 Schemes for representing solids

Most authors (Requicha 1980; Requicha and Voelkler 1982; Mortenson 1985; Mantyla 1984) consider six schemes for representing solids, excluding ambiguous schemes like wireframe representations:

1. Primitive instances
2. Spatial occupancy enumeration
3. Cell decomposition
4. Sweep representations
5. CSG
6. Boundary representations (Brep)

Most current solid modelers are mainly based on CSG (CATSOFT, SYNTHAVISION, PADL-2, TIPS-1) and Brep (CATIA, GWB, EUCLID, ROMULUS, SOLIDESIGN). However, PATRAN-G is based on cell decomposition.

Primitive instances are individual objects within a family called a generic primitive. They are represented by fixed-length tuples of values. For example, a sphere is defined by the tuple <'SPHERE', C, R>, where 'SPHERE' is the name of the family, **C** the center of the sphere, and R its radius. This approach is a kind of procedural model, similar to primitive high-level graphic types, described in Sect. 1.4.2. For example:

type SPHERE = **figure** (C:VECTOR; R:REAL);
          begin
          .
          .
          end;

The primitive instances are easy to use, but they have two severe drawbacks:

- There is a lack of means for combining instances to create more complex structures
- Family-specific algorithms must be included for computing properties of solids

This scheme is no longer used as a pure scheme; however, it may be combined with other approaches to form a hybrid representation, as shown in the next section. The other schemes will be described in Sects. 4.2–4.5. A seventh class of solids, called free-form solids, will be described in Sect. 4.5.6.

4.1.4 Hybrid representations and conversion between representations

None of the schemes for representing solids have properties that are uniformly better than those of other schemes. For this reason, two strategies have been developed—hybrid representations and conversion between representations.

4.1.4.1 Hybrid representations
These are designed by combining the different schemes. For example, the system GMSolid (Boyse and Gilchrist 1982; Sarraga 1982) uses hybrid representations which are CSG-like trees whose leaves are either primitive instance tuples or boundary representations of nonprimitive solids. Another popular scheme is the CSG / sweep hybrid scheme; CSG-like trees have leaves which are sweep representations. Unfortunately, it is difficult to design algorithms for computing the properties of hybrid solids.

4.1.4.2 Conversion between representations
Although there are few algorithms for bidirectional exact conversion, there exist exact and approximate conversion algorithms in one direction. According to Requicha (1980), existing algorithms may be represented by Fig.4.1.
A more recent sweep to CSG conversion algorithm (Vossler 1985) has been added in this schema. This algorithm is described in Sect. 4.4.3. A one-direction conversion from boundary to faceted representation is presented in Sect. 4.5.5. We also describe the bidirectional conversion implemented at MIRALab, between a boundary representation (GWB) and a faceted representation (MIRA) in Sect. 4.7.

4.2 Spatial occupancy enumeration, cell decomposition, quadtrees, and octrees

4.2.1 Spatial occupancy enumeration

In the spatial occupancy enumeration scheme, the solids are represented by a list of **voxels** (volume elements). The voxels are spatial cells occupied by the solid; they are cubes of fixed size and they are located in a fixed spatial grid. Cell size determines the resolution of the representation. Generally, the solid is defined by listing the

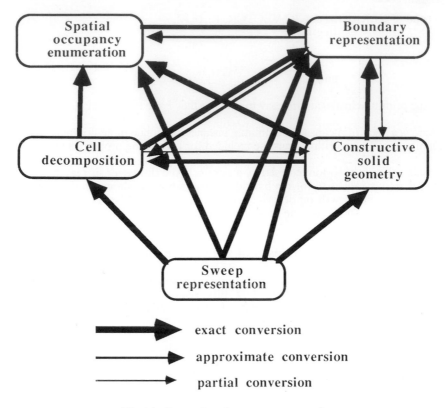

Fig.4.1. Conversions between representations

coordinates of the centers of the cells. Typically, these data are stored as an array of 3D tuples or a **spatial array**. A cell in the array is either occupied by pieces of solid or it is not. The use of spatial arrays has three advantages:

- Spatial arrays are easy to validate
- The access to a given point is easy
- Spatial uniqueness is assured

    However, there are important drawbacks:

- There is a lack of structure between parts of objects
- The representation is expensive in terms of storage
- Spatial arrays are not suitable for modeling certain shapes like complex mechanical parts

4.2.2 Cell decomposition

    Spatial occupancy enumeration is a special case of cell decomposition where the cells are cubical and lie in a fixed grid. A more general way of representing a solid is to decompose it into arbitrary cells and represent each cell in the decomposition. As there are many ways of decomposing a solid into cells, uniqueness is not assured. However, each decomposition is unambiguous. Moreover, this representation provides a means for computing certain properties of solids, like topological characteristics. Cell decomposition is widely used in structural analysis and it is the basis representation in finite elements methods for the numerical solution of differential equations.

Another special case of cell decomposition is the **octree representation**, which uses spatial occupancy enumeration more efficiently than simple spatial arrays. Octrees are a 3D generalization of a 2D representation called **quadtree representation**. In the next sections, we explain the principles of quadtrees and octrees.

4.2.3 Quadtrees

Quadtrees are representations of a 2D object based on the recursive subdivision of a square array into four equally sized quadrants. At any stage of the recursive process, two cases are possible:

1. The object does not uniformly cover the quadrant; it is subdivided into four new quadrants
2. The quadrant is full or empty; no further subdivision is necessary and the quadrant is marked FULL (1) or EMPTY (0). Eventually, the process terminates at the pixel level

An object decomposed in this way can be represented by a binary array of dimension N, where $\log_2 N$ is the maximum level of recursion necessary in the decomposition. However, this representation is too expensive in terms of storage. It is much more efficient to express the arrangement as a tree, whose nodes correspond to the quadrants. This tree is called a **quadtree** (quadratic tree), because each nonleaf node has four sons, corresponding to the four quadrants. A leaf node represent a region that requires no further subdivision.

Figure 4.2 shows an example of a 2D object, with the corresponding binary array representation, the decomposition into quadrants, and the quadtree representation.

Yamaguchi et al. (1984) propose a **triangular quadtree**, which has the advantage of being a projection of an octree (see Sect. 4.2.5). A set of triangular quadtrees TQ is formally defined as follows:

1. $\{0,1\} \subseteq TQ$
2. $<q_{10}, q_{11}, q_{01}, q_{-1,0}, q_{-1,-1}, q_{0,-1}> \in TQ$ if $q_{ij} \in SQ$ for $i \neq -j \in \{-1,0,1\}$

where SQ is a set of side-triangular quadtrees defined by:

1. $\{0,1\} \subseteq SQ$
2. $<q_{00}, q_{01}, q_{10}, q_{11}> \in SQ$ if $q_{ij} \in SQ$ for $\{i, j\} \subseteq \{0,1\}$

4.2.4 Construction of quadtree from polygonal region

Casciani et al. (1984) describe an algorithm which builds the quadtree corresponding to polygonal multiple connected regions starting from their boundary representations.

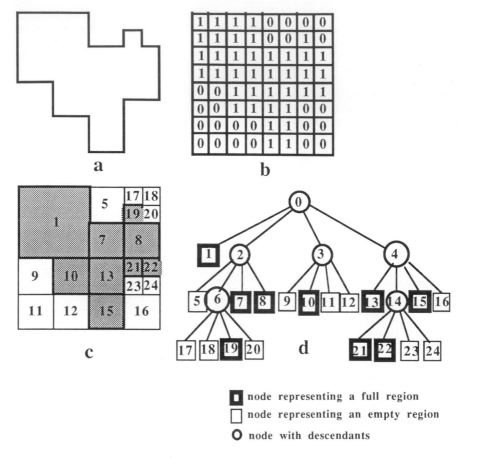

Fig.4.2. a-d Example of quadtree. **a** the 2D object; **b** the corresponding binary array representation; **c** the decomposition into quadrant; **d** the quadtree representation

The algorithm works as follows:

procedure QTREE (Q:CurrentQuadrant; **var** R:Brep);
Determine whether the quadrant has to be subdivided or not
if subdivision is necessary
then
  Store a node 'PARTIAL'
  Provide a geometrical description of the regions lying inside each subquadrant
    using the procedure CLIP (Q,B)
  for each of four subsets B_i of B
    calculate subquadrants Q_i of Q using recursively QTREE (Q_i, B_i)
else
  Add a leaf with 'EMPTY' or 'FULL'

The procedure CLIP (Q,R) performs the subdivision of a set of polygons R into four subsets R_i, lying respectively in the four subquadrants Q_i of Q. CLIP assumes a preprocessing step which sorts all the edges of the input boundaries. The procedure is defined as:

procedure CLIP (Q:CurrentQuadrant; **var** R:Brep);
for each boundary π of R
    Find the index i_0 of the subquadrant Q_{i0} containing the first vertex V_0 of π
    Store V_0 in the list of vertices associated with Q_{i0}
    for each vertex V of π
        Find the index i_1 of the subquadrant Q_{i1} containing V
        Store V in the list of vertices associated with Q_{i1}
        if $i_0 <> i_1$
        then
            Determine the number N of intersections between the segments with endpoints in the i_0-th quadrant and i_1-th quadrant and the clipping lines
            Determine the list L of affected clipping segments
            for each of the N intersections
                Determine the intersection point P between the segment V_0V and the clipping segment
                Store P in the list of intersections associated with the clipping line
                $V_0 := V$
for each of the four quadrants Q_i
    Build up the geometrical description of the subregion R_i using the vertices in Q_i and the lists of intersections along the clipping segments limiting Q_i

The algorithm to determine whether a quadrant Q containing the boundary representation of the polygons R has to be subdivided may be described as follows:

if Q is a pixel then
    if Q is intersected by R
    then Q is full
    else Q is empty
else
    if R is empty
    then Q is empty
    else
        if the distance of every edge of R from the boundary of Q is less than a pixel
        then
            if the center of Q is external to R
            then Q has to be subdivided
            else Q is full
        else Q has to be subdivided

4.2.5 Octrees

Meagher (1982) proposes an extension of the quadtree concept into three dimensions for encoding solids and calls it an **octree**. An octree is a spatially presorted octonary hierarchical tree structure. The octree encoding is similar to the quadtree encoding. A cubic region is recursively subdivided into eight octants, which are cubic regions. Each nonleaf node of an octree has eight descendants.

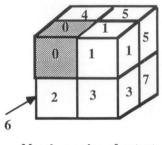

6

Meagher order of octants

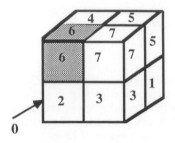

0

Yamaguchi et al. order of octants

Fig.4.3. Order of octants for octree encoding

Yamaguchi et al. (1984) proposes a formal definition of octrees with a more systematic order than the conventional one, as shown in Fig.4.3. Using their order, we show an example of a 3D object with the corresponding octree in Fig. 4.4.

Nodes in the octree are of two basic types—**terminal** and **partial**. As in quadtrees, terminal nodes are leaves either labeled FULL (1) or EMPTY (0). A full leaf represents an octant that is completely filled by the modeled object. An empty leaf represents an octant that lies outside the modeled objects. In a conventional octree as in a quadtree, partial nodes represent an octant which has to be further subdivided.

Yamaguchi et al. (1984) propose an **octree-related data structure** where the leaves of the tree are also allowed to represent cubes which contain a single plane, edge, or vertex of the original object boundary. More formally, Kunii et al. (1985) introduced a BNF definition of octrees, where partial nodes may be **P-nodes** or **S-nodes**. A P-node is a conventional dividing node and an S-node is a special nondividing node, formally represented by S. This S-node arbitrarily specifies the shape of the object boundary and it is considered a full leaf. The BNF definition of an octree o_i is as follows:

$$\textbf{for } i \in \{0, 1, 2, 3, 4, 5, 6, 7\},$$

$$o_i ::= 0 \mid 1 \mid P$$
$$P ::= T \mid S$$

where the oct-tuple $T = <o_0, o_1, o_2, o_3, o_4, o_5, o_6, o_7>$ is an ordered set of octrees and each element of T is an octant. If we represent one octant of a given octree o by o_{xyz}, where $<x,y,z>$ is the position of the octant when we place o in a Cartesian coordinate system, then $T = <o_{000}, o_{001}, o_{010}, o_{011}, o_{100}, o_{101}, o_{110}, o_{111}>$.

With this definition, projecting an octree onto a triangular quadtree using an isometric view is easy and efficient. The isometric view has a special property in that the projection of the edges of cubes in an octree divides the space into triangles. The algorithm is described with examples in the paper by Yamaguchi et al. (1984).

4.2.6 Operations on octrees

Wyvill and Kunii (1985) have introduced addition and subtraction of octrees as follows:

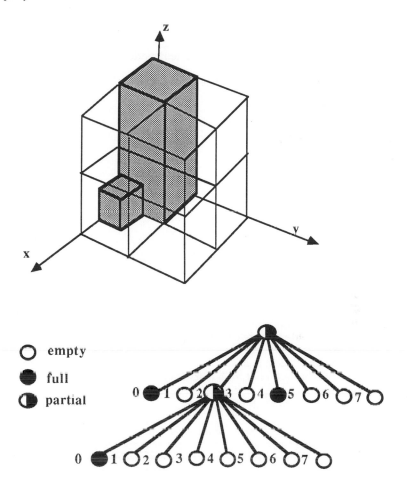

Fig.4.4. Octree representation of a 3D object

addition of two octrees a+b

if a is EMPTY
then result:=b
else
   if b is EMPTY
   then result:=a
   else
    if a is FULL or b is FULL
    then {objects interfere, not allowed}
      else
(*) **if** it is the limit of resolution (see Sect. 4.4.2)
(*) **then** create a nasty cell
        else
        {Subdivide a and b}
         if a is PARTIAL or b is PARTIAL
          then

                    Access the child nodes
                    else
                    if a is a leaf-node or b is a leaf-node
                    then
                        Create child nodes for this leaf-node
                Add the eight elements of a, b recursively

subtraction of two octrees a-b

if a is EMPTY
then result:=EMPTY
else
   if b is EMPTY
  then result:=a
  else
   if b is FULL
  then result:=EMPTY
   else
    if a is FULL and b is a leaf-node
    then
      result:= inverse of b
    else
(*) **if** it is the limit of resolution   (see Sect. 4.4.2)
(*) **then** create a nasty cell
      else
        {Subdivide a and b}
        if a is PARTIAL or b is PARTIAL
        then
          Access the child nodes
        else
          if a is a leaf-node or b is a leaf-node
          then
            Create child nodes for this leaf-node
        Subtract the eight elements of a, b recursively

4.3 Sweep representations

4.3.1 Principle of sweep representations

Sweep representations used in CAD are based on the notion of moving a region along some path. Often, the term **generator** is used to denote the region and the term **director** is used to denote the path or trajectory. Typical examples of sweep representations are cylindrical bodies or revolution bodies. Since sweep representations are one of the basic representations in many solid modeling systems, we have decided to present the concept in this chapter. However, it is essential to understand that surfaces may also be generated using sweeping methods. More generally, we may distinguish several kinds of generators—curves, surfaces and volumes. The sweeping of curves generates surfaces and the sweeping of surfaces produces solids. Volumes may also be swept by the motions of a solid. This latter case is very difficult to process, because of the lack of algorithms. An example will be discussed in Sect. 10.4.5.

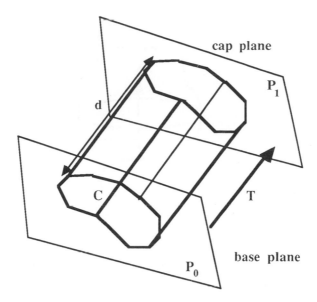

Fig.4.5. Translational sweeping

In the following sections, we shall discuss two particular cases of sweeping—translational and rotational sweepings. We shall consider then the general case of sweeping one curve along another. Finally, we shall explain how sweeping techniques are related to computer animation techniques.

4.3.2 Translational sweeping

An object S_T defined by translational sweeping is obtained by translating a 2D region C along a vector **T** for a distance d, as shown in Fig.4.5. The plane P_0 of the curve is called the **base plane** and the plane P_1 at a distance d is called the **cap plane**.

Special cases are the following:

C is a rectangle area $\Rightarrow$ S_t is a box
C is a disk $\Rightarrow$ S_t is a cylinder
C is any polygonal region $\Rightarrow$ S_t is a prism

4.3.3 Rotational sweeping

Objects generated by rotational sweeping (surfaces of revolution) are obtained by rotating a 2D region C around an axis of rotation **A**. Two elements are important in such a surface—the base point B and the radius function $\rho(s)$, as shown in Fig.4.6.

Typical objects generated by rotational sweeping are revolution bodies, which are obtained by rotating a curve 360^0 around an axis. As shown by Magnenat-Thalmann and Thalmann (1986), numerous objects may be generated by applying evolution laws to the object attributes or to the revolution parameters themselves.

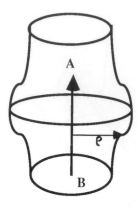

Fig.4.6. Rotational sweeping with the base point B, axis vector A, and radius $\rho=\rho(s)$

More generally, we shall consider the following characteristics in a generalized revolution operation:

1. The axis of revolution is given by two points which may be change during the generation

2. The object may be translated in any direction. Two interesting cases are:
   i. Translation parallel to the direction of the revolution axis; in this case the revolution angle may be several times 360^0
   ii. Translation perpendicular to the revolution axis; in this case the effect of a concentric object is obtained
   More general cases are possible, including any arbitrary motion.

3. The object may be scaled; typically the scale function depends on the revolution angle

4. The orientation of the object may change during the revolution; for example a rotation of the object in the plane of the axis and the center of the object gives a very good twisting effect

5. The shape of the object may change during the revolution as described in Sect. 3.7.2

4.3.4 General sweepings

Another important kind of sweeping is **conic sweeping**, which corresponds to a translational sweeping combined with scaling of the contour.

The method of sweeping was generalized by Lossing and Eshleman (1974) who use a six-component trajectory and generator-orientation curve called a **position-direction (PD) curve**. With this PD curve, an almost unlimited variety of swept solids may be defined.

Consider now the case of a surface obtained by simply moving a polygonal line along another polygonal line as shown in Fig.4.7a.

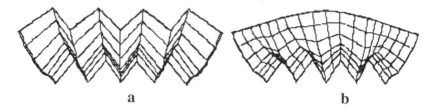

Fig.4.7. Curve C_1 swept along another curve C_2. **a** Without transformation of C_1; **b** With transformation of C_2

The main problem with such sweeping is that it may generate nonhomogeneous objects. Moreover, very little is known about this kind of sweep representation. General sweeping may also involve changes of the swept object during the path, as in Fig.4.7b. This case has characteristics which are very similar to the processing of motion in computer animation.

4.3.5 Sweeping representations from computer animation methods

Magnenat-Thalmann and Thalmann (1986) compared sweeping representations to the motion of objects in animation. Objects move along a path exactly as cross sections of a mechanical part sweep along a curve. The main difference is that in sweeping representations a surface or a solid is constructed by the "motion" of the cross section; in computer animation, at each frame, the moving object is displayed in a different position. In animation, the motion of objects is controlled by laws of evolution which have an essential role (Magnenat-Thalmann and Thalmann 1985a). For example, an object may have a revolution motion around an axis; this means that the angle of rotation changes over time. But how does it change? This is typically an evolution problem. In fact, not only the angle may change, but also the radius.

We now give a similar formulation for objects generated by the motion of a curve or a surface along a path, as in sweeping representations:

1. A generator is characterized by four attributes—shape, position, orientation, and size.
2. A 3D object is generated by moving the generator along a path (the director)
3. During the motion, the generator's attributes are modified according to evolution laws

Several types of evolution laws may be considered.

4.3.5.1 Animation laws based on cosinusoidal functions
There are four typical laws here; for each law, a value between 0 and MAXVAL is returned corresponding to a fraction (FRACT) of the total time:

1. Constant law: $VAL := MAXVAL \cdot FRACT$

2. Acceleration: $VAL := MAXVAL \cdot (1 - COS(\pi \frac{FRACT}{2}))$

3. Deceleration: $VAL := MAXVAL \cdot SIN(\pi \frac{FRACT}{2})$

4. Acceleration then deceleration: $VAL := MAXVAL \frac{(1 - COS(\pi\ FRACT))}{2}$

4.3.5.2 Curved paths and P-curves

The temporal behavior of the position of a point can be easily represented by a **P-curve** (Baecker 1969). A P-curve defines both the trajectory of the point and its location in time. The P-curve has the shape of the trajectory, but a trail of symbols is used instead of a continuous line to depict the path. The symbols are spaced equally in time. This means that the dynamics are represented by the local density of the symbols.

4.3.5.3 Complex evolutive laws

These laws, which are generally procedurally defined, are expressed as analytical functions of time or they may be defined by functions of state variables, computed for example by a continuous simulation method (Magnenat-Thalmann and Thalmann 1986a). It should be noted that the change in the position attribute is considered relative to the current position along the path.

Paths may be created by several methods:

1. Digitizing the curve using one of the methods described in Sect. 1.3.2
2. Improving or modifying the curve using techniques discussed in Chap. 3: Akima local interpolation, ß-spline curve approximation, Kochanek-Bartels spline interpolation

Another kind of sweep representation derives from an animation technique.

One interesting case involves three curves C_1, C_2, and C_3; C1 is swept along C_3 and at the same time it is transformed into C_2 along the path. Moreover, C_1 and C_2 are given with a few constraints on specific points. This is basically the Reeves (1981) **in-betweening technique using moving point constraints**. The principle of the technique is to associate a curve varying in space and time with certain points of the animated object. This curve is called a **moving point** and it controls the trajectory and the dynamics of the point in a similar manner to P-curves. The shape of the curves specifies the path of interpolation. With such a strategy, only the moving points need to be defined; the curves in the keyframes do not have to be numbered and counted.

4.4 Constructive solid geometry

4.4.1 Constructive solid geometry tree

Constructive solid geometry (CSG) is a family of schemes introduced by Requicha and Voelcker (1977) for representing rigid solids as Boolean constructions and combinations of solid components. CSG may be considered a generalization of cell decomposition. In cell decomposition, components are combined using a unique operator, a kind of restricted union, the **gluing** operation that applies only to sets with disjoint interiors. With CSG, the three basic operators are union, intersection, and difference. In CSG, objects are represented as binary trees, called **CSG trees**. Each leaf is a primitive object and each nonterminal node is either a Boolean operator or a motion (translation, rotation) which operates on the subnodes. Each subtree of a CSG tree is a CSG tree and represents a valid solid resulting from the combinations and transformations below it. Formally, a CSG tree may be defined as follows:

```
<CSG tree> ::= <primitive>
               <CSG tree> <set operator> <CSG tree>
               <CSG tree> <rigid motion> <motion arguments>
```

CSG schemes generally have unbounded primitives or primitives that are r-sets. It should be noted that when the primitive solids of a CSG scheme are r-sets, any CSG tree is a valid representation of an r-set if the primitive leaves are valid.

The strength of a CSG system depends on the set of available primitives. Generally, only bounded half spaces are considered in a CSG system. Most commercial systems support half-spaces bounded by planar, conical, cylindrical, spherical, and toroidal surfaces. Figure 4.8 shows a classic example of a CSG tree.

Figure 4.9 shows an image generated using CSG with quadric primitives.

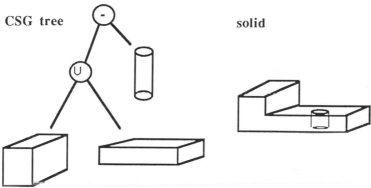

Fig.4.8. An example of CSG tree

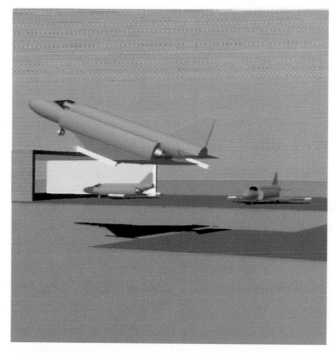

Fig. 4.9. Jetport, by D.Peachey, University of Saskatchewan. The objects in the scene are modeled using CSG with quadric primitives

4.4.2 DAG and RCSG

When the same subobject is used many times in a CSG representation, a directed acyclic graph (DAG) has to be used instead of a CSG tree. As a DAG only provides a description of the object, it is often necessary to convert the description into another representation (e.g. patches) to extract information. Solids may also be directly represented using an octree (Jacklins and Tanimoto 1980; Meagher 1982) or an extended octree (Yamaguchi et al. 1984). Figure 4.10 shows an example of a DAG created by Wyvill and Kunii (1985); it is a crankshaft composed of three objects—slab, tool, and crank. The object is built from two primitive objects—a plane and a cylinder. The operators PLUS (+) and MINUS (-) respectively indicate the union and the difference.

Wyvill et al. (1986a) proposed a reduced version of CSG (RCSG). This structure is a tree with leaves that are of the same form as the ordinary octree. The combination of octree and RCSG structures contains all the information from the original DAG, but the structure is more compact. An example is shown in Fig.4.11.

With this approach, we have to modify the operations on octrees. The new operations are similar to the operations defined in Sect. 4.2.6, but the rules (*) have to be replaced by two new rules:

for addition:
(*) **if** the voxel is of minimum size
(*) **then** create an RCSG node A+B
    else ...

for subtraction:
(*) **if** the voxel is of minimum size
(*) **then** create an RCSG node A-B
    else ...

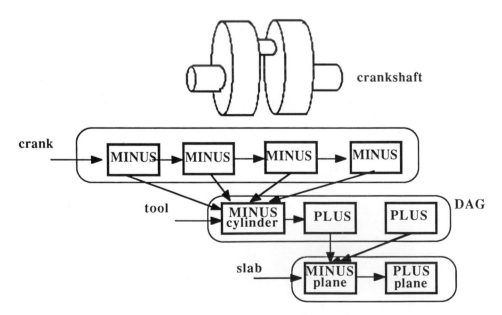

Fig.4.10. DAG of a crankshaft

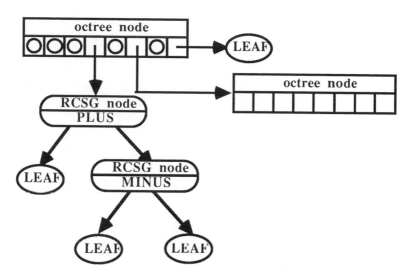

Fig.4.11. An example of a combined data structure (octree + RCSG)

4.4.3 Conversion from sweeping to CSG

Vossler (1985) proposes an algorithm for using sweep outline input methods in a CSG-based solid modeling system. Although this algorithm rarely produces the optimal solution, it produces a single valid decomposition and attempts to minimize the number of primitives and Boolean operations during the decomposition process. The decomposition algorithm searches the input sweep outline until the 2D pattern of one of the simple sweep solids is found. A stack is used to store the name of the solid and the associated Boolean operation. Each time a pattern is found, the complexity of the outline is reduced, either by converting an arc into a line or by deleting vertices. The process continues until the outline no longer encloses any area. The sweep solid is formed by removing the simple sweep solids from the stack and applying the Boolean operations. The algorithm may be expressed as follows:

```
Initialize the stack
while the outline encloses an area do
    Search for a pattern P
    if P does exist
    then
        Determine if P is inside or outside of the current sweep routine
        if it is inside
        then
            operation:= UNION
        else
            operation:=DIFFERENCE
        Construct the simple sweep solid
        Push the solid and the operation onto the stack
        Reduce the current sweep routine by changing an arc into a line and/or
                removing vertices from the outline.
    else
        Break an arc
Construct the solid from the stack
```

4.5 Boundary representations

4.5.1 Properties of a boundary representation

A boundary representation (BR or Brep) represents a solid by a three-level hierarchy of entities—**faces, edges,** and **vertices.** The volume is bounded by a surface; this surface is defined by a collection of faces. Faces are represented in terms of bounding edges and vertices. The faceted representation discussed in Sect. 1.2.2 is a form of boundary representation for defining surfaces. However, a faceted representation may not guarantee a valid solid. For example, in a faceted representation, an edge may be common to more than three edges or two faces may intersect each other. The use of a faceted representation for solid modeling is possible. However, it requires a very complex and expensive validation process. For these reasons, several authors (Requicha 1980; Baer et al. 1979; Mantyla and Takala 1981) have formulated formal and informal rules to define a solid by its boundaries. For example, Requicha (1980) assumes that each boundary representation has a finite number of generic primitive surfaces S_i. Faces F_j of an object with a boundary B should satisfy the following conditions:

1. F_j is a subset of B
2. The union of all F_j equals B
3. Each F_j is a subset of a S_i
4. A face must have an area

Some boundary representations allow faces to be nonplanar; however, this requires additional information on the host primitive surface.
However, even for a simple tetrahedron, validation rules are complex, as shown by Requicha (1980):

1. Each face must have precisely three edges
2. Each edge must have precisely two vertices
3. Each edge must belong to two faces
4. Each vertex in a face must belong precisely to the edges of two faces
5. Vertices must be all distinct
6. Edges may only intersect at a common vertex
7. Faces may only intersect at a common edge or a common vertex

Such conditions are too expensive to validate and it is much more efficient to construct directly valid solids than to verify that they are valid after construction. One way of constructing valid solids is through the use of the Euler operators.

4.5.2 Euler operators

Euler operators were introduced by Baumgart (1975) ; they derive their names from Euler's law: in any simple regular convex polyhedron, the following equation is always satisfied:

$$V - E + F = 2 \qquad\qquad (4.3)$$

where V is the number of vertices, E the number of edges, and F the number of faces.

Table 4.1. Euler operators (Mantyla and Sulonen 1982)

Operator	Explanation
1. MVSF	Make a vertex, a face, and a shell
2. MEV	Make an edge and a vertex
3. MEF	Make an edge and a face
4. KEMR	Kill an edge and make a ring
5. KFMRH	Kill a face, make a ring and a hole
6. KVFS	Kill a vertex, a face, and a shell
7. KEV	Kill an edge and a vertex
8. KEF	Kill an edge and a face
9. MEKR	Make an edge and kill a ring
10. MFKRH	Make a face, kill a ring, and a hole

Equation (4.3) may be generalized for solids:

$$V - E + F = 2 (S - H) + R \qquad (4.4)$$

where S is the number of disconnected components (shells) in the solid, H the number of holes in the solid, and R the number of rings (or cavities) in the faces.

Euler operators are operators which work on the topology of a boundary model. Consider a valid solid, verifying Eq. (4.4); each time an Euler operator is applied, the resulting solid also verifies Eq. (4.4).

Braid et al. (1980) show that five operators (with their inverses) are sufficient to describe any object satisfying Eq. (4.4). In fact, these five operators may be chosen in different ways and several authors (Baumgart 1975; Eastman and Weiler 1979; Braid et al. 1980; Mantyla and Sulonen 1982; Chiyokura and Kimura 1985) propose small variations in the collections of selected operators.

Table 4.1 shows a list of the five operators with their inverses, proposed by Mantyla and Sulonen (1982). Note that operators are named by a sequence of letters with the following meaning:

M = Make (construction operator)   K = Kill   (destruction operator)
V = Vertex   E = Edge
S = Shell   R = Ring
H = Hole

The effects of these operators are shown in Fig.4.12.

It should be noted that Euler operators do not guarantee that a face is always planar. However, the rules of topological integrity are always satisfied because of Eq. (4.4). For example, we may consider the classic example of removing edges from a cube. As shown in Fig.4.13, the generalized Euler equation (Eq.4.4) is verified at each step, although faces are not planar.

A complete example, from Mantyla and Sulonen (1982), is shown in Fig.4.14. Note the effect of the operator KFRMH to create the hole.

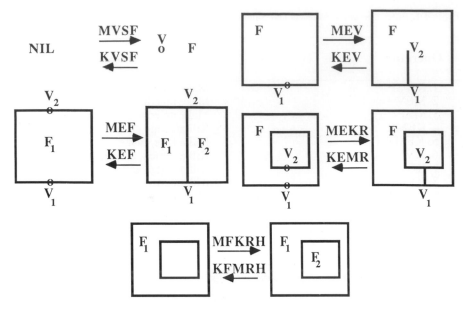

Fig.4.12. Effects of the five main Euler operators and their inverses

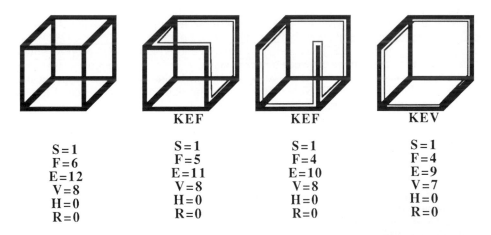

Fig.4.13. Removing edges from a cube. Equation (4.4) is verified at each step; note the nonplanar face, marked with a **thin line**

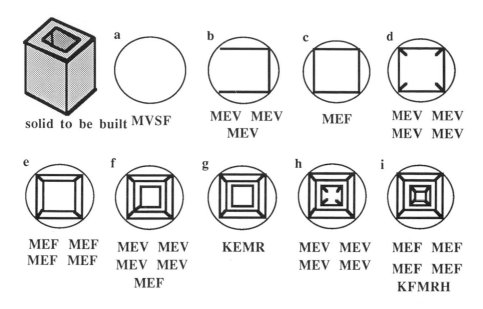

solid to be built MVSF | MEV MEV MEV | MEF | MEV MEV MEV MEV

MEF MEF MEF MEF | MEV MEV MEV MEV MEF | KEMR | MEV MEV MEV MEV | MEF MEF MEF MEF KFMRH

Fig.4.14. An example of a solid constructed with the Euler operators

4.5.3 Join, split and set theory operators in Geometric WorkBench

Geometric WorkBench (GWB; Mantyla and Takala 1981, Mantyla and Sulonen 1982) is a solid modeler based on Euler operators. It defines, manipulates, inverts and analyzes solids. Theoretically, the Euler operators defined in Fig.4.12 are sufficient to build any solid verifying Eq. (4.4). However, in practice, it would be very difficult and expensive to limit a system to these operators. For this reason, GWB provides not only the basic operators but also join and split operators (Mantyla 1983). These operators are described in Table 4.2 and their effects are shown in Fig.4.15.

Mantyla and Sulonen (1982) show that set theory operations may be easily implemented using the basic operators and the join and split operators. They propose a basic algorithm for splitting a solid S by a plane P using two lists—the list of null edges (LNE) and the list of null faces (LNF).

The algorithm may be summarized as follows:

for all edges E of S
   if E intersects P
   then {generate a null edge}
      Calculate the intersection point
      Apply SEMV to E to obtain E, E' and V
      Apply SEMV to E' to obtain E', E'' and V'
      Add E' to LNE
   Combine the null edges using a specific algorithm {see (Mantyla and Sulonen
                                  1982)}

   {create null faces}
   while LNE is not empty **do**
      E:=any edge of LNE
      if E is shared by two identical faces F_1 and F_2

    then
        Add F_1 to LNF
        Apply KEMR to E
    else
        Apply KEF to E
for each face F in LNF
    Apply MFKRH to F
Construct the resulting solids

This algorithm may be easily extended to set theory operations (Mantyla 1983). To implement a set operation between two solids A and B, the first step is to classify the boundary of each of the solids into two components lying in the interior and the exterior of the other solid: AinB, AoutB, BinA, BoutA. The general algorithm to implement A op B is then as follows:

for each edge E of A
    if E intersects the box of B
    then
        for each face F of B
            if E and F intersect
            then
                Store the intersection
        Sort the intersections along E
        Analyze the intersections
for each edge E of B
    if E intersects the box of A
    then
        for each face F of A
            if E and F intersect
            then
                store the intersection
        Sort the intersections along E
        Analyze the intersections
Join the intersections using join operators
Divide A into AinB and AoutB
Divide B into BinA and BoutA
case op **of**
   ∪: Apply the GLUE operator to AoutB and BoutA
   ∩: Apply the GLUE operator to AoutB and BinA
   −: Apply the GLUE operator to AinB and BinA

Translational and rotational sweep operators may also be easily implemented using Euler operators.

4.5.4 Euler operators in MODIF and DESIGNBASE

Modifications of a solid in a boundary representation are not easy to process. For example, changing the size of a hole in a solid requires erasing the hole by adding an appropriate solid and making a smaller hole by subtracting a cylinder. In GWB, such modifications are not performed with the Euler operators but by using the set theory operations described in the previous section.

Chiyokura and Kimura (1985) propose a method of representing the solid design

Table 4.2. Join and split Euler operators

Operator	Explanation
1. SEMV	Split an edge and make a vertex
2. JEKV	Join an edge and kill a vertex
3. SVME	Split a vertex and make an edge
4. JVKE	Join a vertex and kill an edge

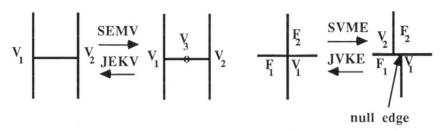

null edge

Fig.4.15. The effects of the join and split Euler operators

process with high-level operations which always use primitive operations to modify the solids. In their system, called MODIF, all primitive operations are stored in a tree structure and the system can quickly regenerate any previously designed solid.

In MODIF, the boundary of a solid is represented as a set of faces defined by loops. Two kinds of loop are possible: P-loops representing face boundaries, consisting of edges, and C-loops representing holes in a face. Edges may be straight lines or cubic Bézier lines. Primitive operations are classifed into three categories:

1. Topological operations which are modified Euler operations
2. Geometric operations
3. Global operations

Table 4.3 shows the list of operations.

Kunii et al. (1985) describe an algorithm for generating a sequence of Euler operators (for MODIF) from octree encoding. The algorithm consists of four procedures:

1. Converting the octree into an extended octree (as already discussed in Sect. 4.2.5)
2. Labeling the entities of the extended octree
3. Generating tables of boundary representation information
4. Generating the sequence of Euler operations

Toriya et al. (1986) propose a system, called DESIGNBASE, which inherits all the characteristics of MODIF. UNDO and REDO operations allow any solid to regenerated. For this, set operations are implemented based on the topology operations described in Fig.4.15. However, two new Euler operators have been added:

MZEV	Make a zero-length edge and a vertex
KZEV	Kill a zero-length edge and a vertex

Table 4.3. The primitive operations in MODIF

Operator	Explanation
A. Topological operations	
1. MEL	Make an edge and a loop
2. KEL	Kill an edge and a loop
3. MVE	Make a vertex and an edge
4. KVE	Kill a vertex and an edge
5. KCLMPL	Kill a C-loop and make a P-loop
6. KPLMCL	Kill a P-loop and make a C-loop
7. MEV	Make an edge and a vertex
8. KEV	Kill an edge and a vertex
9. MEKL	Make an edge and kill a loop
10. KEML	Kill an edge and make a loop
11. MEVVL	Make an edge, two vertices and a loop
12. KEVVL	Kill an edge, two vertices and a loop
B. Geometric operations	
1. TV	Translate a vertex
2. CLB	Change a straight line edge to a Bézier curve
3. CBL	Change a Bézier curve edge to a straight line
4. TB	Translate a control point of a Bézier curve
C. Global operations	
1. TS	Translate a solid
2. RS	Rotate a solid
3. NS	Negate a solid
4. CS	Combine two solids
5. DS	Decompose a solid into two solids

These operators are similar to the operators SVME and JVKE in GWB. An example of a solid generated with DESIGNBASE is shown in Fig.4.16.

4.5.5 Conversion from boundary to faceted representation

Wördenweber (1983) described algorithms to convert a solid from a boundary representation (based on Euler operators) to a faceted representation. This conversion is especially interesting because faceted representations are suitable for fast hidden-surface removal and shading (see Chaps. 5, 6). The conversion is based on a triangulation of all faces of the solid with a minimum number of triangles.

For a simply connected face F with N vertices, an iterative algorithm works as follows:

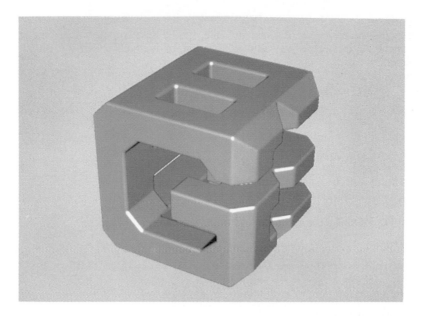

Fig. 4.16. Solid with fillet surface. Courtesy of H.Chiyokura, Ricoh Company Ltd

while N>3 **do**
    Find a vertex **V** where the edges adjacent to **V** make a triangle T, which lies
        inside F and does not interfere with any vertex of F
    Subtract T from F giving F
    N:= number of vertices of F
if N=3
then
    Construct the triangle

For any multiply connected face F with one P-loop PL and H holes (H-loops), the
following algorithm converts it into a simply connected face:

while h > 0 **do**
    Find a pair of vertices V_1 and V_2, where V_1 lies on PL and V_2 lies on an H-
    loop HL; the line segment V_1V_2 lies inside F and should not interfere with
    any edge of any polygon
    Break HL and PL at vertices V_1 and V_2 by splitting the vertices
    Connect the loops by insertion of two new edges between V_1 and V_2
    Redefine the new face as F

4.5.6 Integrating free-form surfaces into a boundary representation

Varady and Pratt (1984) describe techniques for integrating free-form surfaces into the
BUILD solid modeler, which is based on the boundary representation. In particular,
they propose the following operations which involve a solid S and a free-form surface
FF:

1. Sectioning S by FF
2. Replacing the geometry of a selected face of S by the geometry of FF
3. Enlarging S in such a way that it grows until it reaches FF, but only above a selected face of S
4. Adding to S the volume bounded by a part of the boundary of S and FF; this operation is only possible if the bounded volume exists

They also propose **free-form solid primitives**:

1. Projection of a bounded surface region onto another surface, then use of the projection as a face of the solid
2. General sweepings (see Sect. 4.3)
3. Offsetting from a specified surface or surface region
4. Swept solid volumes (see Sect. 4.3)

They also discuss blending and elastic deformation techniques.

4.6 Superquadrics, global and local deformations

4.6.1 Superquadrics

Barr (1981) introduces a new method of defining solids and surfaces using the spherical product of two curves. Mathematically, consider two 2D curves $K(\beta)$ and $L(\mu)$ defined by:

$$K(\beta) = \begin{bmatrix} K_1(\beta) \\ K_2(\beta) \end{bmatrix} \qquad \beta_{min} \le \beta \le \beta_{max} \qquad (4.5)$$

$$L(\mu) = \begin{bmatrix} L_1(\mu) \\ L_2(\mu) \end{bmatrix} \qquad \mu_{min} \le \mu \le \mu_{max} \qquad (4.6)$$

The spherical product $S = K \otimes L$ of the two curves is a surface defined by:

$$S(\beta,\mu) = \begin{bmatrix} K_1(\beta) \; L_1(\mu) \\ K_1(\beta) \; L_2(\mu) \\ K_2(\beta) \end{bmatrix} \qquad (4.7)$$

with $\beta_{min} \le \beta \le \beta_{max}$ and $\mu_{min} \le \mu \le \mu_{max}$

Geometrically, $L(\mu)$ represents a horizontal curve with μ an east-west parameter (like longitude), and $K(\beta)$ represents a vertical curve with β a north-south parameter (like latitude). The surface is created by modulating $L(\mu)$ by $K(\beta)$.

A superquadric $S = K \otimes L$ is defined as the spherical product of superellipses and superhyperbolas K and L. Barr proposes four types of superquadric:

4.6.1.1 Superellipsoids
These are defined by the spherical product of two superellipses **K** and **L**:

$$\mathbf{K}(\beta) = \begin{bmatrix} \cos^{\varepsilon 1}\beta \\ a_3\sin^{\varepsilon 1}\beta \end{bmatrix} \qquad -\pi/2 \le \beta \le \pi/2 \qquad (4.8)$$

$$\mathbf{L}(\mu) = \begin{bmatrix} a_1\cos^{\varepsilon 2}\mu \\ a_2\sin^{\varepsilon 2}\mu \end{bmatrix} \qquad -\pi \le \mu \le \pi \qquad (4.9)$$

ε_1 and ε_2 are two squareness parameters; they are used to pinch, round, and square off portions of the generated solid. We have:

For $\varepsilon_i < 1$, the shape is square

For $\varepsilon_i \cong 1$, the shape is round

For $\varepsilon_i \cong 2$, the shape has a flat bevel

For $\varepsilon_i > 2$, the shape is pinched

a is a vector to rescale the spherical product:

$$\mathbf{a} = \begin{bmatrix} a_1 \\ a_2 \\ a_3 \end{bmatrix}$$

4.6.1.2 Superhyperboloids of one piece
They are defined by the spherical product of a superhyperbola **K** and a superellipse **L**:

$$\mathbf{K}(\beta) = \begin{bmatrix} \sec^{\varepsilon 1}\beta \\ a_3\tan^{\varepsilon 1}\beta \end{bmatrix} \qquad -\pi/2 \le \beta \le \pi/2 \qquad (4.10)$$

$$\mathbf{L}(\mu) = \begin{bmatrix} a_1\cos^{\varepsilon 2}\mu \\ a_2\sin^{\varepsilon 2}\mu \end{bmatrix} \qquad -\pi \le \mu \le \pi \qquad (4.11)$$

a and ε_i have the same meaning.

4.6.1.3 Superhyperboloids of two pieces
These are defined by the spherical product of two superhyperbolae **K** and **L**:

$$\mathbf{K}(\beta) = \begin{bmatrix} \sec^{\varepsilon 1}\beta \\ a_3\tan^{\varepsilon 1}\beta \end{bmatrix} \qquad -\pi/2 \le \beta \le \pi/2 \qquad (4.12)$$

$$\mathbf{L}(\mu) = \begin{bmatrix} a_1\sec^{\varepsilon 2}\mu \\ a_2\tan^{\varepsilon 2}\mu \end{bmatrix} \qquad -\pi \le \mu \le \pi \qquad (4.13)$$

a and ε_i have the same meaning.

4.6.1.4 Supertoroids
These are defined by the spherical product of:

$$K(\beta) = \begin{bmatrix} a_4 + \cos^{\varepsilon 1}\beta \\ a_3\sin^{\varepsilon 1}\beta \end{bmatrix} \qquad -\pi/2 \le \beta \le \pi/2 \qquad (4.14)$$

$$L(\mu) = \begin{bmatrix} a_1\cos^{\varepsilon 2}\mu \\ a_2\sin^{\varepsilon 2}\mu \end{bmatrix} \qquad -\pi \le \mu \le \pi \qquad (4.15)$$

a and ε_i have the same meaning, a_4 is defined by

$$a_4 = \frac{r}{\sqrt{a_1{}^2 + a_2{}^2}} \qquad (4.16)$$

where r is the torus radius.

Superquadrics can be defined by either implicit or parametric equations. The parametric form is used for calculation, since surface points and normal vectors can be generated more easily. However, Franklin and Barr (1981) show that the most efficient approach is the use of methods for generating points on the curve with explicit equations or series approximations.

4.6.2 Global and local deformations of solids

Barr (1984) defines a **globally specified deformation** of a 3D solid as a mathematical function $F(P)$ which explicitly modifies the global coordinates of points in space:

$$Q = F(P) \qquad (4.17)$$

where $P = <p_1,p_2,p_3>$ is the old point and $Q = <q_1,q_2,q_3>$.

A **locally specified deformation** modifies the tangent space of the solid. Global and local deformations are introduced as new hierarchical solid modeling operations. Barr shows that tangent and normal vectors of a deformed surface can be calculated directly from the tangent and normal vector of the undeformed surface and a transformation matrix. The matrix involved is the Jacobian matrix J of the transformation F; the i-th column of J is calculated as:

$$J_i = \frac{\partial F(P)}{\partial p_i} \qquad (4.18)$$

Consider now a surface $S(u,v)$; new vector derivatives are obtained by:

$$\frac{\partial Q}{\partial u} = J\frac{\partial P}{\partial u} \quad \text{and} \quad \frac{\partial Q}{\partial v} = J\frac{\partial P}{\partial v} \qquad (4.19)$$

As the normal vector direction is obtained from the cross product of independent surface tangent vectors, Barr shows that the normal n_Q is obtained as:

$$n_Q = \det \mathbf{J} \, \mathbf{J}^{-1T} \, n_P \qquad (4.20)$$

where n_Q is the new normal vector, and n_P the old normal vector.

Apart from scaling, Barr describes several examples of deformations, using this method:

4.6.2.1 Global tapering along an axis

This consists of differentially changing the length of two global components without changing the length of the third (corresponding to the axis). For example, the equations for a tapering along z are:

$$\begin{aligned} q_1 &= r \, p_1 \\ q_2 &= r \, p_2 \\ q_3 &= p_3 \end{aligned} \qquad (4.21)$$

where $r = f(z)$

4.6.2.2 Global axial twists

This approximately consists of a differential rotation. For example, a global twist around the x-axis is given by:

$$\begin{aligned} q_1 &= p_1 \cos \varphi - p_2 \sin \varphi \\ q_2 &= p_1 \sin \varphi + p_2 \cos \varphi \\ q_3 &= p_3 \end{aligned} \qquad (4.22)$$

where $\varphi = f(z)$

4.6.2.3 Isotropic bend along a centerline parallel to an axis

See (Barr 1984) for details.

4.6.3 Free-form deformations

Another way of deforming solids is proposed by Sederberg and Parry (1986). The technique is referred to as **free-form deformation** (FFD). Physically, FFD corresponds to deformations applied to an imaginary parallelepiped of clear, flexible plastic in which are embedded the objects to be deformed. The objects are also imagined to be flexible, so that they are deformed along with the plastic that surrounds them. Mathematically, consider a local coordinate system (S, T, U) centered in V_0 on a parallelepiped region such that any point V with coordinates $<s,t,u>$ may be written as:

$$V = V + sS + t\,T + u\,U \qquad (4.23)$$

A grid of control points P_{ijk} (i=0 to L, j=0 to M, and k=0 to N) is imposed on the parallelepiped. These points lie on a lattice, and their locations are defined by:

$$P_{ijk} = V_0 + \frac{i}{L}S + \frac{j}{M}T + \frac{k}{N}U \qquad (4.24)$$

FFD are specified by moving the control points from their undisplaced lattice positions. They are defined in terms of a tensor product trivariate Bernstein polynomial (see Sect. 3.4). The deformed point $\mathbf{V'}$ is calculated from the original point $\mathbf{V}$ and the control points $\mathbf{P}_{ijk}$ as follows (see Eq. 3.41):

$$\mathbf{V'} = \sum_{i=0}^{L} \sum_{j=0}^{M} \sum_{k=0}^{N} \mathbf{P}_{ijk}\, B_{iL}\,(s)\, B_{jM}\,(t)\, B_{kN}\,(u) \qquad (4.25)$$

where $B_{iL}(s)$, $B_{jM}(t)$, and $B_{kN}(u)$ are defined by Eq. (3.42) and s, t, and u by:

$$s = \frac{\mathbf{T}\ x\ \mathbf{U}\ \cdot\ (\mathbf{V} - \mathbf{V}_0)}{(\mathbf{T}\ x\ \mathbf{U}\cdot\mathbf{S})}$$

$$t = \frac{\mathbf{S}\ x\ \mathbf{U}\ \cdot\ (\mathbf{V} - \mathbf{V}_0)}{(\mathbf{S}\ x\ \mathbf{U}\cdot\mathbf{T})} \qquad (4.26)$$

$$u = \frac{\mathbf{S}\ x\ \mathbf{T}\ \cdot\ (\mathbf{V} - \mathbf{V}_0)}{(\mathbf{S}\ x\ \mathbf{T}\cdot\mathbf{U})}$$

4.7 Solid modeling at MIRALab

Solid modeling is not the most important area of computer graphics developed at MIRALab; however, as already explained in the introduction to this chapter, the design of certain 3D objects in image synthesis is facilitated by the use of set theory operations. These operations would be very difficult to implement directly in our language MIRA-SHADING, using the normal faceted data structure. For this reason, union, intersection, and difference operations have been added to the language by developping conversion tools from the MIRA-SHADING data structure (MDS) to a Brep data structure (BDS).

In the BDS, each solid is represented by a list of **faces**. The boundary of a face is composed of an outside **loop** and a set of inside loops (**rings**), which are the holes. Each loop is represented by a list of **half-edges**, which correspond to the occurence of a line segment in the face. Each half-edge has a pointer to the **edge** and the **vertex**, which are the first in the loop and a pointer to the other half-edge (making up the same edge). Edges also have pointers to the vertices which determine these edges and pointers to the two faces and the two loops to which they belong.

There are no major problems in the translation from the MDS to the BDS. The solid has exactly the same number of faces, edges, and vertices as the initial figure. Since no holes are allowed in a MIRA-SHADING face, each face has a pointer to a unique loop. Colors and coordinates of each vertex are directly transferred to the BDS. One difficulty arises because the vertices of a face are referenced by indices in the array of the vertices of the figure. This necessitates the creation of a temporary array of pointers to the vertices of the solid; this array allows access to the new vertices with the same indices as the indices used to allow access to the vertices of the figure. Another problem is due to the fact that edges are indirectly defined; inferences are required to find the vertices which bound them and the faces to which they belong. It is also necessary to check before creating it that the edge linking two vertices of a face does not already exist. The list of half-edges which point to a given edge are particularly useful for this control. The equation of the plane of each face and the minimum and maximum coordinates of the solid are also stored in the BDS to facilitate the calculation of the intersections between the faces and the edges (see next section).

The transformation from the BDS to the MDS is simple; the only problem is to eliminate the holes in the face of the solid. The algorithm for a face F works as follows:

Project F onto one of the planes XY, YZ, ZX
for each hole H
    Find a point **P** inside H
    Consider the triangle T formed by **P** and two vertices of the outside loop of H
    Find edges E_i of H intersected by the edges of T and the corresponding
        intersection points I_i
    Divide each E_i at I_i using the Euler operator SEMV
    Link the new vertices (I_i) to the corresponding vertices on the outside loop
        using the Euler operators MEKR and MEF
Make F convex using a recursive algorithm
Delete all useless edges using the Euler operator KEF.

Three set operations have been implemented using this BDS:

SolidUnion(F1,F2,F3)   corresponding to F3:=F1 ∪ F2
SolidIntersection(F1,F2,F3)   corresponding to F3:=F1 ∩ F2
SolidDifference(F1,F2,F3)   corresponding to F3:=F1 — F2

5 Visible surface algorithms

5.1 Object-space and image-space techniques

5.1.1 Problem of hidden lines

Consider the drawing in Fig.5.1a: it is impossible to determine whether this represents the situation as in Fig.5.1b or Fig.5.1c. Fig.5.1a is thus ambiguous, because lines which should be hidden are shown.

In fact, 3D line drawing is generally rather unrealistic; to achieve realism in a computer-generated image, lines which could not really be seen by an observer must first be removed. This process has been a common research problem ever since the first 3D systems were developed; numerous algorithms have been proposed to solve the problem (Sutherland et al. 1974; Griffiths 1978) . They can be classified into two major categories—**object-space** algorithms and **image-space algorithms**. A third category of **list-priority algorithms** is sometimes suggested. This represents a compromise between object-space and image-space algorithms.

Another technique, called **the haloed line effect** has also been proposed by Appel et al. (1979). In this technique, when one line in 3D space passes in front of another, a gap is produced in the projection of the more distant line. This gap is created as if an opaque halo surrounded the closer line.

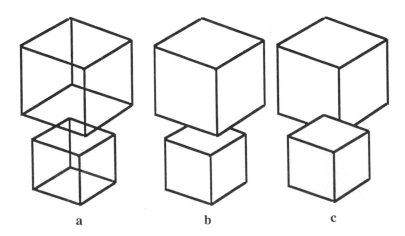

a   b   c

Fig.5.1 a-c. The role of hidden lines

5.1.2 Object-space and image-space algorithms

Object-space algorithms are based on calculations and comparisons between the geometric elements as defined by the user in the 3D space or object space. Although very accurate, their cost increases rapidly with the complexity of a scene. Although several of these algorithms are well-known (Appel 1967; Galimberti and Montanari 1969), they are not yet frequently used. The Appel algorithm, however is conceptually interesting because it has applications in shadow generation (see Chap. 9) and is also considered to be the first to perform **ray tracing** (see Chap. 10). The Appel algorithm is based on the concept of **quantitative invisibility,** i.e., a count of the number of surfaces hiding a vertex of the polygonal objects represented. A line segment is visible only if all points on it have a quantitative invisibility of zero. This technique detects changes in quantitative invisibility along a segment and draws the visible portions.

   Image-space algorithms make intensive use of hardware. They are based on the principle that objects are composed of polygonal faces and one must decide which face is visible at each pixel of the screen. Much more efficient than the previous algorithms, they are also advantageous in terms of cost because the number of pixels remains constant and does not depend on the complexity of the scene. Moreover, these algorithms tie in well with raster technology, which is becoming ever more popular. The best known image space algorithms were developed by Warnock (1969), Watkins (1970), and Catmull (1975).

   List priority algorithms, on the other hand, involve two steps:

1. A step at the level of the object space where the processing consists essentially of establishing a priority list between the various objects.
2. A step at the level of the viewplane where the processing consists mainly of determining the visibility

5.2 Essential tests for hidden-line and hidden-surface algorithms

5.2.1 Outline of algorithms

A hidden-line or hidden-surface algorithm mainly consists of transforming 3D objects into a set of visible line segments or polygons projected onto the viewplane. From the first form to the second form, it is generally necessary to use intermediate representations. All algorithms, in the object space or in the image space, usually involve the same operations and basic tests but not necessarily in the same order. The five basic operations and tests are as follows:

1. **The projection operation**, which transforms from a 3D space to a 2D representation; this has been discussed in detail in Chap. 2
2. **The overlap test**, which is essentially an intersection calculation of two graphic elements
3. **The inclusion test**, which detects whether a point belongs to a face
4. **The depth test**, which determines which points are nearest and which points are furthest from the viewer
5. **The visibility test**, which determines the potentially visible elements of a scene

5.2.2 Overlap test

This test consists of calculating the intersection of graphic elements. Its functions can be summarized by the following operations:

1. Find the points where there is a change in visibility (hidden-line algorithms)
2. Determine whether there is an intersection of two polygons in the viewplane (mixture algorithms)
3. Determine the intersections between objects and a line (hidden-surface algorithms)
4. Calculate the intersection between objects and a line going from the viewer; this operation is very useful for the depth test

The most useful cases of intersections of graphic elements are:

5.2.2.1 Intersection of two lines (within the same plane) given by their equations

$$P_1 = V_1 + \Omega\, N_1 \quad \text{(where } V_1 \text{ is a point of the line and } N_1 \text{ the director vector)}$$
$$P_2 = V_2 + \mu\, N_2 \quad \text{(where } V_2 \text{ is a point of the line and } N_2 \text{ the director vector)}$$

for nonparallel lines, the intersection is:

$$I = V_2 + \frac{(V_{2y} - V_{1y})\, N_{1x} - (V_{2x} - V_{1x})\, N_{1y}}{N_{2x}\, N_{1y} - N_{2y}\, N_{1x}}\, N_2 \qquad (5.1)$$

5.2.2.2 Intersection of a line and a plane given by their equations

$$P_1 = V_1 + \Omega\, N_1 \qquad \text{(where } V_1 \text{ is a point of the line and } N_1 \text{ the director vector)}$$
$$N_2 \cdot P - D = 0 \qquad \text{(where } N_2 \text{ is the normal vector to the plane, D the distance}$$
$$\text{from the origin to the plane, and } P = <x,y,z>).$$

For $N_1 \cdot N_2 \neq 0$, the intersection is:

$$I = V_1 - \frac{N_2 \cdot V + D}{N_1 \cdot N_2} \qquad (5.2)$$

5.2.2.3 Intersection of two polygons within the same plane
This latter case is very frequent and computationally expensive when the intersections of every edge of the first polygon with every edge of the second have to be computed. One common way of avoiding too many tests is to perform a **minmax test**. This test consists of checking if the rectangles bounding the polygons have an intersection. If there is no intersection between the bounding rectangles, there is no intersection between the polygons. Otherwise, a more complicated test has to be performed.

5.2.3 Inclusion tests

The main test consists of checking whether a point **P** lies inside or outside a polygon F given by a list of consecutive vertices $S_1, S_2 \dots S_N$. Two methods are possible:

5.2.3.1 Test on the angles
We denote by Ω_i the angle between the line segment PS_i and PS_{i+1}, as shown in Fig. 5.2.

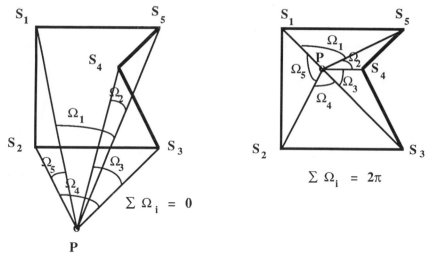

Fig.5.2. Test on the angles

P is inside F when $\sum \Omega_i = 2\pi$ and **P** is outside F when $\sum \Omega_i = 0$.

5.2.3.2 Test on the number of intersection points
Consider a half-line from the point **P** which cuts at least one edge of Γ without passing through any vertex of F (as shown in Fig.5.3). If the number of intersection points of the half-line with the edges of F is odd then **P** is inside F; otherwise it is outside.

5.2.4 Depth test

This test consists of determining which of two elements is nearer to the viewer. Two main kinds of depth test are possible:

5.2.4.1 Test in the object space
A face F is compared with a point-test P_t to detect whether the face hides the point. To perform the test, a line L is considered passing through the point P_t and the eye **E** of the virtual camera. Consider now the intersection point P_f between the line L and the face F. As shown in Fig.5.4, P_t is hidden when:

$$\text{distance } (E,P_t) > \text{distance } (E,P_f)$$

This test is not possible with a parallel projection.

5.2.4.2 Priority test
This test is only possible with an orthographic projection. We assume that the viewplane is the plane XY. Now, consider two faces F_1 and F_2 and their projections PF_1 and PF_2: a point I_{12} is chosen as the intersection of edges of PF_1 and PF_2, as shown in Fig.5.5. By substituting the coordinates X,Y of I_{12} into the equations of the plane of F_1 and F_2, we obtain the values of Z_1 and Z_2. These values are then compared to determine which face is nearer to the viewer.

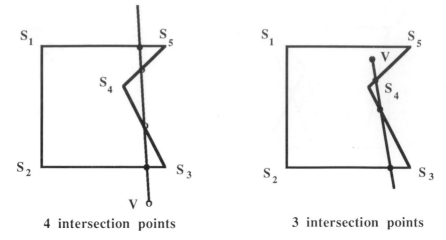

4 intersection points   **3 intersection points**

Fig.5.3. Test on intersection points

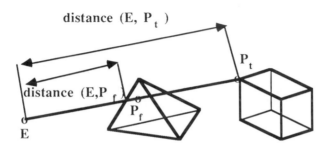

Fig. 5.4. Depth test with a perspective projection

This allows the definition of the concept of **relative priority**: a face F_j has a priority over face F_i (denoted by $F_i <\cdot F_j$) if $Z_i < Z_j$. Problems in determining priorities are shown in Fig.5.6; they may be solved by subdividing the polygons.

5.2.5 Visibility test

The test, presented here may only be applied to convex objects; it determines whether a face is in front of or behind an object. For a given face, the normal vector **N** toward the outside of the object is considered as well as a line passing through a point of the face and the eye of the virtual camera. A vector **K** is chosen on this line as shown in Fig.5.7. The angle Ω is calculated as:

$$\Omega = \cos^{-1} \left(\frac{\mathbf{N} \cdot \mathbf{K}}{|\mathbf{N}||\mathbf{K}|} \right) \tag{5.3}$$

The face is potentially visible when $\Omega \leq \frac{\pi}{2}$; it is not visible if $\Omega > \frac{\pi}{2}$.

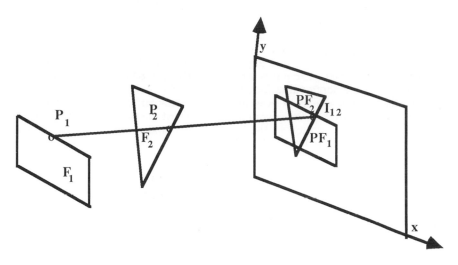

Fig.5.5. Priority test

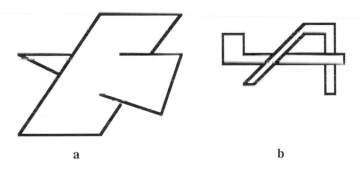

a   b

Fig.5.6. a Penetrating surfaces; **b** cyclic overlap

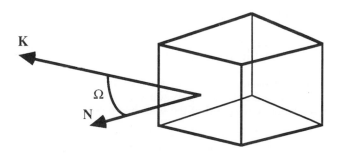

Fig.5.7. Visibility test

5.3 Depth buffer algorithm

Developed by Catmull (1975), this algorithm is the simplest method for hidden-surface removal. However, it requires a **depth buffer** (or **z-buffer**) that consists of an array containing the depth value for each pixel of the image to be displayed. The depth (or z value) of a new pixel to be written to the frame buffer is compared with the depth stored in the z-buffer. If the new pixel is in front of the pixel stored in the frame buffer, the new pixel is written to the frame buffer and the z-buffer is updated. Otherwise there is no action. In pseudo-PASCAL, the algorithm may be described as follows:

> ZBUFFER : **array** [1..MaxX, 1..MaxY] of REAL; {depth buffer}
> INTENSITY: **array** [1..MaxX, 1..MaxY] of ColorType; {frame buffer}

```
for each pixel (X,Y)
    INTENSITY [X,Y] := background color
    ZBUFFER [X,Y] := largest value
for each polygon in the scene
    find all pixels (X,Y) that are within the projected polygon
    for each pixel
    Calculate the depth Z in (X,Y)
    if Z < ZBUFFER [X,Y] {polygon is nearer}
    then
        ZBUFFER [X,Y] := Z;
        INTENSITY [X,Y] := corresponding polygon shading value
```

At the end of scene processing, the array INTENSITY contains the required frame.

It should be noted that this algorithm has been conceptually presented; z-buffer algorithms are generally implemented on graphics terminals which offer the corresponding technology. Several terminals have this kind of hardware, allowing pixels to be written conditionally to the z-value. This means that the frame-buffer and the z-buffer are parts of the terminal; which means, for example, 40 bits/pixel of graphic memory (24 bits for color and 16 bits for depth).

5.4 Scan-line algorithms

5.4.1 Scan-line color-filling algorithm

Scan-line hidden-surface algorithms are based on the same principle as the color-filling algorithm used to fill a single 2D polygon. First, we shall review the fundamental algorithm.

Figure 5.8 shows the basic principle of the method. We have to determine the pixels of a scan-line which are inside a polygon and give these pixels the right color. To avoid checking whether each pixel of the scan-line belongs to the polygon, we use the following strategy:

1. Find the intersections of the scan-line with the polygon
2. Sort the intersections in increasing order of their X-coordinates
3. Fill the pixels between intersection pairs

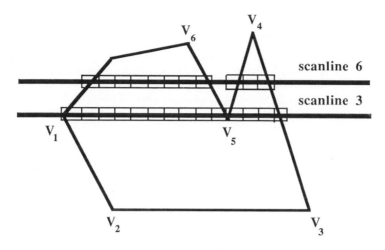

Fig.5.8. Principle of the scan-line method

The calculations of intersections can take a great deal of time. It should be noted that for each scan-line there are only a few edges of the polygon which may have an intersection with the scan-line. We may also assume that an edge which has an intersection with a scan-line has a high probability of intersecting the next scan-line. Moreover, it is possible to compute the X-coordinate (x_{i+1}) of the intersection point of an edge with the scan-line i+1 using the X-coordinate (x_i) of the intersection point computed with the scan-line i:

$$x_{i+1} = x_i + \frac{1}{m} \qquad (5.4)$$

where m is the slope of the edge.

These properties are taken into account in the scan-line color filling algorithm. For each scan-line, only edges which have an intersection are considered; these edges are stored in the **table of active edges** (TAE). At each new scan-line, new intersections are computed using Eq. (5.4) and the TAE is updated. Edges in the TAE are sorted in increasing order of their x-coordinates in order to decide which pixels to color.

TAE may be more easily updated when another table is created: the **table of edges** (TE), including all edges of the polygon sorted in increasing order of their minimum y-coordinate. Each entry of the TE includes the largest y-coordinate of the edge (used to eliminate the edge of the TAE), the X-coordinate of the edge bound which has the smallest y-coordinate, and the value of 1/m.

5.4.2 Scan-line z-buffer algorithm

The main difference between the scan-line color-filling algorithm and the scan-line hidden-surface algorithms is that several polygons are processed instead of a single polygon. This means that polygon identifiers must be added in the TE in order to recognize to which polygon an edge belongs. A **table of active polygons** (TAP) is also updated from the TAE.

Each polygon of the TAP is sequentially processed in order to determine the color of each pixel of the scan-line according to the active polygons. As several polygons may overlap, the color of the pixel is given by the polygon which is the nearest to the observer; this corresponds to the minimum Z-coordinate. This means that the value of the Z-coordinate also has to be stored each time it is less than the currently stored Z-coordinate for this pixel. To obtain the Z-coordinate of a polygon for each point of the scan-line, we use a process which is analogous to the calculation of the X-coordinate of the intersection point with the scan-line in the color-filling algorithm; this means that we store for each edge in the TE the initial Z-coordinate and its variation relative to a variation of 1 along the X-axis.

The z-buffer scan-line algorithm is the simplest scan-line algorithm. It is a special case of the z-buffer algorithm discussed in the previous section. To store the information concerning a scan-line, we use an array called the **scan buffer**, with the color and the depth for each pixel of the scan-line. The color is the value computed by the shading algorithm (see Chap. 6) and the depth is the Z-coordinate. When a scan-line has been completely processed, each pixel of the line is colored using the value in the scan buffer. At the beginning of each scan, the scan buffer is initialized with the background color and a very large depth for each pixel.

The PASCAL array SCANBUFFER is defined as:

```
var
    SCANBUFFER: array [1..RESX] of
                    record
                        INTENSITY: ColorType;
                        DEPTH:REAL
                    end;
```

The heart of the algorithm in pseudo-PASCAL is as follows:

```
for each pixel X on the scan-line
    SCANBUFFER[X].INTENSITY:= background
    SCANBUFFER[X].DEPTH:= maximum real value
for each polygon in the scene
    find the pixels of the scan-line that are within the polygon
    for each of these pixels X
        Calculate the depth Z of the polygon at <X,Y>
        if Z < SCANBUFFER.DEPTH
        then
            SCANBUFFER.DEPTH:=Z;
            SCANBUFFER.INTENSITY:=corresponding polygon shading value
```

At the end of the processing, SCANBUFFER.INTENSITY contains the correct values and is displayed.

5.4.3 Spanning scan-line algorithms

Several authors (Romney 1970; Bouknight 1970; Watkins 1970) have proposed important improvements on the basic scan-line algorithm. They have introduced the concept of **spans**, which are segments of a scan-line along which the same polygon is visible. Examples of spans are shown in Fig.5.9.

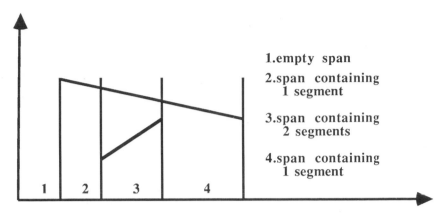

Fig.5.9. Scan-line spans

The three algorithms use sorted lists:

1. A Y-sorted list of polygon edges is utilized to determine which polygons should be considered for the scan-line
2. For each scan-line, an X-sorted list of segments is determined in order to establish a sequential set of spans

The sequence of operations is similar for each algorithm:

```
for each polygon edge
    Sort by the Y-vertex values
for each scan-line
    for each active polygon
        determine the segment obtained by the intersection of the scan-plane and the
            polygon
    Sort the segments by X-vertex values
    Determine the span boundaries
        for each span
            Clip the active segments to span boundaries
            Determine the segment visibility within the span by searching for the closest
                segment in Z
            Display the segment
```

For maintaining the Y-sorted list, a **bucket sort algorithm** is used; but for the X-sorted list, Romney and Watkins find a bubble sort more effective.

Romney suggests taking into account **depth priority coherence**: if penetration is not allowed, and if exactly the same polygons are present, and if the order of the edge crossings is exactly the same on a given scan-line as on the the previous scan-line, then the depth priority of the segments in each span remains unchanged.

Hamlin and Gear (1977) propose a method in which the depth priority may be maintained even if the order of the edge crossings changes by predicting the crossings.

Beatty et al. (1981) provide a complexity analysis of a specific implementation of the Watkins algorithm.

Crocker (1984) generalizes the concept of **invisibility coherence**, introduced by Atherton (1983) (see Sect 5.8) to all scan-line algorithms. Invisibility coherence is a technique for removing portions of a scene that are not likely to be visible. It eliminates surfaces from the active list that are not likely to be visible prior to the processing of the active list for each scan-line in the hidden surface removal process. Information about the Z depth of the pixels of the previous scan-line must be stored to do this.

5.4.4 Scan-line algorithms at object resolution

Sechrest and Greenberg (1982) propose a new algorithm for obtaining, at object resolution and in a polygonal form, the visible surfaces for a scene consisting of nonintersecting opaque polygons. A similar hidden-line algorithm was previously introduced by Hamlin and Gear (1977). Although this algorithm may be considered a scan-line algorithm, a sample is not needed for every scan line. The picture plane is divided into strips of varying width (dependent on the complexity of the picture) defined by the location of the vertices and crossings of the scene, as shown in Fig.5.10.

The procedure for the hidden-line case is as follows:
Find the locally minimal vertices by comparing the endpoints of each edge
            and retaining the lower vertices
Sort them in ascending order by their y location in the picture plane.
Select the next vertex or crossing **P** from the active edge list
if P_y < the y-coordinate of the next locally minimal vertex **M**
then
    Event := **P**
else
    Event := **M**
Update the active edge list
At vertices
    Remove edges that end at Event
    Add edges that begin

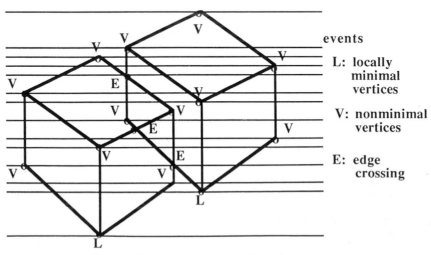

Fig.5.10. Horizontal strips and events

At crossings
    Reorder the edges on the list
if a visible edge ends or is occluded
then
    Write out the coordinate of a visible line

The production of the visible polygons falls into three parts:

1. Creation of visible segments rather than visible lines
2. Extraction of segments surrounding a particular visible region of a polygon
3. Reconstruction to form polygons with the vertices of their contours correctly ordered

5.5 List-priority algorithms

5.5.1 First list-priority algorithms

Schumacker et al. (1969) and Encarnacao (1970) concurrently developed the first list-priority algorithm. The algorithm is applied to objects with triangular faces. When the faces are not triangular, they have to be triangulated by introducing auxiliary edges. The projection must be orthographic and the viewplane is the XY plane.
    The method has three main steps:

1. Preprocessing
2. Priority assignment
3. Visibility determination

    The preprocessing step consists mainly of eliminating all triangles which are perpendicular to the XY plane.
    The priorities are assigned by considering the set of triangular faces $F=\{F_1,F_2,...F_N\}$ and the set of their corresponding projections $P=\{P_1,P_2,...P_N\}$. Each triangle and its projection are supposed numbered and known by their vertices. The ordered pairs $<P_i,\Omega_i>$ are then constructed, where Ω_i is defined as:

$$\Omega_i = \{X| \ X \ \in \ P \ and \ F_i <\cdot P_i\} \tag{5.5}$$

    This may be easily obtained using the minmax test (see Sect. 5.2.2) and the second depth test (see Sect. 5.2.4). There is no risk of cyclic overlap, but penetrating triangles are possible.
    The visibility test is performed by inspecting each pair $<P_i,\Omega_i>$. If $\Omega_i = \emptyset$ then P_i is visible (except auxiliary edges). Otherwise the three edges e_{ik} (k=1 to 3) of P_i are considered. The visibility of e_{ik} relative to P_j (where $P_j \in \Omega_j$) is obtained by determining the intersections of e_{ik} with P_j and by checking whether the bounds of e_{ik} are inside P_j. The different cases of visibility are shown in Fig. 5.11.

5.5.2 Painter's algorithm

    An algorithm, developed by Newell et al. (1972), is based on a simple idea, very similar to the way an artist creates a painting. The idea consists of sorting the scene elements (polygons) in depth priority order based on distance from the viewpoint.

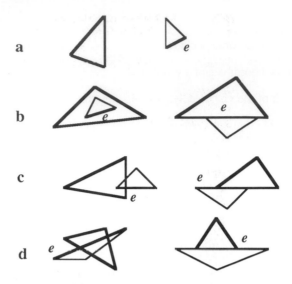

Fig.5.11 a-d. The visibility cases. **a** e is visible; **b** e is invisible; **c** part of e is visible and part is invisible; **d** two parts of e are visible and other parts are invisible

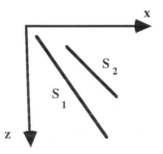

Fig.5.12. S_1 appears before S_2 because $zmin_1 < zmin_2$

When the list is definitive, the elements are simply displayed in the order. The technique seems very simple; however, the sort operation may be very complex, particularly in two cases:

1. When there are cyclic overlaps (see Sect. 5.2.4)
2. When polygons are sorted by their minimum Z-coordinate value and the scene is as in Fig.5.12

The Newell-Newell-Sancha algorithm uses a special sorting technique for solving priority conflicts on the depth priority list. The algorithm may be summarized as follows:

- A preliminary depth priority is performed using the largest value on each polygon
- The polygon P with the largest depth is then compared with the other polygons in the list to determine whether there are any overlaps in depth

- If there is no overlap, P is scan-converted and then displayed and the process is repeated for the next polygon in the list
- If there is an overlap, new tests are performed; if any one of these tests is true, P is scan-converted and displayed and the process is repeated for the next polygon in the list.

The tests are performed in the following order of difficulty:

1. Are the bounding rectangles in the XY-plane for the two polygons disjoint ?
2. Is P on the outside of the overlapping polygon relative to the viewpoint ?
3. Is the overlapping polygon on the inside of P relative to the viewpoint ?
4. Are the projections of P and the other polygon disjoint ?

5.6 Recursive subdivision algorithms

5.6.1 Warnock algorithm

In this algorithm, the screen is divided into windows; three cases are considered for each:

1. There is nothing to be seen in the window—there is no problem
2. What is visible in the window is easy to draw—there is no problem
3. What is visible is too difficult to draw—the window must be subdivided into several smaller windows

The algorithm is typically recursive, ending under one of three conditions:

1. There is nothing to see—the window is colored with the background color

2. The window is reduced to a pixel—since no further subdivision is possible it must be colored with the appropriate color. The pixel-sized window is examined to see if it is surrounded by any of the polygons in the scene. Two cases are possible:

   i) There are surrounding polygons: these are tested (at the pixel center) to see which one is closer to the eyepoint at this pixel location. The pixel is displayed with the color of the closest polygon.
   ii) There is no surrounding polygon: the pixel is displayed with the background color.

3. The window is easy to color; this is possible when:

   i) A single polygon surrounds the window and there are no other polygons in the window. In this case, the window is colored with the appropriate color
   ii) Only one polygon intersects the window. In this case, the window is first colored with the background color and then the portion of the intersecting polygon is colored with the appropriate color
   iii) The polygon closest to the eye surrounds the window. In this case, the window is colored with the color appropriate for the surrounding polygon

The algorithm may be optimized by using the bounding box of the polygons as subdivisions, as shown in Fig.5.13.

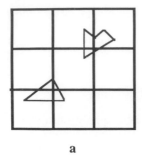   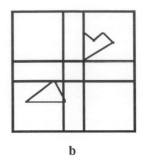

a   b

Fig.5.13. Window subdivisions in the Warnock algorithm. **a** non-optimized; **b** optimized

5.6.2 Weiler-Atherton algorithm

Weiler and Atherton (1977) propose an algorithm which recursively subdivides an image into polygon shaped windows. The algorithm resembles the Warnock algorithm in its method of operation. But the Warnock algorithm is an image-space algorithm because it subdivides until a solution or the predefined resolution is obtained. The Weiler-Atherton algorithm qualifies as an object-space algorithm since it continues to subdivide only until the proper depth order has been established.

The output of the algorithm is in the form of polygons allowing hidden-lines as well as hidden-surfaces. The algorithm involves four steps:

1. A preliminary depth sort
2. A polygon area sort based on the polygon currently closest to the front
3. The removal of polygons behind the polygon currently closest to the front polygon
4. A depth sort by recursive subdivision, if required

The preliminary depth sort is not essential, but it increases the efficiency of the algorithm. For this, an approximate depth-priority list is established using a sorting key. For example, polygons are ordered on the nearest z-value of each polygon.

A copy of the first polygon on the list is then used as a **clip polygon** for the remainder of the list, called the **subject polygons**. This clip polygon and the subject polygons are projected onto the XY-plane before the 2D clipping process. The portion of each subject polygon inside the clip polygon is placed in a list, called the **inside list**. The portion of each polygon outside the clip polygon is placed in a list, called the **outside list**. An example is shown in Fig.5.14.

In the process, the inside list is now examined and any polygons behind the current clip polygon are removed, because they are hidden faces. If any polygon on the inside list is located in front of the clip polygon, the original preliminary depth sort is in error. The algorithm recursively subdivides the area using the erroneous polygon as the current clip polygon and the inside list as input list.

When the recursive subdivision has been completed, the inside list is displayed and the algorithm is repeated using the outside list as input list.

The key element of the algorithm is the **2D polygon-clipping algorithm**. This algorithm is a generalized xy polygon clipper capable of clipping a concave polygon (subject polygon) with holes to the border of another concave polygon (clip polygon) also with holes. The polygons are represented as a circular list of vertices, one for the main contour and one for each of the holes.

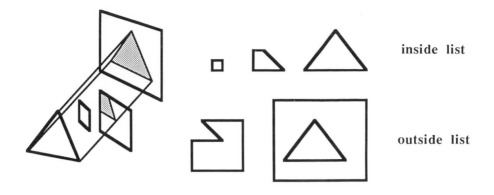

Fig.5.14. Example of clip and subject polygons with the inside and outside lists

The clipping process is as follows:

1. The intersections of the clip polygon and the subject polygon are compared. At each intersection, a false vertex (tagged) is added to the list of vertices of each polygon. A bidirectional link is established between the subject and clip polygon lists for each added vertex (called intersection vertex)
2. Each contour of the subject polygon with no intersection is placed on one of two holding lists: one for boundaries inside the clip polygons, the other for contours outside them. Clip polygon contours outside the subject polygon are ignored. Clip polygon boundaries inside the subject polygon in effect cut a hole in the subject polygon, producing two new contours. In this case, one copy of the clip polygon is placed in each of the holding list (one copy is in reverse order)
3. Two intersection vertex lists are created: one contains the intersections where the clip polygon border passes to the outside of the subject polygon, the other contains those intersections where the clip polygon borders passes to the inside. The intersection type will alternate along the border; this means that only one determination is necessary per contour
4. The clipping is then performed:
   - An intersection vertex (called starting point) is removed from the input list; the clipping is complete when this list is empty
   - Follow along the subject polygon vertex list until the next intersection is found
   - Jump to the clip polygon vertex list and copy the chain of polygon vertices until the next intersection is reached
   - Jump back to the subject polygon vertex list
   - Repeat the three last steps until the starting point is reached; at this stage, the new inside polygon has been closed

   Outside polygons are found using the same process by starting at the initial intersection vertex and the clip polygon vertex list is followed in reverse order

5.6.3 Franklin algorithm

Franklin (1980) proposes an algorithm which eliminates polygons which are clearly hidden and then samples the regions where remaining polygons overlap to find the shallowest polygon within each region. The algorithm is somewhat similar to the Warnock algorithm and the Weiler-Atherton algorithm. However, it is as accurate as the arithmetic precision of the computer and the execution time is linear in the number of faces. It works as follows:

Project and scale the scene to fit a 1 by 1 square on the screen.
Overlay a B by B grid of cells onto the scene, where B is a constant.
for each projected face F
    Determine which cells G, F falls partly or wholly in.
    for each G that contains F
        1: **if** G has a blocking face F_b (the projection of this face covers the cell)
            then
                if F is behind F_b
                then
                    Do not consider this G further with F
                    Go to 1 to process next G;
                  else
                  if F is a blocking face of G
                    then Update F_b to be F
                    else Add F to the set of faces in G
    if F is not added to any G
    then Delete it
for each cell G
    Compare F_b against all the faces on G's set
    Delete from the set any that are behind F_b within G
for each projected edge E
    Determine which cells G passes through
    for each G
        if E is not behind F_b
        then
            Add E to the set of edges in G
    if E is not added to any G
    then
        Delete it from the array of edges
for each cell G
    for each pair of edges $\{E_1, E_2\}$ in G's set of edges
        if there is an intersection between E_1 and E_2
        then
            if the intersection is in G
            then
                Add E_1 to the list of edges intersecting E_2
                Add E_2 to the list of edges intersecting E_1
for each edge E
    Sort the intersection points along E
    Use the sorted points to split E into segments S
    for each segment S
        Find its midpoint **P**
        Find which cell contains **P**
        Compare **P** against all faces F in G
        if **P** is visible
        then
            Draw the segment S
            Add S to the set of visible segments
Determine the regions R of the planar graph formed by the visible segment

for each R
    Find a point **P** in R (e.g., the centroid)
    Find which cell G contains **P**
    Find the closest F in G whose projections contain **P**
    if there is such a face F
    then
        R corresponds to a visible part of F
    else
        R corresponds to the background
    Shade R with the appropriate color

5.7 Algorithms for curved surfaces

5.7.1 Catmull subdivision algorithm

Curved surfaces, also called **patches**, can be used instead of polygons to model free-form curved surfaces. Catmull (1975) proposes a method for producing computer-shaded pictures of such curved surfaces. This method involves three steps:

1. Establishing a correspondance between points on the surface and the pixels
2. Removing hidden parts of patches
3. Calculating light intensities

    The hidden surface algorithm used is Catmull's z-buffer algorithm. Calculation of the light intensity can be performed with the Phong method (see Sect. 6.2) by using an intensity function or by mapping intensities from a picture or a photograph.
    The first step is solved by a recursive subdivision algorithm similar to the Warnock algorithm discussed in Sect. 5.6.1.
    According to Catmull (1975), the algorithm can be described as follows: "If the patch (or subpatch) is small enough so that its projection covers only one sample point, then compute the intensity of the patch and write it into the corresponding element of the frame buffer; otherwise, subdivide the patch into smaller subpatches and repeat the process for each subpatch."
    This method is time-consuming; in practice, it can be used with bicubic patches. However, it is of interest because it produces images of superior quality. Carlson (1982) proposes a modified recursive subdivision to find the space curve which is the intersection of two bicubic patches.

5.7.2 Scan-line algorithms for curved surfaces

More general algorithms for producing shaded images of parametric surfaces are based on scan-line methods. Three different algorithms have been proposed and compared (Lane et al. 1980): the Blinn, the Whitted, and the Lane-Carpenter algorithms. In each, patches are surfaces defined by three bivariate functions:

$$X = X(u,v) \qquad Y = Y(u,v) \qquad Z = Z(u,v) \qquad (5.6)$$

Patches are then transformed to a display space with X going to the right, Y going up, and Z going into the screen. Silhouette edges are defined as curves in the surface for which the Z-component of the normal is zero.

5.7.2.1 Blinn algorithm

This algorithm is an algebraic approach that generalizes the concept of scanning a polygon to scanning a patch. In a first phase, boundary curve and silhouette edge intersections with the current scan-line are determined. All intersection calculations are performed using bivariate Newton-Raphson solutions of the equations. The process results in a list of boundaries for the current scan-line. For each picture element, the Z information for the surface is generated and the required shading can be represented. This algorithm tends to be generally robust and relevant, except when the Newton iteration fails.

5.7.2.2 Whitted algorithm

In this algorithm, bicubic surface patches are defined in terms of "edges" that are cubic curves. Patches have four cubic edge curves. Extremely curved patches may also have additional interior curved edges which subdivide the patch into subpatches. The silhouette curve is approximated by a cubic Hermite interpolation function. After the silhouettes have been determined, intersections of the edges with the scan-line are calculated using Newton's method. Depth and surface normals are then linearly interpolated between the endpoint values of scan-line segments. Visibility is calculated for each segment by comparing the average depth of segment endpoints to establish the priority of segments. Shading is computed using the Phong model (see Sect. 6.2). The major disadvantage of the Whitted algorithm is that it fails if it tries to find silhouettes that do not intersect the boundary of the patch.

   Schweizer and Cobb (1982) propose an algorithm that is partially based on the Whitted algorithm. Their approach consists of two main parts:

1. Preprocessing steps for converting bivariate cubic surface descriptions into a standard internal form and deriving curved-edge polygons; a general surface intersection method is used to detect silhouette edges
2. Rendering of the curved-edge polygons by calculating a cubic approximation to the normal surface and performing an interpolation of the bounding edge normals across the scan-line

5.7.2.3 Lane-Carpenter algorithm

In this algorithm, a polygonal approximation to the smooth surface is derived and the polygons are rendered. A subdivision technique similar to the Catmull algorithm is combined with a polygon scan-line algorithm. This method can be summarized as follows:

1. Patches are sorted by maximum possible Y-values
2. As each scan-line is processed, patches with this maximum possible value are subdivided until:

   i) Any one piece no longer overlaps the scan-line. It is, therefore, placed in the inactive patch list; or
   ii) The patch is within a set of tolerances of being a four-sided planar polygon, at which time it may be processed with a polygon scan-line method

   Variants of the Lane-Carpenter algorithm have been described by Clark (1979) and Riesenfeld et al. (1981).

5.7.3 Blinn algebraic method

The algorithm described in the previous section deals with bivariate parametric surfaces generated by three functions of two variables. Another class of surfaces includes shapes like spheres, cones, and hyperboloids of revolution. These fall into the class of quadric surfaces which are a subset of implicit surface solutions to some equation:

$$F(x,y,z) = 0 \qquad (5.7)$$

Blinn (1982a) proposes a general solution to the imaging problem for such surfaces. The implicit form is ideally suited to raster conversion algorithms. The pixel coordinates are substituted for x and y and the equation is solved for z. Blinn shows how to solve the problem for the summation of several density distributions (see Sect. 14.3.1). The method has been applied to the representation of electron density maps of molecular structures. The results more closely resemble what a real electron density cloud might look like for a covalent bond than do classic molecular models based on intersections of spheres and cylinders.

5.7.4 Visible surface algorithms for intersecting spheres and ellipsoids

Porter (1978) proposes a fast algorithm for the shaded surface display of intersecting spheres. This algorithm is a scan-line algorithm which maintains a list of active spheres (LAS). The algorithm works as follows:

Sort the set of spheres to display in decreasing order of y values
for each scan
   Remove from the LSA all inactive spheres
   Add to the LSA new active spheres
   for each sphere of the LSA
      Compute its intersection with the viewplane using an algorithm similar to the Bresenham algorithm for display of circular arcs (Bresenham 1977)
      Determine the visible points of the intersection using a scan-line z-buffer technique
      Compute the shading for the corresponding pixels

Max (1979) describes a program, called ATOMLLL for representing atoms and molecules with shading and highlights (see Fig.5.15).

This program is an extension of a program called ATOMS (Knowlton and Cherry 1977), which is capable of determining the visible portions of a scene consisting of interpenetrating spheres and cylinders. Both programs keep track of the visible portions of each part in terms of a list of trapezoids. Each trapezoid has two straight vertical sides and two sides, which may be straight lines or arcs of circles. For example, a sphere is represented by two trapezoids, each one having one degenerate vertical side. If this sphere is intersected by a second sphere, the intersection curve is approximated by a circular arc and the trapezoids of the first sphere are subdivided into their visible pieces. In ATOMLLL, trapezoids are colored in vertical raster scan segments.

Knowlton (1981) does not use a z-buffer in the following algorithm based on a model with spheres lighted by the sun, which gives a disk. The algorithm works as follows:

Produce from a file of spheres, a file of disks by associating two disks with each sphere: a light disk centered at the center of the sphere and a black disk backward in z
Sort in z the file of disks
Display the disks by decreasing values of z

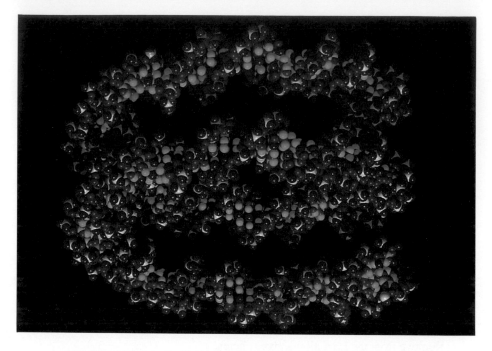

Fig. 5.15. Molecule. By Nelson Max, Lawrence Livermore National Laboratory

for each point covered by a disk
  if disk is light
  then
    if same color
    then color with maximum intensity
    else color with the new value
  else do not color

When a light disk is detected, if the existing pixel is not colored, then the last displayed disk was black. This means there is no intersection, otherwise it is the light disk of another sphere and colors have to be mixed.

O'Rourke and Badler (1979) describe an algorithm to decompose a 3D object into spheres for human modelling (Magnenat-Thalmann and Thalmann 1985b) (see Chap. 9). Hidden surfaces are processed using a depth buffer algorithm adapted to the topology of the sphere. Each sphere is processed as a solid disk (its projection), using the value of the nearest point to the observer as the depth value. For each processed sphere, values in the depth buffer are only modified if the depth of this sphere is less than the current value. With this approach, hidden parts are erased in the depth buffer by overlapping parts. Overlapping spheres have of course similar depth and thus similar intensities; the result is a smoothly shaded picture.

The numerical utility displaying ellipsoid solids (NUDES) system, designed by Herbison-Evans (1978), provides real-time animation of human drawings with hidden lines omitted. The human figures are stick figures fleshed out by ellipsoids. The principle behind the use of ellipsoids is very simple. Assume we have two ellipsoids A and B, where B hides part of A. The points where the elliptical outlines disappear and reappear must be one of the following types:

1. Obscuration points—these are intersection points between the elliptical outlines
2. Interpenetration points—these are the intersections between the outline of ellipsoid A and the section of ellipsoid B which is cut by the plane of the outline of ellipsoid A

These points can generate eight possible arcs. A very simple algorithm involves testing to see whether the center of the arc should be visible; if so, the arc must be visible.

Shaded images have also been generated using the same ellipsoid-based method. Herbison-Evans (1980) proposes a fast method for identifying the ellipsoid that colors a particular pixel. In the case of a z-buffer, the algorithm works as follows:

> **for** each ellipsoid E
> > **for** each $<x,y>$ location
> > > **if** the corresponding point V on E projects onto a pixel P
> > > > Compute the depth z
> > > > **if** $z <$ the current value z_{curr} in the z-buffer
> > > > **then**
> > > > > $z_{curr}:=z$
> > > > > Compute the corresponding color C

Only the appropriate subarea may be scanned by computing beforehand the minimum and maximum extents in x and y of the outline of each ellipsoid.

When no z-buffer is available, the algorithm is as follows:

> **for** each pixel $<x,y>$
> > **for** each ellipsoid E
> > > Compute the depth z
> > > **if** $z <$ the current value z_{curr}
> > > **then**
> > > > $z_{curr}:=z$
> > > > Compute the corresponding color C

The calculation of the depth z for a given position $<x,y>$ and a given ellipsoid involves the solution of a quadratic equation by forming a discriminant and, if this is positive, finding its square root. Time may be saved by prefixing by four tests:

$$x > x_{min}, \quad x < x_{max}, \quad y > y_{min}, \quad y < y_{max} \tag{5.8}$$

Other improvements are described by Herbison-Evans (1980):

- z-boxing and painting front to back
- Testing each pixel against the osculating sphere

5.8 Visible surface algorithms for solids

5.8.1 Scan-line and z-buffer algorithms for constructive solid geometry

A scan-line algorithm for constructive solid geometry (CSG), analogous to the spanning scan-line algorithms, is proposed by Atherton (1983). This algorithm is obtained by integrating a 1D Boolean solution technique into the sequence of

operations described in Sect. 5.4.3. For each span boundary, the 1D Boolean problem
is solved at the first visible point. The modified sequence is now as follows:

> **for** each polygon edge
>   Sort by the Y-vertex values
> **for** each scan-line
>   **for** each active polygon
>   Determine the segment obtained by the intersection of the scan-plane and the
>   polygon
>   Sort the segments by X-vertex values
>   Determine the span boundaries
>   **for** each span
>   (*) Clip the active segments to span boundaries
>   (*) Solve the 1D Boolean problem at the first visible point as specified in
>   the CSG tree
>   (*) **If** the Z-order of segments at boundaries is the same
>   **then** Display the segment
>   **else** Subdivide span at segment intersections and recursively repeat the
>   steps (*) for each new span

Rossignac and Requicha (1986) propose a z-buffer for CSG, which may be
summarized as follows:

> **for** each <x,y>
>   z(x,y) := large value
>   I[x,y]:= background intensity
> **for** each primitive PR of solid S
>   **for** each face F of PR
>   **for** each point **P** in a dense grid on F
>   <x,y> := Projection of **P**
>   d:= |Viewpoint - **P**|
>   **if** d < z[x,y]
>   **then**
>   **if P** on S
>   **then**
>   z[x,y]:=d
>   n:=normal to F at P
>   I[x,y]:= computed intensity

The condition "**P** on S" is evaluated by point-membership classification, i.e., by
an algorithm that determines whether **P** is inside, on the boundary, or outside the
solid.

Okino et al. (1984) also propose an extended depth-buffer algorithm based on
CSG primitives. Their algorithm may be classified as a ray-casting algorithm; it uses
the properties of holes and efficiently calculates the depths of primitives.

5.8.2 Visible surface algorithms for octree-encoded objects

The ability to visit voxels in a spatially predetermined order makes the hidden-surface
problem easy to solve. Doctor and Torborg (1981) propose a very simple function to
display octree-encoded objects. It is based on the ability to traverse a tree so that nodes
are visited in a consistent direction through space. The octree is traversed in a depth-
first manner while processing data elements in a prescribed order. The function is

recursive and frontmost elements are always visited first and the rearmost elements last. The following pseudo-PASCAL function returns a quadtree data element which represents the image directly in front of the octree OCT; QUAD is a quadtree data element representing an area in the image array directly behind the octree region.

```
function DISPLAY(OCT:OCTREE;  QUAD:QUADTREE): QUADTREE;
begin
  if OCT is homogeneous
  then
    if OCT is not empty
    then DISPLAY := quadtree colored according to the material
    else DISPLAY:= QUAD
  else a new quadtree is created; each quadrant of this quadtree is determined
       by the pairs of octants aligned with that quadrant, this is made recursively
       by:
         DISPLAY:=NEWQUAD(
                  SON(OCT,0),DISPLAY(SON(OCT,4),QSON(QUAD,0)),
                  SON(OCT,1),DISPLAY(SON(OCT,5),QSON(QUAD,1)),
                  SON(OCT,2),DISPLAY(SON(OCT,6),QSON(QUAD,2)),
                  SON(OCT,3),DISPLAY(SON(OCT,7),QSON(QUAD,3)))
end;
```

SON(OCT,n) returns a data element from the node OCT and the octant specified by the index; QSON is similar for a quadtree node.

6 Illumination, shading, and transparency models

6.1 Introduction to illumination

If we eliminate the hidden faces of a sphere approximated by polygons and color all visible polygons with the same red color, we will obtain a red circle! This is because our perception of the third dimension is greatly improved by the reflection of light. In the case of a sphere, the different points on its surface do not reflect light in the same way if there are point sources of light. This means that the sphere must not be colored with a uniform color.

Theoretically, there are two extremes of surface type:

- **Ideal specular reflectors**, which are like perfect mirrors (e.g., polished brass, still water)
- **Ideal diffuse reflectors**, which correspond to dull matte surfaces (e.g., cork, chalk)

In fact, most real surfaces are neither ideal specular reflectors nor ideal diffuse reflectors. For this reason, illumination models have been developed. These models break reflection into three components—ambient, diffuse, and specular.

The **ambient** component corresponds to light that is uniformly incident and is reflected equally in all directions by the surface. This ambient light does not come from any single source but is an overall illumination that comes from the surroundings (walls, other objects); it represents in fact a completely distributed light source. No information about the slope of the surface may be obtained from the ambient light, which may be expressed as:

$$I_a = k_a\, C_s \tag{6.1}$$

where k_a is the ambient lighting coefficient and C_s is the color of the surface. The **diffuse** component consists of light that emanates from a point light source but is scattered equally in all directions. This means that the position of the observer is unimportant for this diffuse component. Lambert's law for diffuse reflectors states that the intensity perceived by the observer varies with the cosine of the angle between the light direction L and the normal N to the surface at a given point. This means that the intensity I_d may be computed by the following dot product:

$$I_d = k_d\, C_s\, I_l\, N{\cdot}L \tag{6.2}$$

where k_d is the diffuse reflection constant; this varies from material to material and also depends on the wavelength of the light; its value is always between 0 and 1. C_s is the surface color and I_l is the intensity of the source. Objects possessing only diffuse lighting attributes appear to be made of a dull smooth plastic.

The **specular** component simulates the reflection of light from a surface in some distribution about the angle of incidence. This represents the highlight, i.e., light concentrated around the impact point of the incident ray. The highlight has the color of the source light.

In the next sections, we shall examine several illumination models; we are using the word **model** to mean a mathematical formulation for a description of the reality. An illumination model requires as basic data the properties of the light sources and the properties of the illuminated surface at each point. Typically, an illumination model consists of a formula which computes the intensity of the light from the light position or direction and the normal to the surface at a given point.

6.2 Phong illumination model

6.2.1 Basic model

The first illumination model that took into account the three components of ambient, diffuse, and specular light was devised by Bui-Tuong Phong (1975). Intensity **I** in this model is given by:

$$I = I_a + I_d + I_s \qquad (6.3)$$

where I_a is reflection due to ambient light, I_d is diffuse reflection, and I_s is specular reflection.

Diffuse reflection is defined as in Lambert's law, which means for m_s light sources:

$$I_d = k_d C_s \sum_{j}^{m_s} I_{1j} (N \cdot L_j) \qquad (6.4)$$

where k_d is the diffuse reflection coefficient, N is the unit surface normal, I_{1j} is the intensity of the j-th source, C_s is the surface color, L_j is the vector in the direction of the j-th light source, and m_s is the number of light sources.

Specular reflection is defined as:

$$I_s = k_s C_r \sum_{j}^{m_s} I_{1j} (N \cdot H_j)^n \qquad (6.5)$$

where k_s is the specular reflection coefficient and C_r is the reflective color surface. The exponent n depends on the surface and determines how glossy this surface is; typically n varies from 1 to 200 and would be infinite for a perfect reflector. H_j is the vector in the direction halfway between the observer and the j-th light source (see Fig.6.1) :

$$H_j = \frac{L_j + E}{|L_j + E|} \qquad (6.6)$$

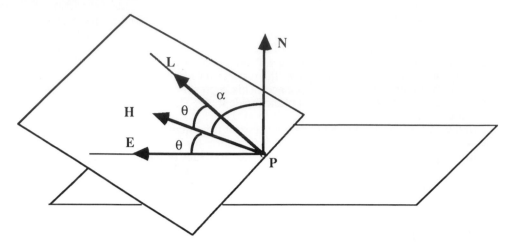

Fig.6.1. Geometry of a light model

Note that the term for I_s is empirical and contains a dot product to the n-th power, which in fact reduces to $\cos^n \alpha$, where α is the angle between the direction of reflection and the viewpoint. Large values of n correspond to metallic and shiny surfaces, while small values correspond to nonmetallic surfaces like paper.

6.2.2 Incremental evaluation along a scan line

There are two dot products in Eq. (6.3) and Phong (1975) has developed an efficient method for their incremental evaluation along a scan line. For this method, the following assumptions are made:

1. A special coordinate system is used with the origin at the point **P** and the Z-axis pointing toward the light source, as shown in Fig.6.2
2. N_p is the normal vector at **P**; it makes an angle i with the Z-axis. The reflected light vector S_p makes an angle 2i with the same axis
3. Only incident angles less than 90^0 are considered
4. If **k** is the unit vector along the Z-axis, then **k**, N_p and S_p are coplanar
5. $|N_p| = |S_p| = 1$

The method determines the unit vector S_p that points along the reflected ray. The vectors S_p and N_p project onto the XY-plane with components $<x_s, y_s>$ and $<x_n, y_n>$, respectively. As these two projections are on the same line (see Fig.6.3), the following equation may be used:

$$\frac{x_s}{y_s} = \frac{x_n}{y_n} \tag{6.7}$$

From assumptions (2) and (3), the component z_n of N_p is:

$$z_n = \cos i \tag{6.8}$$

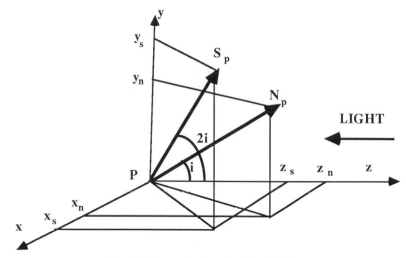

Fig.6.2. Determination of reflected light

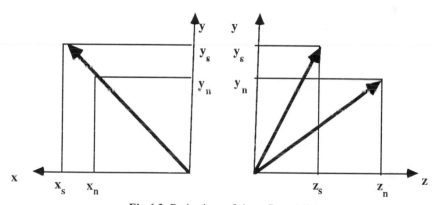

Fig.6.3. Projections of the reflected light

By trigonometry, we may obtain the following expressions:

$$z_s = \cos(2i) = 2\cos^2 i - 1 \tag{6.9}$$

$$x_s^2 + y_s^2 = \sin^2(2i) = 1 - \cos^2(2i) \tag{6.10}$$

From Eqs. (6.7), (6.9), and (6.10), we obtain the three components of the reflected vector S_p:

$$S_p = \langle x_s, y_s, z_s \rangle = \langle 2z_n x_n, 2z_n y_n, 2z_n^2 - 1 \rangle \tag{6.11}$$

In theory, the illumination from a point source should decrease by the square of the distance between it and the surface being illuminated. However, the use of such a relation does not give good results and most authors suggest dividing the diffuse and the specular illumination by the factor C + D, where C is a constant and D_j the distance between the light and the surface. Finally, the modified Phong formula may be rewritten as follows:

$$I = k_a C_s + \sum_j I_{1j} \frac{k_d \, C_s \cdot (N \cdot L_j) + k_s \, C_r \cdot (N \cdot H_j)^n}{C + D_j} \quad (6.12)$$

6.3 Surface shading

6.3.1 What is surface shading ?

Surface shading may be defined as the distribution of light over an illuminated surface. For each type of object model (set of polygons, algebraic surface, patches), shading can be calculated using the reflection models presented in the previous and the following sections. However, reflection models do not directly provide ways of calculating the complete shading of an object, but only the intensity of light at specific points. The shading techniques used depend on the type of object. For polygon meshes, three basic ways of shading objects have been developed—constant shading, Gouraud shading, and Phong shading.

6.3.2 Constant shading

This model, also called **polygonal shading**, involves calculating a single intensity for each polygon. This implies the following assumptions:

1. The light source is at infinity
2. The observer is at infinity
3. The polygons are not an approximation of a curved surface

The two first assumptions are required so that the dot products $N \cdot L_j$ and $N \cdot H_j$ are constant in the calculations of intensity. The third assumption is made because each polygonal facet of an object will have a slightly different intensity from its neighbors. This produces good results for a cube, but very poor ones for a sphere. Moreover, constant shading produces the **Mach band effect**, described by E. Mach, in 1865 as follows: "Wherever the light intensity curve of an illuminated surface (the light intensity of which varies in only one direction) has a concave or convex flection with respect to the axis of the abscissa, that particular place appears brighter or darker, respectively, than its surroundings."

Figure 6.4 shows an example of constant shading.

6.3.3 Gouraud shading

Gouraud (1971) introduced an intensity interpolation shading method that eliminates the discontinuities of constant shading. However, the Mach band effect is still visible where the slope of the shading function changes.

Fig.6.4. Example of constant shading. A frame of *Rendez-vous à Montréal* © 1987 MIRALab,
H.E.C. and University of Montreal

The principle of Gouraud shading is as follows:

1. For each vertex common to several polygons, the normal to each polygon is computed as a vector perpendicular to the plane of that polygon
2. For each vertex, a unique normal is calculated by averaging the surface normals obtained previously (see Fig.6.5):

$$N_t = \sum_{i=1}^{m} \frac{N_i}{m}$$

(6.13)

3. Vertex intensities are calculated by using the vertex normals and one of the light models presented in this chapter
4. As each polygon has a different shading at each vertex, the shading at any point inside the polygon is found by linear interpolation of vertex intensities along each edge and then between edges along each scan-line (Gouraud shading is based on a scan-line algorithm such as the Watkins algorithm). Figure 6.6 shows an example of the interpolation calculation.

Figure 6.7 shows an example of Gouraud shading.

6.3.4 Phong shading

Bui-Tuong Phong (1975) has proposed a normal-vector interpolation shading method. This means that instead of interpolating intensities as in Gouraud shading, Phong interpolates the surface normal vector (as shown in Fig. 6.8).

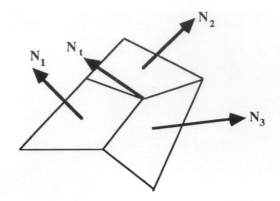

Fig.6.5. Calculation of the vertex normal: $N_t = \dfrac{N_1 + N_2 + N_3}{3}$

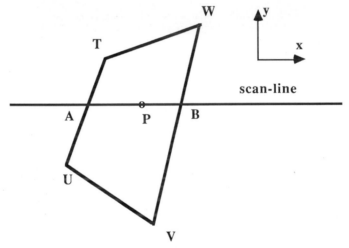

Fig.6.6. Intensity interpolation (Gouraud interpolation)

$$I_A = \frac{I_T (Y_A - Y_U) + I_U (Y_T - Y_A)}{Y_T - Y_U}, \quad I_B = \frac{I_W (Y_B - Y_V) + I_V (Y_W - Y_B)}{Y_W - Y_V}, \quad I_P = \frac{I_A (X_B - X_P) + I_B (X_P - X_A)}{X_B - X_A}$$

With this approach, the shading of a point is computed from the orientation of the approximated normal. With Phong shading, a better approximation of the curvature of the surface is obtained and highlights due to the simulation of specular reflection are much better rendered. However, the method requires more computation, since three normal components must be computed, rather than one shading value, and the vector at each point must be normalized before evaluating the shading function. For this reason, the designer may prefer to choose a different type of shading, according to the kind of object used. The linear interpolation scheme used in the Phong algorithm to approximate the orientation of the normal does not guarantee a continuous first derivative of the shading function across an edge of a polygonal model. In particular,

Fig.6.7. Example of Gouraud shading. © 1987 MIRAI ab, H.E.C. and University of Montreal

Where there is an abrupt change in the orientation of two adjacent polygons along a common edge, the Mach Band effect is possible. This means that a subjective brightness may be visible along this edge. The effect is usually much less visible in the Phong model than in the Gouraud model. However, Duff (1979) shows that Phong shading can produce worse Mach bands than Gouraud shading, notably for spheres and cylinders. Moreover, both techniques render concave polygons incorrectly.

Figure 6.9 shows an example of Phong shading.

Duff (1979) has discovered another great problem in the computer animation of shaded objects with the Gouraud and Phong algorithms. If an object and its light source are rotated together in the image plane, the shading of the object can change contrary to expectations. This is due to the fact that the interpolation of intensities (or normals) is carried out using values on a scan-line, and when objects and lights are rotated, the scan-lines do not cut the edges at the same points. Duff proposes alleviating this problem by interpolating intensities (or normals) in a rotation-independent manner; he avoids the use of values by the use of an appropriate interpolator depending only on the vertices of the polygon.

6.3.5 Fast Phong shading

The original Phong shading method is very expensive, because of the 7 additions, 6 multiplications, one division, and one square-root required per pixel for its evaluation. Duff (1979) shows that Phong shading can be implemented more efficiently by combining the interpolation and reflection equations. For example, for a triangle with surface normals N_1, N_2, and N_3 at the vertices, we may give the following expression for the intensity of the diffuse light (see Bishop and Weimer 1986):

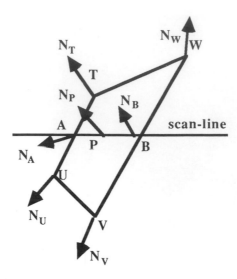

Fig.6.8. Normal interpolation (Phong shading). N_P is calculated by linear interpolation between N_A and N_B; N_A is calculated by linear interpolation between N_T and N_U; N_B is calculated by linear interpolation between N_V and N_W

Fig.6.9. Example of Phong shading. A frame of *Rendez-vous à Montréal* © 1987 MIRALab, H.E.C. and University of Montreal

$$I_d(x,y) = \frac{ax + by + c}{\sqrt{dx^2 + exy + fy^2 + gx + hy + i}} \qquad (6.14)$$

where

$$
\begin{aligned}
a &= \mathbf{L_u \cdot N_1} \\
b &= \mathbf{L_u \cdot N_2} \\
c &= \mathbf{L_u \cdot N_3} \\
d &= \mathbf{N_1 \cdot N_1} \\
e &= 2\mathbf{N_1 \cdot N_2} \\
f &= \mathbf{N_2 \cdot N_2} \\
g &= 2\mathbf{N_1 \cdot N_3} \\
h &= 2\mathbf{N_2 \cdot N_3} \\
i &= \mathbf{N_3 \cdot N_3} \\
\mathbf{L_u} &= \frac{\mathbf{L}}{|\mathbf{L}|}
\end{aligned}
\qquad (6.15)
$$

Using forward differences, this form can be evaluated for successive values of x and y with only three additions, one division, and one square root per pixel.

Bishop and Weimer (1986) describe a new formulation by using a 2D form of Taylor's series and limiting the expansion to the second degree:

$$I_d(x,y) = \Omega_5 x^2 + \Omega_4 xy + \Omega_3 y^2 + \Omega_2 x + \Omega_1 y + \Omega_0 \qquad (6.16)$$

where

$$
\begin{aligned}
\Omega_0 &= \frac{c}{\sqrt{i}} \\
\Omega_1 &= \frac{2bi - ch}{2i\sqrt{i}} \\
\Omega_2 &= \frac{2ai - cg}{2i\sqrt{i}} \\
\Omega_3 &= \frac{3ch^2 - 4cfi - 4bhi}{8i^2\sqrt{i}} \\
\Omega_4 &= \frac{3cgh - 2cei - 2bgi - 2ahi}{4i^2\sqrt{i}} \\
\Omega_5 &= \frac{3ig^2 - 4cdi - 4agi}{8i^2\sqrt{i}}
\end{aligned}
\qquad (6.17)
$$

Using forward differences, this reduces the amount of computation per pixel to only two additions. Similarly, Phong's reflection Eq. (6.3) can be evaluated with only five additions and one memory access per pixel (for ambient term). Finally, Bishop and Weimer also show how to extend the method to compute the specular component with the eye at a finite distance from the scene.

What it is interesting in this approach is that Phong shading is used with only a little more computation per pixel than is required for Gouraud shading. Even with Taylor's approximation, images produced with this fast Phong shading method are indistinguishable from those produced with Phong's method.

6.4 Light transmission

6.4.1 Snell-Descartes law

Some materials, such as water and glass, allow light to travel within them. These materials are said to be transparent. In fact, only part of the light passes through these materials; they may be to a greater or lesser extent absorbent. Other materials completely stop the light: they are opaque. Finally, certain materials allow the light to pass though they do not allow the shape of bodies on the opposite side to be distinguished; these materials are translucent.

In a homogeneous transparent material, the trajectory of the light is a line called a **light ray**. When a light ray changes from one medium to another, it may change direction; this process is called **refraction**. Geometrically, refraction may be described using two fundamental laws (see Fig. 6.10):

1. The incident ray, the normal at the incident point, and the refracted ray are all in the same plane.
2. The sine of the incident angle is in a constant ratio with the sine of the refraction angle; this law is called the **Snell-Descartes law** and may be written as:

$$\sin i_1 = n \sin i_2 \qquad (6.18)$$

where i_1 is the incident angle and i_2 is the refraction angle; n is a constant ratio n_1/n_2, called the **refraction index** of the first material relative to the second.

6.4.2 Simple algorithms based on color combinations

The modeling of transparent bodies forces a choice to be made between realism and performance. A few algorithms take into account almost all physical laws involved; the simplest algorithms do not deal with refraction or with the distance traveled by the ray within the material.

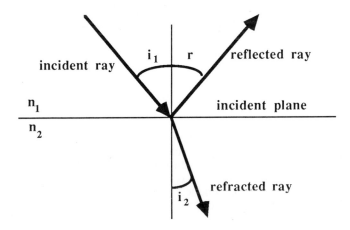

Fig.6.10. Reflection and refraction of light

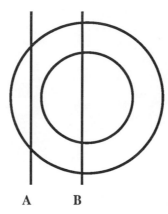

A   B

Fig.6.11. The distance traveled by light in the material is longer for A than B

The omission of refraction has the great drawback that the image behind the transparent material is not deformed as it should be when the light passes through the material. However, this considerably simplifies the calculations, because the coordinates of the image behind the transparent material are not modified; it is, therefore, not necessary to follow the path of each refracted ray to know these coordinates.

To express the absorption of the light by an object, some algorithms use a parameter which defines the quantity of light passing through the transparent material. This transmission factor varies between 0 and 1; 1 represents a completely transparent object and 0 an opaque object. Transparency may then be expressed as a linear combination of the colors of the image behind the transparent material and the material itself.

$$P = t B + (1-t) C \qquad (6.19)$$

where:
P is the color obtained for a pixel of the final image
B is the color of the object behind the transparent object at the same pixel
C is the color of the transparent object if it were opaque
t is the transmission factor

Practically, the colors used in Eq. (6.19) are those calculated by a shading algorithm such as the ones described in the previous section.

Eq. (6.19) does not take into account the distance traveled by the light within the transparent material. Even if we assume that the depth of the transparent body is constant, Eq. (6.19) does not consider the case of curved objects. This means that this equation ignores the fact that the distance traveled by light is longer when the object is curved as shown in Fig. 6.11.

One solution to this problem (Kay and Greenberg 1979) is to compute a transmission factor which is dependent on the curvature of the object. For example:

$$t = t_{min} + (t_{max} - t_{min})\, n_z \qquad (6.20)$$

Fig.6.12. Simulated transparent vase. By D.S. Kay and D. Greenberg D, Cornell University

where:
  t is the transmission factor for a given position
  t_{min} is the minimal transmission factor
  t_{max} is the maximal transmission factor
  n_z is the absolute value of the z-component of the unitary vector normal to the surface for a given position

When the curvature increases, n_z decreases and the value of t tends to t_{min}; when the curvature decreases, n_z increases and the value of t tends to t_{max}. For no curvature, $n_z = 0$ and $t = t_{max}$.

Equation (6.20) does not take into account the distribution of material relative to the curvature. For example, it shows no difference between very thin and thick glass. For very thin glass, the transmission factor should be at a maximum for most of the surface and tends quickly to t_{min} near the borders. For very thick glass, the transmission factor should tend quickly to t_{min} on each side of the point where the curvature is minimal.

One way of expressing the distribution of material relative to the curvature is by the introduction of an exponent in Eq. (6.20):

$$t = t_{min} + (t_{max} - t_{min})(1 - (1 - n_z)^m) \tag{6.21}$$

where t, t_{min}, t_{max}, and n_z have the same meaning as in Equation (6.20), and m is the index of thickness of the transparent object (between 0 and infinity).

Thin glass is simulated with a large value of m and thick glass is simulated with a small value. As the value $(1-n_z)$ is between 0 and 1, it tends to 1 when m tends to 0, and it tends to 0 when m tends to infinity.

An example is shown in Fig.6.12.

6.4.3 Whitted model

Whitted (1980) has improved on the Phong model by using a different interpretation of the direct specular term and additional global illumination terms. The new model has been used as a global illumination model for the ray tracing algorithm introduced by Whitted (1980) and described in Chap. 10. The description of this new model is based on Fig.6.13.

The light intensity I received by an observer from a point on the surface consists of the specular reflection component S and transmission component T. Since surfaces displayed are not always perfectly glossy, Whitted added a term to model the diffuse component as well. Ideally, the diffuse reflection should contain components due to reflection of nearby objects as well as predefined light sources. However, this is computationally expensive, and Whitted retains only the diffuse term from the Phong model. The intensity I according to the Whitted model is:

$$I = I_a + k_d \sum_j I_{lj}(N \cdot L_j) + k_s S + k_t T \qquad (6.22)$$

where:
   I_a is the reflection due to ambient light
   k_d is the diffuse reflection constant
   k_s is the specular reflection constant
   k_t is the light transmission coefficient
   I_{lj} is the intensity of the j-th light source
   N is the unit surface normal
   L_j is the vector in the direction of the j-th light source
   S is the intensity of light incident from the R direction
   T the intensity of light from the P direction

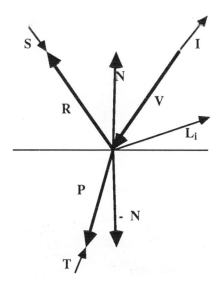

Fig.6.13. The geometry of the Whitted model

The **R** direction is determined by the reflection law:

$$r = i \qquad (6.23)$$

and the **P** direction is obtained using the Snell-Descartes law (6.18).

We may then write the following equations:

$$\mathbf{V'} = \frac{\mathbf{V}}{|\mathbf{V \cdot N}|} \qquad (6.24)$$

$$\mathbf{R} = \mathbf{V'} + 2\mathbf{N} \qquad (6.25)$$

$$\mathbf{P} = \frac{\mathbf{N} + \mathbf{V'}}{\sqrt{n^2 \, |\mathbf{V'}|^2 - |\mathbf{V'} + \mathbf{N}|^2}} - \mathbf{N} \qquad (6.26)$$

where n is the index of refraction.

A ray-traced image generated using this global illumination model is shown in Fig.6.14.

Fig.6.14. A ray traced image based on a global illumination model. Courtesy of T.Whitted, University of North Carolina, Chapel Hill

7 Complex light-source and illumination models

7.1 Complex light sources

7.1.1 What is a complex light source ?

As discussed by Verbeck and Greenberg (1984), a complete intensity calculation must incorporate light-source properties and environmental shadowing effects. An accurate description of physical characteristics of light sources should include three attributes to be modeled:

1. Light-source geometry
2. Emitted spectral distribution
3. Luminous intensity distribution

Most published light-reflection models (described in the previous sections) assume point light sources and do not include the effect of light-source geometries.

In this section, three more sophisticated approaches will be presented: Warn spotlights; the Verbeck-Greenberg approach, which allows the use of complete light-source descriptions; and point light sources with a luminous intensity distribution as proposed by Nishita et al..

7.1.2 Warn spotlights and floodlights

Warn (1983) introduces a model with new lighting controls based on observations of the lights used in a studio of a professional photographer. The two basic lighting controls are **direction** and **concentration**. The main idea behind the model is as follows: for real lights, direction and concentration are produced by reflectors, lenses, and housings; it would be very expensive in CPU time to model these components; a good approach would be to model their overall effect, rather the individual causes.

Warn's directed lights are modeled as the light emitted by a single point specular reflecting surface illuminated by a hypothetical point source of light. As shown in Fig.7.1, the point labeled **LG** is a surface which reflects light onto the object. The light direction vector **L** controls the normal orientation of this single point surface. The hypothetical light source is located along this direction and illuminates the reflector surface, which reflects light on the object.

Now, we can compute the intensity of the reflected light at the point **P** on the object using the Phong model (or any other model) and considering **P** as the eye position. As the hypothetical point source of light is located on the surface normal, the

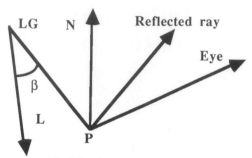

Fig.7.1. Directed lighting model

reflected ray coincides with the light direction vector. The angle between the reflected ray and the vector to the eye (the point **P**) is the angle β between the light direction and the ray from the light position to the point **P**. The intensity at the point **P** from the directed light source is then:

$$I_P = I_1 \cos^c \beta \tag{7.1}$$

where c is the specular exponent of the light reflector surface; if c is large, the beam is narrow, simulating a spotlight. If c is small, the beam is spread out to simulate a flood light. If c=0, we have a point source of light.

From Eq. (7.1), we may compute the intensity seen at the actual eye position from the point **P**:

$$I = \sum_j I_1 \cos^c \beta \; [k_d \; \mathbf{C}_s \cdot (\mathbf{N} \cdot \mathbf{L}_j) + k_s \; \mathbf{C}_r \cdot (\mathbf{N} \cdot \mathbf{H}_j)^n] \tag{7.2}$$

Figure 7.2 shows an image with a spotlight.

Warn has proposed two additional light controls for limiting the area illuminated by a light—**flaps** and **cones**.

Flaps limit the maximum and minimum extents in X-, Y-, or Z-coordinates of the light, as shown in Fig. 7.3. This means that for any point of the object outside the limits of the flap, the light has no effect.

Cones are used to simulate sharply delineated spotlights. As shown in Fig.7.4, the cone size is specified by an angle δ about the light direction. The light has no effect if the angle α between the light direction ray and the ray to the point **P** on the surface is greater than δ.

The four different light controls (concentration, direction, flaps, and cones) can be used together or separately.

7.1.3 Verbeck-Greenberg light-source descriptions

Verbeck and Greenberg (1984) propose very complete light-source descriptions based mainly on light-source geometry and the luminous intensity distribution. Light sources have well-defined geometries that affect the distribution of the light emitted from the source. Three types of emissive geometry may be considered: point sources (0 dimension), linear sources (one dimension) and area sources (two dimensions). Verbeck and Greenberg propose numerical integration techniques to simulate both linear and area sources. Their approach is based on the main characteristics of a

Fig. 7.2. Traditional room. © 1986 MIRALab, H.E.C. and University of Montreal

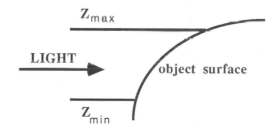

Fig.7.3. Z light-flap

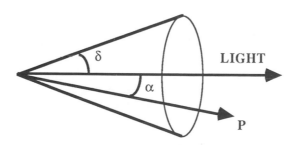

Fig.7.4. Light cone

luminaire—**the luminous intensity distribution**; for example, a floodlight emits light parallel and in one direction, slide projectors focus light, street lights emit light uniformly only over one sector of the surrounding area. The intensity distribution may be seen as a vector field and represented by goniometric diagrams. These diagrams represent a planar slice through the vector field and plot the relative intensity as a function of angular direction.

Verbeck and Greenberg propose redefining the Phong diffuse surface intensity at a point on the surface, including the light-source spatial intensity distribution as specified by the goniometric diagram, and the shadow effects of occluding objects.

For p point sources, the diffuse intensity is:

$$I_{point} = \sum_{j=1}^{p} k_d \, (\mathbf{N \cdot L_j}) \, R_d \, I_{\theta j} \, S_j \qquad (7.3)$$

where R_d is the diffuse reflection curve of the surface material, $I_{\theta j}$ is the relative intensity of the jth light source as specified by the goniometric diagram in the direction (direction to the point from the light), and S_j is the occlusion factor (0 or 1).

A linear light source is approximated by a series of m point light sources; the diffuse intensity is:

$$I_{linear} = \int_{length} k_d \, (\mathbf{N \cdot L_j}) \, R_d \, S_j \, i_{\theta j} \, dx \cong \sum_{j=1}^{m} k_d \, (\mathbf{N \cdot L_j}) \, R_d \, S_j \, i_{\theta j} \, \Delta x \qquad (7.4)$$

where $i_{\theta j}$ is the intensity at the midpoint of segment j of the source, dx is the infinitesimal length of a segment of the source, and Δx is the finite length of the segment.

An area light source is similarly approximated by a series of m point light sources; the diffuse intensity is:

$$I_{area} = \int_{areas} k_d \, (\mathbf{N \cdot L_j}) \, R_d \, S_j \, i_{\theta j} \, dA \cong \sum_{j=1}^{m} k_d \, (\mathbf{N \cdot L_j}) \, R_d \, S_j \, I_{\theta j} \qquad (7.5)$$

where $i_{\theta j}$ is the intensity at the midpoint of area j of the source and dA is the infinitesimal surface element of an area of the source.

According to Verbeck and Greenberg, the method of numerical integration is computationally expensive. However, the results are quite impressive.

7.1.4 Intensity distribution and linear light sources

The distribution of the emission of a point source varies with direction. Nishita et al. (1985) propose the use of point sources with a rotationally symmetric luminous intensity distribution. This distribution may be represented by the curve shown in Fig.7.5. This curve corresponds to the variation of luminous intensity of a lamp including the light center and the illumination axis.

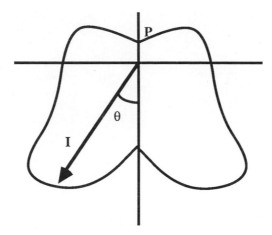

Fig.7.5. Luminous intensity distribution curve. **P** is the point source, **I** is the light intensity $I_1(q)$

Nishita et al. generally use an intensity distribution such as:

$$I_1(\theta) = \frac{I\,(1 + \cos\theta)}{2} \tag{7.6}$$

where I is the intensity at $\theta=0$.

Only key intensity values (e.g., every 10°) are given; in-between values are calculated by linear interpolation using look-up tables for the cosine values.

The illuminance E_1 from a point light source P_1 at an arbitrary point **P** on a face F is calculated as:

$$E_1 = I_1(\theta)\,\frac{\cos\alpha}{r^2} \tag{7.7}$$

where r is the distance between P_1 and **P**, θ is the angle between the illumination axis and the light ray from P_1 to **P**, and α is the angle between the normal of F and the light ray from the source; it is obtained by:

$$\cos\alpha = \frac{d}{r} \tag{7.8}$$

where d is the perpendicular distance between the plane of F and the point light source P_1.

An example is shown in Fig.7.6.

Linear light sources are introduced by Nishita et al. (1985) as linear segments with Lambertian luminous distribution and uniform brightness. Faces that are totally invisible from both end points of the linear source are ignored. When the plane including a face intersects with the linear source, the face receives light from part of the linear source. This means that the linear source must be divided into two parts with the plane. The portion of the visible side of this face is treated as a new light source because the light from the remaining portion is interrupted by the face itself. The illuminance E at an arbitrary point **P** on the face F is calculated as:

Fig. 7.6. Point sources with luminous intensity curves. Courtesy of T. Nishita, Fukuyama University and E. Nakamae, Hiroshima University

$$E = I \int_0^L \frac{\sin \theta \cos \beta}{r^2} dl \tag{7.9}$$

where I is the luminous intensity per unit length of the source, L the length of the source, $\mathbf{Q}$ an arbitrary point of the source, r the distance between $\mathbf{P}$ and $\mathbf{Q}$, and β the angle between the vector $\mathbf{PQ}$ and the normal of the face F.

Nishita et al. (1985) explain how to calculate the integral in Eq. (7.9) in an efficient way by separating the calculation into three cases: the light source is parallel to F, the light source is perpendicular to F, and the light source forms any angle with F. Similarly Nishita and Nakamae (1983) describe area sources and polyhedron sources with Lambertian distribution characteristics of the sources. Brotman and Badler (1984) also introduce polyhedron sources (see Sect. 9.6.2).

7.2 Complex reflection models

7.2.1 Torrance-Sparrow theoretical model

Although the Phong model is very realistic, the specular reflection component is not exact and this has a noticeable effect for nonmetallic and edge-lit objects. This is due to the fact that the intensity of the highlight does not change with the direction of the light source. According to Blinn (1977), this fault is especially apparent in computer animation.

Blinn shows that the theoretical model designed by Torrance and Sparrow (1967) is more realistic. In this model, the surface to be drawn is assumed to be a collection of small mirrors, like facets, that are randomly placed all over the surface. The specular component is considered as reflections coming from all facets oriented in the direction of L'_j. The amount of specular reflection k_s is calculated as:

$$k_s = \frac{DGF}{N \cdot E} \tag{7.10}$$

where N is the unit surface normal, E is the eye direction, D the distribution function of the directions of the facets of the surface, G the amount by which the facets shadow and mask each other, and F the Fresnel factor. Blinn (1977) discusses these factors in detail. For the distribution D, Torrance and Sparrow use a simple Gaussian distribution

$$D_2 = e^{-(\alpha c_2)^2} \tag{7.11}$$

where D_2 is the proportion of facets oriented at an angle α from the average normal to the surface and c_2 is the standard deviation. The corresponding distribution in the Phong approach is:

$$D_1 = \cos^{c_1} \alpha \tag{7.12}$$

The factor G is computed as the minimum of 1 (when there is no interference), G for shadowing (G_{shadow}), and G for masking (G_{mask}). The three cases are shown in Fig. 7.7. Values are calculated as follows:

$$G_{shadow} = 2\frac{(N \cdot H)(N \cdot E)}{E \cdot H} \tag{7.13}$$

$$G_{mask} = 2\frac{(N \cdot H)(N \cdot L)}{E \cdot H} \tag{7.14}$$

where H is the direction of maximum highlights computed as

$$H = \frac{L+E}{|L+E|} \tag{7.15}$$

and L is the unit vector in the direction of the light source. The symbols correspond to those in Fig.6.1.

F is the Fresnel reflection, which is the fraction of the light incident on a facet that is actually reflected as opposed to being absorbed. It may be defined as follows:

$$F = 0.5 \left(\frac{\sin^2(A-B)}{\sin^2(A+B)} + \frac{\tan^2(A-B)}{\tan^2(A+B)} \right) \tag{7.16}$$

where A is the angle of incidence on the microfacet. In our case:

$$A = \cos^{-1}(L \cdot H) \text{ and } B = \frac{\sin A}{n}$$

n is the index of refraction.

It can be shown that the Fresnel formula may be calculated by:

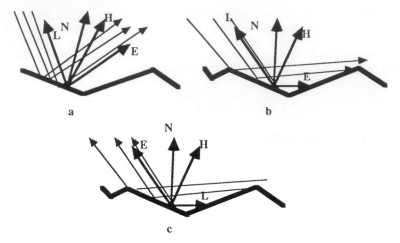

Fig. 7.7 a-c. Three cases. **a** With no interference; **b** with interception of reflected rays; **c** with interception of incident rays

$$F = 0.5 \, \frac{(g-c)^2}{(g+c)^2} \, (1 + \frac{(c \, (g+c) - 1)^2}{(c \, (g-c) + 1)})^2 \qquad (7.17)$$

where $c = \mathbf{E} \cdot \mathbf{H}$ and $g = \sqrt{n^2 + c^2 - 1}$.

Instead of the D_2 function proposed by Torrance and Sparrow and the Phong function, a third function may be used. This function from Trowbridge and Reitz (1975) is based on modeling the microfacets as ellipsoids of revolution:

$$D_3 = \left(\frac{c_3^2}{\cos^2 \alpha \, (c_3^2 - 1)} + 1 \right)^2 \qquad (7.18)$$

where c_3 is the eccentricity of the ellipsoids (0 for very shiny surfaces, 1 for very diffuse surfaces)

Blinn (1977) shows with several examples that the inclusion of the G, F and $1/(\mathbf{N} \cdot \mathbf{E})$ terms has a noticeable effect for nonmetallic and edge lit objects. The use of the D_3 microfacet distribution function provides a better match to experimental data and is, moreover, easier to calculate than D_1 or D_2.

7.2.2 Cook-Torrance model

Cook and Torrance (1982) introduce a more general reflectance model for rough surfaces. This model is based on a reflectance definition that relates the brightness of an object to the intensity and size of each light source that illuminates it. For a given light source, surface, and observer, this reflectance model describes the intensity and spectral composition of the reflected light reaching the observer. The model uses the same symbols as those defined in Fig. 6.1. The vector $\mathbf{H}$ is defined by Eq. (6.6). α is the angle between $\mathbf{H}$ and $\mathbf{N}$ and θ is the angle between $\mathbf{H}$ and $\mathbf{E}$ or $\mathbf{H}$ and $\mathbf{L}$. Consider now the intensity of the incident light E_i per unit projected area and per unit solid angle $d\omega_i$:

$$E_i = I_i \, (\mathbf{N \cdot L}) \, d\omega_i \qquad (7.19)$$

I_i is the average intensity of the incident light.

We may now introduce for each light source, the **bidirectional reflectance R**, defined as the ratio of the reflected intensity I_r in a given direction to the incident energy E_i from another direction (within a small solid angle):

$$R = \frac{I_r}{E_i} \qquad (7.20)$$

From Eqs. (7.19) and (7.20), the reflected intensity reaching the observer from each light source is:

$$I_r - RI_i \, (\mathbf{N \cdot L}) \, d\omega_i \qquad (7.21)$$

We may now split the bidirectional reflectance into specular bidirectional reflectance R_s and diffuse bidirectional reflectance R_d. We may also consider the ambient bidirectional reflectance R_a. The total intensity reaching the observer becomes:

$$I_r = I_{ia}R_a + \sum_j I_{ij} \, (\mathbf{N \cdot L_j}) \, d\omega_{ij} \, (sR_s + dR_d) \qquad (7.22)$$

where s+d=1.

R_a and R_d may be obtained from the measured reflectance spectra for the material and do not depend on the location of the observer. R_s reflects more light in some directions than in others. Assuming that the surface consists of microfacets as defined in the Torrance-Sparrow model, we may write:

$$R_s = \frac{1}{\pi} \frac{DGF}{(\mathbf{N \cdot L}) (\mathbf{N \cdot E})} \qquad (7.23)$$

The symbols used have the same meaning as in the Torrance-Sparrow model. For the D term, Cook and Torrance propose as alternative to the distributions D_1 in Eq. (7.12), D_2 in Eq. (7.11), and D_3 in Eq. (7.18), the Beckmann distribution:

$$D_4 = \frac{1}{m^2 \cos^{-4} \alpha} \, e^{-(\frac{\tan \alpha}{m})^2} \qquad (7.24)$$

This function is similar in shape to the others, but it gives the absolute magnitude of the reflectance without introducing arbitrary constants. However, it requires more computation.

To obtain the spectral and angular variation of F, Cook and Torrance adopt a practical compromise. If the index of refraction n and the extinction coefficient k are known, they use the Fresnel equation; if not, but the normal reflectance is known, they fit the Fresnel equation to the measured normal reflectance for a polished surface. For example, consider Eq. (7.17); at normal incidence, $\theta = 0$, so c = 1, g = n and:

$$F_0 = \left(\frac{n-1}{n+1} \right)^2 \qquad (7.25)$$

which gives for the index of refraction:

$$n = \frac{1 + \sqrt{F_0}}{1 - \sqrt{F_0}} \qquad (7.26)$$

By substituting n into the original Fresnel equation, the factor F is obtained at other angles of incidence.

As reflectance depends on the wavelength and the angle of incidence, the color of the reflected light also depends on the angle of incidence. This has been illustrated by Cook and Torrance (1982) using reflectance spectra for copper. They also show how to simplify the calculation of the color shift from the Fresnel equation. Finally, they generate a series of vases made of a variety of materials, as shown in Fig.7.8.

7.2.3 Hall-Greenberg model and related models

Hall and Greenberg (1983) further improve the Whitted model by including **Fresnel's relationships** for wavelength and angle of incidence, as suggested by Cook and Torrance (1982), as well as the scattering of transmitted light from sources and the attenuation of previous nodes. The model is as follows:

$$I = I^{dif} + I^{spec} + I^{tr} + I^{gdif} + I^{gspec} + I^{gtr} \tag{7.27}$$

where:

$$I^{dif} = \text{diffuse light from light sources} = k_d \sum_j (\mathbf{N} \cdot \mathbf{L}) \, R_d \, I_{1j}$$

$$I^{spec} = \text{specular light from light sources} = k_s \sum_j (\mathbf{N} \cdot \mathbf{H})^n \, R_f \, I_{1j}$$

$$I^{tr} = \text{transmitted light from light sources} = k_s \sum_j (\mathbf{N} \cdot \mathbf{H'})^n \, T_f \, I_{1j}$$

$$I^{gdif} = \text{global diffuse light} = A \, R_d$$

$$I^{gspec} = \text{global specular light} = k_s \, R_f \, R \, F_r{}^{d_r}$$

$$I^{gtr} = \text{global transmitted light} = k_s \, T_f \, T \, F_t{}^{d_t}$$

H is the unit mirror-direction vector based on the reflected ray, and **H'** is the unit mirror-direction vector based on the transmitted ray; R_f is the Fresnel reflectance, T_f the Fresnel transmissivity, A the intensity of the global ambient illumination, R the intensity of the reflected ray, T the intensity of the transmitted ray, F_r the transmittance per unit length of material of the reflected ray, F_t the transmittance per unit length of material of the transmitted ray, d_r the distance traveled by the reflected ray, and d_t the distance traveled by the transmitted ray. Material-dependent coefficients are k_d (diffuse reflection), k_s (specular reflection), and k_t (transmission).

This model is an illumination model for ray tracing. Other extensions of the Torrance-Sparrow and Cook-Torrance models have been proposed. Bouville et al. (1984) describe a model derived from the Cook-Torrance model in which indirect light energy and transparency are computed using radiance theory. Tezenas du Montcel and Nicolas (1985) propose an extension of the Cook-Torrance model which deals with transparency phenomena in a way which ensures consistency with the reflection model. In their approach, transmitted light may be expressed in the same way as reflected light, with bidirectional transmittance for ambient light T_a, diffuse light T_d, and specular light T_s. They propose the following equations to calculate this bidirectional transmittance:

$$T_a = 1 - R_a$$

$$T_d = \frac{T_a}{\pi} \qquad \text{(valid for rough surfaces)} \tag{7.28}$$

$$T_s = \frac{1}{\pi} \frac{DGF_t}{(\mathbf{N} \cdot \mathbf{L})(\mathbf{N} \cdot \mathbf{E})}$$

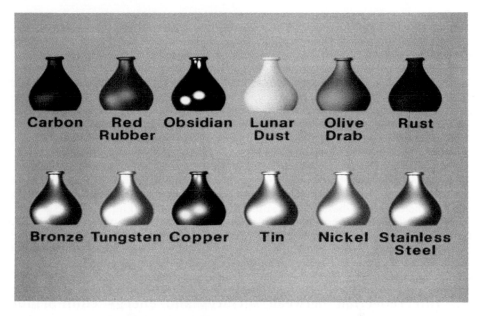

Fig. 7.8. A series of vases by R.L. Cook and K.E. Torrance

The last equation is very similar to Eq. (7.23). F_t is the transmission Fresnel coefficient calculated by Eq. (7.17) with

$$c - \mathbf{H} \cdot \mathbf{L} \text{ and } n = \frac{n_1}{n_2} \tag{7.29}$$

7.2.4 Kajiya anisotropic models

Surfaces like hair, fur, or burnished metals have a characteristic direction and their scattering profiles exhibit anisotropy. For generating such surfaces, Kajiya (1985) proposes a set of **anisotropic lighting models** derived from the laws of electromagnetism. Based on Beckmann's work (Beckmann and Spizzichino 1963), Kajiya proposes a formula for the reflection coefficient, which is suitable for computer graphics:

$$\rho(x, \mathbf{k}_1, \mathbf{k}_2) = \frac{1}{2\, \mathbf{n}_0 \cdot \mathbf{k}_1 A} \int_S \mathbf{n} \; [R(\mathbf{k}_1 - \mathbf{k}_2) - (\mathbf{k}_1 + \mathbf{k}_2)] \; e^{i(\mathbf{k}_1 - \mathbf{k}_2)s} \; dS \tag{7.30}$$

where:

A is the area of the surface over which integration is carried out
$\mathbf{k}_1$ is the incidence vector
$\mathbf{k}_2$ is the emittance vector
$\mathbf{n}$ is the normal vector
s is the surface point

This equation is based on the Kirchhoff approximation for reflection from a rough surface. It approximates the field at any point of the surface by the field which would occur if the surface were replaced by its tangent plane. Kajiya assumes that the incident field is always a plane wave with wave vector $\mathbf{k}_1$.

Equation (7.30) may be used to compute a lighting model which gives the average field power scattered from an arbitrary surface. The integral is calculated using the stationary phase method. For the calculation of the lighting model, Kajiya proposes a method in four steps, where the first three steps are carried out off line:

1. Divide a hemisphere centered about the surface element into a number of discrete cells
2. For each pair of cells, calculate ρ by the integral in Eq. (7.30)
3. The square of the reflectance function $S_{ij} = \rho^2$ is stored for each cell
4. By linearly interpolating S_{ij}, the lighting model is calculated for any pixel (or ray) using the incidence and emittance vector, with respect to the surface frame

For anisotropic surfaces, Kajiya introduces a new mapping technique, called **frame mapping,** which works with any anisotropic model, including a Phong model. The method is based on the Blinn (1978) bump-mapping method (see Sect. 12.4). The idea is to perturb the entire frame bundle instead of the normal. The **frame bundle** for a surface is defined as a local coordinate system given by the tangent, binormal, and normal to the surface. This technique provides a mapping of the directionality of surface features in nature such as hair, fur, and cloth.

7.3 Interreflection between surfaces and energy equilibrium

7.3.1 Radiosity method for diffuse surfaces

None of the models presented in this and the previous section account for the object-to-object reflection between diffuse surfaces. These models are unable to generate the information required for application of the model to situations other than an isolated object suspended in space. To model the interaction of light between diffusely reflecting surfaces, a new procedure has been introduced at Cornell University (Goral et al. 1984; Cohen and Greenberg 1985; Greenberg et al. 1986; Cohen et al. 1986). This procedure, called **the radiosity method**, describes an equilibrium energy balance within an enclosure. It determines surface intensities for diffuse environments independent of observer position. The main assumption in this method is that all emission and reflection processes are ideal diffuse (Lambertian) reflectors. This means that after reflection from a surface the direction of a ray is lost.

The radiosity B_i is the total rate of energy loss from a surface; it is the sum of emitted energy E_i and reflected energy R_i:

$$B_i = E_i + R_i \tag{7.31}$$

The reflected energy may be expressed as:

$$R_i = \rho_i \int_{\text{env}} B_j \, F_{ij} \tag{7.32}$$

where ρ_i is the reflectivity, which is the fraction of incident light that is reflected back into the environment. F_{ij} is the **form factor**, which is defined as the fraction of the energy leaving one surface which lands on another surface. B_j is the radiosity of the other surface. Equation (7.31) shows the relationship between the two surfaces. The radiosity of the first surface is obtained by the sum of two terms—the self-emitted

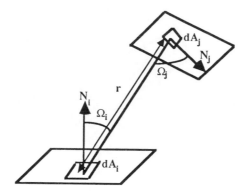

Fig.7.9. Form factor geometry

light and the reflected light. This last term is equal to the radiosity of the other surface multiplied by the fraction of that light which reaches the surface and the reflectivity of the receiving surface.

In this approach, the environment is divided into discrete patches for which a constant radiosity is assumed. This allows the integral (in Eq.7.32) to be approximated by a summation over the patches.

Form factors specify the fraction of energy leaving one patch that lands on another. We assume that the sum of all the form factors from a particular patch to all other patches is equal to unity. Figure 7.9 illustrates the form factor geometry.

The form factor F_{ij} between finite patches is defined as the area average:

$$F_{ij} = \frac{1}{A_i} \int_{A_i} \int_{A_j} \frac{\cos \Omega_i \cos \Omega_j}{\pi \, r^2} H \, dA_j \, dA_i \qquad (7.33)$$

The term H is an additional term to account for the possibility of occluding objects hiding all or part of one patch from another. For nonoccluded environments, H=1.

7.3.2 Hemicube method

Cohen and Greenberg (1985) describe a method for approximating the form factors in occluded environments. The algorithm is based on methods introduced by Nusselt (Sparrow and Cess, 1978). From these methods, it can be seen that any two patches in the environment, which when projected onto any surrounding surface (see Fig.7.10) occupy the same area and location, will have the same form factor value.

For example, each patch is projected onto an imaginary cube located at the center of a patch to perform the necessary hidden-surface computations. Only the half of the cube (**hemicube**) above the patch is visible from the environment. The contribution of each pixel on the cube's surface to the form factor value varies and depends on pixel location and orientation. A delta form factor ΔF_q is calculated for each pixel q on the hemicube. For example, consider the top of the hemicube shown in Fig.7.11.

As $r = \sqrt{x^2+y^2+1}$ and $\cos \Omega_i = \cos \Omega_j = \frac{1}{\sqrt{x^2+y^2+1}}$, the delta form factor is calculated as follows:

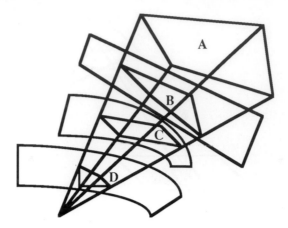

Fig.7.10. Four identical form factors (A, B, C, D)

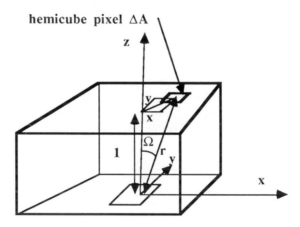

Fig.7.11. Top of hemicube

$$\Delta F_q = \frac{\cos \Omega_i \cos \Omega_j}{\pi r^2} \Delta A = \frac{\Delta A}{(x^2+y^2+1)^2} \tag{7.34}$$

The process is repeated for each patch in the environment by positioning the hemicube at the center of the patch. Finally, the form factor is approximated by:

$$F_{ij} = \sum_{q=1}^{N} \Delta F_q \tag{7.35}$$

where N is the number of hemicube pixels covered by the projection of the patch onto the hemicube.

The form factors are stored in a matrix, which is then compressed into a square matrix by area-averaging the element-to-patch form factors. This matrix is then multiplied by the reflectivities for each color band and solved using a Gauss-Seidel

Fig.7.12. Subtle shading details achieved using the radiosity method. Courtesy of D.P. Greenberg, Cornell University

iterative method to obtain patch radiosities. For each pixel, the location of the ray-patch intersection is computed. The colors are found through a bilinear interpolation of the vertex color values.

An image produced using the radiosity method is shown in Fig.7.12.

Nishita and Nakamae (1985) describe a calculation of interreflection taking into account shadows (see Sect. 9.6.4).

7.3.3 Radiosity method for nondiffuse environments

A more general radiosity method which accounts for all interreflections from both diffuse and nondiffuse surfaces has been introduced by Immel et al. (1986). The new approach consists of calculating an intensity distribution for every surface in the environment, consisting of directional intensities for a number of discrete directions.

The directional analysis method may be summarized in four steps:

1. Environment geometry and material properties are specified in an interactive way. Each surface has to be subdivided into discrete surface patches
2. Geometric and visibility relationships are determined between every pair of patches in the environment
3. From a set of equations, a simultaneous solution for the directional intensities of each patch is performed. Using this global solution, the direction intensity distribution is determined at each vertex grid point on every surface
4. The rendering process consists simply of looking up the intensities that point back to the eye and displaying them

The key to the method is the possibility of precalculating the energy leaving specular surfaces regardless of the viewing direction. This means that successive images of the environment can be rendered from different viewpoints.

The method is a generalization of the radiosity method discussed in the previous section. Here, we have to define the intensity of a point in a certain direction o, called the **directional intensity**. As in Eq. (7.31), this is the sum of the total reflected intensity $I_r(D_o)$ from the point in that direction plus the light emitted $I_e(D_o)$ from the point in that direction :

$$I_t(D_o) = I_e(D_o) + I_r(D_o) \qquad (7.36)$$

Consider now an environment consisting of only two surfaces A_1 and A_2; this is similar to the environment described in Fig.7.9. However, we have to consider directional intensities as shown in Fig. 7.13, which also displays the hemispheres of directions.

Immel et al. (1986) show that for this environment, Eq. (7.36) for the directional intensity from surface dA_1 in direction o is given by:

$$I_{t1}(D_{o1})= I_e(D_o)+I_r(D_{oi})=\varepsilon_1(D_{o1}) + \int_\Omega \rho_1''(D_{o1},D_{i1})\, I_{t2}(D_{o2})\cdot \cos\theta_{i1} d\omega_{i1} \qquad (7.37)$$

where ε_1 is the directional emission from surface 1, ρ_1'' is the bidirectional reflectance of surface 1, $d\omega_{i1}$ is the differential solid angle around surface 1, θ_{i1} is the angle from the normal to surface 1, and Ω is the total solid angle encompassing surface 2 when viewed from surface 1.

The subscripts have the following meanings:

t=total, o=outgoing, i=incoming, r=reflected, e=emitted

The surfaces, visible spectrum, and hemispheres may be made discrete using the following assumptions:

- The surfaces are divided into patches with constant intensities arriving and leaving each patch
- The visible spectrum is divided into a small number of independent wavelength bands
- The hemisphere above the patch is discretized into a finite number of solid angles

Equation (7.37) in a discrete form gives the directional intensity in direction F as the emission in direction F plus the sum of the reflected intensities from discrete directions D, which encompasses the hemisphere above the patch:

$$I_{t1}(F) = \varepsilon_1(F) + \sum_{D=1}^{ND} \rho_1''(F,D)\, I_{t2}(G)\cos\theta_D\, \omega_D \qquad (7.38)$$

where G represents the outgoing direction from patch 2 which points toward patch 1 and is thus in the opposite direction from D.

For more than two surfaces, Eq. (7.38) may be generalized to give the outgoing intensity of a patch i:

$$I_{ti}(F) = \varepsilon_i(F) + \sum_{j=1}^{NP}\sum_{D=1}^{ND} \rho_i''(F,D)\, I_{tj}(G)\cos\theta_D\, \omega_D\, H_{ijD} \qquad (7.39)$$

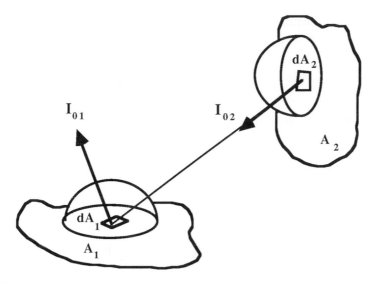

Fig.7.13. Environment of two surfaces with I_{o1} the intensity from dA_1 and I_{o2} the outgoing intensities from dA_2 becoming incoming intensities to dA_1

where NP is the number of patches, ND the number of directions on the hemisphere, and H_{ijD} a factor similar to the H factor in Eq. (7.33):

if patch i sees patch j **then** $H_{ijD}=1$ **else** $H_{ijD}=0$

As in the radiosity method for diffuse environments, the hemisphere may be replaced by the upper half of a cube (hemicube). However, since the intensities may vary directionally, the incoming directions of the receiving patch must be equated with the outgoing directions from the sending patches. Immel et al. (1986) propose replacing a hemicube, which has to be reoriented for each patch, by a full cube (the global cube) surrounding each vertex and oriented along the global axes. With such an approach, if a patch i sees a patch j through the cell oriented in the **d** direction, then the reciprocal cell from patch j is simply in the **- d** direction. The projection of the environment on a global cube surrounding a vertex solves the hidden surface problem providing the H_{ijD} term in Eq. (7.39).

To solve Eq. (7.39), the Gauss-Seidel iterative method is effective as in the radiosity method for diffuse surfaces. The heart of the procedure used in this approach is as follows:

for each patch p
   for each direction d
     {initial estimate for directional intensities I_{pd} is set to the emissions E_{pd}
          of the light sources with all other patch radiosities initially zero}
for each iteration
   for each patch p
     for each direction d
       Set each new intensity I'_{pd} to E_{pd}
for each incoming direction i

   Calculate energy EN_i from i using global cube

for each outgoing direction o

Add $\rho''(p,i,o)\,EN_i$ to I'_{pd} {outgoing intensities are computed from
incoming intensities and bidirectional reflectance}
for each direction d
Replace old intensities with new and test for convergence

7.3.4 Kajiya rendering equation

Kajiya (1986) proposes a general integral equation which generalizes most rendering algorithms. This equation is derived from radiative heat theory and is, like the radiosity Eq. (7.31), an equilibrium energy equation. It balances the energy flowing from one point of a surface to another. However, unlike the radiosity equation, no assumptions are made about the reflectance characteristics of the surfaces. The Kajiya equation is as follows:

$$I(\mathbf{P},\mathbf{P'}) = g(\mathbf{P},\mathbf{P'})\,[\varepsilon(\mathbf{P},\mathbf{P'}) + \int_S \rho(\mathbf{P},\mathbf{P'},\mathbf{P''})\,I(\mathbf{P'},\mathbf{P''})\,d\mathbf{P''}] \qquad (7.40)$$

$I(\mathbf{P},\mathbf{P'})$ is the energy of radiation (transport intensity) passing from point $\mathbf{P}$ to point $\mathbf{P'}$.

The geometry term $(\mathbf{P},\mathbf{P'})$ represents the occlusion of surface points by other surface points. It is 0 for mutually hidden points and 1 / distance$(\mathbf{P},\mathbf{P'})$ for two points $\mathbf{P}$ and $\mathbf{P'}$ visible from each other.

The emittance term $\varepsilon(\mathbf{P},\mathbf{P'})$ represents the energy emitted by a surface at point $\mathbf{P'}$ reaching $\mathbf{P}$.

The scattering term $\rho(\mathbf{P},\mathbf{P'},\mathbf{P''})$ represents the intensity of energy scattered by a surface element at $\mathbf{P'}$ originating from a surface element at $\mathbf{P''}$ and terminating at a surface element at $\mathbf{P}$.

Finally, S is the union of all the surfaces of all the objects in the scene.

Equation (7.40) may be rewritten as:

$$I = g\,e + g\,M\,I \qquad (7.41)$$

where M is the linear operator given by the integral in Eq. (7.40).

Kajiya shows that well-known equations are approximations of Eq. (7.41) e.g., Phong's equation (Eq. 6.12), Whitted's equation (Eq. 6.22) and the distributed ray tracing approach (see Sect. 10.6.2). Kajiya also shows that by defining the radiosity B(P') of a surface element dP' as:

$$dB'(\mathbf{P'}) = d\mathbf{P'}\,\int_S I(\mathbf{P},\mathbf{P'})\,d\mathbf{P} \qquad (7.42)$$

the radiosity Eqs. (7.31) and (7.32) may be rederived.

Kajiya then discusses methods for solving the rendering Eq. (7.41). He proposes an extension of the Monte Carlo Markov chain method to infinite dimensional equations. He also presents a new form of variance reduction, called **Hierarchical sampling**, inspired by stratified sampling. This integral equation approach may be implemented by converting a conventional ray tracer. This new form of ray tracing is called **path tracing**.

8 Antialiasing and motion blur

8.1 Aliasing problem

8.1.1 Aliasing phenomenon

A phenomenon called **aliasing** is a major problem in image synthesis. The term refers to the fact that this phenomenon occurs when a low-frequency signal appears as an "alias" of a high-frequency signal after sampling. Practically, this means that resolution in the object space is infinite when compared with resolution in the display space.

Typically, the effects of the aliasing problem are as follows:

1. A **stairstepping** effect exists along the border of two contrasting surfaces
2. Small objects can **disappear** between the dots because it is possible that no part of them will coincide with a sample point
3. There is a **line breakup effect** when the width of a stripe is of the order of a pixel and misses the center of the pixel
4. The shape and/or size of an object may change depending on the object position. This phenomenon, called **crawling**, occurs when an edge passes through the center of a pixel

The purpose of this chapter is to present techniques used to reduce aliasing in realistic images. For this reason, we do not discuss, except when necessary, techniques for drawing anti-aliased lines. However, several algorithms for this exist, including those of Crow (1978a), Gupta and Sproull (1981), Barros and Fuchs (1979), Field (1984), and Whitted (1983).

8.1.2 Classification of antialiasing methods

Aliasing problems were mentioned early on by Shoup (1973) and Catmull (1974). However, the problem was first systematically studied by Crow (1977), who proposes three classes of antialiasing algorithm:

1. As the aliasing problem is due to low resolution, one easy solution is to increase resolution, causing sample points to occur more frequently. However, this approach has severe limitations, because it also increases the cost of image production. Moreover, point sampling of an unfiltered object is never correct at any resolution
2. The image may be generated at high resolution, and then digitally filtered. This

method, called **supersampling**, eliminates high frequencies which are the source of aliases
3. The image can be calculated by integrating intensities over neighborhoods to yield pixel values. This kind of algorithm is called a **prefiltering algorithm**

The technique of supersampling is simpler than prefiltering. However, the computing of high-resolution images is expensive and slow. In fact, supersampling corresponds to a postfiltering operation.

More generally, supersampling and prefiltering algorithms are based on the concept of **convolution functions**, well known in digital processing. The main difference between the two kinds of algorithms is that supersampling algorithms use discrete convolution and prefiltering algorithms use continuous analytic convolution. Therefore, convolution theory is presented in the next section. Moreover, as simple convolution filters are not always effective for small polygons with an area of less than a pixel or for very thin polygons, prefiltering algorithms may become hidden-surface algorithms at the pixel level, as described in Sect. 8.3.

8.2 Digital-processing convolution theory

8.2.1 Convolution functions

Prefiltering algorithms adjust the pixel attributes of the computed resolution before displaying the image. The basis of prefiltering algorithms corresponds to the signal processing operation of **convolution**. A **filter** is convolved with the image by superposing a filter function over the image function at each pixel position and integrating over the product of the two. Mathematically, the convolution integral is defined as:

$$F(x,y) = \int_{-\infty}^{\infty} \int_{-\infty}^{\infty} h(u,v)\, I(x-u, y-v)\, du\, dv \qquad (8.1)$$

where F is the filtered image, h the convolution function or filter, and I the nonfiltered image.

Based on the Fourier theory, the elimination of all aliasing is theoretically possible by limiting the frequency of the input image in the spatial domain to one-half of the sampling frequency (Oppenheim and Shafer 1975). This means that we have to construct a frequency function which is constant up to the highest representable frequency and then drops to zero. By taking the inverse Fourier transform, we find that this requires convolving the image with (sinx) / x functions. This is not feasible with traditional hardware. The function (sin x) / x must be approximated; the least costly method involves intensity-averaging by area and this is called the **Fourier window method**.

8.2.2 Fourier window method

The intensity of the pixel is computed as a weighted average of the intensities of each region that covers the pixel, as shown in Fig.8.1.

Similarly, an antialiasing version of the Porter algorithm for spherical shading (see Sect. 5.7.4) has also been developed: the list of active spheres is maintained sorted in z. For a pixel partially covered by the boundary of a sphere, color is computed using

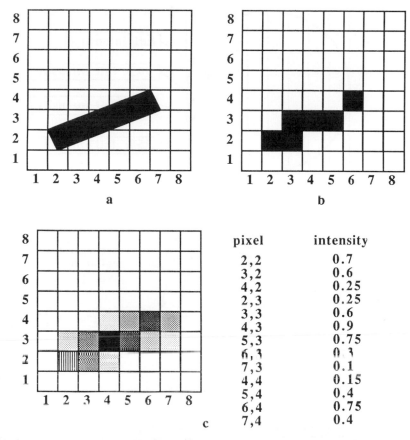

pixel	intensity
2,2	0.7
3,2	0.6
4,2	0.25
2,3	0.25
3,3	0.6
4,3	0.9
5,3	0.75
6,3	0.3
7,3	0.1
4,4	0.15
5,4	0.4
6,4	0.75
7,4	0.4

Fig.8,1 a-c. Antialiasing by intensity-averaging by area. **a** Area to be exactly represented; **b** without antialiasing; **c** with antialiasing

the value stored in the z-buffer. O'Rourke and Badler (1979; see Sect. 5.7.4) use a similar method. A pixel completely covered by a disk receives full intensity; a cell that is partly covered has an intensity proportional to the area of the cell covered, as shown in Fig.8.2.

8.2.3 Fujimoto-Iwata algorithm

Fujimoto and Iwata (1983) describe a method involving the adoption of a filter function that establishes linear relations between the intensity of filtered pixels and the slope and thickness of the vector edge. The filter is a Fourier window and its size is a function of the slope of the vector. Each pixel's intensity is obtained by convoluting the filter function and the line intensity. The integration of the filter function is performed over the region 2(d/2-dx)d (see Fig.8.3). The intensity is proportional to the distance from the vector:

$$\mathbf{I'} = \mathbf{I} \frac{(d-2dx)}{d} \tag{8.2}$$

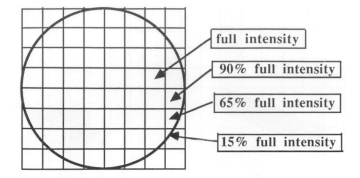

Fig.8.2. Antialiasing in a spherical representation

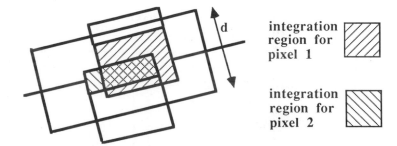

Fig.8.3. The Fourier window in the Fujimoto-Iwata algorithm

Fig. 8.4. Old car designed with propagation control graphs, antialiasing using the Bartlett window.
© 1986 MIRALab, H.E.C. and University of Montreal

Table 8.1. Weightings for a Bartlett window

3 x 3			5 x 5					7 x 7						
1	2	1	1	2	3	2	1	1	2	3	4	3	2	1
2	4	2	2	4	6	4	2	2	4	6	8	6	4	2
1	2	1	3	6	9	6	3	3	6	9	12	9	6	3
			2	4	6	4	2	2	4	6	8	6	4	2
			1	2	3	2	1	1	2	3	4	3	2	1

where I' is the overall intensity, I the intensity of the current pixel, and dx the distance between the pixel and the center line of the vector.

We see that pixel intensity is a linear function of its distance from the center line of the vector. Therefore, the principle of superposition can be applied and the intensity of each pixel can be calculated incrementally without explicit calculation of this distance.

This algorithm is mainly for drawing antialiased lines; however, it may be used as a smooth-edge generator for continuous-tone polygonal images. In such cases, antialiasing occurs only at the edges of the image.

8.2.4 Supersampling using Bartlett window

Any resolution method that combines adjacent pixels into one is a filtering operation. For example, the Fourier window corresponds to a simple average. Better results may be obtained by using the Bartlett window. This filter is approximated by expanding the domain of pixels from which each reduced pixel is averaged and weighting the central pixels more heavily than the peripheral ones. Crow (1981) studied several approximations of the Bartlett window. Comparisons are made using the weighted sum of 9, 25 and 49 high resolution pixels. Corresponding weightings are shown in Table 8.1. An example of image generated using the Bartlett window is shown in Fig.8.4.

8.2.5 More complex convolution functions

This rough approximation of $\frac{\sin x}{x}$ corresponds to convolution with a box function.

It is of course possible to use closer approximations of $\frac{\sin x}{x}$; however this may be computationally expensive. Crow (1977, 1985) compares several convolution functions using the same synthesized test pattern. From this study, it is clear that the most effective filters are the most expensive. In the absence of small high contrasting details, the less expensive filters work well. Moreover, it should be noted that most of the area lying under the (sin x) /x function is in the two-pixel-wide central lobe. This explains the choice of the convolution functions in the study. Figure 8.5 shows the various convolution functions.

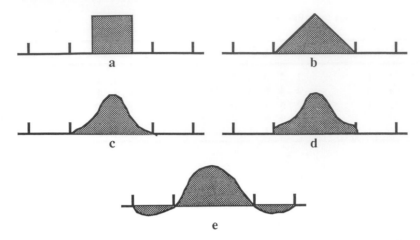

Fig.8.5 a-e. Convolution functions. **a** Box function (Fourier window) across one interpixel distance; **b** triangle across two interpixel distances; **c** central lobe of sin x / x across two interpixel distances; **d** Gaussian distribution across two interpixel distances; **e** weighted sin x / x across four interpixel distances

Turkowski (1982) has introduced a method of calculating antialiasing through the use of coordinate transformations. He has studied the use of the perpendicular point-line distance in evaluating the 2D antialiasing convolution. This means that the antialiasing filter kernel is approximated by a 1D function of the perpendicular distance from a pixel to a line. Extension to polygon rendering has also been described. However, the method does not seem to work for image rendering.

8.3   Hidden surface algorithms with antialiasing

8.3.1 Integrating antialiasing into a hidden surface algorithm

In Chap. 5, several hidden-surface algorithms were presented without reference to the problem of aliasing. In fact, several authors have proposed hidden surface algorithms which include antialiasing techniques by using a filtering process in the rendering algorithm. The two best known prefiltering algorithms are those of Crow (1977) and Catmull (1978). Both algorithms calculate subareas within a pixel whenever a polygon edge passes through it. Crow (1977) properly computes the intensity at a sample point and proposes the implementation of a filtering tiler for convex polygons. Catmull (1978) has proposed a hidden-surface algorithm at the pixel level. The area of a pixel is viewed as a window against which all nearby polygons are clipped. This determines the area of the pixel covered by each polygon. More recent algorithms were proposed by Carpenter (1984) and Catmull (1984).

8.3.2 Crow algorithm

Crow (1977) proposes the implementation of a filtering tiler for convex polygons, which guarantees that each scan-line intersects a polygon in a single segment.

Therefore, for each scan segment, the position and intensity of the end points are passed to the shader-interpolator procedure. Assuming the tiler proceeds from top to bottom and the polygon vertices are stored clockwise, the algorithm works as follows:

Find top vertex
Find next left vertex
Find next right vertex
Find bottom vertex
repeat
  for each left vertex
    Put a new edge block into a queue Q_1
  for each right vertex
    Put a new edge block into a queue Q_2
  for each element of Q_1
    Add weighted area for left edge to corresponding pixels
  for each element of Q_2
    Subtract weighted area for right edge from corresponding pixels
  Generate pixels for middle part of segment
  Increment all edge blocks
until the bottom vertex is reached

Note that an edge block includes the present position, increments yielding the position at the next scan-line, shading attributes, and a count of the number of scan lines remaining until the bottom of the line segment is reached.

8.3.3 Catmull algorithm

Catmull (1978) has introduced a method based on a hidden surface algorithm which is called **a pixel integrator**. The hidden surface algorithm is a scan-line algorithm which works as follows:

Sort all polygons on highest y value
Initialize the active polygon list AP to nil
for each scan-line SC
  Add polygons from y-list that enter on SC to AP
  Initialize the x-bucket to nil and the scan-line buffer to background
  for each polygon P in AP
    Clip off P the piece Q that lies on SC giving P'
    Replace P by P' in AP
    if there are pixels under Q that are completely covered
    then
      Break Q into three pieces: center solid piece and
                two irregular pieces at the ends at the pixel
                boundaries {see Fig.8.6}
    Sort the pieces into the x-bucket according to the leftmost pixel covered
  Initialize the z-list to nil
  for each pixel PX across SC
    Sort every entry at the current x position of the x-bucket into the z-list
    Evaluate the z-list if not empty
    if the piece is solid
    then get its color
    else

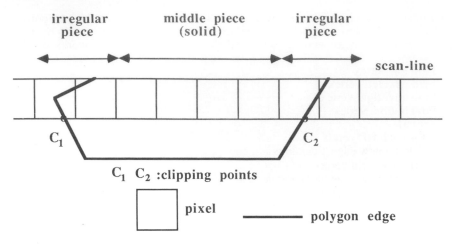

Fig.8.6. Breaking a piece into three pieces

> **if** an irregular piece IP is in front of a solid piece
> **then** find the area of IP over PX to weight the two colors
> **else** call the pixel integrator
> Write the color into the scan-line buffer

The pixel integrator is necessary to find the area of each visible polygon piece in order to determine its contribution to the pixel intensity. The basic algorithm is very similar to the Weiler-Atherton algorithm, described in Sect. 5.6.2. It basically works as follows:

> **procedure** PixelIntegrator (ZL:Z-list; **var** C:COLOR)
> Consider the first polygon P in the z-list ZL
>   {they are assumed in sorted z-order with the first as the closest}
> Look for the first unclipped edge E
> **if** there is no unclipped edge or there is only one polygon P in ZL
> **then** return the color of P weighted by its area
> Clip all polygons in ZL against E
> Put them in two lists L_1 and L_2, one for each side of E
> Set a flag for each edge that lies along the clipping line as it is clipped
> PixelIntegrator(L_1,C_1)
> PixelIntegrator(L_2,C_2)
> Combine C_1 and C_2 to obtain C

8.3.4   A-buffer algorithm

Carpenter (1984) introduces a new algorithm based on an A-buffer (antialiased, area-averaged, accumulation buffer). It may be considered a scan-line algorithm, though it does not require a scan-line order. For antialiasing, more resolution inside the pixel is called for. Carpenter uses a 4x8 bit mask to represent a subpixel polygon. With this approach, clipping one polygon against another becomes a single Boolean operation. The A-buffer data structure is shown in Fig.8.7.

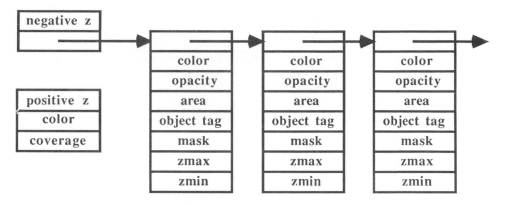

Fig.8.7. The A-buffer structure

In summary, for simple pixels, the buffer contains a positive z-value and a color. Otherwise, it contains a negative z-value and a pointer to a list of fragments sorted front-to-back by the frontmost z. A fragment is a polygon clipped to a pixel boundary.

The A-buffer algorithm uses a Fourier window; this means that the color of the pixel is computed from the area-weighted average of the colors of the visible surfaces contained in the pixel. The heart of the A-buffer algorithm consists of determining the visible fragments and the visible parts of fragments. The algorithm may be considered a reversed painter's algorithm: when neighboring polygons are rendered, the first one will give its color to the pixel and store the fraction of the pixel covered. The neighboring polygon can now blend its color for the pixel with the previous color, knowing what fraction of the polygon is covered by each. The coverages are then summed. The algorithm works as follows:

procedure pack (FL:FragmentList; M:Mask; **var** C:Color; **var** A:REAL);
if this is the last fragment in the list
then
    Return color A and coverage A
else
    Find inside mask M_{in} and outside mask M_{out} {pixel parts inside and outside the
                                                   fragment}
    if M_{out} is not empty
    then
      pack (FL^.next, M_{out} , C, A) {find color and coverage of the rest of the
                                   searched area}
    if the fragment is transparent or overlaps in Z with next on list
    then
      pack (FL, M_{in} , C, A) {find color and coverage of the surfaces behind the
                                 fragment to be filtered by the color of the fragment}
    if nothing hidden behind the fragment affects its appearance
    then
      Return a blend C of the fragment and the outside area A
    else
      if Z's overlap with next fragment
      then

Estimate visibility ratio V_{front}

$$V_{front} = \frac{zmax_{next} - zmin_{front}}{(zmax-zmin)_{front} + (zmax-zmin)_{next}}$$

Estimate the coverage of fragment f_{in} by:

$$f_{in} = V_{front} \, Opacity_{front} + (1-V_{front})(1-f_{next})$$

Blend fragment with what is behind

$$C_{in} = f_{in} \, C_{front} + (1-f_{in}) \, C_{next}$$

Return blend C of inside and outside
    else {just transparent}
        Blend fragment with what is behind
        Return blend C of inside and outside

The colors of inside and outside regions are blended as follows:

$$C = \frac{f_{in} \, C_{in} + f_{out} \, C_{out}}{f_{in} + f_{out}} \tag{8.3}$$

8.3.5 New Catmull algorithm

Catmull (1984) proposes an algorithm that solves the visible surface problem at each pixel independently using a Gaussian filter. A list of polygons is created at each pixel, containing the list of every polygon that overlaps the filter of the pixel. The area of the pixel is defined as the area of the filter even if the filter overlaps other pixels.

The visible surface algorithm at each pixel PX operates on the list L of polygons and works as follows:

Extract from L the closest set of overlapping polygons using a head sort;
        the new list HL is called the head list
if there are no contour edges in the head and if the center of PX is covered at least
    once
then {the pixel is completely covered}
    Call FILTER
    if HL covers all parts of the filter once and only once
    then {calculations for PX are over}
    else
      Call RESOLVER
      Cull obscured pieces
      Call FILTER
else
    Call RESOLVER
    Cull obscured pieces
    Call FILTER

The head sort produces a head list HL composed of two parts: the head H and the tail T with a z gap between. H contains all polygons that are nearest the eye and overlap each other in z but do not overlap any of the remaining polygons in T in z.

The polygons are not completely sorted, because if the polygons of H completely cover the pixel, there is no need to sort the remaining polygons. The head-sort algorithm works as follows:

> Find the polygon P with the nearest z
> Extract all polygons $\{P_i\}$ with the same object tag
> Put $\{P_i\}$ in H
> **for** each P_i
>   **if** P_i does not overlap in z
>   **then**
>   **if** P_i is behind the gap
>   **then**
>   Put P_i in T
> **if** the furthest z in H overlaps the nearest z in T
> **then**
>   Repeat the process with T

The procedure FILTER is applied to a list of polygons L. It convolves each polygon with a circularly symmetric filter that has an arbitrary cross section, chosen to have roughly a Gaussian shape. The process of filtering not only determines the contribution of each polygon but also its area under the filter. The procedure RESOLVER does the clipping necessary at contour edges and intersections. The method is based on the Weiler-Atherton algorithm described in Sect. 5.6.2.

8.4   Edge-inference and specific algorithms

8.4.1 Edge-inference algorithm

Bloomenthal (1983) describes algorithms for the detection and smoothing of edges and the filtering of an image in accordance with the inferred edges obtained from the set of vertical and horizontal segments which form the staircase of the aliased line. The process of edge smoothing may be decomposed into three steps:

1. Finding and tracking of the rastered edges created by the point-sampling process
2. Smoothing of rastered edges
3. Filtering an image along the smoothed edges

8.4.1.1 Tracking process

The tracking process is performed upon a frame of discrete, single-valued regions. The region containing pixel <x,y> may be defined as the set of pixels <x,y> through a four-connected path of pixels, all with the same value as pixel <x,y>. Using a scan-line algorithm, starting points are produced. Once the starting point is known, a region's boundary may be tracked, forming a closed circuit when the starting point is again reached. The algorithm works as follows:

> Take the starting point S
> **repeat**
>   Go up until a corner C
>   **if** C is convex
>   **then**
>   1: Go right until a corner C

```
        if C is convex
        then
            2: Go down until a corner C
                if C is convex
                then
                    3: Go left until a corner C
                        if C is not convex
                        then goto 2
                else goto 1
    else goto 3
until C = S
```

8.4.1.2 Edge-smoothing process
A jag is determined from four sequential corners C_1, C_2, C_3, and C_4 when C_2 - C_1 is parallel to C_4 - C_3 and the distance $(C_2,C_3) = 1$ pixel.

The edge inference algorithm uses a FIFO buffer of nine points to store for a given corner the positions of the four preceding and following points and the length and direction of the segments connecting the points. The location of an eventual new end point for the smoothed edge may be determined from this information.

8.4.1.3 Image filtering
The algorithm works as follows:

```
for each pixel PX in the image which is intersected by the inferred edges
    Compute the percentage P of PX covered by the region
    Use P as a weighting coefficient for averaging the surrounding pixels
    Shade PX as a linear combination of surrounding pixels averaged
        according to whether or not they belong to the region
```

The percentage P is computed using an incremental technique similar to Bresenham's line-drawing algorithm (Pitteway and Watkinson 1980).

8.4.2 Other algorithms

Piller (1980) and Gupta and Sproull (1981) propose parallel processing approaches using special hardware. Fiume et al. (1983) describe a parallel scan conversion algorithm for a general-purpose "ultracomputer." In this approach, a parallel antialiasing algorithm approximates the subpixel coverage by edges using a look-up table. The ultimate intensity of a pixel is the weighted sum of the intensity contribution of the closest edge, that of the "losing" edges, and that of the background.

Guagnan et al. (1983) propose an algorithm for generating antialiased polygons, combining color blending, Gouraud shading, and a z-buffer algorithm. The algorithm is based on a simplification of Crow's algorithm using two pixels on each scan-line. The intensity of each pixel is determined directly by its subpixel position.

Other interesting antialiasing techniques are described in other chapters. In particular, specific techniques have been applied to texture by Blinn and Newell (1976; see Sect. 12.3.2), Norton et al. (1982; see Sect. 12.3.4) and Feibush et al. (1980; see Sect. 12.3.3). Antialiasing in highlighting has been studied in ray-tracing algorithms by Whitted (1980) and Roth (1982; see Chap. 10).

8.5 Temporal aliasing and motion blur

8.5.1 Temporal aliasing problem

As we have seen, spatial aliasing is an effect of spatial undersampling. Temporal undersampling can also be disturbing. Szabo (1978) distinguishes three different temporal effects: the interlace effect, the frame rate update effect, and stroboscopic effects. This kind of temporal aliasing has essentially negative implications on dynamic images; for this reason, we do not discuss these effects here; they have been described in another book (Magnenat-Thalmann and Thalmann 1985b).

There are also several attempts in image synthesis to model motion blur, which corresponds to another form of temporal antialiasing in computer animation. **Motion blur** in photography or cinema is due to the motion of objects during the finite exposure time the camera shutter remains open to record the image on film. Although the simulation of motion blur is mainly useful in computer animation, it portrays the illusion of movement in static images.

Motion blur is currently a very active area of research. As the solution to this problem is strongly related to other problems of image synthesis such as depth of field or fuzzy shadows, new techniques are described in others chapters. In particular, the following techniques are presented:

- An approach based on ray-tracing using a lens and aperture camera model (Potmesil and Chakravarty 1983; see Sect. 10.5.1, 10.5.2)
- The use of distributed ray-tracing (Cook et al. 1984; see Sect. 10.6.2)

Other algorithms will be discussed in the following sections.

8.5.2 Korein-Badler algorithms

Korein and Badler (1983) describe two motion blur algorithms. The first approach is based on intervals during which each object covers each pixel. Object movements are approximated with continuous functions and, within the limits of this approximation, the algorithm determines the precise intervals during which each pixel center is covered by an occluded object. For the temporal interval ΔT covered by the output frame, the algorithm works as follows:

    for each object OB
        for each dynamic attribute
            Find a temporal transformation
        Determine the areas which OB covers during ΔT

    for each pixel PX
        Determine which objects $\{OB_i\}$ cover OB at some time in ΔT
        for each OB_i
            Determine the subinterval $\{\Delta T_i\}$ during which OB_i projects onto PX
        Perform hidden-surface removal by eliminating subintervals associated with
            occluded objects
        Determine the intensity function I of PX on the basis of the remaining
            subinterval and the corresponding attribute functions
        Filter I

The implementation of the algorithm has been limited to objects composed of spheres.

The second approach is based on supersampling. The technique is similar to the corresponding spatial antialiasing technique, but multiple intensity buffers for a single frame are generated, each one corresponding to a different point in time. The intensities of each pixel in the different buffers form a function that can be digitized at a greater resolution than the output frame rate. It may then be filtered to obtain the final image. Although Korein and Badler note a few undesirable effects, the technique is simple to implement and can be used with different methods of image rendering.

8.5.3 Catmull algorithm

Motion blur and depth of field blurring are also possible using the visible surface algorithm for independent pixel processing developed by Catmull (1984) and described in Sect. 8.3.5. Motion blur is accomplished by shrinking the polygons in the direction of the blur. The transformation is relative to the center of the pixel $C = <C_x,C_y>$. We assume a simple velocity $V = <V_x,V_y>$ for each vertex $P = <P_x,P_y>$, which is scaled by the amount S:

$$S = \frac{D}{L+D} \tag{8.4}$$

where L is the length of the xy projection of the motion vector and D is the diameter of the filter.

A transformed vertex P'' is obtained by the following matrix product :

$$P'' = \frac{1}{L^2} P' \, \mathcal{M} \tag{8.5}$$

where $\mathcal{M}$ is the following matrix:

$$\mathcal{M} = \begin{bmatrix} SV_x{}^2+V_y{}^2 & SV_xV_y - V_xV_y \\ SV_xV_y - V_xV_y & V_x{}^2+V_y{}^2 \end{bmatrix} \tag{8.6}$$

and P' is the point in the coordinate system of the pixel; half of the velocity vector is added to center P':

$$P' = P - C + \frac{V}{2} \tag{8.7}$$

Grant (1985) has extended this algorithm to perform the correct analytic calculation in four dimensions.

8.5.4 2 1/2 D Max-Lerner algorithm

Max and Lerner (1985) proposes a 2 1/2 D approach based on sorting the objects in depth and then compositing these images into a single picture, starting from the rear. Layers L_i are characterized by an opacity mask value OP_i and a color value C_i and they are composited from back to front. Each L_i is added to an opaque background of color B to obtain an opaque composite. The process is separated into two steps:

1. Applying the mask to provide an intermediate I
2. Adding L_i to I

The color of the composite CP is given by the two relations:

$$CI = (1-OP_i) \, B \qquad CP = C_i + CI \tag{8.8}$$

where CI is the intermediate color.

Motion blur is included by applying a blur process to both the image and its opacity mask, before doing the composition. The motion blur routine is restricted to translations, implying that each layer has a unique blur direction.

The algorithm blurs a raster image, called by Max and Lerner the instantaneous raster in the direction of the blur vector $<BX,BY>$. It works as follows:

1. Skew the instantaneous raster into a skewed raster S
2. Blur the skewed image S into a blurred raster B
3. Unskew the blurred raster B and combine it with the current composite picture

We shall discuss only the blur step, because the skewing and unskewing processes are very simple.

The skewed raster is blurred by a number of pixels corresponding to the magnitude of the largest blur vector component and written into the blurred raster. Consider a blur in the x-direction, with $BX < NX$, the x-size of the skewed raster. The simple blur, without weighting can be calculated as:

$$B(x) = \sum_{k=0}^{BX} S(x-k) \tag{8.9}$$

A blur with linear weighting is given by:

$$B_2(x) = \sum_{k-0}^{BX} (BX-k) \, S(x-k) \tag{8.10}$$

which can be incrementally expressed as:

$$B_2(x) = B_2(x-1) + (BX+1) \, S(x) - B(x) \tag{8.11}$$

9 Shadows

9.1 Role of shadows

For any realistic computer-generated image, light sources have to be considered as key elements in the scene. However, unless the light source is unique and located at an eyepoint or the illumination is very diffuse, as with an overcast sky, images are not complete without shadows. As noted by Crow (1977a), algorithms for shadows require considerable computation time. Moreover, the main problem is that most algorithms are unable to produce shadows for any object, virtual camera, and light condition, except ray-tracing (Whitted 1980; Kay and Greenberg 1979; Kajiya 1983), which is very expensive in terms of CPU time to be used for computer-generated films. In a computer animation scene, where the lights and/or the cameras are moving, an algorithm which gives perfect results for 100 frames may happen give a bad result for frame 101.

Before studying several algorithms for implementing shadows, we must define the term "shadow." This is the darkness cast by an object that intercepts light. This shadow falls from the side opposite the source of light and, as already mentioned, it is only visible when the eyepoint moves away from the light source.

Crow (1977a) distinghishes three classes of shadow algorithms; Williams (1978) added a fourth. These four classes are as follows:

1. **Shadows generated during the display process**; two different methods were proposed by Appel (1968) and Bouknight and Kelley (1970)
2. **Shadow volume calculations**; the method was introduced by Crow (1977a) and improved by several other authors
3. **Polygon shadow generation with clipping transformations**; the most representative algorithm of this class was proposed by Atherton et al. (1978); the algorithm is based on an object space polygon-clipping algorithm. Earlier, Nishita and Kakamae (1974) published a method for generating shadows based on a convex polyhedron-clipping algorithm
4. **z-Buffer shadows**; the technique was first introduced by Williams (1978) but a new algorithm has beeen recently proposed by Brotman and Badler (1984)

This last approach also simulates penumbrae and will be discussed with another technique introduced by Nishita and Nakamae (1985) in Sect. 9.6.

Finally, we should mention that an elegant way of solving the problem of shadows is by the use of a ray-tracing technique.

9.2 Shadows generated during display process

9.2.1 Appel algorithm

Appel (1968) solves the shadow problem and the hidden-surface problem simultaneously. The algorithm is based on a scan-line technique using structures composed of planar polygonal surfaces. The question of which parts of which surfaces are visible is answered by the technique of **quantitative invisibility**, i.e., a count of the number of surfaces hiding a vertex of the polygonal objects represented. A line segment is visible only if all points on it have a quantitative invisibility of zero. This technique detects changes in quantitative invisibility along a segment and draws the visible portions. In this algorithm, multiple illumination sources and the shadows cast by those sources are possible. The shadow boundaries are computed by projecting points incrementally along the edge of a shading polygon to the surface, which will be shaded. Quantitative invisibility with respect to each light source is used to determine those segment parts which lie in the shadow.

9.2.2 Bouknight-Kelley algorithm

This method is similar to the previous one. However, Bouknight and Kelley (1970) use a hidden-surface algorithm which is already based on a scan-line process. The algorithm is mainly based on the principle that shadows cast by one polygon onto another by point illumination sources are themselves polygons in the 3D space. By projecting the resulting shadow 3D space onto the viewing plane as the original object was projected (see Fig.9.1), it becomes easy to add a second scanning process for keeping track of shadows on each scan-line.

This second scanning operation processes the shadow 3D-space structure and produces data which will be combined with the data obtained from the first scan operation to form the final scan-line intensity (see Fig.9.2).

An important step of the algorithm is the detection of shadows. In particular, it is essential to eliminate as soon as possible the shadow polygons which are unnecessary. In fact, the theoretical number of possible shadows cast is equal to the number of possible pairs of polygons in the structure. However, some of these pairs are useless and should be eliminated. For this reason, Bouknight and Kelley store the shadow pairs in a chained list, with sublists linking all polygons that may shadow a given polygon. These polygons are detected by projecting all polygons onto a sphere centered at the light source. Interference with respect to the light source is tested; all polygon pairs where no interference takes place are discarded.

9.3 Shadow volumes

9.3.1 Crow algorithm

The original algorithm was designed by Crow (1977a). The shadow volume is the space region within which an object "intercepts" light. The boundary surface of the shadow volume is obtained, as shown in Fig. 9.3, by all planes defined by the light source and the contour edges of the original object. This volume is theoretically unlimited; however, it is normally restricted to the view volume. Polygons which bound the shadow volume are added to the list of polygons for display processing,

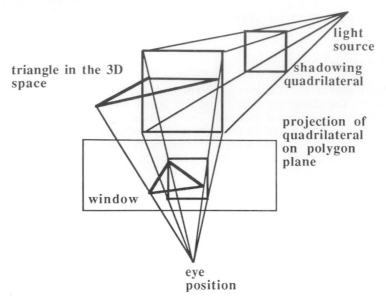

triangle in the 3D space

light source

shadowing quadrilateral

projection of quadrilateral on polygon plane

window

eye position

Fig.9.1. Object and shadow projections

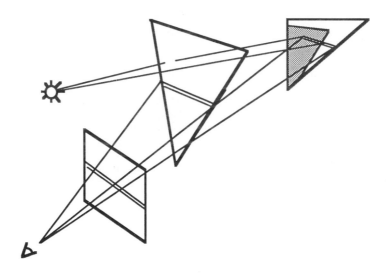

Fig.9.2. The two scanning operations in the Bouknight-Kelley algorithm

just like the polygons of objects. During display processing, shadow polygons are considered invisible, and when they are crossed over a transition inside or outside the object shadow is produced. This means that shadow polygons are included in the z-sort of a scan-line hidden surface algorithm and the parity of the shadow polygons in front of a visible surface is counted to determine whether it is in shadow.

Two kinds of shadow polygons have to be considered—**front-facing polygons** and **back-facing polygons**. Any point in front of a back-facing polygon

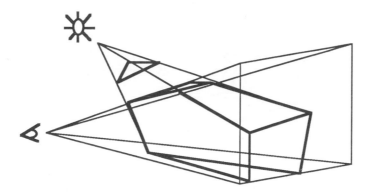

Fig.9.3. The shadow volume

and behind a front-facing polygon is in the shadow. Consider now a line from the camera eye to a polygon. This polygon is front-facing if the shadow volume is entered, but back-facing if is left. A number +1 is given to front-facing polygons, and a number -1 to back-facing polygons. The general idea of the algorithm is to consider a line from the eye to the graphic object and to examine the shadow polygons that are crossed by the line. If the sum of their associated numbers is greater than zero, the pixel is in shadow because more front-facing than back-facing polygons have been entered.

One way of accelerating the algorithm and saving memory is to consider the silhouette of the object as viewed from the light source. This silhouette is obtained by considering the edges of the object. There are two kinds of edges:

1. Edges in the boundary of the object (category 1)
2. Edges shared by two polygons with only one lighted (category 2)

9.3.2 Problems and solutions with shadow-volume algorithm

Problems may occur, as shown in Fig.9.4, where there are edges of both categories in the same object. One way of solving this problem (Bergeron 1985) is to associate a value of 1 to category 1 edges and a value of 2 to category 2 edges. The method is satisfactory except with translucent objects.

Another problem in animation with shadows occurs when the camera eye comes into shadow; in this case, the count of edges is 0 or -1, which means that there is no region of the view volume in shadow. This is due to the fact that the shadow volume is not closed. One way of solving the problem is to calculate the projection of each polygon on the front plane. After a clipping, a shadow polygon is obtained that closes the shadow volume. In these calculations, other special cases may cause difficulties:

1. The light source is between the extremities of the polygon in the direction z (depth) (Fig.9.5a)
2. The object overlaps the front plane (Fig.9.5b)

9.3.3 Polar coordinate approach

For scenes with many small polygons with shadows, Max (1986b) proposes the use of **radial scan lines** in polar coordinates. Consider the line L between the eye E

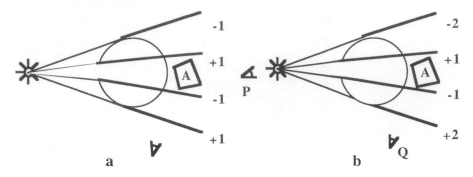

Fig.9.4. a For the observer, the object **A** is erroneously lighted; b for the observer at **Q**, the object is correctly in shadow; however, for the observer at **P**, if the surface is transparent, **A** is erroneously lighted. Note that counters are given for the camera at **Q**

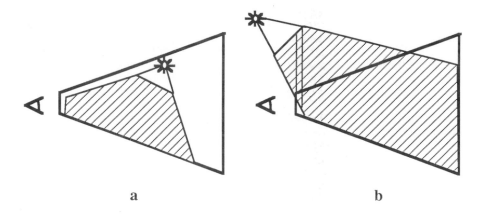

Fig.9.5 a,b. Two special cases

and the light source S; L intersects the picture plane T at a point **P** and a family of scan planes meeting in L intersects T in a family of lines meeting at **P**. Since each scan-plane contains **E** and **S**, the only shadow polygons intersecting a scan plane come from edges which also intersect that scan plane. This approach considerably reduces the sorting of shadow polygons. The algorithm was developed by Max for simulating atmospheric shadows (see Sect. 14.4.2); however, it is quite interesting for conventional shadows.

The algorithm is a polar coordinate modification of Watkins algorithm (see Sect. 5.4.3). It sorts first in θ, next in r, and then simultaneously in z and a shadow distance parameter. The angular coordinate goes counterclockwise and edges are sorted into buckets according to the greatest θ of their end points. As there is a whole circle of values of θ, edges which cross from positive to negative θ must be broken into two parts, one extending from $\theta=\pi$ to the end point with positive θ and one from the other end point until $\theta=-\pi$. The algorithm uses segment blocks containing r, depth and shading information for the left and right edges of the segment, and various pointers. The algorithm works as follows:

Put all edges into θ buckets
for each bucket in order of decreasing θ
   Enter all edges from bucket θ into r sort segment blocks
   Merge all shadow-only segments into shadow sort
   for each visible span generated by the Watkins r- z sort
      Merge back lit polygon segments which satisfy one of the three conditions
         1, 2, or 3 below into shadow sort
      Find intervals I_k of light and shade on the visible span
      for each I_k
         Determine color   {see Sect. 14.4.2 for the atmospheric case}
         Scan convert the information into rectilinear pixel array
      Merge front lit polygon segments which end during the span into shadow
         sort
   Remove edges which terminate at this θ from active r sort
   Update edges for next radial scan line
Output the final image

Note that a polygon is said to be **front lit** if the side facing the viewer also faces the light source. A front lit polygon segment is merged into the shadow sort only after the r processing has completely passed it; otherwise, it would be in shadow itself. Back lit segments are merged when one of the following conditions becomes true:

1. The segment overlaps the span to be rendered and lies at least partly on the sunlit side of the polygon visible in the span
2. The segment is itself about to be rendered
3. The r processing has completely passed the segment

9.4 Object-space polygon-clipping approach

9.4.1 Nishita-Nakamae algorithm

Nishita and Nakamae (1974) describe a method for shadow generation based on a convex polyhedron-clipping algorithm. Hidden-surface removal from any chosen point of view is accomplished by determining the silhouette contours of each polyhedron and using them to define its clipping border. Objects which lie behind a selected polyhedron are clipped to the window defined by the polyhedron's outer boundaries.

Shadowed images are generated by this clipping method in two steps:

1. A view is taken in the direction of the infinite light source. Using the polyhedron clipper, all the hidden surfaces, which are surfaces in the shadow, are found
2. The scene is transformed to a selected viewpoint, and all hidden surfaces are removed by a method similar to the Bouknight-Kelley algorithm

Figure 9.6 shows the principle.
Nishita et al. (1985) propose an extension of the method to treat point sources with luminous intensity distribution, as explained in Sect. 7.1.4. The algorithm detects shadow boundaries on a perspective plane observed from the light source. For simplicity of shadow detection, a partial sphere of lighting is used. This partial sphere bounds a space where the illuminance cannot be neglected.

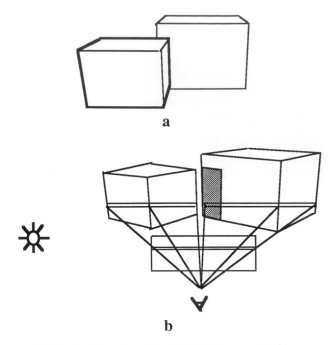

a

b

Fig.9.6 a,b. Principle of the Nishita-Nakamae algorithm

9.4.2 Atherton-Weiler-Greenberg algorithm

Atherton et al. (1978) propose a polygon shadow-generation algorithm based on the object space polygon-clipping algorithm designed by Weiler and Atherton (1977) for hidden-surface removal (see Sect. 5.6.2). This algorithm removes all surfaces that lie behind each unique polygonal area and within its borders. Shadows are created in three steps:

1. Shadow descriptions are found by viewing the environment from the light source
2. By using the hidden surface removal algorithm, illuminated polygons are detected. These polygons are those that are not in shadow and they are determined by considering hidden surfaces removed when viewed from the light source
3. Illuminated polygons are added to the original polygons

The principle is illustrated in Fig. 9.7.

The transformations are performed using view and shadow matrices. The first shadow matrix transforms the polygonal data environment to the environment from a viewpoint at the light source position. Illuminated surfaces are then obtained by using hidden surface removal. The second shadow matrix is used to obtain illuminated surfaces and a copy of the environment at any orientation. This results in a completely shadowed data file. By applying view matrices and the hidden surface removal algorithm, hidden line-removed vector displays or hidden surface-removed halftone displays can be obtained. By using the hidden surface-removal algorithm for each light source, shadowed images with several light sources can be produced.

The object-space polygon-clipping approach offers the advantage that if no light source or object motion (in animation) occur for different camera positions, the shadow information can be saved and reused.

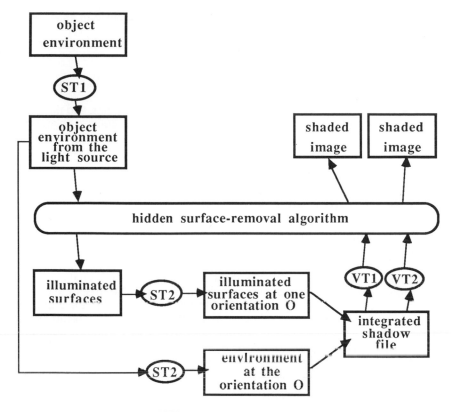

ST1, ST2: shadow transformations
VT1, VT2: view transformations

Fig.9.7. Principle of the Atherton-Weiler-Greenberg algorithm

9.5 z-Buffer shadows

Williams (1978) has described a simple algorithm which utilizes z-buffer visible surface computation to display shadows cast by objects modeled by smooth surface patches. The algorithm works as follows:

1. A view of the scene is constructed from the point of view of the light source. The z-values are computed and stored in a separate shadow z-buffer; the shading values are ignored
2. A view of the scene is then constructed from the point of view of the camera eye. The depth at each pixel is compared with that in the observer's z-buffer. If the surface is visible, a linear transformation is used to map the X,Y,Z points in the observer's view into X',Y',Z' coordinates in the light source view. The Z' value is compared with the Z value at the location <X',Y'> in the shadow z-buffer. Two cases are then possible:

a) The point is not visible to the light source. It is therefore in shadow and is shaded accordingly

b) The point is visible to the light source. It is rendered in the frame buffer at <X,Y>

Williams has modified the second step to render curved shadows on curved surfaces (see Fig.9.8).

The complete scene is computed from the camera eye viewpoint, and the point-by-point transformation to the light source space and consequent shadowing is undertaken as a post-process.

Difficulties in the first step can arise when the light source is punctual and near the visible objects.

9.6   Soft shadows and penumbrae

9.6.1 Umbra and penumbra

As shown in Chap. 6, light sources are generally modeled as either points or directions. However, in the real world, most common light sources have an irregular shape and a finite size, as discussed in Sect. 7.1. Such sources cast shadows involving an umbra and a penumbra. As defined by Crow (1977a), the umbra is that part of the shadow space which receives no light from the source; the penumbra is that area to shadows surrounded by a border area in which a smooth change from shadowed to unshadowed takes place. Calculating a penumbra is very expensive in terms of CPU time and this is the main reason for assuming point light sources. However, in this section, we present two approaches for representing penumbrae.

9.6.2   Brotman-Badler algorithm

Brotman and Badler (1984) propose an approach to modeling distributed light sources and rendering soft shadows with a depth-buffer algorithm. There are, however, certain restrictions on the choice of objects rendered using this algorithm. The most serious is that objects must be a union of convex, closed polyhedral pieces. However, the convexity restriction may be circumvented by splitting a nonconvex object into one or more convex objects. The closed restriction can be circumvented by pasting back faces onto objects to ensure that an outward-facing normal can be determined.

The algorithm uses a modified depth buffer (2D array). Each cell represents a visible point and is described by a record composed of five fields: the depth, the normal, a pointer to object characteristics (color, transmittance, reflectance ...), a pointer to the front-facing shadow polygons, and a pointer to the back-facing shadow polygons. The general algorithm works as follows:

1. All visible objects are rendered into the depth buffer
2. Shadow volumes are computed and counters in the data structure of the depth buffer are modified
3. Preliminary intensity values are computed for the opaque objects, taking into account any effects from the shadows
4. Transparent objects are sorted by Z-values and rendered into a temporary buffer. The intensity values computed are used to attenuate the preliminary values when necessary. With this approach, transparent objects can cast shadows, but cannot have shadows cast on them.

Fig. 9.8. Curve shadows cast on curved surfaces. By Lance Williams, © 1978 NYIT Computer Graphics Lab. Patch subdivision software, James Blinn, background, Paul Xander

Brotman and Badler use distributed light sources defined by intensity, geometric shape, and location. Shapes are modeled as polyhedral surfaces and a set of point sources (that lie on the surface) model the effects of the distributed light source. The point sources are generated using random numbers; more details may be found in Brotman and Badler (1984).

The amount of light reaching any point in the penumbra region is theoretically described by an integration of all the light from visible sources. In practice, once the set of point sources that models the distributed source is generated, the method works as follows:

1. The first operation is to determine shadow volumes resulting from each point source and an object blocking its light
2. Shadow volumes are superimposed to produce the shadow cast by an object intercepting light from a distributed source

The number of shadow volumes surrounding a pixel determines how many points in the point source set of a distributed light source do not illuminate the visible pixel. For every pixel, there is one darkness level associated with each light source. In order to compute this darkness level, it is necessary to perform calculations at two levels—the point-source level and the object level. Figure 9.9 shows an example (taken from Brotman and Badler 1984) where a distributed light source is modeled as three point sources I_1, I_2, and I_3.

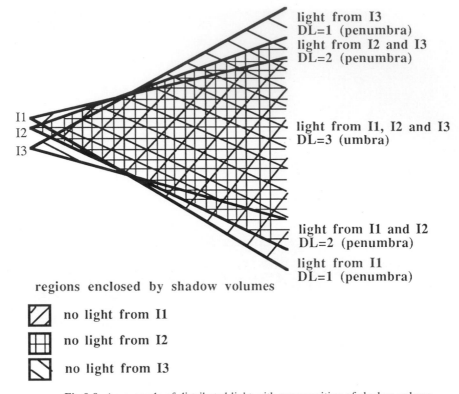

light from I3
DL=1 (penumbra)

light from I2 and I3
DL=2 (penumbra)

light from I1, I2 and I3
DL=3 (umbra)

light from I1 and I2
DL=2 (penumbra)

light from I1
DL=1 (penumbra)

regions enclosed by shadow volumes

no light from I1

no light from I2

no light from I3

Fig.9.9. An example of distributed light with superposition of shadow volume

9.6.3 Umbrae and penumbrae for linear sources

The shadow caused by a linear source, as described in Sect. 7.1.4, also consists of umbrae and penumbrae. Nishita et al. (1985) propose a method to determine the shadow volumes, which is easy to implement because they require objects to be sets of convex polyhedra.

Consider a linear light source with two end points Q_1 and Q_2, a convex polyhedron V, and a face F farther from the light source than V. We define C_1 and C_2 as the two silhouette contours of V when viewed from Q_1 and Q_2. Let C_1' be the projection of C_1 onto F and C_2' be the projection of C_2 onto F. The umbra area is the intersection of C_1' and C_2'. The penumbra area is the minimum convex polygon surrounding C_1' and C_2'. Similarly, if we consider two shadow volumes U_1 and U_2 corresponding to Q_1 and Q_2, the umbra volume is defined as the intersection of U_1 and U_2 and the penumbra volume is the minimum convex volume surrounding U_1 and U_2.

Shadow detection is performed by using the relationships between the shadow volumes and each of the faces. Faces that are totally invisible from Q_1 and Q_2 are ignored. For faces that are visible from either Q_1 or Q_2, the algorithm to obtain the penumbra and umbra boundaries (stored as penumbra loop and umbra loop) works as follows:

if the penumbra volume of the polyhedron V and the face F do not intersect
then
  {there is no shadow cast on F}
else
  Project the contour lines C_1 and C_2 onto F giving C_1' and C_2'
  if one volume U_k, k=1,2 encloses the other one
  then
    C_k' is the penumbra loop and the other projected contour the umbra loop
  else {volumes U_1 and U_2 intersect each other}
    Determine two points P_L and P_R, common to C_1' and C_2' {see Nishita et al. 1985}
    Divide C_1' into two separated strings S_{1A} and S_{1B} using P_L and P_R
    Divide C_2' into two separated strings S_{2A} and S_{2B} using P_L and P_R
    Penumbra and umbra loops are obtained by connecting two strings S_{jX},
      j=1,2 X=A,B

9.6.4 Nishita-Nakamae method for interreflection and shadows

Nishita and Nakamae (1985) introduce a method for indirect lighting with interreflection and shadows results. In order to save time, the penumbrae and umbrae are predetected before scanning for hidden surface removal. As in their original method, first shadow volumes for penumbrae and umbrae formed by a convex polyhedron and a light source are obtained. Then, the penumbrae (or umbrae) on each face are obtained as the intersection areas of penumbra (or umbra) volumes and the face. The procedure works as follows:

1. Input of 3D objects
2. Subdivision of faces into subfaces
3. Classification of faces of each polyhedron for shading into three classes:
   - Faces receiving light from the whole region of the source
   - Faces receiving light from a part of the source
   - Faces receiving no light from the source
4. Obtaining penumbra and umbra volumes
5. Calculation of penumbrae and umbrae on each face
6. Calculation of interreflection of light
7. Determining priority of visibility for a given viewpoint
8. Hidden-surface removal and calculation of direct illuminance at each pixel

The most interesting step is the calculation of interreflection taking into account shadows. As faces in a room are subdivided into subfaces, a test to determine whether or not objects exist between every pair of subsurfaces is required. To reduce the complexity of the test, it is only executed for the four corners of each subsurface. This means that both shadow calculations and illuminance calculation are done at the corner points of subsurfaces. The shadow function v_{ij} for adding shadow influence between corner points P_i and P_j is given by:

v_{ij} = 1 if there are no objects between P_i and P_j
    0 if blocked
The weighting coefficients w_j for the illuminance calculation at P_j is given by:

w_j =   1/4 if P_j is a corner point of polygon
    1/2 if P_j is a point on the edge of polygon
    1 otherwise

Assume a point P_i on the face F_A, a point P_j on the face F_B, and the subsurface A_j surrounding P_j. As the subsurfaces are very small, then the form factor F_{ij} (see Eq. 7.33) may be approximated as follows:

$$F_{ij} = \frac{d_{Aj} \; d_{Bi}}{\pi r_{ij}^4} A_j \tag{9.1}$$

where d_{Aj} is the perpendicular distance between the face F_A and the point P_j and d_{Bi} is the perpendicular distance between F_B and P_i.

The procedure for calculating the shadow functions v_{ij} is complex. Assume a line segment $s = P_m P_n$ consisting of P_j (j=m to n) on a face of a polyhedron F_B as a linear light source. The shadow function v_{ij} for a point P_i on a face of another polyhedron F_A is obtained as follows:

for each v_{ij}
   $v_{ij}:=1$ (j=m to n)
Remove polyhedra behind F_A and F_B
Remove the polyhedra not intersecting the triangle $P_i P_m P_n$ by using bounding
       boxes of the triangle and the polyhedra
Obtain the polyhedra intersecting the plane of the triangle $P_i P_m P_n$
Extract silhouette contours C_k of the polyhedra viewed from P_i
Calculate the intersection between C_k and s
Search the invisible parts PT of s enclosed by C_k when viewed from P_i
for each point P of PT
   $v_{ij} := 0$

Figure 9.10 shows how the shadow function v_{ij} is calculated; examples of w_j values are also shown. An example is shown in Fig.9.11.

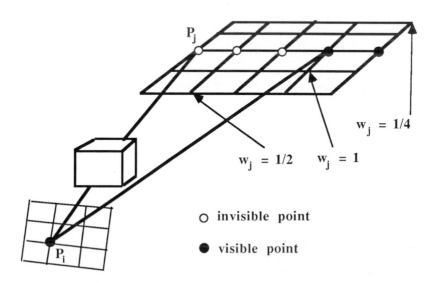

Fig. 9.10. Calculation of the Nishita-Nakamae shadow function

Fig.9.11. Night scenes illuminated by two rectangular sources. Courtesy of T. Nishita, Fukuyama University and E. Nakamao, Hiroshima University

9.7 MIRALab implementation of shadows

As the most used rendering algorithm in the MIRALab software is a scan-line algorithm (other used algorithms are z-buffer and ray-tracing), we chose an algorithm based on the Crow shadow volumes.

This extended shadow-volume algorithm has been incorporated into the MIRA-SHADING language (Magnenat-Thalmann et al. 1985), which is the implementation language of MIRANIM (Magnenat-Thalmann et al. 1985a). To accelerate the calculations of the silhouette, neighbors of the edges of objects are computed. In fact, this calculation has already been performed for each standard object in MIRA-SHADING. Moreover, once this calculation of neighbors is performed for an object, it is still valid even if the object, the camera, or the light changes.

The data structure for an edge is defined in PASCAL as:

```
type EDGETYPE =
    record
        NOVERT: 1..NBMAXVERT; {vertex number in the object}
        NOEDGE: 0..NBMAXEDGES; {edge number in the face}
        NONEIGHB: 0..NBMAXPOLY {number of neighbor polygons}
    end;
```

The silhouette is obtained by inspecting the object polygon by polygon and edge by edge. An edge of a polygon P_i is part of the silhouette if the following condition is true:

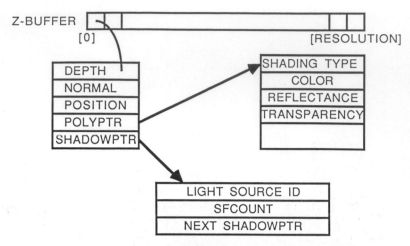

Fig.9.12. Data structure for the scan-line z-buffer with shadows

The ambient light term is then added to I_{total}.

This algorithm can process shadows for nonconvex objects and objects with holes. Examples are shown in Figs.9.13 and 9.14.

(NONEIGHB=0) **or** ((P_i is lighted) **and** (PNONEIGHB is not lighted))

During the building of a shadow polygon, the value of the increment is negative for a back-facing polygon and positive for a front-facing polygon. The absolute value of the increment is 1 for an edge of category 1 and 2 for an edge of category 2.

The display algorithm is a scan-line algorithm. Figure 9.12 shows the data structure used in this algorithm. For each pixel, we store the depth, the normal to the corresponding point, and the position of this point. Two pointers are also stored for each pixel, POLYPTR and SHADOWPTR. POLYPTR is a pointer to the description of the polygon which gives access to the polygon attributes (shading type, color, transparency, reflectance). The SHADOWPTR is a pointer to a list of blocks, each one describing the active light source and a counter.

The algorithm has three steps:

1. All active polygons of an object are scan-converted in the scan-line buffer; information for calculating illumination is stored
2. All active shadow polygons are also scan-converted; for each shadow polygon in front of a visible point, its increment is added to the counter
3. The final intensity of each pixel in the scan-line buffer is computed using the counters $SFCOUNT_i$ in the list accessed via the SHADOWPTR pointer. We have:

$$\text{if } SFCOUNT_i <= 0 \text{ then } I_{total} := I_{total} + I_i$$

The algorithm does not always give good results for transparent objects. The case of an opaque object with a shadow on a transparent object is well-processed (without refraction). However, the shadow produced by a transparent object is incorrect. Only a ray-tracing algorithm would be convenient for this.The camera mode in MIRANIM allows the user to define stereoscopic cameras (see Sect. 2.4.4). In this case, two images are computed, one viewed from the right eye and one viewed from the left. Both images are mixed in a unique image during the scan-line processing using complementary color separation. Shadows may also be produced stereoscopically.

Fig. 9.13. Relax. © 1986 MIRALab, H.E.C. and University of Montreal

Fig. 9.14. Aquarium. © 1986 MIRALab, H.E.C. and University of Montreal

10 Ray-tracing

10.1 Basic ray-tracing algorithm

10.1.1 Principles of ray-tracing

Ray-tracing is an old technique, based on the numerical simulation of geometric optics. Intuitively, it can be seen that light rays can be traced from a light source along their paths until they reach the observer. However, this is a very wasteful approach in computer graphics, because only a few rays coming from a given source actually arrive at the observer (if they ever do). This is why the first algorithms involving ray-tracing carried out the process in the opposite direction, as first suggested by Appel (1968): rays are traced from the observer to the objects in the scene, as shown in Fig. 10.1. The first practical use of the ray-tracing technique in computer animation was the MAGI system (Goldstein and Nagel 1971), which used the algorithm developed by Appel (1968) for solving the hidden-surface problem. Extending this method, MAGI developed the commercial CAD/CAM system SYNTHAVISION. However the most striking application of ray-tracing is the generation of high-quality images involving refraction, reflection, and shadows. The first two implementations of a ray-tracing algorithm for rendering purposes were by Kay and Greenberg (1979) and Whitted (1980).

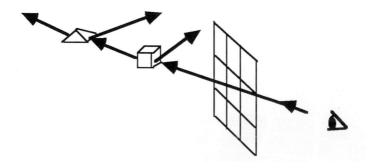

Fig.10.1. The principle of ray-tracing

10.1.2 Kay-Greenberg algorithm

This algorithm is a specific ray-tracing algorithm which takes refraction into account. This means that each ray is modified whenever it strikes a new transparent surface. In a slight modification of the simple algorithm seen in Sect. 6.4.2, the value C is not necessary at the same X, Y location as the new value P, and the transmission factor t is a function of the thickness of the material through which the light ray must travel. The method requires three essential steps:

1. The calculation of refraction vectors
2. The determination of the distortion of the background
3. A strategy for the processing of surfaces

10.1.2.1 Calculation of a refraction vector
Assume a ray of incident direction **I**, passing from the air (index of refraction = 1) to a material with an index of refraction n. A refraction vector **R** is calculated from the Snell-Descartes law using the following formula:

$$\mathbf{R} = \mathbf{S} + \sqrt{1 - |\mathbf{S}|^2}\ \mathbf{N} \tag{10.1}$$

where **N** is the normal vector and **S** is a vector such that $|\mathbf{S}|$ is the sine of the refraction vector and is calculated as:

$$\mathbf{S} = \frac{1}{n}(\mathbf{I} - (\mathbf{I} \cdot \mathbf{N})\ \mathbf{N}) \tag{10.2}$$

10.1.2.2 Distortion of the background
Because of refraction, it is necessary to determine where a ray emerges from the material, given its entering location and direction. To trace the path of a ray through thick material, Kay and Greenberg use the following process:

1. Find a unit vector **U** that defines the direction of the refracted ray by using an approximation of the Snell-Descartes law
2. Find the distance D that the ray must travel within the transparent material
3. Multiply **U** by D to obtain the DX and DY shift values
4. Add DX and DY to the X, Y location. This gives the location of the sight ray as it emerges from the transparent material

Equation (10.3) shows the calculation of the intensity of a transmitted ray:

$$t = T^D \tag{10.3}$$

where t is the transparency for the path of the current ray, T is the transparency for one unit distance, and D is the number of distance units making up the path through the transparent material.

10.1.2.3 Surface processing
This refraction solution was implemented with a z-buffer algorithm. However, several iterations were required, because the surfaces must be processed in inverse order.

10.1.3 Whitted algorithm

The most general ray-tracing algorithm was developed by Whitted (1980), and it is still considered as the basis of all research in this area.

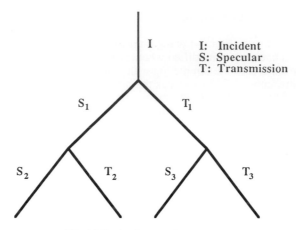

Fig.10.2. An intersection tree

A ray-tracing algorithm consists of shooting pixel rays, computing the intersections of these rays with the objects in the scene, and obtaining the photometric information required to color the current pixel. At each surface struck by a ray, a reflected and/or a refracted ray may be generated.

For each of these new rays, the process must be recursively applied to determine which other surfaces they intersect. For each pixel, an intersection tree must be constructed (see Fig. 10.2).

When the tree has been created, it is traversed, applying an equation at each node to calculate the intensity. With the recursive process, the intensity for the current node is obtained when all its sub-nodes have been evaluated.

The equation applied at each node to calculate the intensity was originally the Whitted illumination model, which was proposed in the same article (Whitted 1980), but other illumination models may also be used, such as the Hall-Greenberg model (see Sect. 7.2.3)

Whitted also introduces bounding spheres to accelerate the intersection tests (see Sect. 11.2.2) and shows how to calculate intersections for polyhedra (see Sect. 10.2) and patches (see Sect. 10.3). He includes antialiasing processing as an integral part of the visibility calculations using a technique similar to the Catmull (1974) subdivision (see Sect. 5.7.1).

10.1.4 Ray-tracing problems

Ray-tracing is a very popular technique, because of the super-realistic images that can be produced. However, it also has disadvantages. The major disadvantage is the time needed to generate an image. Another problem is that there is not enough information associated with a ray to perform good antialiasing.

10.1.4.1 Computation time
One important part of the ray-tracing algorithm is the communication of reflected and transmitted illumination information between the elements of the ray tree. Generally, this is implemented using a pushdown ray stack. Following Kajiya (1983), a skeleton ray-tracing algorithm using a stack can be written as follows:

```
for each pixel
    emit a ray
    push it onto the stack
    while ray stack is not empty do
        for each object
            if no intersection then
                color with background
                exit
            else
                color pixel with the current ray
                pop ray
                generate and push reflection, refraction, and illumination ray
    write the pixel
```

We see that the heart of a ray-tracing algorithm lies in its intersection algorithm. Whitted (1980) stated that up to 95% of CPU time in computing a ray-traced image is spent on the intersection calculations. Note that a comparison of ray-tracing with other techniques such as depth buffer and scan-line algorithms has been carried out by Schoeler and Fournier (1986) displaying scenes on the same hardware.

Various approaches have been attempted to speed up ray-tracing. They may be classified into two categories:

1. Speed up the intersection process itself
2. Reduce the number of ray-object intersection calculations

Various general methods are detailed in the next chapter. However, several authors have also proposed specific algorithms to calculate efficiently the intersection of a ray with various objects: quadrics, polyhedra, algebraic surfaces, parametric surfaces, objects defined by sweeping. The most important algorithms are discussed in Sects. 10.2 - 10.4.

10.1.5 Ray-tracing CSG models

The MAGI original ray-tracing algorithm (Goldstein and Nagel 1971) was based on objects defined by CSG trees. As explained in Sect. 4.4, the CSG model is internally represented as a binary tree. Each leaf node is a primitive object; each intermediate node is the composite object formed by applying the operator (intersection, union, difference) at the node to the subobjects defined by the left and right branches of the node; the root node corresponds to the complete object. Ray-tracing algorithms have one important advantage over scan-line or z-buffer algorithms: they do not need an explicit boundary evaluation of the CSG representation.

The basic CSG ray-tracing algorithm, as described by Roth (1982), works as follows:

Given a ray and a binary tree representing a scene, the ray is classified with respect to the solid. The classification is the information describing the ray-solid intersection. It designates which parts of the ray are inside rather than outside the solid. The process starts at the root of the CSG tree, recursively descends to the bottom, classifies the ray with respect to the primitive solids, and then returns up the tree combining the classifications of the left and right subtrees.

For convex primitives, such as cylinders, cones, boxes, and spheres, there are four possible ray-solid intersection cases:

1. The ray misses the primitive
2. The ray touches the primitive
3. The ray enters and exits the primitive at two different points
4. The ray lies on a face of the primitive

For nonconvex primitives, the classification is more complex.

Ray-object intersection techniques presented in this chapter and techniques of optimization described in the next chapter may be generally applied to CSG models as well as standard surface models. However, reference to CSG models is emphasized in the section on space division (Sect. 11.4).

10.2 Ray-tracing of spheres and polyhedra

10.2.1 Ray-tracing of spheres

Because of the sphere's symmetry, it is a fairly simple process to compute intersections with a ray. An intersection may be tested by finding the minimal distance between the ray and the center of the sphere. If this distance is less or equal to the radius, there is an intersection. For example, suppose the sphere is centered at the point $C = <x_C, y_C, z_C>$ with radius R. The ray is assumed to be given by the following equation:

$$R(t) = R_0 + Vt \qquad (10.4)$$

where $R_0 = <x_0, y_0, z_0>$ is the origin and $V = <x_V, y_V, z_V>$ is a unit vector pointing in the direction of the ray. In Cartesian coordinates, Eq. (10.4) may be rewritten as:

$$<x,y,z> = <x_0 + x_V t, \ y_0 + y_V t, \ z_0 + z_V t> \qquad (10.5)$$

The distance d between C and the ray may be expressed in terms of t using Eq. (10.5):

$$d^2 = (x-x_C)^2 + (y-y_C)^2 + (z-z_C)^2 = (x_0 + x_V t - x_C)^2 + (y_0 + y_V t - y_C)^2 + (z_0 + z_V t - z_C)^2 \qquad (10.6)$$

By setting the derivative equal to zero, we obtain the value t_0 corresponding to the minimum distance:

$$t_0 = -\frac{x_V(x_0 - x_C) + y_V(y_0 - y_C) + z_V(z_0 - z_C)}{|V|^2} \qquad (10.7)$$

The minimum distance d_0 is obtained by substituting t_0 into Eq. (10.6).
The ray intersects the sphere only if:

$$d_0^2 \leq R^2 \qquad (10.8)$$

The intersection points may be easily obtained by solving the quadratic equation:

$$d^2 = R^2 \qquad (10.9)$$

With a sphere centered at the origin, the calculations require only a few floating point operations, so the sphere is often used as a primitive to model more complex objects like ellipsoids. Moreover, bounded spheres are often used to perform preliminary intersection tests on complex objects (see Sect. 11.2.2).

10.2.2 Ray-tracing of polyhedra

For polygonal-based surfaces, the point of intersection between the ray and the plane of each polygon is first calculated. Then, the algorithm checks whether the point is in the interior of the polygon using one of the tests shown in Sect. 5.2.3.

10.3 Ray-tracing of algebraic and parametric surfaces

10.3.1 Ray-tracing of implicit and algebraic surfaces

10.3.1.1 Implicit surfaces

Hanrahan (1983) describes a general method for displaying any analytic surface by ray-tracing. The surface is assumed to satisfy the equation:

$$F(x,y,z) = 0 \tag{10.10}$$

By substituting for the x,y,z coordinates the Cartesian ray Eq. (10.5), we obtain a new equation in the single variable t:

$$F^*(t) = 0 \tag{10.11}$$

The lowest positive solution t_0 of this equation corresponds to the first physical intersection which is the closest point to the anchor. The coordinates of the point may be obtained by substituting t_0 into Eq. (10.5). The incoming ray may be split into additional rays and recursively traced, or an intensity value may be computed. For this, the surface normal is required; it may be calculated by substituting the coordinates of the intersection point into the following equation:

$$N = <\frac{\partial F}{\partial x}, \frac{\partial F}{\partial y}, \frac{\partial F}{\partial z}> \mid_{F=0} \tag{10.12}$$

This general method works only if F* may be derived from F and the first positive solution of Eq. (10.11) may be calculated.

10.3.1.2 Algebraic surfaces

The method works particularly well for algebraic surfaces. An algebraic surface is an implicit surface defined by the equation:

$$P(X,Y,Z) = \sum_{ijk} a_{ijk} X^i Y^j Z^k = 0 \tag{10.13}$$

If we substitute the Cartesian ray Eq. (10.5), we obtain a polynomial equation in t which can be solved by various methods of numerical analysis:

$$P^*(t) = \sum_{i=0}^{d} a_i t^i \tag{10.14}$$

Hanrahan (1983) describes a method for automatically deriving the equation of intersection between the ray and the surface using a symbolic algebra system written in LISP.

Another approach (Faux and Pratt 1979) consists of representing the ray as the intersection of two planes given by the following implicit equations:

$$a_1x+b_1y+c_1z+d_1 = 0 \qquad\qquad a_2x+b_2y+c_2z+d_2 = 0 \qquad (10.15)$$

With Eqs. (10.13) and (10.15), a polynomial equation in one of the coordinates may be obtained. Once the solution for one of the coordinates is found, the other two can be derived using Eq. (10.15).

10.3.1.3 Ray-tracing of Steiner patches

The Steiner patch is the simplest free-form surface, defined by functions $x(s,t)$, $y(s,t)$, and $z(s,t)$. Sederberg and Anderson (1984) show that Steiner patches may be easily ray-traced for two reasons:

1. A Steiner patch may be expressed by an implicit algebraic equation as in Eq. (10.10)
2. The parameter of a point known to lie on the Steiner surface can be computed using closed-form rational polynomial equations in x, y, and z

Steiner patches can be defined by a Bézier control graph consisting of six control points on a warped triangle—one control point on each corner and one along each edge. A weight w_{ij} is assigned to each control point and the surface is defined by:

$$S\ (s,t,u) = \frac{\displaystyle\sum_{i+j\leq2}\Omega_{ij}\ P_{ij}}{\displaystyle\sum_{i+j\leq2}\Omega_{ij}} \qquad (10.16)$$

where:

$$\Omega_{ij} = \frac{2!}{i!\ j!\ (2\text{-}i\text{-}j)!}\ s^i\ t^j\ (u\text{-}s\text{-}t)^{2\text{-}i\text{-}j}\ w_{ij} \qquad (10.17)$$

An essential feature of a Steiner surface (unbounded Steiner patch) is that it is a degree four surface containing a triple point **TP** at the intersection of three double lines. Therefore, for a Steiner surface defined by homogeneous parametric equations in s, t, and u, with each ratio $\frac{s}{u}$ and $\frac{t}{u}$ there corresponds exactly one line that connects that point to the triple point. Using this property, Sederberg and Anderson define such a line as the intersection of two planes P and Q whose orientations vary with s, t, and u. They derive two sets of equations with 12 unknowns each. The algorithm for ray-tracing a surface S is then as follows:

Compute the coefficients of a pair of two parameter families of planes containing **TP**
Compute the variable point on the surface corresponding to the patch parameters
Determine the inverse equations which compute the parameter values of a point which lies on S
for each ray
Express the inversion equations IE as quartic polynomials in the ray parameter
Set up the quartic polynomial QP whose roots are the ray parameter values which correspond to points of intersection
Find the positive roots of QP
Compute the patch parameters of the point of intersection from IE
Compute the shading using the surface normal obtained by the cross product of two directional derivatives

10.3.1.4 Ray-tracing of deformed surfaces

Barr (1986) proposes methods for ray-tracing differentiable surfaces by considering them as deformations of flat sheets. The intersection problem is converted to a new coordinate system in which the surfaces are flat and the rays are bent. For a parametric surface $S(u,v)$, Barr introduces a difference space (D-space) by choosing $D(u,v,t)$ as:

$$D(u,v,t) = S(u,v) - (R_0 + Vt) \tag{10.18}$$

where $R_0 + Vt$ comes from the ray Eq. (10.4).

The D-space is a deformation of a U-space, which is the parameter space. In U-space, 3D difference vectors $<D_1,D_2,D_3>$ are obtained as functions of u, v, and t via Eq. (10.18). In D-space, parametric values of $\begin{bmatrix} u \\ v \\ t \end{bmatrix}$ are obtained as functions of D_1, D_2, and D_3.

The principle of the method is as follows: in D-space, the solution is at the origin, where the difference vector is $<0,0,0>$. The Barr method computes the U-space value which corresponds to $<0,0,0>$ in D-space, inverting Eq. (10.18). This gives our goal:—the intersection values of u, v, and t.

Barr assumes that a point $U = <u_1,v_1,t_1>$ is given as an approximation of the solution values of u, v, and t. He maps U to D-space, by creating the initial difference vector:

$$\mathcal{D}_1 = D(u_1,v_1,t_1) \tag{10.19}$$

from the initial values of u, v, and t.

A difference curve d(s) is then created by connecting $\mathcal{D}_1$ to $<0,0,0>$ in D-space. The inverse image of d(s) is a parametric curve $\mu(s)$ in U-space called the **solution curve**. The end point of $\mu(s)$ which corresponds to $<0,0,0>$ yields the solution values of u, v, and t. Barr (1986) proposes two different choices with their solutions for d(s):

1. $d(s) = s\mathcal{D}_1$ (10.20)

    This curve starts at $\mathcal{D}_1$ when s=1 and ends when s=0 at $<0,0,0>$

2. $d(s,t) = s(t(A-V_0) + B)$ (10.21)

    This curve tends to 0 as s tends to 0

10.3.2 Ray-tracing of parametric surfaces

There are several methods for calculating the intersection between parametric surfaces and rays:
1. Whitted algorithm for bicubic patches (see Sect. 10.1.3)
2. Kajiya algorithm for rational bivariate polynomials (see Sect. 10.3.2.2)
3. Steinberg algorithm for Coons surfaces (see Sect. 10.3.2.3)
4. Sederberg algorithm for Steiner patches (see Sect. 10.3.1.3)
5. Toth algorithm for any parametric surface (see Sect. 10.3.2.4)
6. Joy-Bethabhotla method for surface patches (see Sect. 10.3.2.5)
7. Sweeney-Bartels algorithm for free-form B-spline surfaces (see Sect. 10.3.3.6)

10.3.2.1 Whitted recursive method
In this method, Whitted (1980) generates bounding spheres for each patch. If the bounding sphere is pierced by a ray, then the patch is subdivided into subpatches and bounding spheres are produced for each subpatch. The process continues until the intersected bounding sphere is smaller than a predefined minimum or no more bounding spheres are intersected. This algorithm is similar to the one proposed by Catmull (1975). The method of using a hierarchy of bounding spheres has been generalized by Rubin and Whitted (1980) in a method whereby the object space is represented entirely by a hierarchical data structure consisting of bounding volumes. More details on bounding spheres may be found in Sect. 11.2.2.1.

10.3.2.2 Kajiya algebraic method
Kajiya (1982) transforms the problem of computing a ray-patch intersection into the problem of intersecting two six-degree algebraic curves. The solution to this problem is given by Bezout's theorem (Walker 1950).

10.3.2.3 Steinberg algorithm for Coons surfaces
With bicubic patches, the determination of the point intersection requires the solution of an equation of degree as high as 18. Steinberg (1984) proposes an alternative approach to this problem that requires only biquadratic patches. The method is based on Coons surfaces as described by Eq. (3.33). The basic idea is to split the domains of the parameters u and v at the midpoint. The vector $P(k,t)$ is represented by two quadratics $P_0(k,t)$, $0 \leq t \leq \frac{1}{2}$ and $P_1(k,t)$, $\frac{1}{2} \leq t \leq 1$ with the following conditions:

$$P_0(k,\tfrac{1}{2}) = P_1(k,\tfrac{1}{2})$$

$$P'_0(k,\tfrac{1}{2}) = P'_1(k,\tfrac{1}{2}) \tag{10.22}$$

The blending functions are:

$$F_0(t) = 1 - 2t^2 \quad \text{for} \quad 0 \leq t \leq \tfrac{1}{2}$$

$$F_0(t) = 2(1 - t)^2 \quad \text{for} \quad \tfrac{1}{2} \leq t \leq 1 \tag{10.23}$$

$$F_1(t) = 2t^2 \quad \text{for} \quad 0 \leq t \leq \tfrac{1}{2}$$

$$F_1(t) = 1 - 2(1-t)^2 \quad \text{for} \quad \tfrac{1}{2} \leq t \leq 1$$

Using ray Eq. (10.4), we may express the ray-intercept equation as:

$$S(u,v) = R_0 + Vt \tag{10.24}$$

A direct algebraic method (see Sect. 10.3.1) involves reducing the vector Eq. (10.24) to one equation in one unknown. In our biquadratic case, we may rewrite the equation of the surface as:

$$S(u,v) = T(v) + U(v) u + W(v) u^2 \tag{10.25}$$

where T, U, and W are quadratic vector polynomials.

By using Eqs. (10.24) and (10.25) and eliminating u, we obtain an eight-degree polynomial in v.

10.3.2.4 Toth general method
For surfaces of the form $S(u,v)$, Faux and Pratt (1979) describe how the intersection is obtained as the simultaneous solution of the three nonlinear equations given by the vectorial equation:

$$S(u,v) - \mathbf{V}t - \mathbf{R_0} = 0 \qquad (10.26)$$

This equation can be solved using a method such as the Newton-Raphson method. However, problems occur when there is no intersection or the ray touches the surface. This problem may be solved by minimizing the function $S(u,v) - \mathbf{V}t - \mathbf{R_0}^2$ with respect to u, v, and t.

Toth (1985) also proposes solving the ray surface intersection problem directly using multivariate Newton iteration. His algorithm overcomes the problem of finding a starting point for the Newton iteration by employing techniques from interval analysis. Each iteration of the interval Newton algorithm provides an error bound for the actual root of the system. Then, a binary search scheme identifies regions of parameter space in which the Newton method converges.

10.3.2.5 Joy-Bethabhotla method

Joy and Bethabhotla (1986) describe a new algorithm for ray-tracing parametric surface patches using a quasi-Newton iteration to solve the ray-surface intersection problem. Given the parametric surface $S(u,v)$ and a ray defined by Eq. (10.4), we may compute:

$$F(u,v) = |\mathbf{W}|^2 - (\mathbf{W \cdot V})^2 \qquad (10.27)$$

where

$$\mathbf{W} = S(u,v) - \mathbf{R_0} \qquad (10.28)$$

The function F has essential properties:

1. If a local minimum of F is zero, then this corresponds to a point where the ray intersects the surface
2. Those points where F is a minimum and F>0 indicate that the ray misses the surface by a finite distance

The local minimum is found by using quasi-Newton methods (see Joy and Bethabhotla 1986), which are a generalization of the Toth method.

10.3.3.6 Sweeney-Bartels algorithm for B-spline surfaces

Sweeney and Bartels (1986) describe an algorithm to render B-spline surfaces using ray-tracing. Their method starts with two preprocessing steps:

1. A refinement process consisting of replacing the B-spline representation as a weighted average of the given control vertices with a representation as an average of more control vertices that lie closer to the surface. This refinement process is performed using the Oslo algorithm (Riesenfeld et al. 1980; see Sect. 3.5.4)
2. A second step involving building a tree of nested rectilinear bounding boxes on top of the refined vertices

The leaf nodes of the tree of bounding boxes contain starting values for a Newton iteration. The Kajiya (1983a) algorithm is used to select candidate leaf nodes for further processing by the Newton iteration routine.

For each ray, a linked list of active nodes is maintained by increasing the distance from the ray origin to the closest intersection with the bounding box of the root of the attached subtree.

The core of the algorithm is as follows:

Choose the closest node on the active list and remove it
if the root of the attached subtree is interior to the tree
then
    Consider the four children
if the ray hits the bounding box of a child
then
    Attach the child to an active node
    Sort the node into the active node list
if the root of the attached subtree is a leaf
then
    Use the contained <u,v> parameter values to initiate a Newton process

The Newton iteration finds a pair <u,v> such that a point P(u,v) on the B-spline surface is also a point in a given ray.

10.4 Ray-tracing of surfaces defined by sweeping

10.4.1 Surfaces defined by sweeping

As previously described in Sect. 4.3, complex objects may be generated by sweeping an object along a trajectory. In this section, we shall consider the particular case where the object is a surface. The swept surface to be rendered using ray-tracing may be converted into a collection of polygons, and the technique explained in Sect. 10.2.2 may be applied. However, polygons are apparent and the technique is extremely expensive. More efficient algorithms have been developed which take advantage of the geometric and topological properties of the sweep-defined surfaces. In the next sections, we shall study four special cases of sweep-defined objects:

1. Surfaces defined by a translational sweep — prisms, cylinders
2. Surfaces defined by a conic sweep — cones
3. Surfaces defined by a rotational sweep — surfaces of revolution
4. Surfaces defined by sweeping a sphere

In the latter case, the sweeping operation is somewhat special because the swept object is not a planar contour but a 3D object.

10.4.2 Ray-tracing of surfaces defined by translational sweeping

A surface S_T defined by translational sweeping is obtained by translating a planar curve C along a vector **T** for a distance d, as shown in Fig.4.5. As already stated in Sect. 4.3.2, the plane P_0 of the curve is called the **base plane** and the plane P_1 at a distance d is called the **cap plane**.
    Kajiya (1983a) proposes a method in six steps:

1. Find the intersection point of the ray R with the base plane P_0 and the cap plane P_1
2. Project these points down onto the base plane P_0
3. Project the ray R onto the base plane P_0 to give the 2D ray R'
4. Find the intersections of R' and the contour C
5. Calculate normals at intersection points
6. Transform the results back to view coordinates

Kajiya applies this method using a contour described by a strip tree (Ballard 1981); van Wijk (1984a) similarly describes how to generate objects defined by translational sweeping of cubic splines. The main difference between the two approaches lies in the determination of the intersections (step 4).

10.4.2.1 Kajiya approach

Intersections between the projected ray and the contour are calculated using **strip trees** (Ballard 1981), a hierarchical structure which represents the curve at varying resolutions. The strip tree associated with the curve C is a tree with nodes N(r,c), where c is a portion of C and r a bounding rectangle for c. This bounding rectangle is given by a baseline b and two widths w_1 and w_2. Bounding rectangles are chosen in such a way that each edge of r touches at least one point of c (see Fig.10.3) and the subtrees of node N subdivide c on a point which touches the edge.

The strip tree is generated by the following procedure:

1. Choose as baseline the line segment from the first to the last point of C
2. Scan C for the points m and M corresponding to the minimum and maximum signed distance away from the baseline
3. Divide C at m and M
4. Compute the subtrees recursively

Intersecting the 2D ray R' with the curve defined by the strip tree is straightforward using a recursive process.

10.4.2.2 van Wijk approach

Van Wijk (1984a) uses the local axis frame first introduced by Roth (1982). The object is translated, rotated, and scaled in such a way that the translational vector T is in the z direction, and the distance d is 1. Consequently, the base plane is the plane z=0 and the cap plane is the plane z=1.

The contour is given by a piecewise polynomial description of splines, implemented as a linear list of segments defining the pieces of the curve. Each segment contains the degree of two polynomials u(s) and v(s), their coefficients, and a bounding rectangle for the piece of the curve.

The two values of the parameter t in the ray Eq. (10.4) corresponding to the intersections with the base and cap planes are denoted by t_{min} (smaller value) and t_{max} (larger value).

Consider now the Cartesian equation of the ray (Eq. 10.5). The projection of the ray on the base plane is given by:

$$y_V u - x_V v + x_V y_0 - y_V x_0 = 0 \qquad (10.29)$$

A first rectangle test is performed to detect whether the ray intersects the segment. Then the intersection is calculated by substituting the polynomials u(s) and v(s) of the segment into Eq. (10.29), resulting in a degree 3 polynomial P(s). Intersection points are found by finding the values of the parameter t of the ray Eq. (10.4) corresponding to roots s_0 of the equation P(s) = 0:

$$t = \frac{u(s_0) - x_0}{x_V} \qquad (10.30)$$

with the conditions: $t > t_{min}$ and $0 < s_0 < 1$

A sorted array of n intersection points I[i] is obtained and valid points are then selected using the following algorithm which deletes intersection points beyond the base plane and with the base or cap planes:

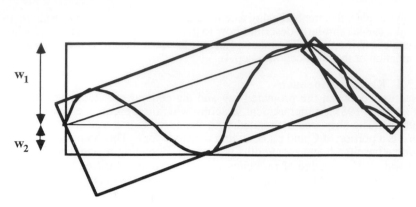

Fig.10.3. Bounding rectangles

if odd(n-i_{max}) **then** n:=i_{max} **else** n:=i_{max}-1;
if odd(n) **then**
    n:=n-1
    for i:=1 **to** n **do** I[i]:=I[i+1]

i_{max} is the index of the point corresponding to t_{max} (assumed to be the intersection with the base plane) in the array I.

10.4.3 Ray-tracing of surfaces defined by conic sweeping

A conic sweep corresponds to a translational sweep combined with a scaling of the contour. Van Wijk (1984a) uses a local axis frame and a strategy similar to the approach for translational sweeping. A point <x,y,z> on a side plane of the object is defined by the equations:

$$x v = y u \quad \text{and} \quad x = z u \tag{10.31}$$

By substituting the value x,y,z from the ray Eq. (10.5) into Eq. (10.31), we obtain:

$$t = \frac{y_0 u - x_0 v}{x_v v - y_v u} \tag{10.32}$$

$$x_0 + x_v t = (z_0 + z_v t) u \tag{10.33}$$

By eliminating t, the following equation is obtained:

$$(y_0 z_v - z_0 y_v)u - (x_0 z_v - z_0 x_v)v + (x_0 y_v - y_0 x_v) = 0 \tag{10.34}$$

Using this linear equation in u and v, the intersection points with the projected ray may be obtained in the same way as for translational sweeping.

10.4.4 Ray-tracing of surfaces defined by rotational sweeping

Surfaces generated by rotational sweeping (surfaces of revolution) are obtained by rotating a curve C around an axis of rotation **A**. As already discussed in Sect. 4.3.3, two elements are important in such a surface: the base point B and the radius function $\rho(s)$, as shown in Fig.4.6.

Two approaches to the ray-tracing of these surfaces have been reported:

1. Surface of revolution based on the rotation of a curve described by a strip tree
2. Surface of revolution based on the rotation of a curve described by bicubic splines

10.4.4.1 Strip tree approach
Kajiya (1983a) proposes a method in which a cut plane π is defined as passing through the ray and parallel to the axis of revolution. The normal n_π to the plane π is given by the cross product:

$$n_\pi = \mathbf{A} \times \mathbf{V} \qquad (10.35)$$

where **V** is the director vector of the ray as in Eq. (10.4).

Intersections between the ray and the two curves formed by intersecting the cut plane with the surfaces are then computed using a strip tree approach similar to the method described in Sect. 10.4.2. To simplify the intersection process, Kajiya uses an algorithm in the $<x^2, y>$ space. The two curves Ω^i representing the intersection of the surface with the plane π are given by the equations:

$$\Omega^i_x = \rho_x - d^2 \quad \text{and} \quad \Omega^i_y = \rho_y \qquad (10.36)$$

where ρ is the square of the original radius curve and d the perpendicular distance of the base point B to the plane π.

Instead of Eq. (10.5), rays are considered as curved using the following equation:

$$R(t) = <(x_0 + x_V\, t)^2, y_0 + y_V\, t> \qquad (10.37)$$

With these equations, the intersection with an extent box may be recursively found. The distance from the ray origin is obtained by solving a degree 4 equation in t. The exact intersection point is then found by substituting in Eq. (10.5).

10.4.4.2 Bicubic spline approach
The van Wijk (1984a) method is similar to the methods used for translational and conic sweeps. The local coordinate system is chosen such that the local v-axis corresponds to the Z-axis and the local U-axis rotates in the XY-plane. The ray is then projected onto the uv plane. As v=z, the value of t corresponding to the intersection point $\mathbf{P} = <x,y,z>$ of the ray with the UV-plane is:

$$t = \frac{v - z_0}{z_V} \qquad (10.38)$$

As the distance from **P** to the uv plane is u, we may write using Eq. (10.5):

$$u = (x_0 + x_V t)^2 + (y_0 + y_V t)^2 \qquad (10.39)$$

Fig.10.4. Glass. Courtesy of J.J. van Wijk, Delft University of Technology, made with the RAYMO
system

From Eqs. (10.38) and (10.39), we obtain:

$$(x_V{}^2+y_V{}^2)v^2+2[-z_0(x_V{}^2+y_V{}^2)+z_V(x_Vx_0+y_Vy_0)]+(x_Vz_0-z_Vx_0)^2$$
$$+(y_Vz_0-z_Vy_0)^2-z_V{}^2u^2=0 \qquad (10.40)$$

By substituting the two spline polynomials into Eq. (10.40), an equation of sixth
degree is obtained. This has to be solved numerically using a method such as the
Laguerre method. Figure 10.4 shows an image generated using this method.
    Bouville et al. (1984) describe a similar method for rendering surfaces of
revolution using ray-tracing. The curve is generated by the B-spline technique and
each cubic section depends on four control points. In the intersection computations,
Benstein-Bézier polynomials are used instead of B-splines, because Bézier control
points are closer to the curve. An example is shown in Fig.10.5.

10.4.5 Ray-tracing of objects defined by sweeping spheres

A series of interesting shapes may be obtained by sweeping a sphere of varying radius
along a 3D trajectory. Van Wijk (1984) formally describes such shapes and proposed
a method to ray-trace them.

10.4.5.1 Object defined by sweeping spheres
Consider a sphere defined by its center $\mathbf{K}=<x_K,y_K,z_K>$ and its radius r and a trajectory
$\Omega(u)$, where u is a parameter such as $u_{min} < u < u_{max}$. When a sphere is swept from

Fig.10.5. A ray-traced image Designer: E.Gihoire. Software: C.C.E.T.T. © GRAVI Productions

$\Omega(u_{min})$ to $\Omega(u_{max})$ along the trajectory $\Omega(u)$ with a radius $r(u)$, a family of spheres is defined by the equation $f(\mathbf{P},u) - 0$, where $f(\mathbf{P},u)$ is defined as:

$$f(\mathbf{P},u) = | \mathbf{P} - \mathbf{K}(u)|^2 - r(u)^2 \tag{10.41}$$

$\mathbf{P} = <x,y,z>$ is a point of the generated object.

10.4.5.2 Ray intersection

The intersection is calculated by substituting the ray Eq. (10.4) into Eq. (10.41); we obtain:

$$f(t,u) = |\mathbf{V}|^2 t^2 + 2(\mathbf{R_0} - \mathbf{K}(u))\cdot\mathbf{V}t + |\mathbf{R_0} - \mathbf{K}(u)|^2 - r(u)^2 \tag{10.42}$$

The equation $f(t,u) = 0$ defines an infinite set of spheres intersected by the ray. Where this equation has coincident roots for t, t is defined as a function of u. It may be shown (van Wijk 1984) that the value of t as a function of u has a minimum or maximum value for an intersection point of a line with the surface. Minimum and maximum values of t(u) are obtained by implicit differentiation of f(t,u).

If only the first intersection point is required, the smallest value of t has to be taken. Otherwise, a validation (described by van Wijk 1984) is necessary.

Bronsvoort and Klok (1985) describe an algorithm for ray-tracing generalized cylinders, that is objects defined by sweeping a 2D contour along a 3D trajectory.

10.5   Depth of field and motion blur

10.5.1 Lens and aperture camera model

Potmesil and Chakravarty (1981, 1982) describe a technique for modeling the effects of a lens and aperture in a virtual camera. Their model allows the generation of synthetic images which have a depth of field and can be focused on an arbitrary plane. Optical characteristics of a lens can also be incorporated. This approach is quite interesting in computer animation (Magnenat-Thalmann and Thalmann 1985b), because it allows selective highlighting through focusing or other optical effects and permits special techniques like fade-in, fade-out, lens distortions, and filtering to be simulated. Image synthesis is based on the generation of point samples of light intensity.

10.5.1.1 Generation of point samples
Point samples of light intensity are generated by the ray-tracing hidden-surface algorithm (Whitted 1980), described in Sect. 10.1.3. From these samples, two types of processing are possible:

1. Direct conversion into a raster image using a pinhole camera model similar to the model described in Chap. 2
2. Conversion by a focus processor into a raster image that is focused and has a depth of field

For an image computed using the pinhole camera model, the 3D scene is sampled at the four corners of each pixel (assumed square). A ray from a sample point in the image plane to the center of projection is extended into the scene and intersected with the nearest surface element. The intensity of the sample point and the maintenance of information about reflected and refracted rays in a tree are processed as in the Whitted algorithm (see Sect. 10.1.3). The intensity of a pixel is computed by averaging its four point samples. Antialiasing is performed by recursive subdivision of pixels into 2x2 regions and repetition of the sampling and averaging processes at the four corners of each new region. Finally, the intensity of the pixel is obtained by a weighted sum of the intensity of the regions.

For focused images, sampled values are saved in a file from nodes of the shading tree. This file will be the input file for the focus processor. A sample i consists of the values x''_i, y''_i, z'_i, r_i, g_i, b_i, id_i where

- x''_i and y''_i are coordinates of the sampled point in the image plane coordinate system
- z'_i is the accumulated distance along the camera's optical axis of the currently intersected 3D surface point; z'_i is expressed in the 3D coordinates system
- r_i, g_i, b_i are the RGB values contributed by the currently intersected 3D surface point
- id_i is a identification number

10.5.1.2 Focus processor
Image (de)focusing is obtained by introducing a circle of confusion as a projection of a point onto the image plane. Diffraction effects are studied by determining the light intensity distribution within the circle of confusion for unfocused points.

The raster image is generated using the sampled values, the geometric camera model, and the lens and aperture parameters.

The focus processor models the output raster image as an array of square pixels. A pixel $<j,k>$ covers an image area $<x''_j,y''_k> x <x''_{j+1},y''_{k+1}>$. The final intensity $q(j,k)$ of pixel $<j,k>$ is computed separately for each primary color using the following equation:

$$q(j,k) = \frac{\sum_{i=1}^{N} f(x''_i,y''_i)\ h\ (j,k,x''_i,y''_i,z'_i)}{\sum_{i=1}^{N} h\ (j,k,x''_i,y''_i,z'_i)} \tag{10.43}$$

N is the number of input samples in the image. The input function $f(x''_i,y''_i)$ at point $<x''_i,y''_i>$ is a delta function of magnitude equal to the color values r_i, g_i, b_i. The impulse-response function h is the point spread function (PSF), explained in Potmesil and Chakravarty (1982); it gives the response of the system over the area of pixel $<j,k>$ due to the input function $f(x''_i,y''_i)$. It is calculated as the integral of the intensity-distribution function I over pixel $<j,k>$:

$$h\ (j,k,x''_i,y''_i,z'_i) = \int_{x''_i}^{x''_{i+1}} \int_{y''_k}^{y''_{k+1}} I\ (z'_i, \sqrt{(x''-x''_i)^2+(y''-y''_i)^2})\ dx''dy'' \tag{10.44}$$

The focus processor uses the lens and aperture parameters to compute tables of the h functions at equally spaced intervals z' between the nearest and the farthest points in the image. Values of the h function are calculated using Eq. (10.44) at the z' coordinate of the table for all the pixels within the square area circumscribing the circle of confusion. Then the processor distributes the intensity of each input point to output pixels according to the values stored in the table nearest to the sample z' depth. Intensities are calculated using Eq. (10.43).

Figure 10.6 shows an image generated using this method.

10.5.2 Motion blur

Potmesil and Chakravarty (1983) propose an extension of their model to motion blur by redefining the two stages of image generation as the ray-tracing step and a motion blur step.

10.5.2.1 Ray-tracing step

The ray-tracing hidden-surface program generates intensity sample points of an instantaneous image, identifying points which are in motion and giving the image path of the projected motion. In fact, what is necessary for the motion-blur step is the list of samples of an image frame with a list of motion paths of the individual objects, time of the frame exposure t_{frame}, and the exposure duration T_{frame}.

10.5.2.2 Motion-blur processor

A motion-blur processor generates motion blur by convolving moving points with optical system-transfer functions; these functions are derived from the path and the velocity of the objects and the exposure time of the virtual camera. The processor separates sample points of a moving object with the same path $r'(t)$ into a raster image i_1. Motion blur PSF h (x'',y'',x',y') is computed as a raster image i_2 from t_{frame}, T_{frame} and the path $r'(t)$ by the following equation:

a   b

Fig.10.6. Image of a transparent carafe generated with **a** the pinhole camera model and **b** the lens and aperture camera model by Michael Potmesil, Rensselaer Polytechnic Institute and Indranil Chakravarty, Schlumberger-Doll Research

$$h\ (x'',y'',x',y') = \frac{1}{\sqrt{(\frac{dx'(t)}{dt})^2 + (\frac{dy'(t)}{dt})^2}} \qquad (10.45)$$

The images i_1 and i_2 are then convolved into a blurred image i_1*i_2. An example is shown in Fig.10.7.

10.6   Antialiasing, stochastic sampling, and distributed ray-tracing

10.6.1 Antialiasing and stochastic sampling

Aliasing is one of the major problem of ray-tracing. To avoid it, oversampling methods as described in Chap. 8 may be applied. As previously shown in Sect. 8.2, the correct display value at a pixel p is a weighted integral of shades in the neighborhood of the pixel:

$$p = \int_A h(x,y)\ I(x,y)\ d(x,y) \qquad (10.46)$$

where A is the pixel area of the function I(x,y) which is the non-filtered image and h(x,y) is the filter.

As the convolution integral Eq. (10.46) cannot be easily calculated directly, conventional oversampling methods use a regular array of points to approximate the ideal image.

Typical conventional oversampling is calculated as:

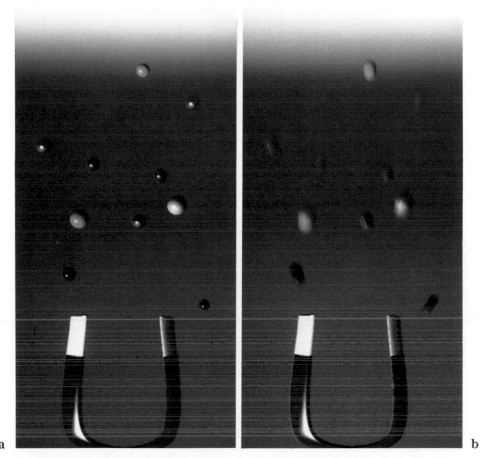

Fig.10.7 a,b. Magnet attracting metallic balls. **a** Instantaneous exposure; **b** Finite-time exposure. By Michael Potmesil, AT&T Bell Laboratories and Indranil Chakravarty, Schlumberger-Doll Research

$$v = \sum_i w_i \, I \, (x_i, y_i) \qquad\qquad (10.47)$$

where $I\,(x_i, y_i)$ are sampled values of the nonfiltered image at predefined positions $<x_i, y_i>$.

As stated by Dippé and Wold (1985), this approach tends to create false patterns that are easily perceived. For example, with an oversampling as in Fig.10.8 (see Purgathofer 1986), the method will completely fail for a set of regular patterns with a high image frequency because of Shannon's sampling theorem (Pavlidis 1982).

By randomizing the locations of the sample, irregular patterns may be generated. This means that stochastic methods can be used to generate different classes of irregular sampling patterns. In summary, regular sampling patterns produce consistent errors, and stochastic sampling produces inconsistent errors thus avoiding regular patterns.

.01	.02	.04	.02	.01
.02	.05	.08	.05	.02
.04	.08	.12	.08	.04
.02	.05	.08	.05	.02
.01	.02	.04	.02	.01

Fig.10.8. Examples of weights for supersampling

For ray-tracing, stochastic sampling means stochastically selecting viewing rays. A stochastic set of points in the image is chosen, the corresponding rays are cast, and these rays are traced recursively throughout the scene in the conventional manner (see Sect. 10.1.3).

Dippé and Wold (1985) propose the use of two different stochastic sampling techniques—Poisson sampling and jittered sampling.

For Poisson sampling, the sample points are uniformly distributed over the image using standard pseudorandom methods. The total number of samples is the product of the sampling rate and the image size in each dimension. Minimum distance Poisson samples are approximated by generating uniformly distributed sample points but only retaining sample points that satisfy the minimum separation with all previously retained sample points.

For jittered sampling, the jittered sample pattern is derived from a regular pattern calculated in an incremental manner. A pseudorandom jitter is added to each sample point.

Dibbé and Wold use adaptive stochastic sampling; they take an initial set of samples in the region about each pixel. If the error estimate based on these samples is too large, additional samples are placed in the region until the error estimate is sufficiently low.

10.6.2 Distributed ray-tracing

Distributed ray-tracing is a new approach introduced by Cook et al. (1984). They suggest oversampling not only according to pixel area, but also for various other effects at the same time: depth of field, motion blur, fuzzy shadows, translucency, and fuzzy reflections. In this approach, the rays are distributed in time so that rays at different spatial locations are traced at different instants of time.

Mirror reflections are determined by tracing rays from the surface in the direction of the mirror. Blurred reflections may be calculated by distributing the secondary rays about the mirror direction. Similarly, translucency is obtained by distributing the secondary rays about the main direction of the transmitted light. With this translucency, the objects seen through translucent objects are not distinct. Penumbrae, as defined in Sect. 9.6, are also calculated by distributing the secondary rays.

Depth of field is calculated by starting with the traditional ray from the center of the lens through point p on the focal plane. A point q on the surface of the lens is selected and the ray from q to p is traced. This calculation is performed using the focal distance and the diameter D of the lens calculated by:

$$D = \frac{F}{n} \qquad (10.48)$$

where F is the focal length of the lens and n the aperture number.

The motion-blur problem is also solved by distributing the sample points in time. For any complex path of motion, the position of the object may be computed at specific times and changes in visibility and shading are correctly accounted for.

10.6.2.1 Distributed ray-tracing algorithm
The algorithm works as follows:

Choose a time for the ray and move the objects accordingly
Construct a ray from the center of the lens to a point of the screen
Trace a ray from an arbitrary location on the lens to the focal point of the original ray
Determine which object is visible
Calculate the shadows
for each light source, trace a ray from the visible point to an arbitrary location in the light; the number of rays traced to a location in the light should be proportional to the intensity and projected area of that location as seen from the surface
for reflections, trace a ray in an arbitrary direction about the mirror direction from the visible point; the number of rays traced in a specific location should be proportional to the amount of light from that direction that is reflected toward the observer
for transmitted light, trace a ray in an arbitrary direction around the direction of the transmitted light from the visible point; the number of rays traced in a specific location should be proportional to the amount of light from that direction that is transmitted toward the observer

10.6.3 Stochastic sampling in distributing ray-tracing

Cook et al. (1984) have suggested oversampling for various effects at the same time. This oversampling can also be done in a stochastic way. Lee et al. (1985) consider the case of a point X in an n-space A. The convolution integral may be written as:

$$p = \int_A h(X)\, I(X)\, dX \qquad (10.49)$$

Consider X as an n-dimensional random variable with probability density function $h(X)$. Then, the value of the integral in Eq. (10.49) is $E(h(X))$, the expected value of h. Now, let $X_1, X_2, ... X_N$ be independent identically distributed random variables with density function $h(X)$. Consider the following unbiased estimator for $E(h(X))$:

$$h_N = \frac{1}{N} \sum_{i=1}^{N} h(X_i) \qquad (10.50)$$

Lee et al. construct a sampling scheme so that the variances of their estimates

$$VAR(h_N) = E(h_N - E(h(X)))^2 = \frac{E(h^2(X)) - E(h(X))^2}{N} = \frac{VAR(h(X))}{N} \qquad (10.51)$$

throughout the scene are less than or approximately equal to a threshold value T.

As the variance at each point is not known a priori, they use the following approximation S_N^2 for VAR $(h(X))$:

$$S_N^2 = \frac{1}{N} \Sigma \, (h(X_i) - h_N)^2 \tag{10.52}$$

The number χ_β^2 (N-1) is defined in such a way that:

$$\text{Probability } [\frac{N \, S_N^2}{VAR(h(X))} < \chi_\beta^2 \, (N\text{-}1)] = \beta \tag{10.53}$$

The core of the distributed ray-tracing algorithm is as follows:

repeat

Draw samples
Compute and keep the incremental sums of $h(X_i)$ and $h^2(X_i)$

until $\dfrac{S_N^2}{\chi_\beta^2 \, (N\text{-}1)} < T$

The test in Eq. (10.53) is constructed so that:

$$\text{Probability } [\frac{VAR(h(X))}{N}) < \frac{S_N^2}{\chi_\beta^2 \, (N\text{-}1)}] = 1\text{-} \beta \tag{10.54}$$

and so the probability of stopping when $\dfrac{VAR(h(X))}{N} > T$ is less than β.

For the choice of the values T and β, Lee et al. (1986) propose calculating T as follows:

$$T = \frac{M}{\chi_\beta^2 \, (Z\text{-}1)} \tag{10.55}$$

where M is the maximum or worst case variance that will be tolerated for a scene and Z the maximum number of samples to be allowed. Lee et al. also propose precalculating and storing in a table the values of $T \, \chi_\beta^2$ (N-1) for N=1 to Z. The value of β serves to spread the values of the table between 0 and M.

Purgathofer (1986) proposes another approach based on the statistical t-test. Consider N samples X_i, i=1 to N, with a mean m_X and standard deviation s. The true mean of the population lies within an interval of width 2d around m_X with probability Ω if

$$t_{1-\Omega,N-1} \, s \, \frac{1}{\sqrt{n}} \le d \tag{10.56}$$

where t is the tabled value for the t-test with N-1 degrees of freedom and error probability $1-\Omega$. So, if the approximated value of every pixel lies within a 2d-wide interval around the optimal value with probability Ω, this can be computed very simply by incrementing the number of samples until Eq. (10.56) is satisfied. However, Eq. (10.56) is only valid for a large enough N, which implies the calculation of a necessary minimum number of samples by another approach.

10.7 Ray-tracing at MIRALab

10.7.1 Organization of ray-tracing option at MIRALab

Ray-tracing has been implemented at MIRALab using a very classic approach. Ray-tracing coexists in the MIRA-SHADING language with three other display algorithms—wire-frame, scan-line, and z-buffer. This means, for example, that specifications of light sources, transparency or shadows can be carried out by the ray-tracing or the scan-line algorithm. This allows the user to render progressively a 3D scene in the following order:

1. Wire-frame
2. Painter's algorithm
3. z-buffer with constant shading
4. Scan-line with constant shading
5. z-buffer with Gouraud shading
6. Scan-line with Phong shading
7. Ray-tracing

Selection of the display algorithm is performed (for the programmer) by a call to the procedure DISPLAY_ALGORITHM. This procedure initializes a certain number of variables necessary to the display algorithm. An object F in MIRA-SHADING is displayed as soon as a statement **draw** F is called. The action taken by the draw operation is dependent on the display algorithm:

1. For wire-frame and z-buffer algorithms, the **draw** statement consists of writing the object into the frame buffer
2. For scan-line and ray-tracing algorithms, the **draw** statement only inserts the object into a list of objects to be displayed

In this latter case, display processing is itself started by a call to the statement **image**.

10.7.2 Structure of display processing

Display processing may be summarized as shown in Fig.10.9. The procedure zzzzIMAGE (corresponding to the statement **image**) either calls the procedure SCAN_LINE or the procedure RAY_TRACING. Only the latter procedure is described in this section.

The RAY_TRACING procedure is mainly a loop on the pixels corresponding to the current viewport. It calls procedure FPHI to calculate world coordinates corresponding to the current pixel by converting from screen coordinates to viewport coordinates then to window coordinates, and finally to the world coordinates using the values of the viewup vector, the viewplane normal, and the view reference point.

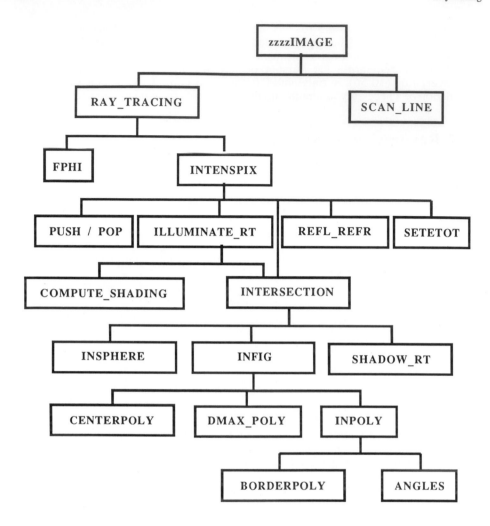

Fig.10.9. Basic organization of ray-tracing in MIRA-SHADING

The procedure INTENSPIX basically works in the same way as the skeleton presented in Sect. 10.1.4. It calculates the total intensity for the pixel and constructs a tree for reflected and refracted rays. It first checks whether the primary ray (received as parameter) intersects an object (procedure INTERSECTION); if there is no intersection, the pixel is colored with the background color.

In case of an intersection, INTENSPIX pushes the ray onto a stack and checks whether there are reflected and refracted rays. These rays are defined and are then also placed on the stack; the direction of the reflected and refracted rays are determined by the procedure REFL_REFR. The procedure then pops the first ray from the stack and repeats the intersection search until one of the following conditions is met:

1. **There is no intersection between the ray and any object**:
   Transmit the background color to the source ray
   Delete the element from the stack
   Pop the next ray

2. **The stack limit is reached**
   Transmit a null intensity using the procedure SETETOT
   Pop the next ray

3. **An intersection has been detected**
   Calculate the intensity at the intersection point using the procedure ILLUMINATE_RT
   Add ambient light and intensity of the refracted and reflected rays generated by the current ray
   Divide by an attenuation factor dependent on the distance
   Transmit the intensity using the procedure SETETOT
   Delete the element on the stack
   Pop the next ray

   Repeat the operations until the stack is empty

The procedure ILLUMINATE_RT computes diffuse and specular contributions, modifies these values using the concentration factor (when the light is a spotlight as defined by Warn), and computes the shadow impact if necessary.

The procedure INTERSECTION is the most important and the most expensive procedure of the ray tracing module. It detects whether there is an intersection between a ray and objects; this test (by the procedure INFIG) is only performed when a test with a bounding sphere (procedure INSPHERE) is positive (see Sect. 11.2.2 for information about bounding spheres). For facet-based objects, the procedure INFIG also uses a preliminary intersection test with the bounding circle (procedure CENTERPOLY and DMAX_POLY) of each facet. The intersection test between the ray and a polygon is performed by the procedure INPOLY, which detects if the ray passes through the border of the polygon (procedure BORDERPOLY) or inside the polygon (using the procedure ANGLES based on the method of angles, described in Sect. 5.2.3). If the shadow option has been selected, INTERSECTION calls SHADOW_RT to add the shadow factor of all intersected objects and returns this shadow value.

11 Optimization techniques for ray-tracing

11.1 Survey of optimization techniques

11.1.1 Classification of techniques

As previously explained in Sect. 10.1.4, various approaches have been developed to speed up ray-tracing. These may be classified into two categories:

1. Methods for speeding up the intersection process itself
2. Methods for reducing the number of ray-object intersection calculations

Several of the techniques presented for saving CPU time also provide elegant solutions to the aliasing for ray-traced images (e.g., cone tracing, beam tracing, and space subdivision methods).

11.1.2 Techniques for speeding up intersection process

11.1.2.1 Software solutions
As previously indicated in Sects. 10.2-10.4, several authors propose specific algorithms for efficiently calculating the intersection of a ray with various objects: quadrics, polyhedra, algebraic surfaces, parametric surfaces, objects defined by sweeping. Another way of reducing the computational expense of ray-traced images is to enclose complex objects with simpler objects, such as spheres or parallelepipeds. These enclosing objects are called bounding volumes. If a ray does not intersect the bounding volume, then the intersection with the complex object does not have to be calculated. Bounding volume techniques are discussed in Sect. 11.2.

11.1.2.2 Hardware solutions
Nishimura et al. (1983) have developed LINKS-1, a parallel pipelined multimicrocomputer system for ray-tracing. With this machine, an image to be generated is divided into several subimages and each of the computers generates one or more subimages independently. LINKS-1 is currently being used for computer-generated films by the Japanese commercial production house TOYO-LINKS.

Plunkett and Bailey (1985) propose the vectorization of a ray-tracing algorithm. This is possible because the intersection calculations belonging to the diffcrent pixels and the intensities of the different pixels are calculated independently. Figure 11.1 shows an image produced using this approach.

Cleary et al. (1986) have analyzed the performance of a multiprocessor algorithm for ray-tracing. They use a cubic and a square array of processors with only local communication between near neighbors.

Fig.11.1. Solid geometric model of a Cincinnati Milacron T3-726 electric robot. By Dave Blunkett/ Mike Dailey, Purdue CADLAB

11.1.3 Techniques for reducing number of ray-object intersection calculations

Two categories of algorithms have been proposed for reducing the number of intersections:

1. Algorithms which extend the concept of a ray (cone tracing and beam tracing) and use the spatial coherence of polygonal environments or the coherence of rays. These are presented in Sect. 11.3
2. Algorithms based on space subdivision; these are discussed in Sect. 11.4

In addition, Hall and Greenberg (1983) have proposed an original method, called **adaptive tree-depth control.**

11.1.4 Adaptive tree-depth control

This method is based on the observation that the percentage of an image that is comprised of reflective and transparent surfaces is generally low. By controlling the depth of the intersection tree during the ray-tracing process, there is a significant computational saving. Hall and Greenberg approximate the upper boundary of the contribution of any node of the tree to the final color of the sample point by considering the intensity of every node on the tree to be maximum. The first node of the tree contributes 100% to the final color of the sample point. The maximum contribution of the children for any parent node may be evaluated by computing the contributions for the reflected and transmitted children. By multiplying the approximate maximum contributions, we can compute the maximum cumulative contribution of the child node to the sample point. The depth of the tree may then be adaptively controlled by establishing a cutoff contribution threshold.

11.2 Bounding volumes

11.2.1 Bounding volumes and clusters

Determining the intersections of a ray with a particular object may be computationally very expensive. One simple way of eliminating the unnecessary intersections is to perform a preliminary intersection test of the ray with a **bounding volume** (also called an **extent**) of the object. If there is no intersection between the ray and the bounding volume, it is certain that the ray does not intersect the object. Otherwise, an expensive test is required. This technique works well only if the intersection test with the bounding volume is much more efficient than the test with the object. This implies that the bounding volume must be very simple, for example, a sphere, rectangular parallelepipeds, ellipsoids.

The technique of bounding volumes was suggested by Clark (1976) and implemented by Whitted (1980). However, Brooks et al. (1974) had previously used a tree-structured object description in which the branches were arbitrarily oriented rectangular parallelepipeds that enclosed subvolumes of the object.

The concept of bounding volumes has also been extended to **clusters**. Objects are grouped together and clustered within a single bounding volume when they are in close proximity. Clusters of clusters may also be created in a hierarchical way and a multilevel tree may be constructed with the objects as leaves. The top level is first tested; then, if necessary, the hierarchy is recursively descended. The recursive process is stopped when:

1. There is no intersection, or
2. There is an intersection at the bottom level; an intersection test is required with the object (at the corresponding leaf)

In the following sections, we shall present the most common bounding volumes. We shall then discuss the selection of bounding volumes based on void areas.

11.2.2 Simple bounding volumes

11.2.2.1 Bounding spheres
As explained by Rubin and Whitted (1980), the use of spherical bounding volumes substantially reduces computation time. For this reason, this kind of bounding volume is very often implemented in current ray-tracing software. In Sect. 10.2.1, we have shown that because of the sphere's symmetry, it is a fairly simple process to compute intersections with a ray. An intersection may be tested by finding the minimal distance between the ray and the center of the sphere . If this distance is less or equal to the radius, there is an intersection. As already noted, with a sphere centered at the origin, calculations only require a few floating point operations.

As stated by Kajiya (1983a), spheres are particularly simple to check for intersection, but have the defect of not fitting most objects very closely. For this reason, use is often made of bounding boxes.

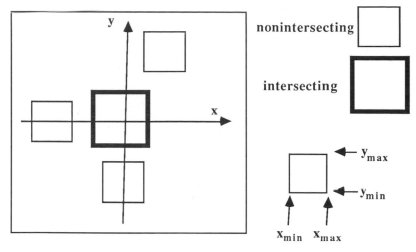

Fig.11.2. Two-dimensional bounding box test

11.2.2.2 Bounding boxes

A box is a rectangular parallelepiped and carrying out a test in three dimensions with a box is computationally expensive. On the other hand, it is relatively easy to transform the 3D bounding box test into a 2D sign test. By using translations and rotations, the ray is made coincident with the z axis. The same transformations are then applied to the object and the bounding box. There is an intersection between the ray and the bounding box when the following condition is true in the translated and rotated coordinate system:

$$x_{min} \, x_{max} < 0 \text{ and } y_{min} \, y_{max} < 0 \tag{11.1}$$

where $x_{min}, x_{max}, y_{min}$ and y_{max} are the limits of the transformed bounding box, as shown in Fig.11.2.

11.2.2.3 Bounding volumes for fractals

In Sect. 13.4.4, the ray-tracing of fractals, as introduced by Kajiya, is discussed. Two types of bounding volumes for fractals are presented: "cheese-cakes" (Kajiya 1983a) and ellipsoids (Bouville 1985).

11.2.3 Selection of optimal bounding volumes

The selection of optimal bounding volumes is difficult. As stated by Kajiya (1983a), bounding volumes should satisfy two criteria:

1. They should be tight, which means that they should enclose the object leaving little void area
2. They should allow an efficient intersection test with a ray

So far, we have emphasized the second criterion in describing bounding spheres and bounding boxes. We now discuss an approach for satisfying the first criterion—void areas.

11.2.3.1 Void areas and cost functions

Weghorst et al. (1984) have introduced the concept of a **void area**, which is the difference in the projected areas between the bounding volume and the object. The projection is an orthographic projection onto a plane perpendicular to the ray and passing through the origin of the ray. If we omit the second criterion above, we could simply minimize the void areas for all rays to obtain an optimal bounding volume, the object itself. As this is definitively not advantageous, another strategy is required which takes into account the cost of intersection. Weghorst et al. propose minimizing the following cost function T to select the bounding volume:

$$T = b\,B + i\,I \qquad\qquad (11.2)$$

where:
   b is the number of times that the bounding volume is tested for intersection
   i is the number of times that the object is tested for intersection
   B is the cost of testing the bounding volume for intersection
   I is the cost of testing the object for intersection

For a given object, b and I are generally constant, but B and i change with the shape and size of the bounding object. Unfortunately, a decrease in i corresponds to an increase in B and vice versa, which means that it is not easy to minimize T.

Weghorst et al. propose a method in which different bounding volumes (spheres, boxes, cylinders) are automatically assigned to the objects in a scene. The selection is made by minimizing the product of an associated complexity factor (which measures the relative complexity of the intersection test) and the volume of the potential bounding shape. This volume corresponds to void areas for all directions. Examples are shown in Figs.11.3-11.5.

Fig.11.3. Camera. By H. Weghorst, G. Hooper, and D.P. Greenberg, Cornell University

Fig.11.4. Pool room. By H. Weghorst, G. Hooper, and D.P. Greenberg, Cornell University

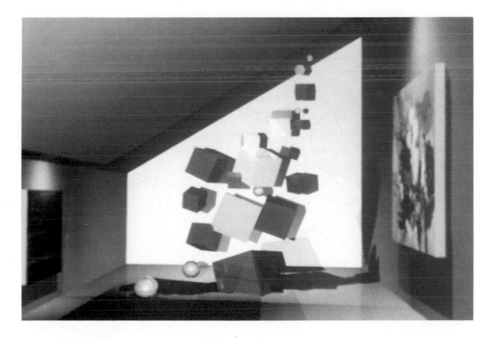

Fig.11.5. A ray-traced image using void areas. By H. Weghorst, G. Hooper, and D.P.Greenberg, Cornell University

11.2.4 Kajiya plane-sets and object hierarchies

Kajiya (1986) proposes a new type of bounding volume which can be made to fit convex hulls arbitrarily tightly. Objects are bounded with volumes constructed of arbitrary planes described by the Cartesian equation:

$$Ax + By + Cz = D \tag{11.3}$$

where $N = <A,B,C>$ is the normal vector to the plane and D the distance from the plane to the origin.

Kajiya defines a **slab** as the region between two parallel planes π_1 and π_2 characterized by the pair of values of D: $\{D_1 , D_2\}$; the normal N is of course the same and is called by Kajiya a plane-set normal. Different bounding slabs are possible simply by changing N. Figure 11.6 shows a 2D representation of slabs.

The bounding volume is obtained by the intersection of a set of bounding slabs (at least three), which implies a set of plane-set normals. Example of sets of plane-set normals are:

$\{<1,0,0>, <0,1,0>, <0,0,1>\}$ rectangular parallelepiped

$\{\frac{1}{\sqrt{3}}<1,1,1>, \frac{1}{\sqrt{3}}<-1,1,1>, \frac{1}{\sqrt{3}}<-1,-1,1>, \frac{1}{\sqrt{3}}<1,-1,1>\}$ eight-sided parallelepiped

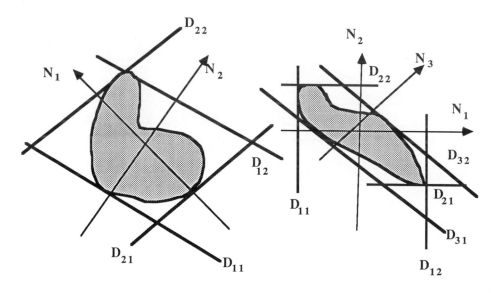

N_i **i-th plane set normal**

$D_{i1} \; D_{i2}$ **distances for i-th plane-set**

Fig.11.6. Two-dimensional examples of slabs

As the bounding volumes exist in world space, a modeling transformation (3x3 matrix $\mathcal{M}$ and a translation $\mathcal{T}$) must be applied. This modeling transformation is associated with each object in the database.

For **polyhedra**, the bounding volumes are determined by computing the bounding volume enclosing the vertices. Three steps are necessary:

1. Transform the vertices P_k: $P_k' = P_k \mathcal{M} + \mathcal{T}$ (11.4)
2. Project each transformed vertex onto each normal N_i: $d_{ik} = P_k' N_i$ (11.5)
3. Compute the pair $\{D_1 , D_2\} = \{\min\{d_{ik}\}, \max\{d_{ik}\}\}$

For **implicit surfaces**, the Kajiya method is:

Apply the transformation $\mathcal{M}$ to each point $P = <x,y,z>$ satisfying the implicit
    equation $F(x,y,z) = 0$
for each P
  Project it onto the normal N_i

After a few arrangements, an equation is obtained which is solved by the method of Lagrange multipliers.

For **compound objects**, the bounding volume of two bounding volumes is the pairwise minimum of each D_1 and the pairwise maximum of each D_2.

The **ray-volume intersection** is computed as the intersection of the intervals obtained as a result of each ray-slab intersection. Ray-slab intersections are themselves obtained by substituting the ray Eq. (10.4) into the plane Eq. (11.3), corresponding to the two planes bounding the slab.

Kajiya introduces **object hierarchies** by defining the extent of a particular node in the hierarchy to be the combined extent of all that node's children. With this approach, for any ray missing the bounding volume at a given node, the node's entire subtree may be discarded.

A corresponding hierarchy traversal algorithm has been developed. For a given ray R:

Compute the dot products and reciprocals
t:= the distance to the nearest object O hit so far
p:=nil {pointer to O}
while heap is nonempty and distance to top node < d **do**
    Extract candidate C from heap
    if C is a leaf
    then
      Compute R-object intersection
      if R hits C and distance < d
      then
        t:=distance
        p:=C
    else
      for each child Ch of C
        Compute R-bounding volume intersection
        if R hits the bounding volume
          Insert Ch into the heap

The Kajiya approach is very efficient and has been used for the production of two sequences: *The Magic Egg* and *Trees*.

11.3 Use of coherence in ray-tracing

11.3.1 Image coherence versus object coherence

Two kinds of coherence may be used to reduce the cost of a ray-tracing algorithm:

Image coherence is based on the fact that the intensities of two neighboring pixels are more likely to be the same than to be different. This means that it is not necessary to shoot one ray for each pixel. A typical algorithm using this approach has been proposed by Broonsvort et al. (1984): the image is generated with a low resolution (e.g., macropixels of 8x8 pixels). Only a few rays are calculated, while the intensities of other pixels are computed from the measured intensities of neighboring pixels. However, for complex images, this image coherence drops to a low level and the gain is small.

Object coherence is based on the relationship between objects in the environment and this information is used to reduce the number of intersections. A typical object coherence method is that described by Coquillard (1985). Only objects close to the ray are considered. The Coquillard algorithm adaptively subdivides a plane containing the projection of the box enclosures of the objects. It uses a data structure which defines the adjacencies of the projections of the box enclosures of the object to speed up execution.

11.3.2 Cone tracing

Amanatides (1984) proposes the use of an extension of rays to include a spread angle and virtual origin, which allows a ray-tracer to area sample the scene using a cone instead of an infinitely thin ray. The spread angle is defined as the angle between the center line of the cone and the cone boundary as measured at the apex of the cone. It is important to choose the spread angle so that when the ray is sent from the eye, the radius of the cone at the distance of the virtual screen is the width of the pixel.

Two complex calculations are required in such an approach:

1. The intersection between the cone and the object to be ray-traced. Three cases are described by Amanatides—spheres, planes, and polygons
2. The fraction of the cone that is blocked by the object; this information will be useful to perform antialiasing as shown below

11.3.2.1 Intersection between sphere and cone
Consider a sphere with center **C** and radius R and a cone with an apex **S** and a spread angle A. The intersection test begins by finding the point **P** on the cone's center line closest to **C** and the distance d between **P** and **C**. There is no intersection between the cone and the sphere if :

$$Q \tan (A) + \frac{R}{\cos (A)} < d \qquad (11.6)$$

where Q is the virtual origin, which is the distance from **S** to **P**. Figure 11.7 shows the cone and the sphere.

The fractional coverage of the sphere within the ray is determined by finding the area of intersection of two circles, the outline of the sphere, and the outline of the cone where it is closest to the sphere. Amanatides suggests the use of a polynomial to determine this partial coverage. Kirk (1986) proposes precalculating the percent

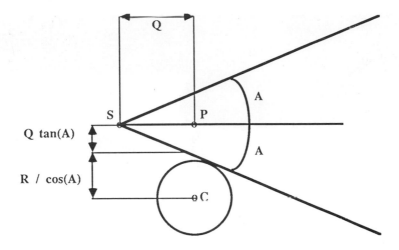

Fig.11.7. Cone and sphere

coverage for a range of values and storing it in a table. A filtering function may be incorporated into the table, so that the resultant values are prefiltered. Distances greater than the desired filter radius have a weighting of zero. This is performed by convolving the area of the intersection with the following function:

$$W = \cos^2 (0.5 \, \pi \, \frac{D}{F})$$ (11.7)

where W is the weight for a given point, D is the distance from the cone center line and F is the filter radius. Kirk uses an approximation by breaking the cone into small rectangular areas; the weights calculated for each area are then summed and the total is normalized so that a completely covered cone has a 100% weighting:

$$W_N = \frac{1}{W_C} \sum_i A_i \cos^2 (0.5 \, \pi \, \frac{D_i}{F})$$ (11.8)

where W_N is the normalized weighting, W_C the nonnormalized weighting for a completely covered cone for a given point, A_i is an area, and D_i is the distance from the cone center line for each area.

11.3.2.2 Intersection between plane and cone of spread angle A

If the intersection between the center line of the ray and the plane is behind the origin of the ray, the plane is discarded. Otherwise, the test for intersection consists of comparing the spread angle A and the angle Ω between the center line L of the ray and the plane normal N.

The fractional coverage of the plane is calculated by finding the area of intersection between the cross section of the cone and a half plane. From the angles A and Ω, we may calculate the distance d between the center of the circle and the edge of the half plane. The area of intersection is computed from the distance d using a polynomial approximation. The Kirk method above may be also used.

Fig.11.8. Ray-tracing with cones. Courtesy of John Amanatides, University of Toronto

11.3.2.3 Intersection between polygon and cone of spread angle A
The vertices of the polygon are projected onto a plane perpendicular to the director vector of the cone. Then, the intersection between the circular cross section and the polygon is performed by calculating the distance from the center of the circle to each edge. The area of intersection may be calculated as in the previous case.

11.3.2.4 Antialiasing
As stated by Amanatides, the fractional coverage information is sufficient to perform simple area antialiasing. No small detail may "fall between the cracks" as the ray covers the whole pixel. This means that only one ray per pixel is sufficient regardless of scene complexity.

Figure 11.8 shows an image generated using cone tracing.

11.3.3 Beam-tracing and coherent ray-tracing

11.3.3.1 Ray coherence
Heckbert and Hanrahan (1984) made the observation: "In many scenes, groups of rays follow virtually the same path from the eye," this means that neighboring rays have essentially the same object intersection tree. Similarly, Speer et al. (1985) defined the term **ray coherence**. The ray currently being traced from the viewpoint is checked against the object intersected by the previous ray from the viewpoint. A check of all other objects in the scene is only necessary if the current ray does not intersect this object.

Two methods of exploiting this coherence have been proposed:

- The use of beams instead of rays
- The use of a cache

11.3.3.2 Beam-tracing

Instead of tracing rays, Heckbert and Hanrahan trace beams through a scene consisting of polygonal objects. This restriction allows beams to be approximated by pyramidal cones.

A recursive beam tracer is used with the viewing pyramid as initial beam. Beam surface intersections are computed using 2D polygonal set operations. The closest beam-surface intersection is determined by searching a depth-sorted list of polygons (Newell et al. 1972) as described in Sect. 5.5.2. The first visible polygon is found by intersecting the beam with the first polygon in the list. The set operations involved in this algorithm must handle concave polygons containing holes. Heckbert and Hanrahan propose using an algorithm such as the Weiler-Atherton algorithm described in Sect. 5.6.2.

For each beam-polygon intersection, the beam is fragmented and new beams are created for the reflected and transmitted swaths of light. These new beams are redirected with a 4x4 homogeneous matrix transformation and recursively traced.

The recursion is terminated in the following cases:

- The maximum tree depth is reached
- The intensity contributed by the branch does not make a perceptible difference (see the technique of adaptive tree depth control, Sect. 11.1.4)
- The size of the polygon is below some threshold

It should be noted that the 4x4 matrix, used in the beam-tracer algorithm, represents a linear transformation. This means that refraction is not always correctly rendered.

The beam tracer builds an intermediate data structure, called the **beam tree**, which is very similar to the classic ray tree (Whitted 1980) described in Sect. 10.1.3. The links in a beam tree represent beams of light and the nodes contain a list of surfaces intersected by a beam. It is important to note that all the secondary beams also have polygonal cross sections. In the case of reflection, shadows, and refraction (under certain assumptions), the new beams are again pyramidal cones. This allows an entire beam to be traced at once using a recursive polygonal hidden surface algorithm such as the Weiler-Atherton algorithm. The size of the beam tree S_B is a natural measure of the coherence C in an image:

$$C = \frac{S_R}{S_B} \qquad\qquad (11.9)$$

where S_R is the size of the average ray tree size, calculated as the total number of nodes in the tree divided by the number of pixels.

11.3.3.3 Caching

Speer at al. (1985) propose a coherent ray-tracing algorithm that uses the path generated by the last ray-set to predict the path of the current ray-set. Instead of attempting to trace many rays simultaneously, these authors retain the intersection tree for one more program iteration. The ray tree is a kind of cache; a cache hit occurs if the next ray intersects the same object. Otherwise, a miss occurs.

There is a problem with this approach when the same object may be hit by the next ray and another object blocks the ray before it hits that object (see Fig.11.9).

Speer et al. propose the use of a cache with two types of information—the last object intersected and a logical "container." This container is a cylinder of security starting at the point of origin of a ray and ending at the point of intersection with an object and with the central axis aligned with the ray. If a corresponding ray from the next ray-set does not intersect the side of the cylinder and intersects the same object intersected by this ray, then that object must be the foremost object intersected by the corresponding ray. Figure 11.10 shows an image generated using this coherent ray-tracing algorithm.

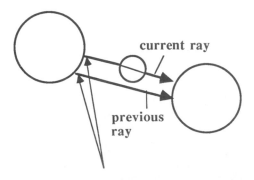

Fig.11.9. Problem when another object blocks the ray before it hits this object

Fig.11.10. Coherent ray-tracing. By L.Richard Speer, Tony D. DeRose and Brian A. Barsky, University of California, Berkeley Computer Graphics Laboratory, 1985

Hanrahan (1986) examined this algorithm for sphere beam tracing and found that there were many cache misses because the container is much smaller than the beam cross section. He proposed the use of a cache containing the last sphere hit and a list of potential blocking spheres. He proposes to order the searches in a way which maximizes the probability that a cache hit will occur. The cache is organized as a tree and the search takes place in breadth-first order so that coherent regions are completely computed before moving onto the next region. The method is similar to the common seed fill or boundary fill algorithm used in paint systems (see Magnenat-Thalmann 1985b, Sect.5.8).

11.4 Space division for ray-tracing

11.4.1 Hierarchy of bounding volumes and space division

Clark (1976) uses hierarchical geometric representations to speed both clipping and visibility calculations. Each level of the hierarchy consists of bounding volumes which enclose the lower levels. Terminal nodes represent primitive object elements such as polygons.

Rubin and Whitted (1980) propose using a similar strategy to reduce the number of intersection tests. They describe a scene using a hierarchical tree of bounding boxes. Since the bounding volumes of the children lie entirely within the bounding volumes of the parent, the child volumes need only be searched if the ray intersects the parent volume. Figure 11.11 shows an image generated using this method.

An alternative approach is to decompose space into a set of disjoint volumes containing a list of those surfaces contained within each volume. The total number of objects in each volume has to be a small number, which implies a fine subdivision. The search for an object intersection proceeds along the path of the ray through the subdivision.

Four approaches have been proposed:

- Techniques based on a space decomposition with an octree
- Techniques based on a binary space partitioning tree (BSP tree)
- Techniques based on digital differential analyzers (DDA)
- Techniques based on CSG models

11.4.2 Space decomposition with an octree

11.4.2.1 Glassner algorithm
Glassner (1984) describes a ray-tracing algorithm using a division of the space into small compartments, keeping a list of all the objects that reside in each of these compartments. Each time a ray is started, the compartment in which it originated is determined. The ray is followed and compared against the objects it hits in this compartment. Two cases are possible:

1. One or more objects are intersected, the color value of the closest is returned, and the tracing for this ray is finished
2. No object is intersected, the process has to be repeated with the projection of the ray into the next compartment

The octree structure (see Sect. 4.2.5) is the perfect scheme for breaking up space into such compartments. Volumes with high object complexity are recursively

Fig.11.11. A scene composed of curved and polygonal objects. Courtesy of T.Whitted, University of North Carolina, Chapel Hill

subdivided into smaller volumes generating new nodes in the tree. The octree storage technique is a slight variation of the technique described by Gargantini (1982). Each octree node consists of a name, a subdivision flag (set if the node has been subdivided), center and size data, and an object-list pointer. A node is located by hashing the name and then following a linked list of all nodes that hash that number starting at a given point in a table.

Glassner intersects the object with each of the six planes bounding the voxel. If any point of intersection lies within the side of the voxel (square), the object is kept. Otherwise, some point within the object is examined and the object is discarded if the point is outside the voxel.

The algorithm for the movement to the next voxel in the path of the ray is to find a point guaranteed to be in that voxel. For solving this problem, we need two values:

- The largest value t_m of t that the ray may assume within a voxel; t is the parameter in the ray equation (Eq. 10.4)
- The length L of the side of the smallest voxel

The point is found by moving the distance $\frac{L}{2}$ perpendicular to each face in which t_m lies. The problem with this approach is that the determination of t_m requires calculating intersections of the ray with the six planes that bound the voxel.

Figure 11.12 shows examples generated using this approach.

11.4.2.2 The Wyvill-Kunii algorithms

Wyvill and Kunii (1985) describe a ray-tracer which also operates on an octree structure. Their algorithm is based on the directed acyclic graph (DAG) structure,

Fig. 11.12. Space subdivision for fast ray-tracing. Image software and geometry by Andrew Glassner

described in Sect. 4.4.2. Rays are traced backward from the viewpoint to a source light. Each ray is followed through the structure until it encounters a nonempty voxel. At this point, the intersection points of the ray with the voxel boundary are found. These points are then transformed back to the primitive's space using the inverse matrix associated with the octree leaf. In the case of reduced CSG structures (see Sect. 4.4.2), Wyvill et al. (1986a) describe how to find intersections for all objects in the voxel corresponding to a RCSG node.

The correct intersection is found as follows:

Find all the intersections and order them by distance from the ray source
while there is an intersection **do**
  for the nearest intersection point **I**
    construct points **A** and **B** on the line of the ray such that

        A is ε units closer to the ray source than **I** and **B** is ε units farther.
    if A is outside the object and **B** is inside
    then
      I is the correct intersection point
      exit
  Remove **I** from the list of points

Wyvill and Kunii propose an improvement of the Glassner algorithm to skip quickly over empty voxels. They also have to find a point which is guaranteed to be in the next voxel.

The algorithm which avoids most of the intersection calculations is as follows:

Consider a ray from $\mathbf{P}$ to $\mathbf{Q}$ within the voxel v bounded by $\mathbf{L}$ and $\mathbf{H}$

Consider the distance $\mathbf{D}=\mathbf{Q}-\mathbf{P}$ and the exit point $\mathbf{E}$ of the voxel v

Find $\mathbf{R}=<R_x,R_y,R_z>$ such that R_i is the distance from $\mathbf{P}$ to $\mathbf{E}$ in the direction i

Find t such that $t = \text{Min} \left(\left|\frac{R_x}{D_x}\right|, \left|\frac{R_y}{D_y}\right|, \left|\frac{R_z}{D_z}\right|\right)$

The point $\mathbf{P} + t\,\mathbf{D}$ is guaranteed to lie on the voxel boundary. However, the above calculations do not work with integers. Therefore, Wyvill and Kunii propose calculating a new point $\mathbf{P'}$ from an old point $\mathbf{P}$ as follows:

for i:=x **to** z **do**
   if $D_i \geq 0$ **then** $R_i := H_i - P_i$ **else** $R_i := L_i - P_i - 1$;
k:=x;
for i:=y **to** x **do**
   if $|R_k D_i| > |R_i D_k|$ **then** k:=i;
for i:=x **to** z **do**

   if i=k **then** $P'_i := P_i + R_i$ **else** $P'_i := P_i + D_i \frac{R_k}{D_k}$;

11.4.3 Method based on BSP trees

Kaplan (1985) proposes a method called **space tracing**, which consists of preprocessing the data structure describing the scene: space is recursively subdivided with respect to three planes parallel to the coordinate axes. The database is organized in a binary tree, called a binary space partitioning (BSP) tree introduced by Fuchs et al (1980). This BSP tree is built in such a way that the nonterminal nodes contain the identification of a partition plane, which divides the space into two half spaces. Terminal nodes may be either empty nodes or box nodes. A box node describes the cubical space region, which is reached by passing through all points of binary decision of the higher nonterminal nodes. Each box node contains a list of primitive objects intersecting the box.

The ray-tracing process is very similar to the Glassner technique:

1. **for** each ray
    Traverse the BSP tree in order to determine to which terminal box BX the ray
        origin $\mathbf{R_0}$ belongs
    if $\mathbf{R_0}$ is outside the known space
      then
        Terminate the process {an empty node is reached}

2. **for** each object OB of the list associated with BX
    Find the ray-surface intersection.
    Put it in a list L

3. Sort L
    Find the intersection point $\mathbf{IP}$ with the object of the box which is nearest to $\mathbf{R_0}$
    {IP is the impact point of the ray with the scene}

4. **if** the ray does not intersect any object in the box
    Find the exit point of the ray by calculating the intersection with all box faces, in
        order to obtain a new ray origin
    Repeat the process at step 1 until an impact point is found or the ray leaves the
        known space.

11.4.4 Methods based on digital differential analyzers

Fujimoto et al. (1986) propose a method which determines the next voxel in the path more easily but has the disadvantage of using more space. They introduce a new data structure, called spatially enumerated auxiliary data structure (SEADS). SEADS may be viewed as a 3D extension of the raster grid, with pixels becoming voxels (orthogonal cuboidal cells). The volume along the path of the ray is found using a 3D incremental line drawing algorithm. This is a 3D extension, called 3DDDA, of a conventional 2D digital differential analyzer (DDA) algorithm, as described by Rogers (1985). A basic DDA algorithm is a method for rasterizing a line from $P_1 = <x_1, y_1>$ to $P_2 = <x_2, y_2>$ by solving the governing differential equation:

$$\frac{dy}{dx} = c \qquad \text{or} \qquad \frac{\Delta y}{\Delta x} = \frac{y_2 - y_1}{x_2 - x_1} \qquad (11.10)$$

The solution is:

$$y_{i+1} = y_i + \Delta y = y_i + \Delta x \frac{y_2 - y_1}{x_2 - x_1} \qquad (11.11)$$

In a simple DDA, the largest of Δx and Δy is chosen as one raster unit.

This line generator algorithm may be viewed as a very efficient tool for identifying rectangular pixels pierced on a raster grid. Fujimoto et al. (1986) modify a DDA algorithm in order to identify not some but all pixels pierced by the line (see Fig.11.13).

The 3D extension is carried out by using two synchronized DDAs working in mutually perpendicular planes that intersect along the driving axis; 3DDA is applied along the ray direction and it directly identifies all three indices of the cell, which means that intersections are processed without any multiplication or division.

Figures 11.14 and 11.15 show images generated using the modified DDA algorithm.

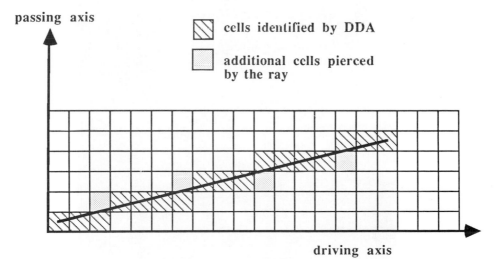

Fig.11.13. Modified DDA

Fig.11.14. Antialiased spherical DNA containing 7011 atoms of various kinds. By Akira Fujimoto, Graphica Computer Co.

Fig.11.15. CG Tokyo '85 containing 10 584 objects. By Akira Fujimoto, Graphica Computer Co.

Nemoto and Omachi (1986) describe an adaptive subdivision algorithm for rapid ray-tracing implemented on parallel architecture using a 3D computer array. The 3D space of a scene to be rendered is divided into several subdivisions by a plane perpendicular to a coordinate axis. Each computer of the 3D array is assigned to one subregion and maintains only the object descriptions contained within that subregion. Each computer has six connections to neighboring computers in order to pass messages about rays and redistribution. Initial rays from the eyepoint are created by all computers in parallel.

As an image is divided into subimages, each computer creates the initial rays which pass through its own subimage. Then, each initial ray is transferred to the appropriate subregion where the initial ray starts. Each ray is then tested for intersection with those objects within the subregion. Rays that exit a subregion are passed to neighboring subregions via connections between computers. For redistribution, the boundary surface between two subregions is slid by one unit and a part of the load for one subregion is transferred to the other subregion.

A 3D DDA algorithm, similar to the Fujimoto-Iwata algorithm, is used to trace rays.

11.4.5 Pure CSG approach

Arnaldi et al. (1987) propose an arbitrary spatial subdivision based on the scene configuration. Instead of using a regular subdivision like Glassner or Kaplan, they use an irregular division with the CSG tree directly. In order to simplify subdivision preprocessing, each primitive is replaced by its bounding box and minimized using the operators of the initial CSG tree. There are two steps in the spatial subdivision:

1. **In 2D,** the infinite plane containing the virtual screen is chosen as the specific plane for a subdivision into two dimensions. Each bounding volume is projected onto the plane, according to the position of the virtual camera, in order to obtain a rectangle, which is decomposed into its four line segments. This set of line segments is then used for producing a partitioning of the screen (see Fig.11.16) by the technique of BSP described by Fuchs et al. (1980; see Sect. 11.4.3).
   A segment is selected from among the set of available segments. The line passing through this segment determines a binary partition of the plane. The remaining segments are distributed in the two regions created and the process is recursively applied until all segments have been processed. Each part of the plane may be empty or may contain primitives.

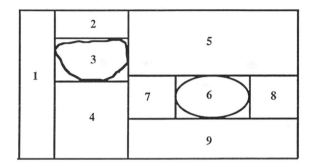

Fig.11.16. Two-dimensional subdivision into 9 regions

screen

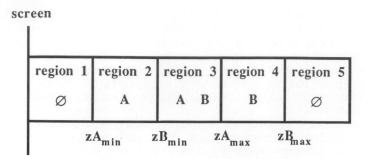

Fig.11.17. Subdivision in the z-direction

2. **In 3D**, each nonempty region is then subdivided along the third dimension. As shown in Fig. 11.17, the 3D extension of the screen part is decomposed along the z-axis, depending on the distribution of the primitives. In our example, the region has, after the first step, two primitives A and B, with the minimal and maximal values zA_{min}, zB_{min}, zA_{max}, zB_{max}. These values allow the 3D region to be subdivided into subregions, which may contain primitives or not.

To solve the problem of passing from one region to another, following a ray, additional information on connectivity is stored for each region. This information is expressed using pointers, specific to certain corners of the region. A corner pointer allows passage directly from one region to an adjacent region. With this structure, it is possible to pass from any one region to another.

The model used is the CSG model. From a classic binary tree, depending on the primitives in each box, a few simple construction rules are sufficient to perform the restriction of the initial tree with respect to the primitives of the given box. The method consists of traversing the initial tree to rebuild gradually the restriction during the ascent of the tree. For a given node N, consider restrictions A and B of their subtrees and the Boolean operator op. The algorithm works as follows:

```
if N is a primitive
then
    if N belongs to the region
    then restriction(N) := N
    else restriction(N) := ∅
else
    if N is a node
    then
        if A is empty
        then
            if B is empty
            then
                restriction(N) := ∅
            else
                if op = union
                then
                    restriction(N):=B
                else {intersection or difference}
                    restriction(N):= ∅
```

```
          else {A nonempty}
            if B is empty
          then
              if op = intersection
              then
                  restriction(N):= ∅
              else {union or difference}
                  restriction(N):= B
          else {B nonempty}
              restriction(N) := A op B
```

As a primitive may be distributed between several regions, the same ray-primitive intersection may be computed several times. In order to avoid these redundant calculations, Arnaldi et al. (1987) number each ray and associate with each primitive an additional data structure called a mailbox. After any computation of a ray-primitive intersection, the ray number and the intersection values are stored in the mailbox. Before any subsequent ray-primitive intersection, the ray number is compared with values in the mailbox to detect whether the intersection has already been computed.

11.4.6 Areas on screen

Sears and Middleditch (1984) propose an approach based on the division of the projection plane into disjoint regions, each enclosing a unique set of pixels. For a single light source at the observer's position, the algorithm works as follows:

Add the required viewing transformation to the root of the volume tree
Push all transformations from internal nodes to the leaves
Find the smallest axially aligned rectangular bound for the projection in the picture
    plane of each primitive volume's bounding box
Use the horizontal and vertical edges of these bounds to delimit rectangular regions
    R_{ij} (see Fig.11.18)
for each inner rectangular region R_{ij}
    Grow an auxiliary tree containing only those primitives whose associated
        rectangles contain that region
    Find the front face of the volume corresponding to each pixel on the picture plane
    Determine the color of each pixel from the front face attributes and the surface
        normal

11.4.7 Partitioning environment to accelerate shadow-testing operation

Shadow testing in a ray-tracing algorithm is the most computationally expensive operation, because each object in the environment must be tested to see if it occludes each light source for every ray-intersection point. To reduce this shadow-testing time, Haines and Greenberg (1986) propose a method which involves generating **light buffers**. A light buffer is defined using two algorithms:

1. A procedure to partition the environment with respect to the position of each light
2. A procedure to test whether a given point is in shadow by using this partitioned definition of the environment

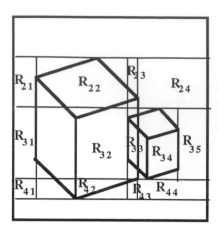

Fig.11.18. Examples of rectangular regions in the projection plane

A light buffer is a cube-shaped frame surrounding a light source. Each face is associated with one of the orthogonal axes within the environment and has a gridwork of cells (squares). Each cell may be considered a small window through which the light source can look; it contains a list of object surfaces that can be seen from the light. Three pieces of information are stored in each element of the list—the object number, the face number, and the relative depth value This approach is somewhat similar to the Franklin hidden-surface algorithm (see Sect. 5.6.3).

Haines and Greenberg use a modified scan-line algorithm to determine rapidly which object surfaces are seen within which grid squares. The basic procedure is to cast all polygons onto each face of the light buffer cube. Transformation, clipping, and culling are performed for each polygon, six times for each light buffer. The Cohen-Sutherland algorithm is used to determine whether a polygon is possibly within the viewing frustrum. Then, polygons facing away from the light are culled by determining the polygon's normal. Remaining polygons are projected onto the light buffer face; the scan-line algorithm is used to project the polygons onto the image plane. To avoid aliasing, all grid squares adjoining the part of the scan line covered by the polygon are marked. A final test is carried out to ensure that each polygonal surface is marked into at least one grid square. Then, for each marked grid square, the closest depth for each polygon is calculated.

During shadow testing, the light buffers are accessed for each view ray-intersection point, and a list is retrieved of all surfaces that might occlude the light ray. Each polygon in the list must be tested until an occlusion is found or until the depth of the potentially occluding polygon is greater than the intersection point.

This method works for opaque polygonal surfaces; Haines and Greenberg also describe how to extend it to nonpolygonal and transparent surfaces.

12 Texture

12.1 What is texture ?

12.1.1 Introduction

Computer-generated images can achieve a high degree of realism with hidden-surface removal and shading. However, in many cases they tend to look artificial because surfaces appear very smooth. Images of metallic or plastic cups, for example, look very realistic, but images of oranges or human skin do not. Almost all physical surfaces, in fact, have a detailed structure visible to the human eye. This detailed structure, called texture, provides a great deal of information about the nature of the surface.

12.1.2 Kinds of texture

Kaufman and Azaria (1985) describe five primary approaches to texture synthesis based on mathematical models or derived from texture analysis techniques:

1. Texture synthesis using a syntactic approach
2. Texture generation using a statistical approach
3. Texture synthesis using a growth model
4. Computer drafting approach
5. Texture synthesis using stochastic modeling

This last category is strongly related to fractals and will be discussed in detail in the next chapter. A different kind of texture called artificial texture will also be briefly presented in the next section.

Three major methods are very popular for generating sophisticated synthetic images:

1. **Texture mapping** consists of "painting" a picture onto a smooth surface or adding a pattern to the surface; the surface still appears smooth
2. **Bump mapping**, also known as normal perturbation, adds the appearance of roughness to the surface. The method consists of perturbing the normal vector, which is used in the light calculations
3. **Solid texturing** uses texture functions defined throughout a region of 3D space

Finally, texturing techniques are now greatly influenced by ray-tracing algorithms and two methods, introduced by Carey and Greenberg (1985), will be presented in a specific section:

1. Ray-traced geometric texture
2. Ray-traced spectral texture

12.2   Methods derived from texture analysis

12.2.1 Syntax-based texture

This method was introduced by Fu and Lu (1978, 1979) and consists of dividing a given texture pattern into **fixed-size tiles**. Each tile is associated with a tree representation, where each node corresponds to a pixel in the tile. A basic tile is generated using a tree grammar :

$$G = (V,r,P,S) \text{ over } <S,r>$$

where V is a set of terminal and nonterminal symbols, S is a set of terminal symbols, S is the start symbol, r is the rank associated with S members, and P is a set of production rules in the form of a one level tree with r children.

A stochastic tree grammar allows irregular patterns to be generated. A probability Pr(k) is associated with each production rule $P_k \in P$; this is the probability that the rule is selected and avoids regularity by introducing a certain turbulence in the texture.

As the coherency between neighboring basic tiles is a problem, a set of higher syntax rules is also introduced for the placement of different basic tiles.

12.2.2 Statistically based textures

These methods have been mainly used to generate gray-level textures. Textures may be produced using Markov chains (Chellappa and Kashyap 1981, 1981a; Cross and Jain 1981; Hassner and Slansky 1980), whose states are the set of gray levels {G} with limiting distribution {P(G)}. Unfortunately, the use of Markov random field texture models requires a large amount of storage and CPU time, especially in the case of multigray-level textures (Monne et al. 1981) or best-fit textures (Garger and Sawchuk 1981). For this reason, a binary texture simulation method has been proposed by Garber (1979). In this method, a functional value is given corresponding to the conditional probability that the next pixel in the generation process is a black pixel, given a black-and-white pattern in its neighborhood.

Another approach has also been proposed by Schachter and Ahuja (1979)—mosaic models. Contiguous piecewise patterns are created using random mosaic models and bombing models. Applications of this method include bubble holes on the surface of cement, leaves on the ground, pebbles on the beach, and small stones on the surface of asphalt.

As a specialist in flight simulators, Schachter (1980) proposes a method of generating long-crested wave models. The model uses the sums of three crested, narrow-band noise waveforms. Applications of this technique simulate orchards, forests, rocky terrains, water, and deserts.

12.2.3 Textures based on growth model

A systematic and complex method has been introduced by Yokoyama and Haralick (1978). The model simulates the growing process in nature by introducing three major operations which are applied to cells:

12.2.3.1 Seed distribution operation

This operation distributes values (called seeds) to the cells; this distribution may be deterministic or random.

12.2.3.2 Skeleton growth operation

This operation expands the seeds into skeleton shapes; at each iteration, the skeleton expands its shape to a neighboring cell in a randomly generated direction. Only the new-grown cells become bud cells (seeds) for the next iteration.

12.2.3.3 Muscle growth operation

This operation is similar to the skeleton operation, but every grown cell becomes a bud cell.

These operations produce a symbolic mother image. In a second phase, relative images are generated by applying specific probability transformations to the value of the mother image.

12.2.4 Textures based on computer drafting approach

These methods were originally designed for drafting with a pen-plotter; however, they also can be used for a raster scan display.

Mezei et al. (1974) describe a method for plotting patterns of natural objects such as rocks, wood, brush, bark, and fur. In this method, a collection of symbols (lines, curves, quadrilaterals, ovals) is chosen and distributed on the surface with a dense, uniform random pattern. For example, the texture of fur is composed of irregular lines with different directions depending on the location; for rocks, curved lines are distributed on several faces in 3D; for brushes, lines are distributed on a cylindrical surface.

Yessios (1979) proposes drafting algorithms which generate graphic representations of stones, wood, plants, and soil. In these algorithms, a regular pattern is built first and is then disturbed by randomly shifting points in X and/or Y directions. For stone walls, Yessios simulates the building process by dealing with one stone at a time or by manipulating the lines corresponding to the joints of the wall. The wood-grain drafting algorithm is based on disturbances to concentric ellipses.

12.2.5 Artificial texturing

Schweitzer (1983) has described a texturing method which approximates the texture changes caused by distance from the viewer and orientation of a surface without attempting to render exactly a realistic texture. According to the author, artificial texture is a means of providing an inexpensive aid to visualizing the shape of a shaded surface. For this kind of texturing, no knowledge of the type of object space data is required; however, depth and normal information should be available at each pixel. The artificial texture is composed of individual texture elements, called **texels**. The size of each texel is a function of the depth of the element from the projecting plane. The shape of the texel is a function of the surface orientation over the texel as well as the orientation of the texel itself. The last texture gradient providing perceptual information is the density gradient. There are two different types of density gradient—compression and convergence. Compression is a decrease in distance between texels due to the perspective transformation of elements at a greater depth from the viewer. Convergence is a result of elements projected closer together when the surface is at a slant to the viewer.

Implementation is based on a modified z-buffer image file as input. At each pixel, the input z-buffer contains normal and intensity information. The shape of each texel is determined by projecting pixels surrounding the texel center onto the plane defined by the center normal. For texel density, the algorithm is implemented using a simple density function for texel positions, such as placing them at equal x, y screen intervals. Density information in both directions is produced using approximate areas covered by each pixel's boundaries rather than the distances between pixel centers.

12.3 Texture mapping

12.3.1 Introduction

Catmull (1975) shows with his algorithm (Sect. 5.7.1) that photographs, drawings, or any picture can be mapped onto bivariate patches. However, this approach fails when the number of points to be displayed on a patch is less than the number of elements in the picture to be mapped. Catmull suggests alleviating the problem by mapping areas rather than points onto points, subdividing the patch and the picture at the same time.

In fact, this image mapping corresponds to the transformation from one coordinate system (texture space) to another (3D space). If both spaces are expressed using parametric coordinates, we may define mapping function as:

texture space: (t,u)   3D space: (v,w)

v=F(t,u) and w=G(t,u) or t=H(v,w) and u=I(v,w)

Figure 12.1 shows an image with texture mapping.

Fig.12.1. A carafe modeled by 15 bicubic patches with a mapped image of a ship. By Michael Potmesil, Rensslaer Polytechnic Institute

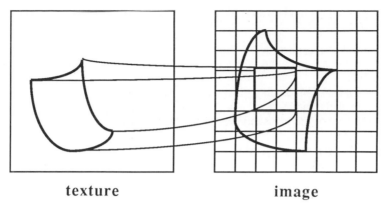

texture   **image**

Fig.12.2. Region of texture pattern corresponding to picture element

12.3.2 Blinn-Newell technique

Blinn and Newell (1976) propose an extension of the Catmull technique by introducing a more sophisticated filtering method: in effect, applying a controlled blur to the pattern to be mapped. This is implemented by computing a weighted average of the regions in the pattern definition function. The shape of this weighting function is determined using digital signal-processing theory. The quadrilateral formed in texture definition space by the (u,v) corners of the pixel forms the base of a square pyramid, which is used to weight the texture values. This function was originally used by Crow (1977) to solve the aliasing problem in computer-synthesized shaded images, as shown in Chap. 8. In the texture mapping case, the 2x2 region surrounding the given picture element is inverse mapped to the corresponding quadrilateral in the (u,v) parameter space, as shown in Fig. 12.2.

The values in the texture pattern within the quadrilateral are weighted by a pyramid distorted to fit the quadrilateral when summed. It should be noted that the derivation of the quadrilateral on the texture pattern is based on the assumption that the parametric lines within a picture element are linear and equally spaced so that a simple affine transformation may be used.

12.3.3 Antialiasing filters

Feibush et al. (1980) propose a method for eliminating aliasing effects of textured polygons by equivalently filtering both the texture and the edges of the polygons. In this approach, the polygons may be planar, concave, or contain holes. A texture defined by a 2D array of texture points is assigned to each polygon and completely covers its surface. Three coordinate systems are used in this method:

1. A 2D texture definition space (in the XY-plane) TS
2. The 3D object space OS
3. The image space IS

For the texture-filtering algorithm, a convolution mask CM, whose shape is determined by the weighting function of the filter, is centered at each display pixel. Each pixel has a bounding rectangle which is the smallest rectangle that completely bounds the pixel's convolution mask.

The texture-filtering algorithm for a given view of the object to be textured works as follows:

Make a list of the portions of the polygons visible in image space (the display polygons D_i), using the Weiler-Atherton algorithm (see Sect. 5.6.2)
for each D_i
   Make a list of all display pixels dp_j whose bounding rectangle is completely or partially within D_i
   Make a list of the intersections of each bounding rectangle with D_i
   for each dp_j
      (*) Transform its bounding rectangle from IS to OS then to TS
         {to simplify the selection of texture points, a rectangle is constructed around the bounding quadrilateral, which includes extra points}
   Transform the parent polygon of D_i from OS to TS
   Clip the rectangle around the CM quadrilateral against the parent polygon
   for each texture point TP_k
      Transform TP_k to OS and then to IS
   Clip the transformed texture points against the bounding rectangle of the CM in IS to eliminate the extra points selected in (*)
   Filter the selected texture points by computing the weighted average of their color values

For pixels near an edge of a polygon, the intensity is only partially determined by the texture filter, because its convolution mask covers more than one display polygon. The contribution of a polygon to a pixel must be determined by filtering the edge. This contribution is the percentage of the volume of the entire cone that is above the polygon. The calculation of this volume U works as follows:

Initialize U to zero
Clip DP against the bounding rectangle of CM
for each vertex V_i of the clipped polygon
   Construct a triangle T_i with the following sides:
      S_1: line segment between V_i and the next vertex clockwise V_{i+1}
      S_2: line segment between V_i and the pixel
      S_3: line segment between V_{i+1} and the pixel
for each T_i
   Construct the perpendicular $P_\perp$ from the pixel to S_1 giving two right triangles
      $T_{i_1}^R$ and $T_{i_2}^R$
   Calculate the two volumes U_{i1} and U_{i2} above $T_{i_1}^R$ and $T_{i_2}^R$
   if $P_\perp$ is inside T_i
   then
      Calculate the volume U_i above T_i as: $U_i := U_{i1} + U_{i2}$
   else
      Calculate the volume U_i above T_i as: $U_i := U_{i1} - U_{i2}$
   if $S_2 \times S_3$ is negative
   then
      $U := U + U_i$
   else
      $U := U - U_i$

The method may be accelerated by using the base and the height of each triangle as indices to a look-up table that contains the volume above this triangle for the given weighting function.

12.3.4 Clamping method

Norton et al. (1982) propose a very different method, called **clamping**. This is a method for antialiasing textured surfaces by bandwidth limiting in object space.

Consider a visual texture on a plane defined by an intensity function $I(x,y)$. When such a textured surface is displayed on a raster-scan device, the function has to be converted to an array of pixel intensities. The texture may be displayed by directly sampling the intensity function, taking $I(P(u,v))$ proportional to the intensity of the pixel at screen coordinates $<u,v>$. $P(u,v)$ is defined as the perspective transformation converting $<u,v>$ to coordinates $<x,y>$ on the textured surface.

Aliasing is avoided by taking the convolution integral at screen coordinates $<u_0,v_0>$:

$$\iint I(P(u-u_0,v-v_0)) \; h(u,v) \; du \; dv \qquad (12.1)$$

This integral is explained in Sect. 8.2 (see Eq. 8.1) and may be approximated by discrete sampling methods.

Norton et al. evaluate this integral using another method; they perform a Fourier transform, transferring the problem to the frequency domain. Bandwidth limiting is performed separately for each pixel. Three simplifications are assumed:

1. A simple box filter is used
2. The perspective transformation is locally approximated by a linear transformation
3. The actual value of the convolution integral is approximated by the low-order terms in a power-series

Norton et al. show that the average I_m of $I(x,y)$ over a parallelogram centered at $<x_0,y_0>$ may be expressed as:

$$I_m = e^{ikx_0+ily_0} \; \max \, (0, \, r \, ((k \, x_1+i \, l \, y_1)^2 + (k \, x_0+i \, l \, y_0)^2)) \qquad (12.2)$$

By decreasing the constant r, it is possible to increase the area over which the filter acts, increasing the size of the box in the box filter.

The term max(...) is called the **clamping function**; it has the effect of forcing (or clamping) the oscillate term (to which it is multiplied) to its local average value.

Similarly, consider a rectangular filter; a rectangle on the screen will map to a quadrilateral via the perspective transformation P. We may approximate the quadrilateral by a parallelogram (first-order approximation). If the rectangle R in screen coordinates is centered at $<x_0,y_0>$ with a width $2\Delta x$ and a height $2\Delta y$, $P(R)$ is the parallelogram defined as:

$$P(x_0,y_0)+(P(x_0+\Delta x,y_0)-P(x_0-\Delta x,y_0)) \; s+(P(x_0,y_0+\Delta y)-P(x_0,y_0-\Delta y)) \; t \quad (12.3)$$

with $-1 < s,t < 1$

We may average over this parallelogram similarly to Eq. (12.2) and obtain:

$$e^{i\,\mathbf{K}\cdot\mathbf{X}} \; \max \, (0, \, r \, ((\mathbf{K}\cdot\mathbf{V}_1)^2 + (\mathbf{K}\cdot\mathbf{V}_2)^2)) \qquad (12.4)$$

where $\mathbf{V}_1 = P(x_0+\Delta x,y_0) - P(x_0-\Delta x,y_0)$ and $\mathbf{V}_2 = P(x_0,y_0+\Delta x) - P(x_0,y_0-\Delta y)$ represent the changes in object space coordinates respectively associated with horizontal and vertical screen displacement of one pixel. The clamping function is max(...); $\mathbf{K}$ is a vector $<k,l>$ and $\mathbf{X}$ a vector $<x,y>$.

12.3.5 Texture mapping in scan-line order

There are two great difficulties in texture mapping: aliasing and the time required to transform a picture onto the projection of some patch. As we saw in the previous paragraphs, the procedure usually involves performing an inverse mapping of a pixel onto a surface texture. However, this is difficult mainly because inverse mapping does not take place in scan-line order.

Catmull and Smith (1980) introduced a method that carries out the mapping in scan-line order both in scanning the texture map and in producing the projected image. The texture surface is transformed as a 2D image until it conforms to a projection of a polygon placed arbitrarily in 3D. In other words, the 2D region bounded by a unit square is mapped into a 3D surface which is projected back into 2D for final viewing. There is a great advantage to this approach: the 2D transformation may be decomposed into two simple transforms, one in horizontal scan-line order and one in vertical scan-line order.

Catmull and Smith also propose performing the light calculations on a square canonical polygon and then transforming the results. Normals for a polygon are determined and stored in the frame buffer. A stream processor can then interpolate the normals to obtain normals at higher resolution. The complete approach may be summarized as:

1. Transform eye and lights relative to canonical polygon
2. Fill the canonical polygon normal frame buffer with normals at low resolution
3. Generate normals at high resolution using cubic splines
4. Normalize the normals
5. Implement the lighting function by dotting the normal at each pixel with vectors to the lights and the eye
6. Transform the results into position into the frame buffer yielding the shaded polygon
7. Use the intensity of each pixel in the texture as the color in the lighting function

12.3.6 Mip mapping and summed-area-tables

To reduce the sampling difficulties in the projection of a flat source image onto a curved surface, Williams (1983) proposes the use of prefiltered source images in the form of a pyramidal parametric prefiltering and sampling geometry. This is based on a pyramidal structure with both intra- and interlevel interpolation. For an image represented as a 2D array of samples, interpolation is necessary to produce a continuous function of the parameters u and v. A third parameter D may move up and down a hierarchy of corresponding 2D functions, with interpolation between the levels of the pyramid providing continuity. Figure 12.3 shows a pyramidal organization called "mip" mapping.

With this approach, many images of varying resolution are derived from the original by averaging down to lower resolution. In a lower resolution version of the texture, each pixel represents the average of some number of pixels in the higher resolution version. The technique requires several tables. Since only a limited number of tables may be stored, values from two adjacent tables must be blended to avoid obvious differences between areas of texture represented at different resolutions.

Figure 12.4 shows an image generated using mip mapping.

Crow (1984) proposes the use of a single table, called a **summed-area table**, in which each texture intensity is replaced by a value representing the sum of the intensities of all pixels contained in the rectangle defined by the pixel of interest and the lower-left corner of the texture image. Consider an arbitrary rectangle of the upper-right corner UR, lower-right corner LR, upper left corner UL, and lower-left corner

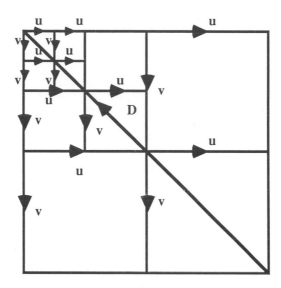

Fig.12.3. Principle of pyramidal parametrics (mip mapping)

Fig. 12.4. Sunstone by Ed Emshwiller and Lance Williams. © 1983, NYIT Computer Graphics Lab

LL. The sum of intensities over this rectangle may be found by taking a sum and two differences of values from the table:

Start with the table entry at UR
Subtract the table entry at LR
Subtract the table entry at UL
Add the table entry at LL {because the area lying below and to the left of the rectangle has been subtracted twice}

The texture coordinate at a pixel is calculated by an incremental bilinear interpolation. At each pixel, the texture coordinates are found by adding horizontal increments (constant over a scan segment) to the coordinates from the previous pixel. Increments are also used to allow incremental interpolation of the texture coordinates of the end points of one scan segment from those of the previous one. A pair of vertical texture coordinate increments may then be computed by incremental interpolation between the vertical increments at the scan segment ends. The texture rectangle is determined by taking the maximum of the absolute values of both x-coordinates and similarly for the y-coordinates, using vertical and horizontal increments.

Glassner (1986) proposes an improvement of the summed-area table method in order to compensate for errors that arise from the inclusion of texture lying outside the pixel. He gives methods for constructing a filter which is 1 only inside the transformed pixel and 0 everywhere else. The filter may be obtained to different degrees of precision and even to an adaptive precision. The new technique is partly based on the use of an auxiliary table which contains local estimates of the texture variance.

12.3.7 Two-part texture mapping

Most of the methods described in this section assume that either the texture pattern has been predistorted to compensate for the distortion of the mapping, or the curved surfaces are represented parametrically. The problem of mapping undistorted planar textures onto arbitrarily represented surfaces is not insignificant. Bier and Sloan (1986) propose solving the problem by using a two-part mapping. The principle is as follows:

1. Find a mapping S from the texture plane $<x,y>$ to a simple intermediate surface $<X_1,Y_1,Z_1>$ in 3-space
2. Find a second mapping O from the intermediate surface to the object surface $<X_2,Y_2,Z_2>$

Barr (1984a) previously used such a two-part mapping, called **decal projection**; the intermediate surface was a quadric surface.

For the first mapping S, Bier and Sloan discuss the use of four different intermediate surfaces:

12.3.6.1 Plane mapping
This is the simplest and least useful, because it complicates the O mapping. The plane mapping may be written as:

$$S : <x,y> \rightarrow <ax,by>$$

where a and b are scaling factors.

12.3.6.2 Cylinder mapping
This mapping is more useful, especially when final objects are solids of revolution. The mapping for a cylinder defined parametrically as a set of points $\langle\theta,h\rangle$ is as follows:

$$S : \langle x,y\rangle \rightarrow \langle \tfrac{ax}{r}+\theta_0, by+h_0\rangle$$

where a and b are scaling factors, r is the radius of the cylinder, and $\langle\theta_0,h_0\rangle$ is the selected position on the cylinder for the center of the 2D artwork.

12.3.6.3 Box mapping
This is a general-purpose mapping; however, it generates clipping problems, discontinuities, and undesirable contiguity.

12.3.6.4 Sphere mapping
There are high distortions in mappings from a plane to a sphere. However, we may use stereographic projections to map to two hemispheres, which implies a low distortion but a discontinuity at the equator. The stereographic projection is defined as:

$$S : \langle x,y\rangle \rightarrow \langle \tfrac{\zeta}{x'}, \tfrac{\eta}{x}\rangle$$

with $\zeta = \tan\phi\cos\theta,\;\; \eta=\tan\phi\sin\theta$ and $\xi= \dfrac{\sqrt{1+(1+\zeta^2+\eta^2)}}{2}$

For the second mapping from the intermediate surface IS to the object OB, Bier and Sloan present four techniques:

1. **reflected ray**
   Fire a ray R from the eyepoint to OB
   Compute the reflected ray R'
   Follow R' until it reaches IS

2. **OB normal**
   Follow a line in the surface normal direction until it reaches IS

3. **OB centroid**
   Follow a line from the centroid of OB through the point of interest on the surface of OB until it reaches IS

4. **IS normal**
   Follow a line from an IS point in the direction of the IS normal until the line reaches the surface of OB.

Bier and Sloan study the different combinations of S and O mappings. Only five combinations are considered further (see Bier and Sloan 1986). The rest are eliminated because of poor invertibility or poor continuity. The reflected ray method is not considered because it is viewing-dependent. The five good combinations are:

1. Cylinder mapping - IS normal
2. Box mapping - OB centroid
3. Box mapping - IS normal

4. Sphere mapping - OB centroid
5. Plane mapping - IS normal

A simple technique for mapping polygonal images onto 3D quadrilateral-based surfaces used in the MIRALab implementation is described in Sect. 12.7.1.

12.4 Bump mapping

12.4.1 Simulation of wrinkled surfaces

Blinn (1978) describes a method which uses a texturing function to alter slightly the direction of the surface normal before using it in the intensity calculations. This technique was previously used by Batson et al. (1975) to generate shaded relief images. Blinn uses a function F(u,v) that measures the displacement of the irregular surface from an ideal smooth one. A new point Q on the wrinkled surface is given by the following equation:

$$Q = P + FU \qquad (12.5)$$

where P is the original point and U the unitary normal vector. Figure 12.5 shows a cross section of a smooth surface (v is constant), the function F(u), and the corresponding cross section of the wrinkled surface.

The problem is how to calculate the new normal. We assume that $P=<x,y,z>$, where x=x(u,v), y=y(u,v), and z=z(u,v). Consider the normal vectors to the surface in P:

$$P'_u = \frac{\partial P}{\partial u} = <\frac{\partial x}{\partial u}, \frac{\partial y}{\partial u}, \frac{\partial z}{\partial u}>$$

$$P'_v = \frac{\partial P}{\partial v} = <\frac{\partial x}{\partial v}, \frac{\partial y}{\partial v}, \frac{\partial z}{\partial v}> \qquad (12.6)$$

P'_u and P'_v define a tangent plane to the surface at the point P. The cross product of both vectors is a vector normal to the surface:

$$N = P'_u \times P'_v \qquad (12.7)$$

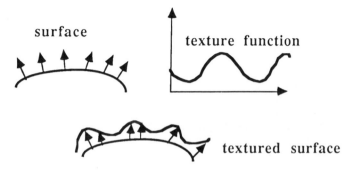

Fig. 12.5. Principle of normal perturbation

We may now rewrite Eq. (12.5) as:

$$Q = P + F \, \frac{N}{|N|} = P + F \, n \qquad (12.8)$$

The new normal **M** may be calculated as:

$$M = Q'_u \times Q'_v = (P'_u + F'_u \, n + F \, n'_u) \times (P'_v + F'_v \, n + F \, n'_v) \qquad (12.9)$$

By considering that F is negligably small, we obtain:

$$M = P'_u \times P'_v + F'_u \, (n \times P'_v) + F'_v \, (P'_u \times n) + F'_u \, F'_v \, (n \times n) \qquad (12.10)$$

The last term is zero and the first term corresponds to **N**:

$$M = N + D \qquad (12.11)$$

with

$$D = F'_u \, (n \times P'_v) - F'_v \, (n \times P'_u) \qquad (12.12)$$

12.4.1.1 Geometric interpretation

1. As shown in Fig. 12.6, an amount from the two vectors $(N \times P'_u, N \times P'_v)$ in the tangent plane to the surface is added to the original normal **N**. This amount is proportional to the u and v derivatives of F.
2. The vector **M** may be viewed as coming from rotating the original vector **N** about some axis in the tangent plane to the surface. This axis vector is obtained by calculating the cross product:

$$\begin{aligned} N \times M &= (F'_u \, (N \times (n \times P'_v)) - F'_v \, (N \times (n \times P'_u)) \\ &= |N| \, (F'_v \, P'_u - F'_u \, P'_v) = |N| \, A \end{aligned} \qquad (12.13)$$

A is a vector perpendicular to the vector $< F'_u, F'_v >$, as shown in Fig.12.7. The angle of rotation is then:

$$\theta = \arctan \frac{|D|}{|N|} \qquad (12.14)$$

To summarize, the perturbed vector **M** may be calculated at any desired u and v value and scaled to a length of 1. The result is then passed to the light intensity calculation procedure in place of the actual normal.

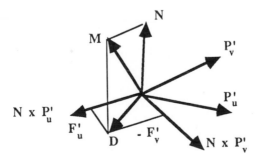

Fig.12.6. Geometric interpretation of the new normal

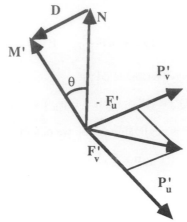

Fig.12.7. Rotation of the normal vector

Cook (1984) extends the bump maps into **displacement maps**; this means that the location is perturbed as well as the surface normal. The advantage of this technique is to solve partly the silhouette problems that arise when bump maps are used to make beveled edges.

12.4.2 Bump function

The choice of the function F is very important. Blinn proposes different techniques:

- F is defined analytically as a bivariate polynomial or bivariate Fourier series; this is generally an expensive approach because of the larger number of coefficients required
- F is defined by a look-up table LTABLE using a doubly indexed array of values between 0 and 1; the results are not very smooth unless an enormous array is used
- F is defined by a look-up table LTABLE as in the previous case and an interpolation is performed for values between table entries. The following is a PASCAL implementation by bilinear interpolation:

```
var LTABLE: array[1..64,1..64] of REAL;

function VALUE(U,V:REAL): REAL;
var
  IU,IV:INTEGER;
  DU,DV,L00,L10,L01,L11,LU0,LU1:REAL;
begin
  IU:=TRUNC(64*U);
  DU:=64*U-IU;
  IV:=TRUNC(64*V);
  DV:=64*V-IV;
  L00:=LTABLE[IU+1,IV+1];
  L10:=LTABLE[IU+2,IV+1];
```

```
    L01:=LTABLE[IU+1,IV+2];
    L11:=LTABLE[IU+2,IV+2];
    LU0:=L00+DU*(L10-L00);
    LU1:=L01+DU*(L11-L01);
    VALUE:=LU0+DV*(LU1-LU0)
end;
```

B-splines can be used, but Blinn shows that a cheaper, continuous interpolation scheme for derivatives consists of taking the difference of the interpolated function along the parametric directions:

```
EPSI=1/64;
FU:=(VALUE(U+EPSI,V)-VALUE(U-EPSI,V))/(2*EPSI);
FV:=(VALUE(U,V+EPSI)-VALUE(U,V-EPSI))/(2*EPSI);
```

Table entries can be generated algorithmically. However, when irregular textures are required, the best approach is to construct a table manually. This can be achieved with a video frame buffer and a painting program that utilizes a digitizing tablet to control the alteration of the table values. The user "paints" in the function values; black areas correspond to small values of the table and white areas to large ones.

12.4.3 Shadows for bump-mapped surfaces

Bump mapping produces realistic images but does not show the shadows that the bumps cast on nearby parts of the same surface. Max (1986) proposes a method for finding these shadows from precomputed tables of horizon angles, listing, for each position entry the elevation of the horizon in a sample collection of directions. These tables are developed for bumps on a standard flat surface, and then a transformation is applied so that the same tables can be used for an arbitrary curved parametrized surface patch.

To simulate shadows, a separate shadow map is needed for every light source direction. Max uses a sunset model, where the sunset time is determined by the angle of elevation of the western horizon, as viewed from a given point. The horizon elevation angle is the maximum angle of elevation from the given point to any other terrain point located directly to its west. Assume a flat patch and a nonnegative bump function $F(u,v)$. In spherical coordinates (φ,θ) with the pole along the z-axis, the unit vector $\mathbf{L}$ to the light source is given by $\mathbf{L}=<\sin\varphi\cos\theta, \sin\varphi\sin\theta,\cos\varphi>$. The horizon angle in the direction corresponding to θ completely determines the shadow pattern for any $\mathbf{L}$ vector in the plane. The table of horizon angles $\beta(u,v,\theta)$ is indexed by the surface parameters u and v and the angle θ. Max has shown that it is sufficient to sample the parameter θ at only eight values corresponding to east, north-east, north, north-west, west, south-west, south, and south-east. In-between values are obtained by interpolating the angle β between two adjacent θ values. The result is compared with the angle f to determine whether a point is in the shadow. Tables developed for flat patches may be used for an arbitrary curved parametrized surface patch by scaling the bump size to the patch size. For this purpose, Max has proposed a new formulation of the Blinn Eq. (12.8) for a perturbed surface as:

$$\mathbf{Q} = \mathbf{P} + F \frac{\mathbf{N}}{\sqrt{|\mathbf{N}|}} \qquad (12.15)$$

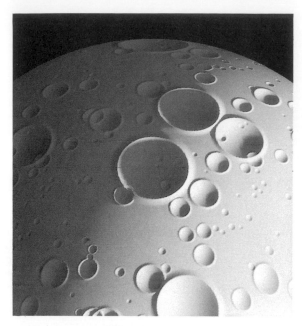

Fig. 12.8. A view of the moon. By Nelson Max, Lawrence Livermore National Laboratory

The corresponding perturbation is given by the equation

$$\mathbf{D} = \frac{F'_u \, (\mathbf{N} \times \mathbf{P}'_v) - F'_v \, (\mathbf{N} \times \mathbf{P}'_u)}{\sqrt{|\mathbf{N}|}} \qquad (12.16)$$

To achieve the technique of shadows for bump-mapped surfaces, Max also defines an affine transformation B. This transformation brings a wrinkled surface S defined on a standard flat patch to a position which approximates P_w at the point $P_w(u_0,v_0)$, where P_w is a wrinkled surface corresponding to the curved patch **P**:

$$B(u,v,w) = (u-u_0)\mathbf{P}'_u(u_0,v_0)+(v-v_0)\mathbf{P}'_v(u_0,v_0)+w\frac{\mathbf{N}}{\sqrt{|\mathbf{N}|}}+P(u_0,v_0) \qquad (12.17)$$

Figure 12.8 shows a view of the moon, with a bump texture formed by randomly adding craters of random size. The shadows are cast from one rim to the other, on craters near the terminator of the sunlit region. A sun of angular diameter 1.5 was used, giving realistic penumbrae.

12.5   Solid   texture

12.5.1 Solid texture functions

We saw in the last section that existing techniques which apply a texture to an object are restricted to parametrically defined surfaces. Several authors (Peachey 1985; Perlin

1985; Brossard et al. 1985) propose texture algorithms that can be applied to any 3D surface. This approach is commonly called **solid texturing**.

A **solid texture function**, as defined by Peachey (1985), for a shading parameter ρ is simply a texture function defined at the points on a surface in terms of their 3D coordinates rather than their surface coordinates u and v:

$$\rho = \rho(x,y,z) \qquad (12.18)$$

Such a solid texture function is generally defined throughout a given volume of space and is often made periodic so that it is defined at all points in the space. The 3D scene coordinates of the point being rendered may be used as an argument of the texture function; however, it is often more convenient to use a local coordinates system.

As indicated by Perlin (1985), the solid texture approach has several advantages over texture mapping:

1. Shape and texture become independent
2. The database is extremely small

12.5.2 Choice of solid texture functions

In 2D, digitized texture plays an important role, but in 3D synthetic textures are more flexible than digitized textures. For this reason, it is essential to find adequate functions to define these textures. In this section, we present a number of popular functions introduced by Peachey and Perlin.

1. **Bombing** has already been mentioned in Sect. 12.2.2. It is a stochastic texture model which consists of randomly dropping bombs of various shapes, sizes, and orientations onto the texture space. A 3D extension may be easily implemented by using spherical bubbles as bombs.
2. **Fourier synthesis functions** may be used to simulate marble. The solid texture function consists of a sum of sinusoidal functions of <x,y,z>. Details of the MIRALab implementation of marble functions are found in Sect. 12.7.8.
3. **Projection functions** are a class of solid texture functions based on 2D textures projected through 3D space.
4. **Combination functions** are functions which produce a solid texture function from several simpler solid texture functions.
5. **Noise functions** are scalar valued functions which take a 3D vector argument and have the following properties: statistical invariance under rotation, a narrow bandpass limit in frequency and statistical invariance under translation. For example, a simple random surface texture may be created by using:
   color = white * noise(point)
   The instantaneous rate of change of noise() along the x, y, and z directions provides a simple way of specifying a normal perturbation. Perlin uses this function to create waves.
6. A **turbulence function** provides a realistic representation of turbulent flow and may be used to simulate the appearance of marble, fire, clouds, bubbles. The turbulence function may be created using a noise function. Details of the MIRALab implementation of the turbulence function may be found in Sect. 12.7.6.

12.6 Ray-traced textures

12.6.1 Surface properties

Texture is an important surface property; other surface properties are geometry, roughness, shininess, finish, color, pigmentation, opacity, and transparency. Carey and Greenberg (1985) distinguish three categories of surface properties: macroscopic surface geometry, microscopic surface geometry, and spectral surface properties.

Macroscopic geometry includes surface characteristics much larger than the wavelengths of visible light. Microscopic geometry describes physical characteristics of the surface which are approximately equal to the size of the wavelength of the light. Spectral properties are wavelength-dependent functions like absorption, reflection, and transmission.

Carey and Greenberg propose a set of methods based on ray-tracing to simulate these surface properties especially in the case of heterogeneous materials. These methods are discussed in the following paragraphs and Fig.12.9 shows an image generated using these methods.

12.6.2 Macroscopic geometry

Complex shapes may be represented by combining a geometric surface like a polygon or a cubic surface with a geometric perturbation function such as a bump in the Blinn technique (see Sect. 12.4).

Carey and Greenberg (1985) incorporate a concept similar to the Blinn bump method into a ray tracing system. The method is straightforward because reflected and transmitted rays are sent out from the point of intersection of the primary ray. The direction of these spawned rays is dependent on the primary ray direction and the surface normal. The ray propagation paths are substantially altered just by perturbing the normals as in the Blinn method.

Fig. 12.9. Textured bathroom. By R.J. Carey RJ and D.P. Greenberg , Cornell University

12.6.3 Microscopic geometry

Microscopic geometry is sometimes referred to as roughness, glossiness, or sheen. The basic concepts of microscopic geometry have been described by Torrance and Sparrow (1967) and were previously discussed in Sect. 7.2.1. Microscopic geometry is defined by the sizes and the orientations of microfacets comprising the surface. Because of the storage limitations, microfacet distribution is considered instead of individual microfacets.

Carey and Greenberg (1985) propose varying the diffuse and specular reflection coefficients by using a perturbation algorithm similar to the normal perturbation method. However, they impose two constraints: the sum of the values of the coefficients must be one, and the specular coefficient increases when the specular exponent (average distribution of the microfacets of the surface around the mirror direction) increases. Texture maps are perturbation functions which represent deviations from the average roughness terms. Carey and Greenberg propose using random functions, procedural models, fractal functions (see Chap. 13), theoretically based models, and pattern generators.

12.6.4 Spectral properties

Proper material characteristics may be simulated using wavelength-dependent functions such as reflection/transmission and light emission spectra. Carey and Greenberg propose a method for simulating heterogeneous spectra for realistic surfaces and materials using a perturbation method similar to the geometric perturbation method. The surface is assigned mean surface spectral curves and a spectral perturbation function, which is applied to the mean spectra. A perturbation range is also assigned which defines the maximum and minimum bounds of the perturbed spectral curve. This approach is very useful for introducing imperfections into surface reflectivity by discretely storing the perturbation function.

The average transparency of a material may also be perturbed by a similar method. Irregularities in transparency are introduced by varying the amount of absorption of transmitted light by the material per unit distance traveled.

Heterogeneous materials are simulated by combining several spectral curves into a single material. The concentration of the various materials varies with respect to position on the surface using a Boolean "mixture function."

12.7 Implementation of textures at MIRALab

12.7.1 Mapping of 2D polygon-based images onto 3D surfaces

A common case of texture mapping is the mapping of 2D polygonal images onto 3D ruled or free-form surfaces defined with m x n quadrilateral facets. This restriction is not so severe, because any free-form surface (Coons, Bezier, B-spline, ß-spline surfaces), sphere, cylinders, revolution surfaces, cones, parabolic cones may be tranformed into a surface composed of m x n quadrilateral facets.

The method for mapping the image has four steps:

1. Generate an m x n grid and cut the image according to the grid
2. Clip the image using the Sutherland-Hodgeman algorithm
3. Map the grid onto the 3D surface

Fig.12.10. Japanese puppets. © 1985 MIRALab, H.E.C. and University of Montreal

4. Create the texture; this texture is created as an independent part of the original object. This means that the texture may also be used as an independant object that has taken the 3D shape

The technique may be used for any 2D polygonal image; in particular, it is possible to generate polygonal patterns on a rectangle and then map the textured rectangle onto the 3D surface.

Figure 12.10 shows an image generated using this technique.

12.7.2 Solid texturing: method of 3D spaces

The method of 3D spaces is based on the following principle: the use of 3D spaces (texture, transparency, color, fog) where objects are placed during the display process. For example, in the case of a texture, each point of the object surface corresponds to a point in the texture space giving the values of texture to apply to this point. This method allows the easy application of texture, color, transparency, and fog to any object, whatever its shape and representation. Moreover, this method ensures the continuity of the texture across the whole object, because texture is not dependent on object shape, as shown in Fig.12.11.

To apply such 3D spaces, it implies that when the object moves, the spaces must follow the object. To achieve this, inverse transformations must be applied to the object coordinates.

There are two main techniques for defining texture space which correspond to the techniques described in Sect. 12.4.2:

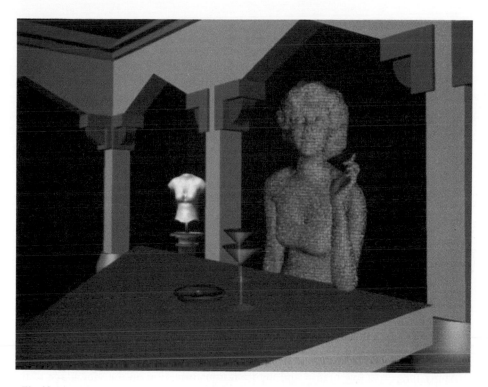

Fig.12.11. Texture space. A frame of *Rendez-vous à Montréal* © 1987 MIRALab, H.E.C. and
University of Montreal

1. A 3D texture function T is defined as:

$$T: <x,y,z> \rightarrow T(x,y,z) \text{ from } R^3 \text{ to } R$$

   This function is evaluated during the display process. This means that if a pixel
   represents a part of the object which is textured, the position in the texture space is
   transmitted to the texture function which returns the texture value.
2. A 3D array of texture is defined before the display process; then, an interpolation is
   performed to obtain the texture value at display time.

   The first approach implies evaluating the function for each pixel, which may be
very expensive at high resolution; however, the second approach is also very
expensive because the array is 3D; for example, if we consider an array of 64 x 64 x
64, we have to compute and store 262 144 values.

   To simplify the use of the texture space, the coordinates may be normalized
between <0,0,0> and <1,1,1>. The user has to define the texture space between
<0,0,0> and $<x_{max},y_{max},z_{max}>$; these dimensions may be different from the
dimensions of the object to be textured. In this case, the texture space may be repeated
several times. For example, suppose that the dimensions of the object are between
<0,0,0> and <100,50,400> and the dimension of the texture space are between
<0,0,0> and <50,25,100>; the texture space will be repeated twice in x, twice in y,
and four times in z.

12.7.3 Calculations of partial derivatives

For 3D texture functions, we have to generalize the equation:

$$\frac{dF}{dx} = \frac{F(x+1)-F(x-1)}{2} \tag{12.19}$$

into two equations:

$$\frac{\partial F}{\partial U} = F'_U = \frac{F(P+\Delta U) - F(P-\Delta U)}{2\Delta U} \tag{12.20}$$

$$\frac{\partial F}{\partial V} = F'_V = \frac{F(P+\Delta V) - F(P-\Delta V)}{2\Delta V} \tag{12.21}$$

Practically, this means that the displacement value along the axis is dependent on the figure and must be calculated; in particular, it is necessary to take into account the transformations which were applied to the figures and the perspective transformation.
The following steps are necessary:

1. Find the extrema of the original figure:
   $<x_{min},y,z>$ $<x_{max},y,z>$ $<x,y_{min},z>$ $<x,y_{max},z>$ $<x,y,z_{min}>$ $<x,y,z_{max}>$
   where $<x,y,z>$ is the center of the original figure
2. Apply to these points the transformations (rotations, scalings, translations) which were applied to the figure
3. Apply the perpective matrix and the final transformation on the viewplane to the points
4. Compute the number of resulting pixels for each axis X, Y, and Z
5. Compute the displacement; this means that for each of the three axes, we have a number of pixels NX in X and NY in Y

12.7.4   3D texture functions

Any function $T(x,y,z)$ may be theoretically used as a 3D texture function. Practically, however, functions have to be adequately chosen. For example, the following functions are particularly suitable:

1. $T(x,y,z)=Fact \sin[2\pi(Ax+\frac{B}{10}[C \ random(x,y,z)+1+\cos(2\pi \ Dy)])]$ $\qquad$ (12.22)

This function produces regular patterns which may be perturbed by the addition of a random factor of irregularity. Examples are shown in Fig.12.12.

2. $T(x,y,z)=-Fact \dfrac{e^{-N^2R}}{D}$ $\qquad\qquad$ (12.23)

with $R= \sqrt{(x-x_0)^2+(y-y_0)^2+(z-z_0)^2}$ and $N=\dfrac{4}{D}$

This function is very suitable for simulating holes which are randomly positioned.

Fig.12.12 a-d. Solid textures. © 1985 MIRALab, H.E.C. and University of Montreal

12.7.5 Color and transparency spaces

Color and transparency may be modified or even defined at each point of an object. If we consider color, three approaches are possible:

1. Color variation is related to the original coordinates
2. Color variation is related to the current coordinates
3. Color variation is dependent on the texture space (perturbation of the normal); for example, Fig. 12.13 was produced by relating the color space to the texture space.

A very interesting class of color functions is defined as follows:

$$COLOR.R := Fact\ COLOR.R$$
$$COLOR.G := Fact\ COLOR.G$$
$$COLOR.B := Fact\ COLOR.B$$

where Fact is defined as

$$Fact := 0.5 + 0.5[\sum_i C_i (\sin(w_i x + P_z) + 1) \sum_i C_i(\sin(w_i z + P_x) + 1)] \quad (12.24)$$

with $C_{i+1} = \dfrac{C_i}{\sqrt{2}}$ $w_{i+1} = 2w_i$ $P_z = K_1 \sin(2\pi z)$ and $P_x = K_2 \sin(2\pi x)$

Fig.12.13. Color space. © 1985 MIRALab, H.E.C. and University of Montreal

Regularity of the color function is controlled by the factors K_1 and K_2.

This class of functions may also be used to represent terrains as in Gardner (1984), or trees, if we also use transparency (Gardner 1985). This approach will be discussed in Sect. 15.2.3. Fog simulation using a similar technique is also presented in Sect. 15.7.3.

12.7.6 Set of primitives

The MIRALab implementation of materials using the solid texturing method is based on a set of primitives.

12.7.6.1 RANDOM

The first primitive, called RANDOM(**P**), is essential and is used to add a random contribution to a regular organization without breaking the continuity. A random value between 0 and 1 is returned for any point **P**. The function is continuous for each of the three axes X, Y, and Z, but returned values for two sufficiently different points are independent. The value of the function at a given location P(x,y,z) is computed as follows: if x, y, and z have integer values then the value of RANDOM(**P**) is given by a hashing function used to index an array filled with random values. Otherwise, a linear interpolation is used between the value of RANDOM at each of the eight points with integer coordinates surrounding **P**.

12.7.6.2 VECRANDOM

The primitive VECRANDOM(**P**) returns a random vector with three random mutually independent components.

12.7.6.3 TURBULENCE

This function is used to simulate a turbulent flow into a regular structure. TURBULENCE(**P**, N) is a continuous function which returns a value between 0 and 1. The level of detail of turbulence is controlled by the parameter N in a way similar to the parameter involved in fractals (see Chap. 13).

Solid texturing has also been used to represent phenomena such as fire and clouds. These techniques will be discussed in Chap. 15.

12.7.7 Wood textures

Wood textures are obtained by a perturbation of colors in the space of equidistant concentric cylinders. Each cylinder is colored dark brown and each intercylindric space is colored light brown. Any object textured using this method appears as if it were cut from a tree. The natural character is emphasized by a light perturbation of the cylinders using the continuous function RANDOM in order to avoid perfect circular arcs. Two different kinds of wood texture have been implemented:

12.7.7.1 Wood with gradation
Between each cylinder, there is a gradation between two different brown colors as shown in Fig.12.14. Moreover, the upper limit of the gradation region is also perturbed using the function RANDOM. With this strategy, between two cylinders there is first a dark brown region, then a gradation from dark brown to light brown, then a region of light brown.

12.7.7.2 Wood with a collection of radial line segments
Between two cylinders, radial line segments are produced with a varying width dependent on the distance to the previous cylinder. Radial line segments are colored dark brown and drawn on a light brown color for the intercylindric space.

This approach is more realistic, because it is more similar to nature al state. However, it is much more expensive in CPU time. Figure 12.15 shows an example.

In our approach, cylinders have a Z-axis which means that any surface parallel to the Z-axis will have a texture similar to a board cut along the tree trunk. Any surface perpendicular to the Z-axis will have a texture with concentric circles.

12.7.8 Marble texture

The marble texture is given using periodic streaks or vertical planes (the thickness and the color have to be supplied by the user), which are perturbed using the function TURBULENCE. In fact, a color value is assigned to the point <x,y,z> according to the value taken by $X_1 = \sin (Ax + B\ TURBULENCE\ (<x,y,z>))$. With this approach, the color streaks are repeated but not the perturbation of the streaks, because this perturbation is determined by TURBULENCE, which is based on RANDOM.

As X_1 takes only values in the range -1 to 1, we have only to distribute the colors

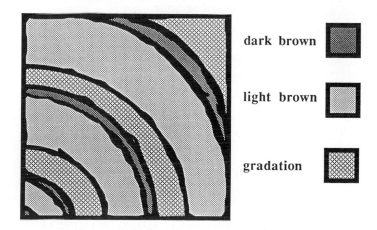

dark brown

light brown

gradation

Fig.12.14. Wood with gradation

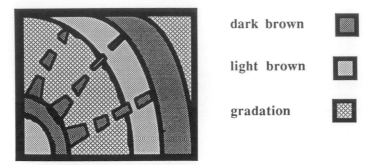

Fig.12.15. Wood texture using radial line segments

along a line segment of length 2 to determine completely the marble texture;. Three colors (provided by the user) are involved C_1, C_2, and C_3; their amounts (thickness of the streaks) are represented by Q_{2D}, Q_{1A}, and Q_{1B} (which are also provided by the user). Note that $Q_{3D} = 2 - (Q_{2D}+Q_{1A}+Q_{1B})$.

There is a gradation from the color C_2 to the color C_1 and from the color C_3 to the color C_1, but not from the color C_2 to the color C_3. This approach is very similar to the nature of marble, which is formed by the solidification of different mineral layers previously deformed by turbulent forces.

Figure 12.16 shows an example.

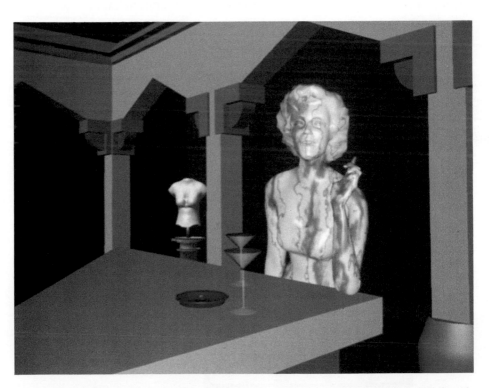

Fig.12.16. Marble texture. A frame of *Rendez-vous à Montréal* © 1987 MIRALab, H.E.C. and University of Montreal

13 Fractals and stochastic models

13.1 Mandelbrot fractal geometry

13.1.1 Intuitive approach to fractal objects

Complex natural subjects such as coastlines, mountains, galaxies, and clouds would seem to be beyond rigorous description for scientists. How can one model a jagged and wild mountain using Euclidean geometric methods? It is not possible because of the irregular (in the Euclidean meaning of the term) shapes of the real world.

However, Mandelbrot (1975, 1977, 1982) has studied the structure of these complex natural objects and succeeded in describing them by introducing a new kind of geometry **fractal geometry**. He shows that objects constructed in this geometry, called **fractal objects**, can represent the shape of mountains, the pattern of stars in the sky, and fluid networks in the organism. Fractal geometry has become a new field of mathematics and it seems to provide a clearer look at our universe.

But what exactly is a fractal ? Our tendency is to perceive things only in one, two, or three dimensions. With fractals, Mandelbrot goes a step beyond this by introducing fractional structures that occupy the space between points (0D), lines (1D), planes (2D), and volumes (3D). A line is a line, but a line with infinite wiggles, called a fractal curve, will eventually fill a sheet of paper; there is a progression from one to two dimensions. This intuitively means that a fractal curve cannot be described as 1D, but it has **a fractional dimension**. Moreover, fractal curves contain an infinite variety of detail at each point along the curve, so it is not possible to know exactly what the length is. This is the first characteristic of fractal geometry.

A fractal object has a second important characteristic which is **self-similarity**. An object with exact self-similarity has the following property: each small portion, when magnified, reproduces exactly a larger portion. This feature is also essential for modeling most complex natural objects. For example, consider the case of a plane flying high above a coastline. The coastline is very rough and jagged at a distance; but it is also rough and jagged close up. In other words, the details have the same general kind of shape as the overall structure. However, we cannot say that the coastline is exactly self-similar. In fact, objects in nature rarely exhibit self-similarity; they possess a related property, **statistical self-similarity**. Typically, a coastline is a statistically self-similar object.

13.1.2 Koch curve

A very well-known example of a fractal curve is the Koch curve, which is obtained by repeatedly scaling an original curve and using the reduced pattern to replace the middle third of the line segments in the curve. Consider now a curve containing two segments

(Fig.13.1a). A copy of this original curve is taken and considered a pattern. This pattern is then reduced by a factor of one-third. Each segment of the original curve is divided into three equal portions and the middle portion is replaced by the reduced pattern. The result is shown in Fig.13.1b. The process may now be repeated by again reducing the pattern by a factor of one-third; dividing each segment of the second curve (Fig.13.1b) into three equal portions and replacing the middle portion by the new reduced pattern, which is called by Mandelbrot a **generator**. The third curve obtained is shown in Fig.13.1c.

The process may be indefinitely repeated, and we may observe that the number of segment lines at each step is multiplied by 4. As the length of each segment is 1/3 of the segment line in the previous step, the length of the curve increases by a factor of 4/3 at each step. Finally, this means that the length of the fractal curve tends to infinity as more as detail is added.

13.1.3 Fractal dimension

What is now the dimension of the Koch curve? To answer this question, consider first a line segment; this has a similar scaling property, i.e., it may be divided into N identical parts without changing its length; each part is scaled down by a factor $r=1/N$ from the whole. Similarly, when a surface is subdivided into N equal parts without changing its area, each part is scaled down by a factor $r = 1/N^{1/2}$ from the whole. In 3D, a solid cube may be divided into N equal cubes without changing the total volume; in this case, each small cube is scaled down by a factor $r = 1/N^{1/3}$ from the whole. We may generalize this approach and say that any K-dimensional self-similar object may be divided into N equal parts; each part is scaled down by a factor r given by :

$$r = \frac{1}{\sqrt[K]{N}} \tag{13.1}$$

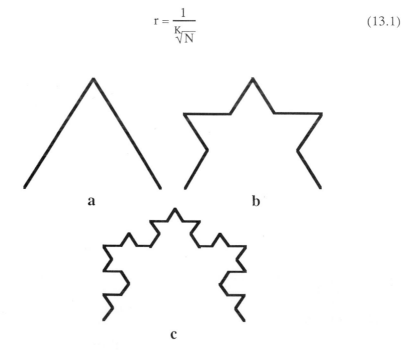

Fig.13.1 a-c. Principle of the Koch curve construction. **a** Original curve; **b** Curve after first step; **c** Curve after second step

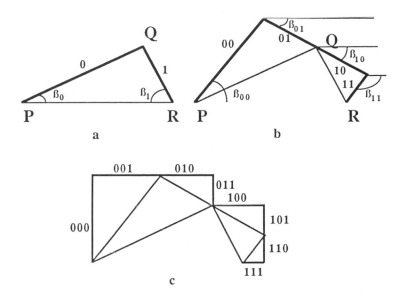

Fig.13.2 a-c. Construction of fractal curve. **a** Original curve; **b** after step 2, angles are noted; **c** after step 3

Now, we may isolate K, which is the dimension:

$$K = \frac{\ln N}{\ln \frac{1}{r}}$$

(13.2)

This is the formula used to calculate the dimension of a fractal object. In the case of the Koch curve, any segment is composed of four subsegments (N=4) and each segment is scaled down by a factor $r = \frac{1}{3}$. We obtain $K = \frac{\ln 4}{\ln 3} = 1.2619...$ This means that the Koch curve has a fractal dimension of about 1.26.

13.1.4 Method for generating fractal curves

Consider first a simple example composed of two segments PQ and QR (Fig.13.2a). For the Koch curve, the fractal curve is generated by replacing each segment of the curve by a reduction of the original curve (the generator). At step S, the curve includes N^S segments. These segments may be numbered in the order in which they were built using a number of S digits in base N. Figure 13.2b shows the second step and Fig.13.2c explains the third step.

In order to build the curve, we must know the angle $ß_i$ between each segment i and the segment PR. We need to know the length l_i of the segment i relative to the length of PR. As shown in Table 13.1, there are two very simple rules:

1. For the angle:

$$ß_i = \sum_k ß_k$$

(13.3)

Table 13.1 Number, angle, and length of generated segments

Segment number i	Angle β_i	Relative length l_i
0	$\beta_0=30^0$	$l_0=\sqrt{3}/2$
1	$\beta_1=-60^0$	$l_1=1/2$
00	$\beta_{00}=\beta_0+\beta_0=60^0$	$l_{00}=l_0\,l_0=3/4$
01	$\beta_{01}=\beta_0+\beta_1=-30^0$	$l_{01}=l_0\,l_1=\sqrt{3}/4$
10	$\beta_{10}=\beta_1+\beta_0=-30^0$	$l_{10}=l_1\,l_0=\sqrt{3}/4$
11	$\beta_{11}=\beta_1+\beta_1=-120^0$	$l_{11}=l_1\,l_1=1/4$
000	$\beta_{000}=\beta_0+\beta_0+\beta_0=90^0$	$l_{000}=l_0\,l_0\,l_0=3\sqrt{3}/8$
001	$\beta_{001}=\beta_0+\beta_0+\beta_1=0^0$	$l_{001}=l_0\,l_0\,l_1=3/8$
010	$\beta_{010}=\beta_0+\beta_1+\beta_0=0^0$	$l_{010}=l_0\,l_1\,l_0=3/8$
011	$\beta_{011}=\beta_0+\beta_1+\beta_1=-90^0$	$l_{011}=l_0\,l_1\,l_1=\sqrt{3}/8$
100	$\beta_{100}=\beta_1+\beta_0+\beta_0=0^0$	$l_{100}=l_1\,l_0\,l_0=3/8$
101	$\beta_{101}=\beta_1+\beta_0+\beta_1=-90^0$	$l_{111}=l_1\,l_0\,l_1=\sqrt{3}/8$
110	$\beta_{110}=\beta_1+\beta_1+\beta_0=-90^0$	$l_{110}=l_1\,l_1\,l_0=\sqrt{3},8)$
111	$\beta_{111}=\beta_1+\beta_1+\beta_1=-180^0$	$l_{111}=l_1\,l_1\,l_1=1/8$

where β_k is the angle of segment k and k is a digit of the number i. For example, $\beta_{101}=\beta_1+\beta_0+\beta_1$.

2. For the segment length:

$$l_i = \prod_k l_k \qquad (13.4)$$

where l_k is the length of the segment k and k is a digit of the number i. For example, $l_{101}=l_1\,l_0\,l_1$.

In summary, at step S, the fractalization of a curve of N line segments is as follows:

1. Angles and segment lengths are determined relative to the first and the last vertex of the curve.
2. The i-th segment is obtained by decomposing the number i into S digits in base N; the angle and the segment length are determined using Eqs. (13.3) and (13.4).

Another example of a fractal curve is shown in Fig.13.3.

13.2 Formal approach: fractional Brownian motion

13.2.1 Definition of fractional Brownian motion

As a mathematical model for random fractals, Mandelbrot and Van Ness (1968) have introduced the term **fractional Brownian motion (fBm)**, which is an extension of the well-known concept of Brownian motion used in physics. fBm denotes a family of

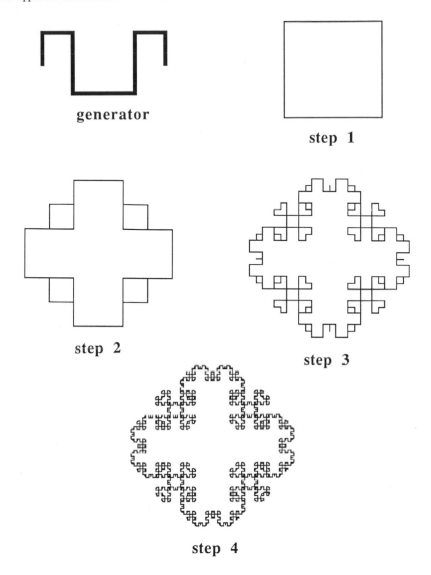

generator

step 1

step 2

step 3

step 4

Fig.13.3. An example of a fractal curve

1D Gaussian stochastic processes, providing useful models for natural time series. Mandelbrot uses these models to approximate a wide range of natural phenomena such as terrains and landscapes. We give a description of fBm based on the work of Fournier et al. (1982).

Let u be a real parameter such that $-\infty < u < \infty$, and let w be defined as the set of all values of a random function; w is assumed to belong to a sample space W. Ordinary Brownian motion $B(u,w)$ is a real random function with independent Gaussian increments such that $B(u+\Delta u,w)-B(u,w)$ has mean 0 and variance $|u_2-u_1|$. $B(u_2,w)-B(u_1,w)$ is independent of $B(u_4,w)-B(u_3,w)$, if $[u_1,u_2] \cap [u_3,u_4] =\varnothing$.

Let H be such that $0 < H < 1$ and let b_0 be an arbitrary real number. **The reduced fBm** is a random function $B_H(u,w)$, which represents the moving average of $B(u,w)$ weighted by $(u-s)^{H-0.5}$ and is defined by:

$$B_H(0,w)= b_0 \qquad\qquad (13.5)$$

$$B_H(u,w)-B_H(0,w) = \frac{1}{\Gamma(H+1/2)}\{ \int_{-\infty}^{0}[(u-s)^{H-0.5}-(-s)^{H-0.5}]dB(s,w))+ \int_{0}^{u}(u-s)^{H-0.5}dB(s,w)\}$$

Note two important points:

- When H=0.5, $B_H(u,w)$ degenerates into ordinary Brownian motion
- The increments of fBm are stationary and statistically self-similar, which is essential for fractal applications as shown in Sect. 13.1

13.2.2 Internal and external consistency

Before presenting algorithms to simulate fBm, it is essential to discuss the requirements of such algorithms. The first quality of an algorithm is its **efficiency**, because high-quality images often require 10^5 or even 10^6 sample points. Two other properties are also essential—internal consistency and external consistency.

Internal consistency is the reproducibility of the modeling primitive at any position in an appropriate coordinate space and at any level of detail. This means that the characteristics of the primitive should be independent of its position and orientation in space. Moreover, scale consistency should also be maintained.

External consistency refers to the continuity properties of adjacent modeling primitives. Typically, in a polygonal environment, this means that the same function with the same parameters must be applied to the same vertex for all faces which have this vertex.

It should be noted that internal and external consistencies are more difficult to maintain for stochastic sample paths than for primitives such as polygons or even high-order curves and surfaces.

13.2.3 Mandelbrot algorithms for calculating fBm

Mandelbrot proposes various methods for calculating discrete approximations of fBm. These methods may be classified into three categories:

13.2.3.1 Shear displacement processes
In this method, Mandelbrot (1975) uses a fractional Poisson field in N dimensions, where with each point **P** there corresponds a value $F(P)$, which is the sum of an infinite collection of steps whose directions, locations, and amplitudes are three sequences of mutually independent random variables. Mandelbrot uses this method to develop stochastic models for relief and the shape of coastlines.

13.2.3.2 Modified Markov processes
With this method (Mandelbrot 1971), a sum of two terms is computed: a Markov-Gauss process (low-level frequency) and a weighted sum of M Markov-Gauss processes (high-level frequency). This approximation to discrete fractional Gaussian noise is called by Mandelbrot **fast fractional Gaussian noise**.

12.2.3.3 Fast Fourier transform filtering

In this third approach (Mandelbrot 1977), a pseudorandom generator produces a **white noise** W(t). This noise is filtered using a transfer function T(f), which is a fast Fourier transform. This method was used to produce some of the most impressive fractal images.

These methods have advantages and drawbacks: the first method has a time complexity of $O(N^3)$ for surfaces and the two others have a complexity of only $O(N\log N)$. However, the second method seems to be valid for only one dimension, and for the third one the main drawback is that the entire sample must be computed at once.

13.3 Random midpoint displacement algorithms

13.3.1 Justification for algorithm of recursive subdivision

For synthesizing realistic mountains, the classic representation using geometric models does not produce esthetically pleasing images; but Mandelbrot theory gives good results. However, for producing numerous frames as in computer animation, the direct application of this theory is very expensive, as we have shown in Sect. 13.2. For this reason, Fournier et al. (1982) introduce a simplification of the Mandelbrot methods. They propose a **recursive subdivision algorithm** to generate approximations of the sample path of 1D Brownian motion. The method is much more efficient than previous methods; however, as pointed out by Mandelbrot (1982a), it sacrifices mathematical purity for execution speed in its approximation to fBm.

An algorithm of recursive subdivision is justified by two facts, which provide the variance for the expected value of the increment of the process:

1. Mandelbrot and Van Ness (1968] have shown that the conditional expectation value of $B_H(\frac{u}{2},w)$ is $\frac{1}{2}B_H(u,w)$ when $B_H(0,w)=0$. This value is independent of the parameter H. The property of self-similarity gives the variance
2. fBm is self-similar with H as coefficient of self-similarity; this means that $B_H(u+\Delta u,w)-B_H(u,w)$ and $B_H(u+h\Delta u,w)-B_H(u,w)$ have the same distribution if the latter is rescaled by a factor of h^{-H}

13.3.2 Recursive algorithm and one-dimensional primitives

The method corresponds to the construction of a "fractal polyline" primitive from an initial deterministic line segment. It recursively subdivides the interval, as shown in Fig. 13.4 and generates a scalar value at the midpoint. This value is taken as a displacement of the midpoint at each step in the recursion and is used as an offset from that midpoint along a vector normal to the original segment. This offset d is calculated by the following equation:

$$d = s.GAUSS (s_d, t_m) \qquad (13.6)$$

where GAUSS is a function that returns a gaussian random variable with zero mean and unit variance, sd is the seed and tm is the middle of the interval $(t_1+t_2)/2$, and s is the current standard deviation given by:

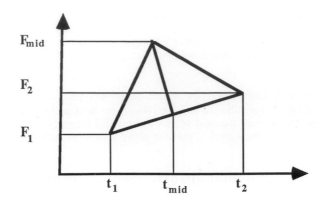

Fig.13.4. Subdivision of an interval

$$s = k \, 2^{-iH} \tag{13.7}$$

where i is the iteration level, k a scale factor and H the fractal dimension.

The following is a MIRA-2D implementation of the algorithm which subdivides the interval $[t_1, t_2]$ based on the formulation by Fournier et al (1982).

```
procedure FRACTAL(T1,T2,EPSI,H,SCALE:REAL; SEED:INTEGER);
var
  F1,F2,RATIO,STD:REAL;
  procedure SUBDIVIDE(F1,F2,T1,T2,STD:REAL);
  var
    FMID,TMID:REAL;
  begin
   if (T2-T1) > EPSI then
    begin
      TMID:=(T1+T2)/2;
      FMID:=(F1+F2)/2+GAUSS(SEED,TMID)*STD;
      STD:=STD*RATIO;
      SUBDIVIDE(F1,FMID,T1,TMID,STD);
      SUBDIVIDE(FMID,F2,TMID,T2,STD)
    end
    else lineabs  <<T2,F2>>
  end;
begin
  F1:=GAUSS(SEED,T1)*SCALE;
  F2:=GAUSS(SEED,T2)*SCALE;
  moveabs <<T1,F1>>;
  RATIO:=2**(-H);
  STD:=SCALE*RATIO;
  SUBDIVIDE(F1,F2,T1,T2,STD)
end;
```

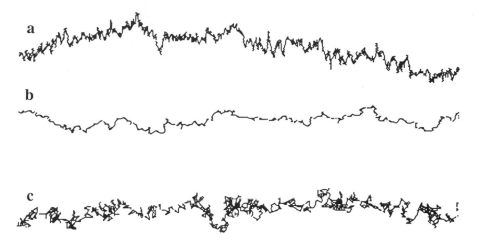

Fig.13.5 a-c. Three fractal polylines. **a** Perturbation in y; **b** perturbation in the direction of the normal to the subsegment; **c** perturbation in x and y

It should be noted that this is an approximation of fBm, which is neither stationary, nor self-similar. However, the algorithm is efficient, because only a few operations are required to generate a sample point.

Modifications of the algorithm to generate the middle points are discussed in Sect. 13.5 on the MIRALab implementation.

One-dimensional fractal primitives can be combined in arbitrary ways to represent natural phenomena such as rivers or coastlines. By choosing an appropriate value for H, it is possible to generate realistic shapes.

Figure 13.5 shows three differents fractal polylines; the first (Fig.13.5a) was obtained using a perturbation in y; the second curve (Fig.13.5b) was obtained by using the normal to the subsegment as the direction of perturbation; in the last case (Fig.13.5c), the midpoint perturbation is performed in x and y.

13.3.3 2D primitives

Fractal polygons can be created similarly to fractal polylines. For example, surfaces consisting of triangles can be easily used to represent stochastic surfaces. Each triangle is subdivided into four by connecting the midpoints of the sides as shown in Fig. 13.6. The positions of the midpoints are obtained by the same process as for polylines.

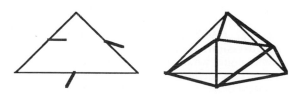

Fig. 13.6 Principle of fractals using triangles

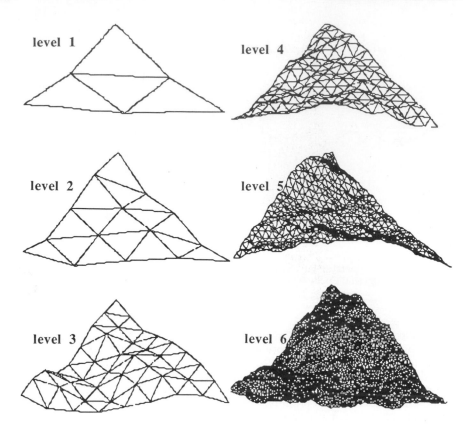

Fig.13.7. Generation of a fractal surface

One of the most important problems to be solved is external coherence: how to move the middle of the edge when it is shared by several triangles. One solution is to store the seed of the random function for the vertices and keep a hashtable to retrieve the midpoints, unperturbed, along the edges of the original polygons. A complete example with several levels of recursion is presented in Fig.13.7.

Figure 13.8 shows the case of an object with quadrilateral faces; the method is very similar and each face is subdivided into four faces. Unfortunately, these faces may be nonplanar and may cause problems at the rendering phase.

Triangular edge subdivision is context independent because no information is passed between adjacent triangles. According to Miller (1986), this leads to the creasing problem, which is the occurrence of creases or slope discontinuities along boundaries. Fournier et al. (1982) propose another method, called by Miller the **diamond-square subdivision**. Rather than subdividing only edges, a square is used to generate its center point, which then leaves holes that are surrounded by data in a diamond arrangement. This method of subdivision takes values from neighboring regions and so it is context dependent. Creasing problems in this second method are still present. Moreover, both methods generate surfaces passing through the original points, which may cause bumps and dents.

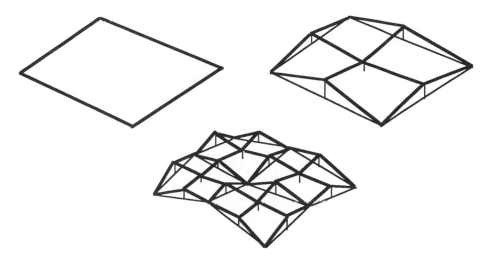

Fig. 13.8. Three steps in the generation of quadrilateral fractals

Miller (1986) proposes a new subdivision method which guarantees C^1 continuity but produces surfaces which do not pass through the original points. The method is called **square-square subdivision**. The new points are generated on a square which is half the size of the existing square. The new values are taken in the proportion 9·3·3·1, the nearer points having the greater weighting. In the limit, the interpolant is a biquadratic surface which is smooth and continuous in surface normal.

Figure 13.9 compares triangle-edge subdivision, diamond-square subdivision, and square-square subdivision.

13.3.4 Texture based on recursive subdivision

The recursive subdivision method introduced by Fournier et al. (1982) may als extended to texture generation using the approach suggested by Haruyama and Bai (1984). Complicated random textures are generated by perturbing normal vector the surface by means of this recursive subdivision. There are advantages to this method: no original texture pattern is needed, only a small amount of data is required, and properties of the texture may be changed simply by adjusting a few parameters.

Normal vectors may be perturbed using two methods that we shall first explain for a straight line segment P_1P_2:

13.3.4.1 Angle perturbation
As shown in Fig.13.10, consider two normal vectors N_1 and N_2 with the associated perturbed vectors F_1 and F_2; Ω_1 and Ω_2 are the angles between the normal vectors, and the perturbed vectors. Ω_1 and Ω_2 are Gaussian variables with a mean 0 and standard deviation Ω_s.

A perturbed vector F_m at the midpoint $\dfrac{P_1+P_2}{2}$ is calculated by the subdivision technique. The angle is defined as an approximate fBm function along the line segment P_1P_2. This angle has the mean $\dfrac{\Omega_1+\Omega_2}{2}$ and the standard deviation $\Omega_s 2^{-h}$, where h is a self-similarity parameter.

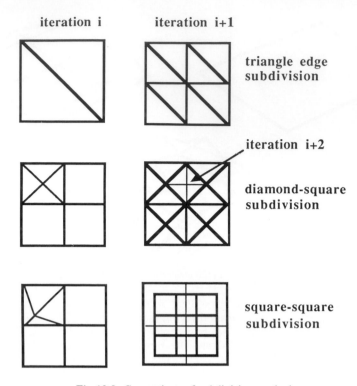

Fig.13.9. Comparison of subdivision methods

13.3.4.2 Vector perturbation

This second method is more efficient because of the lack of trigonometric calculations. As shown in Fig.13.11, perturbed vectors are $F_1 = \dfrac{N_1 + S_1}{|N_1 + S_1|}$ and $F_2 = \dfrac{N_2 + S_2}{|N_2 + S_2|}$, where N_1 and N_2 are the normal vectors and S_1 and S_2 the perturbing vectors. S_1 and S_2 are defined as $S_1 = \langle S_{1x}, S_{1y} \rangle$ and $S_2 = \langle S_{2x}, S_{2y} \rangle$ where S_{1x}, S_{1y}, S_{2x} and S_{2y} are Gaussian variables with a mean 0 and standard deviation S_s. By the subdivision algorithm, the perturbing vector S_m is calculated at the midpoint $(P_1 + P_2)/2$ as an approximate fBm with a mean $\langle \dfrac{S_{1x} + S_{2x}}{2}, \dfrac{S_{1y} + S_{2y}}{2} \rangle$ and standard deviation $\langle S_s 2^{-h}, S_s 2^{-h} \rangle$.

Textures on a parametric curve or a parametric surface may be obtained using a very similar approach. Figure 13.12 shows a surface $Q(u,v)$ with perturbed vectors $F(u,v)$ calculated as:

$$F(u,v) = \frac{N(u,v) + S(u,v)}{|N(u,v) + S(u,v)|} \qquad (13.8)$$

$S(u,v)$ is generated as a function of fBm and $N(u,v)$ is obtained by taking the cross product of the two vectors $\dfrac{\partial Q(u,v)}{\partial u}$ and $\dfrac{\partial Q(u,v)}{\partial v}$ and renormalizing.

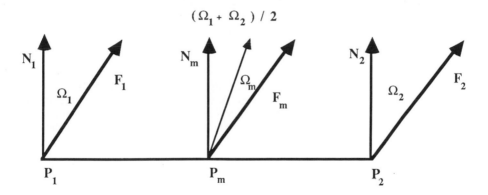

$(\Omega_1 + \Omega_2) / 2$

Fig.13.10. Angle perturbation

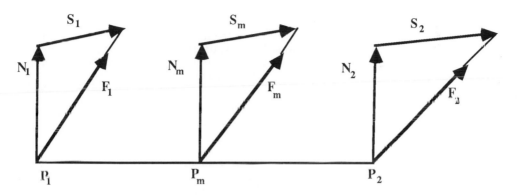

Fig.13.11. Vector perturbation

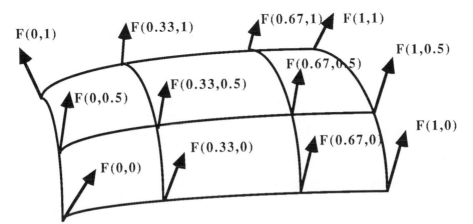

Fig.13.12. Perturbed normals on a parametric surface $Q(u,v)$

13.4   Other researches on fractals

13.4.1 Introduction

Research in fractals and stochastic modeling is still very active. In particular, techniques for postponing the database amplification step as long as possible are very popular. For example, Fournier and Milligan (1985) propose a group of techniques for generating complex images in a display processor operating directly on the frame buffer. In particular, reentrant stochastic subdivision and filtering at the frame buffer level are studied. The display processor, acting directly on the frame buffer, receives sparse 3D geometric data, generates dense 2D stochastic arrays, and determines their color, shade and visibility before writing the final image.

In the next sections, we shall briefly discuss three areas of investigation: iterated function systems, fractals in 3D, and ray-tracing of fractals.

13.4.2 Iterated function systems

As has been shown in this chapter, fractals objects used to model natural phenomena are generally based on fBm. Control of these fractals is provided by the dimension parameter and by scaling. According to Demko et al. (1985), it is not clear if such a control is sufficient to model plants and trees. For these reasons, these authors introduce fractals based on **iterated function systems** (IFS).

An IFS on a k-dimensional space is defined by a set of maps $M=\{M_1,M_2,...,M_n\}$ and a set of probabilities $\{P_1,P_2,...,P_n\}$ such as $\sum_i P_i=1$. A random walk in the k-dimensional space is then defined as follows:

- At the point Q_0, a map M_{i0} is randomly chosen with the probability P_{i0}
- The next position in the walk is then $Q_1=M_{i0}(Q_0)$
- At the point Q_1, a map M_{i1} is randomly chosen with the probability P_{i1}
- The next position in the walk is then $Q_2=M_{i1}(Q_1)$
  and so on indefinitely

Each IFS has a unique attractor, which is typically a fractal set or more formally it is the set theoretical union of the images of itself under the functions in the IFS. Intuitively, this attractor is the set about which the random walk eventually clusters. Demko et al. also introduce a P-balanced measure of the IFS which quantifies this clustering by ascribing a sense of density to the attractor.

Using an IFS with four maps, an image of a maple leaf has been generated as the attractor of this IFS. However, the most interesting part of this research is that the method also provides the possibility of solving the inverse problem: given the geometry of an object, determine an IFS that will approximately generate this object. The technique is based on tiling the original object with two or more affinely transformed copies of itself. Each transformation used to create a tile corresponds to one map in the IFS. The object would be exactly generated if the self-tiling were exact.

13.4.3 Geometric fractals in   three dimensions

Norton (1982) describes a system for generating and displaying geometric fractals in three-dimensions. The algorithm used to generate the surfaces, well adapted for an array processor, requires a great deal of space and time. As 3D surfaces are assumed to

Fig.13.13. Three-dimensional fractal. Courtesy of Alan Norton, IBM T.J. Watson Research Center, Yorktown Heights, New York

have an interior and an exterior, the technique is based on "point determinations;" this means that calculations determine whether a point is inside or outside a specified invariant set. The technique involves iterating a function repeatedly and keeping track of the points which satisfy certain criteria. A 3D grid is used; the output of the algorithm consists of a list of boundary points on the grid. The surface is displayed using a two-stage method:

1. Assign illumination intensities to each vertex by imagining a light source
2. Produce an image depending on viewer direction

The resulting surfaces are shaded and displayed using z-buffer type algorithms. A 3D fractal is shown in Fig.13.13.

13.4.4 Ray-tracing of fractals

13.4.4.1 Kajiya algorithm
Kajiya (1982) has introduced a method of intersecting rays with fractal surfaces computed using a recursive subdivision algorithm. The surface is modeled as a large number of triangles; the X- and Y-coordinates of the vertices are set on an isometric grid and the Z-coordinates are generated recursively as explained in Sect. 13.3. The algorithm, which involves calculating all the intersections between rays and polygons, is of course impractical, because a typical scene requires the tracing of a million rays on the surface of a million polygons. To cut dramatically the number of intersections to be computed, Kajiya proposed generating the fractal surface and tracing it at the same time, thereby discarding very early the parts of the surface which do not contribute to the current pixel. In this algorithm, it is necessary to determine the extent that must enclose a fully evolved facet at any iteration level.

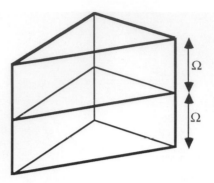

Fig.13.14. The cheesecake extent

The Kajiya rendering algorithm maintains a list of active nodes which are to be traded by the current ray. A facet is a polygon representing the surface at this level of recursion, and the extent encloses the surface given by the subtree at N. A node is active if its extent intersects the ray and no primitive polygonal facet shadows it. Assume that the fractal surface can be represented as a tree of branching ratio four with a facet and an extent associated with each node. The algorithm works as follows:

Remove the closest node N from the active node list. For each of the four extents E_i, if there is an intersection with the ray, add the corresponding nodes N_i to the active node list. If the new nodes contain primitive facets that intersect the ray, then remove all nodes shadowed by the closest facet from the active node list.

13.4.4.2 Kajiya cheesecake
The key to the performance of the algorithm lies in the specification of the extents. Kajiya proposes a cheesecake extent, which is a triangular prism centered on the triangle to be evolved, as shown in Fig.13.14.

This extent is formed by taking the convex hull of the facet translated in z by a distance $\pm \Omega$. For a minimum value of Ω, we have a tight extent. The problem is: how to choose Ω. As a fractal surface is stochastically defined, it is not possible to predict with complete certainty its variation. It implies that we just have to choose Ω to guarantee a very high (more than 99%) chance of the cheesecake enclosing the fully evolved surface. For example, for a surface following a Gaussian distribution, the probability that the center point extends beyond the cheesecake is twice the tail of the distribution.

13.4.4.3 Bouville approach
Bouville (1985) finds a problem with the cheesecake extent: since the variance of displacement decreases as we approach the vertices of the triangle, the extent becomes too broad. He proposes the use of two other types of boundary volumes—ellipsoids and bounding volumes with spherical triangles. In the first case, the major problem is the positioning and sizing of the ellipsoids. As the variance of displacements is zero at vertices of the triangle, these vertices should be on the ellipsoid surface. Moreover, one ellipsoid axis must be in the direction of the displacements. As suggested by Roth (1982), ray Eq. (10.4) is transformed so that the intersection computations are performed in a more adequate coordinate system. Bouville proposes a method (see Bouville 1985) to transform the ellipsoid into a sphere centered at the origin and of unit radius.

The second case has been proposed, because the sphere is well-suited to the surface in the z-direction but leaves large voids in the X- and Y-directions. These areas can be removed by intersecting the sphere S with the half-space H delimited by the three planes parallel to the Z-axis, each containing one edge of the triangle. The resulting volume is delimited vertically by two spherical triangles, whose vertices are the same as the plane triangle, and laterally by three disks of radius $\sqrt{1.5}$. The intersection is then easy to perform by calculating the intersections of the ray with S and H.

Miller (1986) proposes a method of ray tracing fractals in the case of reflections in water (see Sect. 15.3.3)

Figures 13.15 and 13.16 show examples of ray-traced fractals.

13.5 Fractals and stochastic modeling at MIRALab

13.5.1 Fractals based on recursive subdivision

At MIRALab, fractals have been implemented based on the recursive subdivision. Fractal polygons are created using algorithms similar to those described in Sect. 13.3. In particular, subdivisions of meshes of triangles and quadrilaterals are widely used. Figure 13.17 shows the generation of an image using this method.

In this section, we describe the implementation of the recursive subdivision for triangles and emphasize innovative techniques to choose the midpoints in the subdivision (Magnenat-Thalmann et al. 1987). Before explaining how the technique was implemented, we should define the operation. It consists of receiving an object F_1 and generating a fractal surface F_2 composed of triangles with edges of a length less than a predefined value DIMEDGE. The fractal surface F_2 is generated from the original object F_1; if this object is not a mesh of triangles, it is first triangulated.

At each step, each triangle has to be subdivided into four smaller triangles, as discussed in Sect. 13.3. When triangles are subdivided, it is essential to pay attention to the external consistency. In this case, consistency means that if two adjacent triangles share the same edge which is too long, they will have to share the same new generated vertex. To solve this problem, new vertices are generated using a hashtable of records with a key consisting of the numbers of the two vertices defining an edge.

The general algorithm is as follows:

for each triangle of the original object
    for each edge of the triangle
        if the edge has a length ≥ DIMEDGE
        then
            if a vertex has not already been generated for the pair of vertices
            then
                Calculate a new vertex between the two vertices and record it into the
                    hashtable

Fig.13.15. Ray-tracing of fractals. By C.Bouville, C.C.E.T.T., Cesson-Sévigné, France

Fig.13.16. Tahoe afternoon; experimental ray-tracing software used to render fractal mountains, clouds, and ripples. Courtesy of P.Wattenberg, Sandia National Laboratories

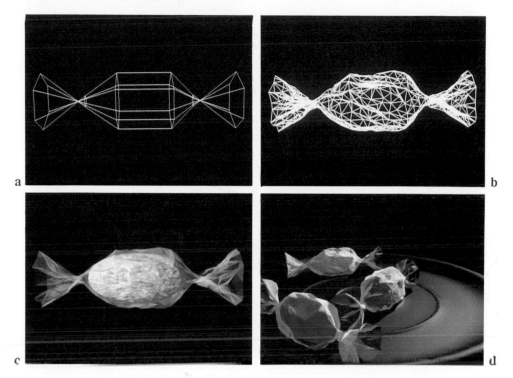

Fig.13.17 a-d. The generation of fractal surfaces: candies. © 1986 MIRALab, H.E.C. and University of Montreal

13.5.2 Controlling choice of midpoint in recursive subdivision

When an edge is too long, it is subdivided by a process similar to that described in Sect. 13.3. However, a more extensive way of choosing the midpoint has been developed (Magnenat-Thalmann et al. 1987). The midpoint is randomly generated inside a revolution volume where the axis is the edge itself. Now, we may completely define our FRACTAL operation by the means of the procedure:

procedure FRACTAL(F1:FIG; DIMEDGE, ECC, DISP:REAL; **var** F2:FIG)

Three parameters allow control of the recursive subdivision DIMEDGE, ECC, and DISP. DIMEDGE is the maximum length that may have an edge on the fractal surface. ECC defines the eccentricity of the smallest cylinder surrounding the revolution volume. It represents the ratio between the cylinder radius and its length. When ECC has a large value, the fractal surface is more irregular. For ECC=0, all generated points are on the axis, which means that the shape of the figure is not changed, but triangles are smaller. With a small value of ECC, there are only small irregularities. Figure 13.18 shows the effect of the ECC parameter. DISP is a parameter which specifies the displacement of the revolution volume toward the segment center. Fig.13.19 shows interesting values of DISP and the corresponding shape of the revolution volume. Interesting combinations of the parameters ECC and DISP are also presented for a single tetrahedron in Fig.13.20.

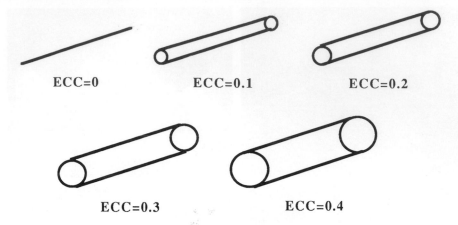

ECC=0   ECC=0.1   ECC=0.2

ECC=0.3   ECC=0.4

Fig.13.18. Effect of the ECC parameter

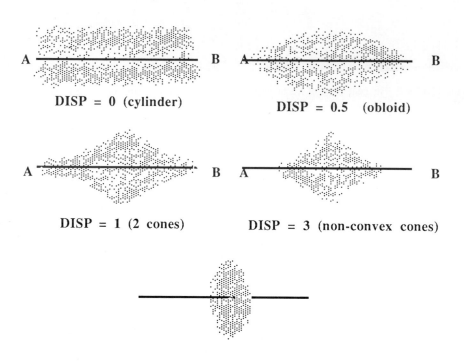

A ——————————————— B   A ————————————————— B

DISP = 0 (cylinder)   DISP = 0.5   (obloid)

A ——————————————— B   A ——————————————— B

DISP = 1 (2 cones)   DISP = 3 (non-convex cones)

Fig.13.19. Effect of the DISP parameter

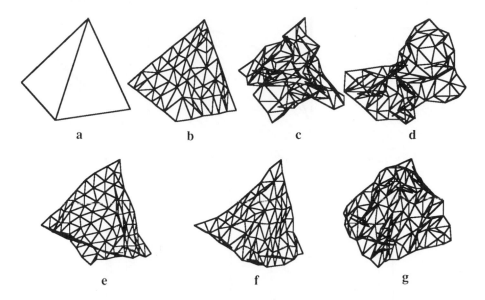

Fig.13.20 a-g. Combinations of the parameter ECC and DISP for a single tetrahedron. **a** original tetrahedron; **b** THR=6, ECC=0, DISP=2; **c** THR=6, ECC=1, DISP=2; **d** THR=6, ECC=3, DISP=2; **e** THR=5, ECC=0.1, DISP=100; **f** THR=5, ECC=0.1, DISP=5; **g** THR=6, ECC=0.1, DISP=1

13.5.3 Algorithm to generate midpoint

The revolution volume is determined from the parameters ECC and DISP. When we consider the half-volume in the reference system <0,1> x <0,1>, we may use the formula:

$$y = x^{DISP} \tag{13.9}$$

Figure 13.21 shows the function for different values of DISP.

The function may be easily applied to the axis using a reference system transformation with B_1 and B_2, two perpendicular vectors, normalized and perpendicular to the axis as shown in Fig.13.22. Let B_3 be a vector along the axis with a random length. B_3 is calculated using Eq. (13.9) and a random value H between 0 and 1. The z-value, between 0 and 1, is obtained as follows:

$$\frac{\int_0^z \pi\, (x^{DISP})^2\, dx}{\int_0^1 \pi\, (x^{DISP})^2\, dx} = z^{2DISP+1} = H \tag{13.10}$$

$$z = H^{\frac{1}{2DISP+1}} \tag{13.11}$$

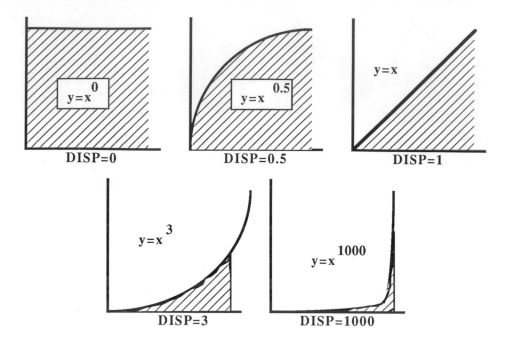

Fig.13.21. Examples of functions $y=x^{DISP}$

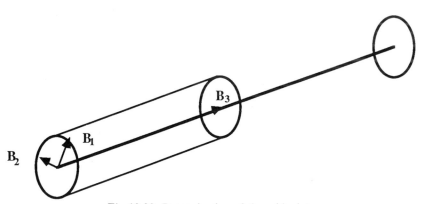

Fig.13.22. Determination of the midpoint

Fig.13.23. Chessboard. © 1986 MIRALab, H.E.C. and University of Montreal

13.5.4 Stochastic textures

At MIRALab, Burgess (1987) proposes a perturbation of the normal length using stochastic processes. The degree of absorption of the light by the surface is changed by modifying the length of the normal at the points corresponding to the pixels of the surface. The equation of the perturbed normal is as follows:

$$\mathbf{N'} = d\,\mathbf{N} \qquad\qquad (13.12)$$

with $d = |S|$ if $|S| \leq 1$ $d=1$ otherwise

S is the result of an fBm function computed from the values of h and the scale factor as explained in Sect. 13.3. The seeds used for the pseudorandom generator of the normal law centered at zero are derived from the initial seed given by the user, with h and the scale factor given by the user at the surface creation.

Figure 13.23 shows an image of such textures.

14 Fuzzy and soft objects

14.1 Phenomena modeling

In the real world, many objects do not have smooth, well-defined, and shiny surfaces. Their shapes are irregular and ill-defined and may change with time. These objects are called **fuzzy objects** by Reeves (1983). Fuzzy objects can of course be represented by geometric primitives. For example, Schachter (1983) describes the simulation of cumulus cloud layers by a concatenation of cloud groups, each consisting of about 75 sun-shaded ellipsoids confined to a circular envelope. Schachter also shows how smoke trails can be simulated by strings of long, thin, translucent ellipsoids. The results, however, are quite unrealistic, although they are useful especially in the case of flight simulators.

More realistic models for natural objects have been created and their application will be further discussed in Chap. 15. Csuri et al. (1979) have proposed a model for representing a cloud of smoke. The cloud is first generated by a 3D mathematical approximation. Then, a 2D array of the intensities is created by ray-tracing. A procedure model has been well described by Marshall et al. (1980) and is one of the first attempts to model objects as collections of particles. Blinn (1982) has produced images of the rings of Saturn using light-reflection functions for simulating clouds and dusty surfaces. The technique consists of simulating light passing through and being reflected by layers of particles. Fractal surfaces (see Chap. 15) may also be used to model fuzzy objects; for example, clouds may be constructed using fractals; unfortunately, there is a lack of dynamic aspect to the images.

The traditional separation of image synthesis into object modeling and image rendering is not always well-adapted to any image. Fractals are typical examples where there is a strong interaction between the object modeling and rendering phase. Furthermore, as already discussed, some objects change in shape and appearance. This change may be spontaneous or in response to surroundings; objects that change in this way are called **soft objects** by Wyvill et al. (1986b). With such objects, not only object modeling and image rendering have to be considered as a whole, but motion has also to be integrated into the design process. We call **phenomena modeling** the activity that consists of modeling objects and motion at the same time. Examples of applications of phenomena modeling are clouds, water, fire, and smoke and also living forms. Time-dependent procedural models are a very flexible way of defining phenomena. Procedural models (Newell 1975; Clark 1976; see Sect. 1.4) have proved to be a very flexible way of defining graphic objects. Associated with data flow methods (Hedelman 1984), procedural methods provide a useful approach to image composition and animation. A procedural model is generally represented by a procedure and its parameters. By modifying the parameters, an instance of the model is changed.

In the following sections, we present four different kinds of procedural model which are very suitable for the design of natural phenomena.

1. Particle systems introduced by Reeves (1983)
2. Soft objects generalized by Wyvill et al. (1986, 1986b,c) and based on Blinn (1982a)
3. Light scattering techniques introduced by Blinn (1982) and refined by Kajiya (1984) and Max (1986b)
4. Analog cellular automata defined by Thalmann (1986) from von Neumann's theory (1966)

Applications and more specific techniques will be discussed in Chap. 17, which presents all approaches to the implementation of phenomena modeling of, e.g., fire, clouds, trees, water.

14.2 Particle systems

14.2.1 Reeves method

A systematic method for modeling fuzzy objects called the **particle systems method** has been developed by Reeves (1983). A particle system is a collection of particles that together represent a fuzzy object. Over a period of time, particles in the system are born, move, change, and die.

Reeves describes how to compute each frame in a motion sequence with the following steps:

1. Generate new particles by means of controlled stochastic processes and assign them individual attributes
2. Extinguish particles whose lifetime is over
3. Move and transform the remaining particles according to their dynamic attributes
4. Render the image of the living particles in a frame buffer

The number of particles generated at a given frame NP_f can be determined by an equation involving either the mean number of particles MP_f generated at a frame and its variance VP_f:

$$NP_f = MP_f + RANDOM \cdot VP_f \qquad (14.1)$$

or the mean number generated per screen area MP_{sf} and its variance VP_{sf} per screen area:

$$NP_{sf} = (MP_{sf} + RANDOM \cdot VP_{sf}) \times SA \qquad (14.2)$$

where RANDOM is a function that returns a distributed random number between -1 and 1 and SA is the screen area.

The mean number of particles generated by frame MP_f may vary over time as a function of the frame number f:

$$MP_f = MP_{f0} + \Delta MP \cdot (f-f_0) \qquad (14.3)$$

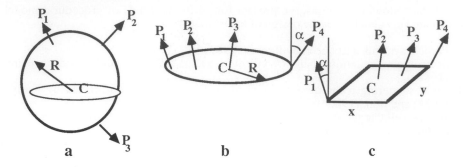

Fig.14.1 a-c. Particle system shapes. P_i are the particles. **a** Sphere of center C and radius R; **b** circle of center C and radius R in the xy plane; α is the ejection angle; **c** rectangle of center C and edges xy; α is the ejection angle

14.2.2 Particle attributes and dynamics

For each new particle generated, values are determined for the following attributes: initial position, velocity, size, color, transparency, shape (sphere or rectangle), and lifetime. Initial values may also vary over time by giving an average value and the variance or the maximum variation. For example, the initial color COL is given by:

$$COL = M_{COL} + RANDOM \cdot V_{COL} \qquad (14.4)$$

where M_{COL} is the mean color and V_{COL} the maximum variation.

The system also has a generation shape, which defines a region into which newly born particles are randomly placed. Figure 14.1 shows three different kinds of system shape.

Global dynamic attributes such as "rates of change" are also defined in the particle system to control motion and transformations. A particle is killed when its lifetime reaches zero, accomplished by decrementing the current lifetime at each frame.

14.2.3 Particle rendering

Particle rendering can be complex because particles can hide each other and transparency and shadows are also often required. However, for explosions and fires, Reeves (1983) describes a very simple algorithm based on the assumption that each particle is displayed as a point light source.

A pixel gains light when it is covered by a particle; the amount depends on attributes like the particle's transparency and color. A particle's size and shape determine the covered pixels. A hierarchy of particle systems can also be defined to control complicated fuzzy objects.

In Reeves' work, particle systems do not intersect with other surface-based modeling primitives. Objects modeled using other techniques are composited together with particle system objects in a postrendering compositing stage (see Chap. 16). This compositing stage is performed by splitting the image of the particle system into subimages based on clipping planes defined in the model coordinate space. An experiment for combining particles and polygons is described by Wyvill et al. (1985), but they consider particles as single pixels or spheres, which may be very expensive in terms of CPU time. An algorithm which integrates particle and polygon rendering has been developed by Magnenat-Thalmann et al. (1986) based on an A-buffer algorithm. This algorithm is described in detail in the next section.

14.2.4 Integrating particle and polygon rendering using A-buffer algorithm

This rendering method (Magnenat-Thalmann et al. 1986) is based on a scan-line A-buffer algorithm, which is an extension of the processing of translucent polygons. Particle locations are first calculated in the eye coordinate system and then in the image coordinate system using the same procedure as that used for polygons. Each particle is considered a translucent surface; this means that it is possible to use the same strategy as for the processing of translucent polygons. In our case, the algorithm used is based on the idea of an **A-buffer** or accumulation buffer as introduced by Carpenter (1984) for antialiasing processing (see Sect. 8.3.4). In this case, the A-buffer is an array of elements composed of three fields: the depth of the nontranslucent pixel, a pointer to the sorted list of translucent pixels, and a field for shadow processing. In PASCAL, the data structure is as follows:

```
type
    TypPtPixcl = ↑PixelStruct;
    DepthBufType = array [0..Resolution] of
                        record
                            Depth: DOUBLE; (*depth of the nontranslucent pixel *)
                            PixelSt: TypPtPixel; (* sorted list of translucent pixels *)
                            InfoSh: RecShadow  (* informations for shadows*)
                        end;
    PixelStruct =   record
                        next: TypPtPixel;
                        Depth: DOUBLE; (* pixel depth *)
                        TT: REAL; (* transparency coefficient *)
                        PixelSt: TypPtPixel;
                        case BOOLEAN of
                            FALSE: (CC: Color); (* color for pixcl shading *)
                            TRUE: (Sh: RecShadow) (*informations for shadows*)
                    end;
```

The list of translucent pixels contains translucent pixels found coming from polygons and pixels belonging to particles, sorted according to their depth. Particles are distinguished from translucent pixels, using negative values for the transparency coefficient.

The final color of the pixel is found by computing the following index of luminance:

$$\text{lumin} = \ln \left(\frac{r+g+b}{3} + i \right) / 2 \qquad (14.5)$$

where **r**, **g**, and **b** are the color values of the current processing particle; the average value of the R, G, and B components of the particles for the pixel are then multiplied by **lumin** to obtain the final color of the pixel.

The formula for calculating lumin is rather empirical; however, it seems appropriate because it increases significantly when there are extra particles for a pixel with few particles but not for a pixel with many existing particles.

14.2.4.1 Time and memory optimization

The use of a sorted list of translucent pixels is very practical, because it allows particles to be combined with polygons, even with translucent polygons. However, it tends to become very expensive when the number of particles accumulated for a pixel is too high. This is because the list for the pixel is too long during the sort stage. In fact, Magnenat-Thalmann et al. (1986) note that if the size of the list per pixel is limited to 30 particles, there is no difference on a Raster Technologies One/80 terminal (1280x1024x24 bits) except if the average of the transmission coefficient for these particles is less than 0.1. But, in terms of time optimization, there is a gain by a factor of 10-15.

For each scan-line intersecting a particle, a pointer to this particle is inserted into the bucket of particles corresponding to this scan-line. This indicates that this particle is active for this scan-line. Processing of these particle buckets is similar to the processing of an edge bucket in a regular scan-line algorithm. With this approach, a list of active particles is always stored.

Before the display of the scan-line, particles of the current scan-line are inserted into the list of active particles, because they become active for this scan-line. After the calculation of the intensities for the current scan-line, particles which become inactive for the next scan-line are removed from the list of active particles. A particle becomes inactive when the following condition is detected:

$$NoScanLine+1 > YPosScreen+Size$$

With this approach, particle systems may be present in any animation scene involving polygon-based primitives and free-form surfaces. Figure 14.2 shows an animated sequence of a Japanese pagoda destroyed by fire; a wind is blowing on the fire.

Other realistic effects such as transparency, 3D texture by bump mapping, image mapping, fractals, shadows, light spots, fog, and stereoscopic cameras may coexist with particles. Moreover, any scene involving particles may be computed with antialiasing. However, with this algorithm, particles may not produce shadows.

14.2.5 Applications and extensions of particle systems

Particle systems were used to produce the Genesis Demo sequence from the Lucasfilm Ltd. movie *Star Trek II: The Wrath of Khan*. In particular, a wall of fire was successfully rendered and will be discussed further in Sect. 15.5.1. Fireworks have also been modeled using particle systems.

The modeling of clouds as particle systems is much more complex because particles cannot be rendered as point light sources but must be considered individual light-reflecting objects. Cloud models are also very complex because of their shape, atmospheric factors, and shadows. Reeves (1985) proposes shading models for particle systems. However, the algorithm is very specific to the rendering of trees and will be discussed in Sect. 15.6.3.

Figure 14.3 shows an image with Reeves particles systems.

Other extensions to Reeves' work have been proposed. In particular, Wyvill et al. (1985) introduce particles as fuzzy balls with a radius of influence. At the rendering stage, a particle is treated as a sphere of radius r, with varying translucency. The edge of the sphere is almost perfectly translucent, contributing almost nothing to the image, while at the center the full color intensity of the particle is added to the pixel value. A negative exponential function is used to provide a smooth transition between the two extremes:

Fig.14.2. Pagoda. © 1986 MIRALab, H.E.C. and University of Montreal

Fig.14.3. White sands. By Alvy Ray Smith © 1986 Pixar; all rights reserved. The flowering plants are grown in three dimensions from a single cell using an algorithmic computer model, written by the artist and based on mathematics by A.Lindenmayer, P.Hogeweg, and B.Hesper. The grass was contributed by William Reeves, using his procedural modeling technique called particle systems. The compositing software is by Thomas Porter and the hidden-surface software by Loren Carpenter. The picture was rendered using an Ikonas graphics processor and frame buffers. The resolution is 512x488, 24 bits/pixel. The Chinese (also Japanese) in the upper left-hand corner is the artist's name and is part of the piece

$$f = e^{-\frac{d^2}{s^2}} \qquad (14.6)$$

This gives the fraction of the intensity to be added to the image at a distance d from the center of the particle; s^2 is proportional to the radius of influence r.

Yaeger et al. (1986) describe a specific application of special particle systems for modeling the planet Jupiter. Particles are moved using a real physical model based on fluid mechanics. The particle renderer produces 2D output, which serves as a texture map in a polygonal rendering system.

Another extension developed at MIRALab includes Brownian motion of particles and will be further described in Sect. 14.6.

14.3 Soft objects

14.3.1 Blinn algebraic surfaces

Blinn (1982a) describes an interesting approach for the purpose of displaying molecular models. It is based on a mathematical model similar in form to a simulation of electron density maps. In quantum chemistry, the electron is represented in an atom by a density function $\Psi(x,y,z)$ of the spatial location. For example, for a hydrogen atom:

$$\Psi(x,y,z) = e^{-ar} \qquad (14.7)$$

where $r = \sqrt{(x-x_1)^2+(y-y_1)^2+(z-z_1)^2}$ and x_1, y_1, and z_1 are the coordinates of the atom.

For a collection of atoms, we may sum the contribution of each atom:

$$\Psi(x,y,z) = \sum_i b_i\, e^{-a_i r_i} \qquad (14.8)$$

where $r_i = \sqrt{(x-x_i)^2+(y-y_i)^2+(z-z_i)^2}$

Similarly, Blinn shows that the net density contribution of one atom may be calculated as:

$$\Psi_i(x,y,z) = T\, e^{\frac{B_i r_i^2}{R_i^2} - B_i} \qquad (14.9)$$

where B_i is a parameter that alters the blobbiness of the object and R_i is the radius of the atom. T is a threshold amount that we may consider as 1, according to Blinn.

Once the surface is described by the summation of terms like those in Eq. (14.9), Blinn used a straightforward technique to render this surface. The algorithm has been previously presented in Sect. 5.7.3. For each pixel location, the defining algebraic equation reduces to a univariate equation in z. The solutions to this equation yield the z-depth of the surface at that pixel.

When the number of atoms is large, the summation of $\Psi_i(x,y,z)$ terms is too expensive in terms of CPU time. For this reason, Blinn suggests taking into account only atoms which are close to the scan ray.

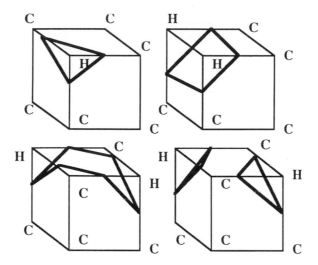

Fig.14.4. Cubes with cold and hot vertices. *C* cold, *H* hot

14.3.2 Scalar fields

The technique introduced by Blinn corresponds to an approach where objects are described by a scalar field. The scalar field is a mathematical function defined over a volume of space. In the Blinn approach, the field is based on the field of electron density around an atom. Wyvill et al. (1986b) show that a wide variety of shapes can be represented by a suitable choice of field function. In their method, called **soft objects**, the function represents arbitrary shapes when the isosurfaces (surfaces of constant function value) are plotted. The function, therefore, depends on a set of given independent key points. A radius of influence R is defined and the contribution to the field made by any key point beyond its radius of influence is zero. The contribution at the position of the point itself is the maximum value 1.

From these assumptions, Wyvill et al. derive the field function:

$$C(r) = a\frac{r^6}{R^6} + b\frac{r^4}{R^4} + c\frac{r^2}{R^2} + 1 \qquad (14.10)$$

where r is the point <x,y,z> and R the radius of influence; a, b, and c are constants with the approximate values:

$$a = -0.44444 \quad b = 1.888889 \quad c = -2.444444$$

To define the isosurface of value F, Wyvill et al. use a simple polygon mesh. The part of the space occupied by the surface is divided by a 3D grid into small cubes. The algorithm then proceeds in three steps:

1. All the cubes which are intersected by the surface are found as follows: for each key point, the field is calculated at a succession of adjacent grid points along one axis until a point with a field value less than F is encountered. This point and the previous one form the end points of one edge of a cube which is intersected by the surface

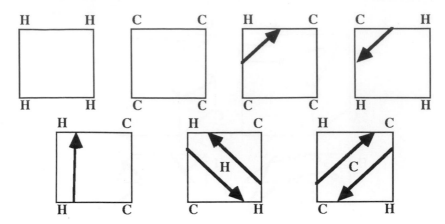

Fig.14.5. Different cases for connecting intersections. *C* cold, *H* hot

2. Each cube obtained in the first step is then examined to see whether or not its neighbors are intersected by the surface. If a neighbor is intersected, the neighbors of this cube are then inspected and so on until all the cubes intersected by the surface have been found

3. For each cube intersected by the surface, we have only eight field values at the vertices. From this, a set of polygons is constructed, which represents a part of the isosurface that intersects the cube. The process is as follows: first, points which approximate the intersection of the isosurface with the edges of the cube are found. These are then connected to make the polygons. If we suppose that the value of the function for the isosurface is F, any vertex whose function value is greater than F is called HOT and any other is called COLD. Examples are shown in Fig.14.4

The algorithm works as follows:

```
for each edge of cube <p,q>
    if p is HOT and q is COLD  or p is COLD and q is HOT
    then create intersection <p,q>;
for each face of the cube
  Create edges according to Fig.14.5
while edges remain do
  start:=any edge
  polygon:={start};
  Remove start from edge array;
  next:=successor of start;
  while next <> start do
     polygon:=polygon+{next};
     Remove next from edge array
  Output polygon
end;
```

Note that for two adjacent vertices p (COLD) and q (HOT) with field values F_p and F_q, the intersection I of the isosurface with pq is computed by taking as distance d from p to I:

$$d = \frac{F - F_p}{F_q - F_p}$$

(14.11)

Fig.14.6. Soft objects. By B.Wyvill, C.McPheeters and G.Wyvill, University of Calgary

This linear interpolation is reasonable when the cubes are small enough.
Figure 14.6 shows an image generated using soft objects.

14.4   Volume density scattering   models

14.4.1 Blinn low-albedo approximation

This approach was developed for the problem of studying the rings of Saturn. It consists of statistically simulating the light passing through and being reflected by clouds of similar small particles. The basic model assumes a cloud of spherical reflecting particles of radius r, positioned randomly in a layer of thickness T with n particles per unit of volume. Figure 14.7 shows the layer.

The angle α between **L** and **E** is very important and is called the **phase angle**. A function characterizing the total brightness of a particle is the phase function $\varphi(\alpha)$. We need a way of determining the total brightness function B of a fuzzy object. Blinn(1982) makes a series of simplifying assumptions and obtains the following result:

$$B = \frac{\omega}{\mu} \varphi(\alpha)\, S \ + \text{Tr Col} \tag{14.12}$$

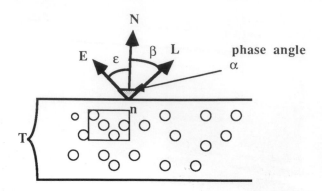

Fig.14.7. Geometry of a cloud layer. n is the number of particles per unit of volume, N the normal, E the emission direction, L the incident direction, T the layer thickness, α the phase angle, β the incident angle and ε the emission angle

where ω is the albedo, which is a measure of the reflectivity of the particle, μ is the cosine of the emission angle, $\varphi(\alpha)$ is the phase function, S is the scattering probability, Tr is the transparency of the fuzzy object, and Col is the background color.

Assuming that the albedo ω is near 0 (low albedo), Blinn has shown that the scattering probability may be calculated as:

$$S = \frac{\tau}{\mu} e^{-\tau/\mu}$$ (14.13)

and the transparency may be written as follows:

$$Tr = e^{-\tau/\mu} + \omega \, \varphi(\pi)$$ (14.14)

where τ is the optical depth. This means that light traveling through a fuzzy object of optical depth τ is attenuated by the factor $e^{-\tau}$.

For the phase function $\varphi(\alpha)$, several possibilities exist, depending on the assumptions:

1. Constant function: $\varphi(\alpha)=1$
2. Anisotropic function: $\varphi(\alpha)=1 + x \cos(\alpha)$ where x is a property of the material
3. Lambert function: $\varphi(\alpha)=\frac{8}{3\pi} (\sin \alpha + (\pi-\alpha) \cos \alpha)$
4. Rayleigh diffraction function: $\varphi(\alpha) = \frac{3}{4} (1+ \cos^2 \alpha)$
5. Henyey-Greenstein function: $\varphi(\alpha) = \dfrac{1-g^2}{(1+g^2-2 \, g \cos \alpha)^{3/2}}$; which is the equation
   of an ellipse of eccentricity g in polar coordinates; g depends on the material

Blinn has applied his model to a cloud of reflective ice particles in orbit about Saturn–the rings of Saturn. More details will be given in Sect. 15.4.1.

14.4.2 Atmospheric scattering

Max (1986a,b) also proposes a single scattering model for light diffusion through haze. Assume, as shown in Fig. 14.8, the light source (sun) at infinity with $\mathbf{L}$ a unit vector in the direction of the light, $\mathbf{U}$ a vector from the eye (at origin) along a viewing ray R, and H a height above which no data in the model extend.

Two angles are defined—the angle θ between R and the vertical and the angle ϕ between $\mathbf{L}$ and the vertical. Assume that the haze has constant density and absorbs a fraction b dr of the light along an infinitesimal length dr of the ray R.

The intensity at distance r through the haze may be written as:

$$I(r) = I(0) \, e^{-br} \qquad (14.15)$$

Now consider a nonshadowed interval $\mathbf{AB}$ on the ray R. From Fig. 14.8, we may write that the intensity reaching a point $\mathbf{P} = s\mathbf{U}$ on the interval $\mathbf{AB}$ is:

$$I = I_0 \, e^{-b(H - s\cos\theta)\sec\phi} \qquad (14.16)$$

where I_0 is the sunlight intensity at height H.

As the point $\mathbf{P}$ is at a distance s from the eye, the scattered light is further attenuated by a factor $\exp(-bs)$. Finally, the total light I_T reaching the eye, scattered from the interval between $\mathbf{A} = s_i\mathbf{U}$ and $\mathbf{B} = s_{i+1}\mathbf{U}$, is now:

$$\int_{s_i}^{s_{i+1}} \rho \, I_0 \, e^{-bH\sec\phi \, - \, bs(1-\cos\theta\sec\phi)} \, ds \qquad (14.17)$$

where ρ is the scattering coefficient.

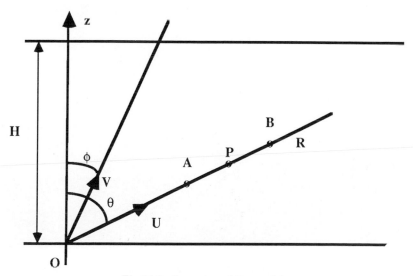

Fig.14.8. Geometry of the model

This integral has a solution of the form:

$$C_1 (e^{-C_2(s_{i+1})} - e^{-C_2(s_i)}) \qquad (14.18)$$

where C_1 and C_2 are constants depending on the ray.

The calculation may be extended to layered fog by assuming that the scattering coefficient may be expressed as:

$$\rho = \beta\, b(z) \qquad (14.19)$$

where β is a constant depending on the angle between the viewing ray and the sun direction.

The total scattered energy E_s is obtained by adding up the integrals from each of the illuminated segments along the ray from the eye to a surface point.

For the output color, Max uses the following equation:

$$\mathbf{F} = T\,\mathbf{S} + (1\text{-}T)\,\mathbf{H} + E_s\,\mathbf{E} \qquad (14.20)$$

where $\mathbf{F}$, $\mathbf{S}$, $\mathbf{H}$, and $\mathbf{E}$ are color vectors with r,g,b components, $\mathbf{F}$ is the output color, $\mathbf{S}$ the surface color, and $\mathbf{E} = \mathbf{I}\text{-}\mathbf{H}$ is the extra glow corresponding to the difference between the haze color in shadow ($\mathbf{H}$) and illuminated ($\mathbf{I}$).

Figure 14.9 shows an image generated using this model.

Fig.14.9. Sunlight coming through a break in the clouds. By Nelson Max, Lawrence Livermore National Laboratory

14.4.3 Ray-tracing approach

The Blinn low albedo approximation suffers from a number of defects when used to model clouds, simply because clouds have a very high albedo. Kajiya (1984) proposes a more general scattering model which models multiple radiative scattering against particles with high albedo. The author states that his representation may also model media which absorb and emit light such as flames.

Blinn has assumed a value of the albedo ω near 0. For an albedo near 1 (high albedo), Kajiya uses a method which provides a perturbation solution with a series of forced conservative scattering equations. He expands the scattering equation into spherical harmonics and solves the system by relaxation.

Kajiya (1984) proposes a new technique for ray tracing volume densities without any viewing or lighting restrictions. He separates the rendering process into two steps:

14.4.3.1 For each frame (or sometimes less frequently)

The radiation is driven from light source i through a density array $\rho(x,y,z)$ into an array $I_i(x,y,z)$, which holds the contribution of each light source to the brightness of each point in space. The array $I_i(x,y,z)$ is computed as:

$$I_1(x,y,z) = e^{\kappa/\rho \int_\Gamma r(\gamma)\, d\gamma} \tag{14.21}$$

where κ is the absorption coefficient, ρ the density of matter in the volume extent, and Γ the path:

$$\Gamma = \Gamma_{x,y,z} = <x(t),y(t),z(t)> \tag{14.22}$$

The integrated optical path length along a particular ray is calculated by bilinearly sampling and summing the density array along the ray.

14.4.3.2 for each ray trace

The ray is first culled against a bounding rectangular prism as an extent. The brightness B is calculated by Romberg integration as:

$$B = \int_{\lambda_1}^{\lambda_2} A\, C\, \rho(x(t),y(t),z(t))\, dt \tag{14.23}$$

λ_1 is the beginning of the path between the eye and the farthest visible volume element. It is the maximum value between 0 and the distance to the nearest intersection with the bounding extent. λ_2 is the ending of the path. It is the minimum distance to the nearest intersection point with the rest of the world database and the distance to the farthest intersection with the bounding extent. A is the amount of attenuation due to absorption and scattering of the material visible to the eye:

$$A = e^{-r I'} \tag{14.24}$$

where:

$$I' = \int_{\lambda_1}^{t} \rho(x(t'),y(t'),z(t'))\, dt' \tag{14.25}$$

C is the brightness contribution of each light source to the brightness of the particular point:

$$C = \sum_i I_i(x(t),y(t),z(t))\ p(\cos\theta_i) \qquad\qquad (14.26)$$

where $p(\cos\theta_i)$ is the phase function depending on the phase angle θ_i.

Kajiya describes an application of his diffuse rendering algorithm to a cloud model, which is discussed in more detail in Sect. 15.4.1.

14.5 Cellular automata

14.5.1 Lifegame approach

As described by Gardner (1971), John Conway's Lifegame belongs to a class of simulation games. The basic idea is to start with a simple configuration of organisms one to a cell and then observe how this changes as genetic laws for births, deaths, and survival are applied. Laws (or rules) are applied at each generation. Rules have to be chosen very carefully in order to meet three criteria:

1. No initial pattern should be proved to grow without limit
2. There should be initial patterns which seem to grow without limit.
3. After a certain number of periods, patterns should terminate in one of three ways:
   i) Fading away by overcrowding or isolation
   ii) Entering a stable period without any more change
   iii) Entering an endless cycle of two or more periods

Conway's classic game may be formulated using an unlimited checkerboard, which is in fact a 2D array of cells with two possible states (dead or alive). There are three transition rules:

Birth rule: each empty cell adjacent to exactly three living organisms is a birth cell. This means that an organism will be born at the next generation

Death rule: each living organism with one or no neighbors dies from isolation; each living organism with four or more neighbors dies from overpopulation

Survival rule: each living organism with two or three neighbors survives to the next generation

14.5.2 Theory of cellular automata

Conway's Lifegame is in fact a trivial and well-known application of a more general theory called the **theory of cellular automata** (Wolfram 1984). Lifegame provides a good example for explaining the conceptual framework of the theory. John von Neumann (1966) originally developed the theory of cellular automata. He used it to prove the capacity of a machine to reproduce itself. This was, however, only a specific component of what would have been a more general theory of complex natural and artificial automata. His premature death left incomplete most of his work on automata. Von Neumann's work in fluid mechanics and the fact that existing analytical methods were inadequate for obtaining information for the solution of nonlinear partial differential equations led him into computation and the study of automata (Burk 1966).

Except for Borto's doctoral thesis (Borto 1975), this theory of automata is more often used in the areas of logic and computation than in more analytical applications.

A **cellular automaton** (Demongeot et al. 1985; Lobry and Reder 1985) is a cellular space or set of cells with the following properties:

1. The cells are regularly distributed in an N-dimensional space
2. Each cell can possess, in a given generation, a state chosen from a finite set
3. A configuration of the cellular automaton is defined as the set of states of all the cells in a given generation
4. The state of a cell in a generation depends exclusively on the states of the neighboring cells
5. A transition function defines the state of a cell from the states of those in its neighborhood in the previous generation

An important feature of cellular automata is that all state transitions occur at the same time in discrete time steps, forming successive generations as the model evolves. The aim of the game is to find an initial configuration which evolves over many generations.

Cellular automata can serve as explicit models for a wide variety of biological, chemical, and physical processes: biological pattern formation, snowflake formation, turbulent fluids. Current models of natural systems are usually based on partial differential equations. Cellular automata provide alternative and complementary models.

14.5.3 Analog cellular automata

Thalmann (1986) defines **an analog cellular automaton** as a homogeneous spatial organization in one, two, or three dimensions of interconnected finite state automata. The state of each automaton is characterized by the use of real numbers that correspond to some physical characteristics of the system being modeled (position, velocity, color, surface normal). State transitions functions are defined on these real numbers and are applied to all automata at the same time using information from the state of neighboring automata. Each application of these rules forms a generation. To implement the model, we set up an initial configuration assigning a certain value to some automata. The rest of the configuration remains in a stable state.

Analog automata may be easily implemented in structures corresponding to MxN grids. In computer graphics, typical examples are a class of polygon-based objects, made up of MxN polygons. For example, ruled surfaces, like cylinders or revolution surfaces, and free-form surfaces, like Coons, Bézier, or ß-splines, may be represented as an arrangement of MxN polygons.

Consider now P_{ij}, each polygon of such an object. To each P_{ij}, we may associate a state S_{ij}. This state changes with time t according to a transition function T :

$$S_{ij}(t+1) = T(S_{ij}(t), S_{i-1,j}(t), S_{i,j-1}(t), S_{i+1,j}(t), S_{i,j+1}(t)) \qquad (14.27)$$

We may also consider that a state S_{ij} is characterized by L state variables $W_{ij}{}^k$ with a transition function T^k defined for each state variable. If the state variables are independent, we define:

$$W_{ij}{}^{k}(t+1) = T^{k}(W_{ij}{}^{k}(t), W_{i-1,j}{}^{k}(t), W_{i,j-1}{}^{k}(t), W_{i+1,j}{}^{k}(t), W_{i,j+1}{}^{k}(t)) \quad (14.28)$$

$$i=1,M \qquad j=1,N \qquad k=1,L$$

If the state variables are not independent, we have:

$$W_{ij}{}^{\{s\}}(t+1) = T^{\{s\}}(W_{ij}{}^{\{s\}}(t), W_{i-1,j}{}^{\{s\}}(t), W_{i,j-1}{}^{\{s\}}(t), W_{i+1,j}{}^{\{s\}}(t), W_{i,j+1}{}^{\{s\}}(t)) \quad (14.29)$$

where $W_{xy}{}^{\{s\}}(t)$ means $W_{xy}{}^{1}(t), W_{xy}{}^{2}(t), ..., W_{xy}{}^{L-1}(t), W_{xy}{}^{L}(t)$

An implementation of surfaces based on analog cellular automata has been developed at MIRALab. This implementation is discussed in Sect. 14.6.

This Lifegame approach may be compared with traditional methods for surface modeling and rendering. The method is particularly adapted to situations where a formal physical or mathematical model is too complex to be directly implemented. In particular, analog cellular automata may be used to model perturbations of surfaces by natural phenomena such as wind. In this case, the best strategy is as follows:

1. Decompose the complex perturbation into several simpler perturbations
2. Find the right transition function to be applied to the state variables

This transition function is the main problem of the method. For complex systems like waves, where the direction of waves has to be distinguished, velocity distribution has to be considered, as will be discussed in Chap. 15.

14.6   Fuzzy objects at MIRALab

14.6.1 Control of particle systems at MIRALab

The main defect of procedural models is that they require programming and are, therefore, generally inaccessible to noncomputer specialists. For this reason, we have introduced interactive control of procedural models into our extensible director-oriented animation system MIRANIM (Magnenat-Thalmann et al. 1985a). With this approach, a user may define his own evolution laws in particle systems.

Systems may be initialized by interactive commands and then updated by animation blocks, and the laws may return any state variables. For example, we may obtain the position of the center of a particle system and consider it as the interest point for the camera. With this approach, the possibility of defining any evolution law within an animation system may provide many new possibilities for motion. Systems are controlled using seven commands: CREATESYST, SHAPESYST, SHAPEVOL, MOTIONSYST, MOTIONVOL, ORIENTATION, and STATUS. These commands, described in Sect. 17.4.2, are responsible for locating the invariable fields of a system (particle shape, system shape, acceleration) and for initializing the variable fields (velocity, center position, generator point). The generator point may represent either the point from which particles seem to emerge (this is the general rule) or the point where particles seem to converge if the initial surface is a circle or a rectangle with a negative ejection velocity. The use of a generator point considerably decreases the complexity of the calculations of the direction of the initial velocity of particles.

14.6.2 Evolution of particle systems

For each particle system, an animation block called EVOLUTIONx (where x is the system number) is activated. It controls the initial attributes of each new particle generated and global attributes like "rates of change." The blocks are activated by an interactive command as follows:

    EVOLUTIONx <initial time> <duration> <parameters>

There are 17 attributes, which are described in Sect. 17.4.3.

Each attribute may be constant or vary according to any predefined law or procedural law. Particle motion may be controlled in different ways:

1. By using predefined MIRANIM laws (linear motion, circular motion, harmonic motion)
2. By using Brownian motions: when a small particle is immersed in a liquid, it can be seen under a microscope to move in a zigzag motion. In our model, we assume that a particle moves along three 1D lines (along the axes X,Y, and Z) where it may hop from one point to either of its two neighboring points with equal probability. To obtain a law which gives the position at any time of a particle with such a motion, we have to store a global state variable for each particle. These variables are modified by an animation block and the law merely gives the current position by accessing the state variables
3. By using laws based on simultaneous differential equations (Magnenat-Thalmann and Thalmann 1986a)
4. By using procedural laws

Only in the last case does the user add his own dynamics by programming.

With this approach, any evolution law may be applied to each variable in the block. For example, the size rate of a particle may vary linearly from 1 to 2 in 10 s or the average color of new particles may oscillate between red and green in a period of 0.5 s.

The EVOLUTIONx blocks work as follows:

for each system
  Compute the number of particles to be generated
  Determine the viewing parameters to be used in accordance with the associated
      virtual camera
  while there are particles to process
    if a particle has to die
    then
      Replace it by a new particle
    else
      Make the particle older
          {This means that each characteristic changes according to the given
            parameters; the new position is calculated}
    Process the next particle

the dynamic characteristics of the system are changed: center position, velocity, generator point

14.6.3 Surface definition based on cellular automata

In this case, we consider a 2D space of MxN cells, represented by a matrix STATE. STATE[I,J] is the state variable which characterizes the cell <I,J>. This state variable is a vector which defines the displacement of the position of a vertex of the polygonal mesh. The surface is considered to have MxN vertices.

Three operations have to be defined in order to control the cellular automata :

14.6.3.1 Initialization of automata

INITSTATE(F,NU,NV,STATE,VAL)

This operation has to calculate for a given surface F, the number of vertices NU and NV. It then initializes the matrix STATE to the value VAL.

14.6.3.2 Simulation of perturbation

MODIFY(STATE,U,V,VAL)

This operation simulates a perturbation VAL at the coordinates U,V; it may be called at any time to initialize a first generation or to modify an existing state. In fact, it corresponds to adding the value VAL to the component STATE[U,V].

14.6.3.3 Application of transition function

GENERATION(STATE, NU,NV,NTIMES,TRANSIT)

This operation applies the state transition function TRANSIT to the array STATE based on the theory of cellular automata. NTIMES corresponds to the number of generations. The function TRANSIT corresponds to the function T^k defined in the previous section and it has the same parameters.

We have a fourth operation which adds to each vertex <I,J> of the surface F the value of the corresponding STATE[I,J]. This operation is called STATESURF(STATE,F).

A PASCAL implementation of analog cellular automata is as follows:

```
const NUT=100; NVT=100;
type MATRIX=array [0..NUT,0..NVT] of VECTOR;

    procedure  INITSTATE (F:FIG;var NU, NV:INTEGER; var
                      STATE:MATRIX;  VAL:VECTOR);
    var U,V,NBVERT,NBFACES:INTEGER; EXIT:BOOLEAN;
    begin
        NBVERT:=NBVECTORS(F);
        NBFACES:=NBPOLYGONS(F);
        NV:=1;
        EXIT:=FALSE;
        while (NV < TRUNC(SQRT(NBFACES)+1) and not EXIT do
        begin
            NU:=NBFACES div NV;
            if (NV+1)*(NU+1) = NBVERT then EXIT:=TRUE;
            NV:=NV+1
        end;
        NV:=NV-1
        for U:=1 to NU do
            for V:=1 to NV do STATE[U,V]:=VAL
    end;
```

```
procedure  MODIFY (var STATE: MATRIX; U,V:INTEGER;
                        VAL : VECTOR);
begin
   STATE[U,V]:=VAL
end;

procedure GENERATION (var STATE:MATRIX;
                         NU,NV,NTIME :INTEGER;
         function TRANSITION (V1,V2,V3,V4:VECTOR) : VECTOR);
var STATE2:MATRIX;
    HORZ,HORZM,HORZP,VERT,VERTM,VERTP,U,V,K:INTEGER;
begin
   for K:=1 to NTIMES do
   begin
      for U:=1 to NU do
      begin
         HORZ:=NU;
         HORZM:=((U+NU-2) mod NU)+1;
         HORZP:=(U mod NU)+1;
         for V:=1 to NV do
         begin
            VERT=NV;
            VERTM:=((V+NV-2) mod NV)+1;
            VERTP:=(V mod NV)+1;
            STATE2[U,V] := TRANSITION(STATE[HORZP,VERT],
                            STATE[HORZ,VERTP],
                            STATE[HORZ,VERTM],
                            STATE[HORZM,VERT])
         end
      end;
      STATE:=STATE2
   end
end;
```

14.6.3.4 Transition functions

The role of the transition function is essential. At each generation, this function is applied to each cell and determines the real impact of the neighbors. There is of course no limitation on the number of potential transition functions. For simple cases, we have limited our investigations to the following functions:

- Average of the neighbor values
- Maximum (or minimum) of the neighbor values
- Vector with coordinates which are the maximum (or minimum) corresponding coordinates of the neighbors
- Vector which has the maximum (or minimum) length from among the neighbors
- Vector which has the maximum (or minimum) sum of coordinates from among the neighbors

The GENERATION operation always examines the four neighbors (in the 2D case) of each cell. We need to solve the problem for the borders of the array. Three approaches are possible:

1. Using constant automata that are not updated surrounding the array
2. Connecting the border automata to themselves
3. Connecting opposite sides of the array, making a kind of torus (in 2D automata)

14.6.4 Solid textures based on cellular automata

As shown in Chap. 12, any function $T(x,y,z)$ may be theoretically used as a 3D texture function. Practically, however, functions have to be adequately chosen. In our "Lifegame" approach, we use the STATE matrix (defined this time as a matrix of real numbers), obtained by the cellular automata to characterize the perturbation of the normal to the surface. However, as the texture function has to be in terms of three coordinates, a correspondence between the cells and the points on the surface should be computed. These calculations are very time-consuming and cannot be carried out. An approximate method which is much less expensive consists of projecting the surface onto a specific plane and then applying the values determined by the automata. The algorithm is as follows:

1. The figure is first normalized
2. The figure is rotated around the X (angle α_1) and Y (angle α_2) axes in order to make the main axis parallel to the Z-axis. The main axis is determined by averaging the normals to all faces in the figure. If the average is 0, we arbitrarily choose the normal to the first face
3. The figure is translated in such a way that the minimal limits correspond to the X- and Y-axes (translation vector: $<-x_{min},-y_{min}>$)
4. The figure is scaled to correspond to the dimensions of the STATE matrix (scale vector: $<\frac{U}{(x_{max}-x_{min})}, \frac{V}{(y_{max}-y_{min})}>$)

We finally obtain a new transformation matrix to be applied to the figure before rendering:

$$\mathcal{M} = \begin{bmatrix} \dfrac{U\cos\alpha_1}{x_{max}-x_{min}} & \dfrac{V\sin\alpha_1\sin\alpha_2}{y_{max}-y_{min}} & -\sin\alpha_1\cos\alpha_2 & 0 \\[2ex] 0 & \dfrac{\cos\alpha_2}{y_{max}-y_{min}} & \sin\alpha_2 & 0 \\[2ex] \dfrac{U\sin\alpha_1}{x_{max}-x_{min}} & -\cos\alpha_1\sin\alpha_2 & \cos\alpha_1\cos\alpha_2 & 0 \\[2ex] -x_{min} & -y_{min} & 0 & 1 \end{bmatrix} \qquad (14.30)$$

The corresponding bump function is as follows:

```
function BUMP(X,Y,Z:REAL): REAL;
var U,V:REAL; p1,p2,q1,q2,U1,U2,V1,V2: INTEGER;
begin
    (*the transformation matrix is applied to the point <X,Y,Z> *)
    U:=Mat[1,1]*X+Mat[3,1]*Z+Mat[4,1];
    V:=Mat[2,1]*X+Mat[2,2]*Y+Mat[3,2]*Z+Mat[4,2];
    (*transformation from the real space [0,NU] x [0,NV] to an
        integer space [1,NU] x [1,NV] *)
    if (U>=NU) or (U<0) then U:=0;
    if (V>=NV) or (V<0) then V:=0;
    U1:=TRUNC(U+1); V1:=TRUNC(V+1);
    p1:=U1-U; q1:=1-p1; p2:=V1-V; q2:=1-p2;  (*weight calculations*)
```

if U1=1 **then** U2:=NU **else** U2:=U1-1; (*circular arrays*)
if V1=1 **then** V2:=NV **else** V2:=V1-1;
BUMP:=p1*q2*STATE[U1,V]+p1*q2*STATE[U1,V2]+
      q1*p2*STATE[U2,V1]+q1*q2*STATE[U2,V2]
end;

Figure 14.10 shows an example in which the perturbations are defined using a uniform random generator:

for U:=1 **to** NU **do**
  for V:=1 **to** NV **do**
    if RANDOM > 0.65 **then** MODIFY(STATE,U,V,RANDOM-0.5)/4)

The function TRANSIT(R_1,R_2,R_3,R_4) is defined as:

$$\text{TRANSIT} := \frac{2R_1 + 0.5R_2 + R_3\cos R_2 + R_4}{4.5}$$

Fig.14.10 a,b. A surface *a* without texture; *b* with a solid texture computed using the Lifegame approach. © 1986 MIRALab, H.E.C. and University of Montreal

15 Natural phenomena

15.1 Synthesis of natural phenomena: a challenge

Buildings may be easily simulated using a computer. Flight simulators were one of the earliest applications of computer graphics, and most CAD systems are used to model machinery and circuits. However, specialists in computer graphics have from the beginning been attracted to the possibility of creating 3D images involving natural phenomena. Yet, natural phenomena are surely the most difficult objects to synthesize by computer.

The reader may now feel that it is not so difficult to generate a 3D image involving natural phenomena: fractals may be used for mountains, volume densities for clouds, and particle systems for fire. This is certainly true; we have presented in previous chapters the basic theories for representing most natural phenomena. In particular, natural phenomena can be effectively represented by fuzzy objects, fractals, and solid textures. However, we have not yet explored the complete potential of such theories. Moreover, there are other models which have been developed specifically for these phenomena.

This chapter presents the different practical approaches to the representation of various natural phenomena: terrain, mountains, water, clouds, fire, trees.

15.2 Representation of terrain and mountains

15.2.1 Early terrain models

Some of the first terrain pictures were produced by Dungan et al. (1978) using a texture tile technique. With this 2D technique, a specific texture approximation is assigned to a surface within an image. Another technique of simulating terrain was proposed by Dungan (1979). In this terrain model, an array of height values H(U,V) is created from a Defense Mapping Agency terrain file. This array is a set of point surface representations at a uniform resolution in which the indices have implicit positional information. The image is created from the database using a masking priority algorithm. In this algorithm, the visible surface representation is found by searching along the line of sight through each pixel and comparing the height of the database with the ray. The first surface representation that appears at or above the ray is the visible surface. Shadows are produced from the height array and a sun vector. A shadow height is calculated at each array position by interpolation back toward the sun, where the sun vector lines up with an array position. Shadow heights are kept at array positions in shadow. Finally, shadows are added to the reflectance map texture.

Terrain models based on a database require a large amount of storage. For this reason, Marshall et al. (1980) have proposed **procedure models** based on the work of Brooks et al. (1974) and Newell (1975). Procedure models compute the exact specification of an object guided by the parameters that serve as input to the model. Procedure models have two important advantages: first, they save a great deal of storage in the description of a terrain; second, they are able to send information about the object generated to other procedure models. Marshall et al. (1980) have described a procedure model for trees which will be presented in Sect. 15.6.1. However, the general methodology may be applied to a complete terrain. Such a terrain model is based on the fact that a procedural model can take as its primitive elements the output of other procedure models. This leads to a hierarchical organization as shown in the example of Fig.15.1.

A difficult problem for the user is the generation and display of a large expanse of terrain stretching to the boundaries of the object space. To solve this problem, a data generation routine displays a quadrilateral grid (of variable resolution) which can be warped in X, Y, or Z to create mountains peaks and rolling hills. Each intersection of a vertical and horizontal line can be warped with a cursor. Once the data are converted into display format, a procedure model can be defined that will position plains, mountains, and hills to build a complex terrain model.

Max (1981) has represented islands as elliptical paraboloids. An island k is given by:

$$P_k(x,y) = Z_k - e_k (x-X_k)^2 - f_k (x-X_k)(y-Y_k) - g_k (y-Y_k)^2 \qquad (15.1)$$

where $<X_k,Y_k,Z_k>$ is the highest point on the paraboloid.

Rolling hills are simulated by superimposing cosine terms:

$$Q_k(x,y) = P_k(x,y) + \sum_j a_{jk} \cos (l_{jk} x + m_{jk} y) \qquad (15.2)$$

Each island is formed from three paraboloids of different colors: a shallow brown paraboloid for the beach, a steeper brown paraboloid for the cliffs, and a green paraboloid for the rolling hills.

15.2.2 Fractal-based terrains and mountains

Mandelbrot's fractal geometry (1971, 1975, 1977, 1982) provides both a description and a mathematical model for complex shapes such as landscapes, mountains, terrains, craters, coastlines. By using a statistically self-similar coastline, Mandelbrot has produced a series of views at increasing magnification of a fractal landscape. In each succeeding view, a portion of the coastline, indicated by a small box, is magnified to obtain the next view. What is essential in this series of views is that each view looks like a different part of the same landscape at the same magnification.

For generating fractal landscapes, almost all algorithms add random irregularities, but, in fact, the fractal dimension determines the amount of detail at different distance scales. Sometimes, the choice of the fractal dimension gives unrealistic rough surfaces; the height variations have to be scaled by a power law.

In order to give the impression of a lunar landscape in an image, Voss (1985) describes how circular craters were added using a fractal distribution of crater sizes. A rising fractal planet was generated using a random walk on a sphere. This walk is the sum of many independent steps; each independent surface displacement encircles the sphere in a random direction and divides it into two hemispheres, which are displaced relative to each other in height.

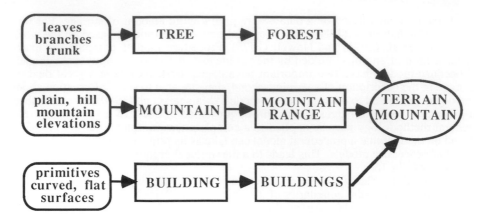

Fig.15.1. A hierarchy of procedure models

Several authors (Mandelbrot 1975; Fournier et al. 1982) have also shown that coastlines are best represented by curves with matching stochastic properties. For example, empirical data suggest that the stochastic characteristics of the Australian coastline are nearly identical to those of 1D fractional Brownian motion with H=0.87 (Mandelbrot 1977). Fournier et al. (1982) have also generated fractal polylines very similar to the Australian coastline using their recursive subdivision algorithm, described in Sect. 13.3.

Another interesting application by Fournier et al. (1982) is the generation of a planet using stochastic parametric surfaces. The method is similar to the quadrilateral subdivision described in Sect. 13.3 but applied to bicubic Bézier patches.

Finally, we should mention a parallel processing algorithm (Miller 1986) for the rendering of height fields which is exact and distributes the load evenly between the processors. The algorithm uses an intermediate spherical projection. The advantage of the method is that the visible surface calculation for the viewing sphere is independent of the viewing direction, and the processing may use planes which pass vertically through the terrain map.

15.2.3 Textured quadric surfaces

The realism of fractal surface images is achieved only by rendering hundreds of thousands (or even millions) of planar faces, which is very expensive in terms of CPU time. However, limiting the number of faces limits the realism of the images. For this reason, Gardner (1984) has defined a level of realism which reduces the computation problem to manageable proportions by adopting a style similar to impressionist painting. Instead of painting shapes without expanding effort on details, results are produced using simple curved surfaces and texture patterns.

Scenes are composed of a set of convex objects, with each object defined by one quadric surface and N bounding planes, where N can be zero. This approach avoids the computation of intersections between quadrics and ensures that all surface boundaries are at most second-order.

The key to the Gardner approach is the determination of the portions of the boundary curves which are visible in the image. The strategy consists of projecting all surface boundaries onto the image plane. Then, all key points at which boundary and surface visibility changes are determined on each boundary. These key points are then

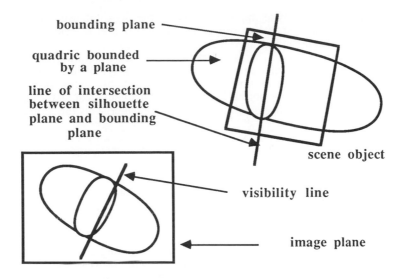

bounding plane

quadric bounded by a plane

line of intersection between silhouette plane and bounding plane

scene object

visibility line

image plane

Fig.15.2. Image curves in the Gardner algorithm

used to determine a scan-line list of visible boundaries and surfaces. Figure 15.2 shows the most important elements of the strategy.

1. The **limb curve** is the projection of the quadric silhouette. If we consider rays starting from the eyepoint and going to the image plane, the limb curve corresponds to the set of image points for which the rays are tangential to the quadric surface.
2. Curves of intersection between the quadric and its bounding planes are then projected giving **the intersection curves**.
3. To determine which boundary curve segments are visible, Gardner introduces the concept of a **visibility line**. A visibility line for a building plane is defined as the projection on the image plane of the line of intersection between the quadric silhouette plane and the bounding plane. This visibility line can be used to determine the visibility of any point on the limb curve relative to a particular bounding plane and the visibility of any point on the intersection curve related to that plane.
4. For objects with more than one bounding plane, **an intersection line** is introduced; it is defined as the image of the intersection between two bounding planes. This line corresponds to the portion of the intersection curve of one bounding plane defined to be visible relative to the other.

Given all image boundary curves and lines, we must now find which boundary segments are visible by determining key points. The key points of boundary visibility are:

- Curve extrema (minimum and maximum z)
- Contact points, which are points of tangency between the limb curve and an intersection curve
- Intersection points, which are points of intersection between an intersection line and an intersection curve related to a common plane
- Triplet points, which are image points of the corner intersections of three bounding planes

Visibility is determined by testing the key points; the algorithm uses a list of visible key points sorted on z in scan-line order. The determination of priorities between different objects is also taken into account in the algorithm.

The representation of natural surface detail is produced by texturing. Detail may be simulated efficiently by modulating surface shading intensity. For efficiency reasons, Gardner chooses to produce texture values only for visible scene surface points corresponding to image sample points. He proposes a mathematical texturing function which represents natural surface detail in a statistical manner. This function is defined as:

$$T(x,y,z) = \sum_i C_i \frac{\sin\,(w_i x + PX_i) + 1}{2}) + \sum_i C_i \frac{\sin\,(w_i x + PY_i) + 1}{2}) \qquad (15.3)$$

where PX_i and PY_i are phase shift functions which introduce irregularities. For low values of n, Gardner proposes to define PX_i as a sinusoidal function of y, and PY_i as a sinusoidal function of x for producing natural-looking patterns.

Modulation of the shading intensity is done by computing a weighted average of the surface shading intensity and the texture function Eq. (15.3) at each visible point. The texture function is also used to simulate amorphousness of trees (see Sect. 15.6).

Figure 15.3 shows an image generated using textured quadric surfaces.

Fig. 15.3. Trees and hills modeled by textured quadric surfaces. By Geoffrey Y. Gardner, Grunman Corporate Research and Development Center

15.3 Representation of water

15.3.1 Early models of water waves

Natural scenes very often involve water; however, water is difficult to represent by computer. The main reason is that water is usually in motion. Shape depends on this motion and this makes it very difficult to model because hydrodynamics models are too complex to use. Other difficulties are caused by the optical properties of water.

Several authors have proposed methods to represent waves in water. Whitted (1980) was one of the first to attempt to render water waves for the film *The Compleat Angler*. Using ray-tracing, he animated realistic reflections from ripples in a small pool. The ripples were created by bump mapping the pool surface. The surface normal was perturbed according to a sinusoidal function. Schachter (1980) proposed long crested wave models, using the sum of narrow band noise waveforms. Demos et al. (see slide in technical set, SIGGRAPH '81) produced an image for Pyramid Films using cycloidal waveforms. Greene (see slide in technical set SIGGRAPH'82) used sine waves and bump mapping to produce the image "Night Castles." Norton et al. (1982) used frequency limited (clamped) analytical functions to model waves, according to the theory explained in Sect. 12.3.4.

A simple wire-frame model of sea waves was used in the computer-generated film *Dream Flight* (Thalmann et al. 1982). The sea is basically represented by a series of parallel lines perpendicular to the eye direction. Waves are simulated by the application of a transformation obtained by applying to each point the matrix T defined as:

$$T = \begin{bmatrix} DIR_x & DIR_y & DIR_z \\ NOR_x & NOR_y & NOR_z \\ DNR_x & DNR_y & DNR_z \end{bmatrix} \tag{15.4}$$

DIR is the wave direction, usually parallel to the plane XZ; NOR is the normal vector to the sea, usually parallel to the Y-axis; DNR is computed as the cross product of vectors DIR and NOR.

The following function is also applied:

$$\begin{aligned} V_x &= V_x \\ V_y &= V_y + A \sin(V_x \cdot CYC + \varphi) \\ V_z &= V_z \end{aligned} \tag{15.5}$$

A is the wave amplitude; CYC is the wave cycle defined as $\frac{K}{A}$, where K is a constant (e.g. K=0.2); φ is the phase.

Similarly to Schachter, Max (1981) uses combinations of linear waves fronts. The equation for the surface of a long crested wave train is:

$$z(x,y,t) = -h + A \cos(lx + my - \omega t) \tag{15.6}$$

A is the amplitude; h is the distance of the mean sea level below the eye at $z = 0$; <l,m> is a wave vector such that:

$$l^2 + m^2 = k^2 \tag{15.7}$$

where k is the wave number:

$$k = \frac{2\pi}{\lambda} \qquad (15.8)$$

λ is the wavelength and w is the angular frequency in radians per second defined as:

$$w = k\,c \qquad (15.9)$$

c is the velocity defined as:

$$c = \sqrt{\frac{g}{k}} \qquad (15.10)$$

where g is the acceleration of gravity.

In the linear first approximation, the wave trains may be summed to represent the complete surface:

$$f(x,y,t) = -h + \sum_j a_j \cos(l_j x + m_j y - \omega_j t) \qquad (15.11)$$

Max also proposes using Stokes' method for turbulent water or periodic irrotational waves of finite amplitude. In this case, if the waves are symmetrical about their peaks at x=0, Stokes uses successive approximations of the Fourier series:

$$z(x,t) = \sum_{n=1}^{\infty} a_n \cos n\,k\,(x - ct) \qquad (15.12)$$

Max only uses the second-order term of Eq. (15.12) and adds it to the sum Eq. (15.11).

Figure 15.4 shows sea waves produced by Max.

Linear fronts used by Max have a notable deficiency. They form a self-replicating pattern when viewed over any reasonably large area. To avoid this problem, Perlin (1985) uses spherical wave fronts emanating from point source centers. For any wave source center, the surface normal is perturbed toward the center by a cycloidal function of the center's distance from the surface point. The new normal **N'** is calculated as:

$$\mathbf{N'} = \mathbf{N} + \psi\,(\mathbf{P} - \mathbf{C}) \qquad (15.13)$$

where **P** is the point, **C** the center, and **N** the old normal; ψ is defined as:

$$\psi\,(\mathbf{V}) = \frac{\mathbf{V}}{|\mathbf{V}|} \cdot \text{cycloid}(|\mathbf{V}|) \qquad (15.14)$$

Perlin creates multiple centers by using the direction of the function Dnoise() (see Sect. 12.5.2) over any collection of widely spaced points:

for I:=1 to N do CENTER[I]:=DIRECTION (DNOISE(I * VECT))

where DIRECTION(V) is the unit length direction of the vector V and VECT is the vector <100,0,0>.

Fig. 15.4. Carla's Island. By Nelson Max, Lawrence Livermore National Laboratory

To improve the realism, Perlin distributes the wave front spacial frequencies using a 1/f relationship of amplitude to frequency. In this case, Eq. (15.13) is replaced by:

$$N' = N + \frac{\psi\,((P - C)\,f\,)}{f} \qquad (15.15)$$

15.3.2 Recent water wave models

Several recent methods have been proposed for the modeling of water waves. These methods are different and do not all address exactly the same problem. In fact, there are several classes of possible water waves:

- Tides
- Seismic waves
- Internal waves
- Surface gravity waves
- Surface tension waves

15.3.2.1 Peachey model

Peachey (1986) proposes a model for waves and surf which only deals with surface gravity waves. The ocean surface is represented as a single-valued function of three variables:

$$y = f\,(x,z,t) \qquad (15.16)$$

where <x,y,z> is a 3D point of the surface and t the time.

This wave function is a sum of several long-crested linear waveforms W_i with amplitude A_i:

$$f(x,z,t) = \sum_i A_i\, W_i(x,z,t) \tag{15.17}$$

where W_i is defined as:

$$W_i(x,z,t) = w_i\, FRACTION(\Omega_i(x,z,t)) \tag{15.18}$$

where w_i is the wave profile, FRACTION is the fractional part function, and $\Omega_i(x,z,t)$ the phase function.

The values of the wave profile function $w_i(u)$ may be interpreted as vertical displacements of the ocean surface from the rest position. Peachey proposes the use of wave profile functions, changing according to the wave steepness S and the depth ratio δ. The steepness is defined from the height H of the wave and the wavelength λ as:

$$S = \frac{H}{\lambda} \tag{15.19}$$

The depth ratio is expressed as:

$$\delta = \frac{d}{\lambda_i^{deep}} \tag{15.20}$$

where d is the depth of the water and λ_i^{deep} the deep-water wavelength:

$$\lambda_i^{deep} = \frac{gT_i^2}{2\pi} \tag{15.21}$$

with g the acceleration of gravity at sea level and T_i the wave period.

The steepness S controls a linear blending between:

1. A sinusoidal function (for S small):

$$w_i(u) = \cos(2\pi u) \tag{15.22}$$

2. A sharp-crested quadratic function (for S large):

$$w_i(u) = 8\,|u\text{-}0.5|^2 - 1 \tag{15.23}$$

The phase function $\Omega_i(x,z,t)$ at any time t may be expressed as:

$$\Omega_i(x,z,t) = \Omega_i(x,z,t_0) - \frac{t\text{-}t_0}{T_i} \tag{15.24}$$

Peachey ignores the time dependence of Ω_i and describes the phase at a fixed time t_0. To include wave refraction effects due to effects of depth on wavelength and speed, the phase function must be evaluated as an integral of a depth-dependent phase-change function over the distance from the origin to the point of interest. In one dimension:

$$\Omega_i(x_i) = \int_0^{x_i} \Omega_i{}'(u)\, du \tag{15.25}$$

where $\Omega_i'(u)$ is calculated as in the constant-depth case by:

$$\Omega_i'(u) = \frac{1}{\lambda_i} = \frac{1}{C_i T_i} \qquad (15.26)$$

where C_i is the propagation speed, which may be expressed by the Airy model as:

$$C_i = g \frac{\lambda_i}{2\pi} \tanh \left(\frac{2\pi d}{\lambda_i}\right) \qquad (15.27)$$

Peachey simulates the spray from breaking waves using particle systems as described in Sect. 14.2. Waves break when the speed Q_m of circular motion of the water in the crest of the wave exceeds the speed C of the wave itself. Initial positions of the particles are at the crest of the wave, and initial velocity is in approximately the same direction as the wave motion with a speed of Q calculated as:

$$Q = \frac{Q_m}{\pi S_{max}} \qquad (15.28)$$

where S_{max} is the desired maximum steepness at the break point and:

$$Q_m = \pi S C \qquad (15.29)$$

A stochastic perturbation is also added to the particle velocity to reduce uniformity.

Particle systems are also used to simulate the spray resulting from waves striking obstacles.

The rendering of this wave model is carried out using an adaptation of the Lane-Carpenter algorithm (see Sect. 5.7.2.3) for parametric surfaces to the case of single-valued functions of two variables. The algorithm is incorporated in a novel implementation of the A-buffer (see Sect. 8.3.4). Particle systems are separately rendered and then integrated with other surfaces.

Figure 15.5 shows an image generated using the Peachey model.

15.3.2.2 Fournier-Reeves model
Fournier and Reeves (1986) also describe a model for modeling refraction and surf, but emphasize depth effects. They consider particles (motion) on a free surface with the XY-plane in the direction of the sea at rest and the Z-axis pointing up. Each particle describes a circle around its rest position $P_0 = <x_0, y_0, z_0>$. In the Z-plane, the equations of motion are:

$$x = x_0 + r \sin \Phi \qquad (15.30)$$
$$y = y_0 + r \cos\Phi \qquad (15.31)$$

where Φ is the phase angle:

$$\Phi = k x_0 - \omega t \qquad (15.32)$$

This corresponds to the trochoid represented in Fig.15.6.

Fig. 15.5. Waves on Babbage Beach. By D. Peachey, University of Saskatchewan

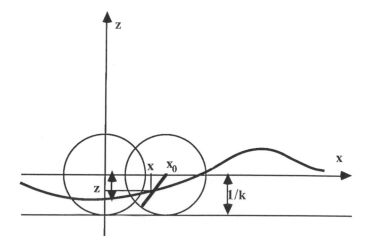

Fig.15.6. The trochoid

In a similar manner to the Peachey model, we may write the following equations:

$$H = 2r \tag{15.33}$$

$$\lambda = \frac{2\pi}{k} \tag{15.34}$$

$$T = \frac{2\pi}{\omega} \tag{15.35}$$

$$C = \frac{\lambda}{T} = \frac{\omega}{k} \tag{15.36}$$

in deep water:

$$\lambda = \frac{gT^2}{2\pi} \tag{15.37}$$

$$C = \frac{gT}{2\pi} \tag{15.38}$$

where H is the wave height, λ the wavelength, k the wave number, T the period and C the phase speed (speed of travel of the crest).

Several modifications are proposed by Fournier and Reeves to this basic model:

1. Take into account the direction of the wave by performing a 2D rotation in the orbit plane
2. Model the effect of the wind on the top of the crest by redefining the phase angle in (Eq. 15.32) as:

$$\Phi = kx_0 - \omega t - \mu (z \ z_0) \Delta t \tag{15.39}$$

where μ is a coefficient of proportionality which has an impact on the shape of the waves, and Δt is the time
3. Take into account the effect of the depth d at the point P_0. Fournier and Reeves show that the new phase angle may be calculated as:

$$\Phi = -\omega t + \sum_0^{x_0} k_\infty \frac{\Delta x}{\sqrt{\tanh (k_\infty d(x))}} \tag{15.40}$$

where d(x) is the depth at the position x and k_∞ is the wave number at infinite depth
4. Model the waves breaking on the shore. In this model, circles are flattened into ellipses, the major axis is oriented toward the slope of the bottom γ in the direction of the wave travel, and the length of the major axis is increased. For this, Equations (15.30) and (15.31) are replaced by:

$$x = x_0 + r \cos \alpha \ S_x \sin \Phi + \sin \alpha \ S_z \cos \Phi \tag{15.41}$$

$$y = y_0 + r \cos \alpha \ S_z \cos \Phi + \sin \alpha \ S_x \sin \Phi \tag{15.42}$$

with:

$$\sin \alpha = \sin \gamma \, e^{-k_0 d} \tag{15.43}$$

$$S_x = \frac{1}{1 - e^{-k_x d}} \tag{15.44}$$

$$S_z = S_x (1 - e^{-k_z d})$$ \hfill (15.45)

where k_0, k_x and k_z are scaling factors

Breakers are caused when the particle speed is greater than the phase speed and the curvature of the surface is high. When a breaker is detected, spray and foam are generated; both are rendered using particle systems (see Sect. 14.2).

To give designers control over the shape of the ocean, the model includes multiple trains of waves. A wave train is a rectangular box on the surface of the sea containing waves of the same basic characteristics and of the same phase origin. The overall randomness of the ocean is achieved by a combination of small variations within a train and large variations between trains.

15.3.2.3 Pool model

Wyvill et al. (1986d) describe waves on water in the restricted case of pools. Their best results are obtained by adding waves from point sources. The waves are generated using a main source and secondary sources (see Fig.15.7). These secondary sources are placed so that they represent reflected images of the primary source in the sides of the pool. This means that where the waves meet the sides of pool, their shape is consistent with the expectation that any wave meets a reflection of itself at the edge.

15.3.2.4 Waves by analog cellular automata

Thalmann (1986) describes the modeling of a water surface as an application of analog cellular automata. According to the traditional model of cellular automata, the plane is divided into a lattice of small regular cells. The values of the state matrix correspond to a region of the surface and represent a displacement in the Y-axis from the XZ-plane. So, to model for instance the ripple made by a rock piercing the surface of water, an initial configuration is built by modifying the position value of a few automata. Applying the state transition function will form a wave front in successive generations, emerging from the disturbed automata and having the same shape as the perturbation. For example, the simulation of the trail left by a boat moving on water is presented in Sect. 15.7.1.

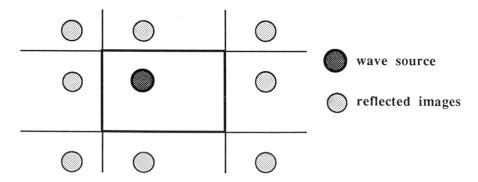

Fig.15.7. Waves in a rectangular pool

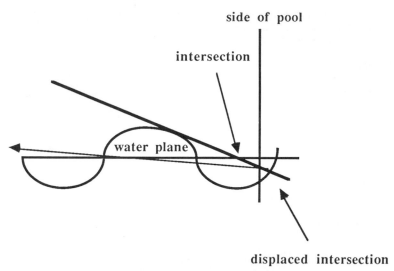

Fig.15.8. Displacement mapping

15.3.3 Optical properties

Max (1981) uses a functional approximation to the shape of his waves and performs direct ray tracing. The ray intersections are found by iteration. Ten to fifteen percent of rays are reflected twice by the water surface. For this purpose, Max uses the following technique: the first crest of the wave of largest amplitude in front of the reflected ray is approximated by a parabolic cylinder, tangential to the crest and with the same curvature as the Stokes wave at the crest. The normal to the actual wave at the <x,y> position of the piercing point is then used to find the second reflected ray.

Perlin (1985) uses his solid texture mapping to render his waves with a scan-line algorithm.

Wyvill et al. (1986d) compare three different methods: approximation using polygons, wave functions used as a texture map, and an application of displacement mapping (Cook 1984; see Sect. 12.4.1). The idea of this last method, which is certainly the best, is to calculate an ordinary point of intersection with the plane surface, which is the water. Then, the point of intersection is modified to make it nearer or further from the eye, along the line of sight, according to the wave function. The modified point of intersection should then be checked back against adjacent objects. For example, in Fig.15.8, the intersection of the ray and plane surface is in front of the pool's side, but the modified intersection is behind.

Figure 15.9 shows an image generated using this method.

The reflection of light in water is a complex problem, because there may be many water waves per pixel when the regions are distant. This implies tracing many rays per pixel for ray-tracing rippling water. Miller (1986) proposes a method consisting of perturbing rays vertically but not laterally, by the water. This allows reflections of distant hills in water to be modeled quite realistically, using a parallel approach as described in Sect. 15.2.2. Since reflected light is only scattered vertically, the light scattered toward an observer lies within a range of vertical angles from the point on the water surface. This is like a **fan** of light rays incident on the water. Miller considers the water as flat with a normal perturbation with superimposed sine waves. The waves have two effects: they perturb the center of the fan and spread the fan

Fig. 15.9. Swimmer. By G.Wyvill, A. Pearce, and B.Wyvill, University of Calgary

based on the curvature of the wave. For each water pixel, a fan is generated based on the projection distance and the perturbation and spread of the water wave. The plane slice of the height field is projected and clipped to that fan and the intensities are averaged over the fan.

Kirk (1986) produced images showing two spheres floating underneath a surface with reflective and transmissive properties chosen to simulate clear water. The method is based on cone tracing (see Sect. 11.3.2) and the texturing function is based on four sine wave products (see Eq. 15.3), with various phases and amplitudes.

15.4 Representation of sky, atmosphere, clouds, and fog

15.4.1 Techniques and models for generating clouds

At the end of the 1970s, Csuri et al. (1979) created images of a smoke cloud. A 3D approximation of a particular cloud was generated, then a kind of ray-tracing was used to create a 2D array of the intensities in the image. The cloud was implemented as a procedure model with the following parameters: wind velocity, particle concentration, rate of emission and height of source.

The functional model described in Sect. 14.4.1 was designed by Blinn (1982) for the synthesis of the rings of Saturn. According to the author, the extension of this model to the simulation of an arbitrary varying spatial density function of scatterers, with multiple reflections and different amounts of shadowing from any direction is not straightforward. The rings of Saturn consist of a cloud of reflective ice particles in orbit about the planet. The optical depth, albedo, and size distribution of scattering particles in the rings vary with the radius from the planet. Blinn also simulates a cloud layer with a random texture pattern.

Voss (1983) has fractally generated densities with a series of plane parallel models. For this, he has adapted Blinn's procedure by modeling a sandwich of several Blinn models. Voss (1985) also states that clouds and areas of rain are the natural shapes where fractal behavior has been experimentally verified over the widest range of distance scales. He proposes realistic **fractal clouds** which represent temperature or water vapor density as a function of 3D position. A more accurate display may be obtained by allowing local light scattering to vary with the temperature distribution $T(x,y,z)$.

Perlin (1985) creates background clouds by composing a color spline function with his TURBULENCE function.

Kajiya (1984) has generated **3D optical density functions** using his diffuse rendering algorithm (see Sect. 14.4.3). The images are generated from a numerical model for cumulus convection. The model incorporates the equations of motion, continuity, condensation, and evaporation. Convective motions of the atmosphere, latent heat of vaporization of water, and frictional effects are also taken into account in this model. According to the author, cloud simulation starts in a convectively unstable atmosphere; then a heat source (the sun) is applied at the base of model. A warm layer of air forms close to the ground and starts to rise; when most air has risen enough to be supersaturated, the cloud starts forming. The image of the cloud is generated from the density function, which is directly taken from the mixing ratio of liquid water in the atmosphere at each 3D grid point.

Gardner (1984) has also produced clouds using a refinement of the technique of textured quadric surfaces (see Sect. 15.2.3). He assigns a threshold value for the texture function and defines the cloud to be translucent at any image point where the texture falls below the threshold. Artificial boundaries between the visible and invisible portions of the texture surface are softened by varying the translucence linearly as the texture function crosses the threshold. The technique was demonstrated by Gardner in an image which shows a sky plane textured with variable translucence to simulate a cloud layer. A more systematic model has been developed by Gardner and is described in the next section.

Finally, we should mention the clouds produced by Kirk (1986) using cone tracing (see Sect. 11.3.2). The method is based on the mapping onto a surface of the amount of light that the surface diffuses. This diffusion weight is a fraction of the incoming light transmitted and the remainder is divided between being absorbed and being diffused. A plane with this property modulated by a calculated texture gives an appearance of a soft cloud with a small amount of light absorption and mostly diffuse radiation.

15.4.2 Gardner cloud model

Gardner (1985) introduces a new model of clouds which allows the simulation of arbitrary cloud scenes. Different types of clouds may be viewed from various distances and angles: cirrus clouds (wispy clouds at high altitude), stratus clouds (layer clouds at low altitude), and cumulus clouds (heap clouds at low altitude). The cloud model uses three basic elements: a sky plane, ellipsoids, and a mathematical texturing function.

The sky plane is modeled by a plane parallel to the ground plane, assumed to be the XY-plane. The equation of the sky plane at an altitude A is then:

$$P(x,y,z) = Z - A = 0 \qquad (15.46)$$

The gross 3D cloud structure is based on ellipsoids expressed as follows:

$$Q(x,y,z)=Q_1x^2+Q_2y^2+Q_3z^2+Q_4xy+Q_5yz+Q_6xz+Q_7x+Q_8y+Q_9z+Q_{10}=0 \quad (15.47)$$

The mathematical texturing function used is very similar to the texturing function for terrains (Eq. 15.3); it is a "poor man's Fourier series":

$$T(x,y,z) = k\sum_i C_i[\sin(FX_ix+PX_i)+T_0]+\sum_i C_i[\sin(FY_iy+PY_i)+T_0] \quad (15.48)$$

T_0 is a parameter for controlling the contrast of the texture pattern and k is a parameter which has a maximum value of 1 for $T(x,y,z)$.
Frequencies FX_i and FY_i and coefficients C_i are chosen as follows:

$$FX_{i+1} = 2F_i \qquad\qquad FY_{i+1} = 2Y_i \qquad\qquad C_{i+1}=0.707\ C_i \qquad (15.49)$$

PX_i and PY_i are **phase shift functions** which introduce irregularities. Gardner proposes the following functions:

$$PX_i = \pi/2 \sin (FY_{i-1}y) + \pi \sin (FX_i\ z\ /\ 2) \qquad (15.50)$$
$$PY_i = \pi/2 \sin (FX_{i-1}x) + \pi \sin (FX_i\ z\ /\ 2)$$

The shading intensity is calculated as:

$$I = (1-a)\ \{(1-t)[(1-s)I_d + sI_s] + tI_t\} + a \qquad (15.51)$$

where I_d is the intensity due to diffuse reflection, I_s is the intensity due to specular reflection, I_t is the intensity contributed by the texturing function $[I_t=T(x,y,z)]$, a is a fraction of surface reflection due to ambient light, t is a fraction of texture shading, and s is a fraction of specular reflection.

The translucence of the sky plane and the ellipsoids is modulated by defining a threshold value for the texturing function. For ellipsoids, translucence is increased at the boundary using the limb curve (see Sect. 15.2.3). The modulated translucence is calculated as:

$$TR = 1 - \frac{I_t - T_1 - (T_2 - T_1)\ (1 - g(x,z))}{D} \qquad (15.52)$$

where T_1 is the threshold at the center of the limb curve, T_2 is the threshold at the boundary of the limb curve, D is a range of texturing function values, and $g(x,z)$ is the normalized limb curve.

Using this model, Gardner has produced various very impressive images. High cirrus layers, stratus layers, and thick cumulus clouds are simulated using a 2D model based on a single textured plane in the sky. Complex clouds are produced by linking several ellipsoids. Horizontal cloud formations are modeled using clusters of ellipsoids and vertical cloud formations are simulated by pushing the ellipsoids upward. Gardner clouds are shown in Fig. 15.10.

Fig. 15.10. Clouds. By Geoffrey Y. Gardner, Grunman Corporate Research and Development Center

15.4.3 Simulation of fog

The easiest way to add fog to an image involves modifying the color of the object after lighting calculations. Fog space is strongly related to the position of the object relative to the eye. For example, to simulate a light fog on the floor, the fog function takes into account the height of a point of the figure. If a point of the object is lower than a certain height, then it is affected by fog and, depending on the distance to the eye, the point will be more or less whitened by fog. To simulate a fog which is not limited to the floor, we may use the distance between the object and the eye and assume that the object will be less visible when it is far away and consequently whiter.

Fog effects may also be simulated by combining an image with the background color. The fog is deeper when the distance between the considered point and the eye is longer.

Schachter (1983) proposes modifying the color C of a surface element due to distance fading as follows:

$$C' = C\,e^{-\gamma d} + H\,(1 - e^{-\gamma d}) \tag{15.53}$$

where d is the distance to the surface element, γ the fading constant, and H the horizon color.

Fog may also be considered as a characteristic of the camera as proposed by Magnenat-Thalmann and Thalmann (1986b). Fog for the camera is defined by giving the distance where the color is 50% mixed with the background color.

Example of fog implementations at MIRALab are discussed in Sect. 15.7.3.

15.4.4 The Nishita-Nakamae model of sky light

The most natural light is commonly called **daylight** and is generally rendered by a combination of ambient light and directional light (sun). This approach does not correspond to reality as explained by Nishita and Nakamae (1986), who propose another approach. Daylight is modeled as a combination of direct sunlight (directional light) and **skylight**. Skylight is considered as emanating from the sky dome which surrounds the earth. The sky dome is treated as a hemisphere of very large radius. As the intensity of skylight (skylight luminance) is not uniform, Nishita and Nakamae divide the sky dome into bands, which themselves do not necessarily have uniform luminance.

The illuminance at a given point in the scene is a combination of light from the sky and light reflected from the ground and/or surrounding objects. Interreflection of light between objects in the scene must also be considered.

For unobstructed sky, the illuminance at a point **P** is calculated with the following assumptions:

1. **P** is considered as the center of the dome and the center of the coordinate system
2. The coordinate system is also defined so that **P** is in the XY-plane, which is horizontal
3. The XY-plane is also the base of the sky dome of radius r
4. N-band sources are defined by cutting the hemisphere by planes, including the X-axis
5. A band source k is characterized by its angle of elevation Ω_k (see Fig.15.11) and its width $2\Delta\delta$
6. Each band may be subdivided into sky elements; such an element has a constant luminance and may be considered as a point source P_s
7. P_s is measured by two angles: the angle α from the X-axis to the sky element and the angle Ω from the XY-plane to the sky element

The illuminance $E_k(\alpha)$ due to the band source k between 0 and α may be calculated as follows:

1. For uniform sky (constant sky luminance L_0):

$$E_k(\alpha) = 0.5\ d_k\ (\alpha - \cos\alpha\ \sin\alpha)\ L_0 \tag{15.54}$$

with

$$d_k = \cos(\delta_k - \Delta d) - \cos(\delta_k + \Delta d) \tag{15.55}$$

2. For non-uniform sky :

$$E_k(\alpha) = d_k \int_0^\alpha L(\alpha,\delta_k)\ \sin^2\alpha\ d\alpha \tag{15.56}$$

where $L(\alpha,\delta_k)$ is the sky luminance at P_s.

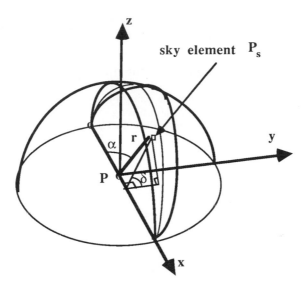

Fig.15.11. Model of the distribution of sky luminance

For obstructed sky, the illuminance by the source in the visible region between α_1 and α_2 is calculated as $F_k(\alpha_2)$ $E_k(\alpha_1)$. An algorithm for calculating the visible parts of the sky is described by Nishita and Nakamae (1986).

To take into account reflected light, Nishita and Nakamae assume that the illuminance of each face F is uniform. Therefore, the illuminance may be obtain by substituting L_0 in Eq. (15.54) to the luminance of F.

15.5 Representation of fire

15.5.1 Fire based on particle systems

The wall-of-fire element in the Genesis Demo sequence from the movie *Star Trek II: The Wrath of Khan* was generated using a two-level hierachy of particle systems. A top-level system generates particles which are themselves particle systems. These particle systems form expanding concentric rings on the surface of a planet. The starting times of these particle systems vary, which produces an effect of an expanding wall of fire.

Various attributes of the individual particle systems are inherited from the top-level system but vary stochastically: average color, rate of change of the colors, initial mean velocity, generation circle radius, ejection angle, mean particle size, mean lifetime, mean particle generation rate, mean particle transparency parameters. The particles are mainly red with a touch of green. The heart of the explosion has a hot yellow-orange glow which fades off to shades of red elsewhere. The cooling of a glowing piece of material is simulated by the rate of change of the colors: green and blue components drop off quicker than the red component. When the intensity of particles falls below a minimum value, the particles are killed as their lifetime expires. The wall of fire was generated using 400 particle systems and contained over 750 000 particles.

A computer-generated animation sequence showing a pagoda destroyed by fire has also been produced at MIRALab and is described in Sect. 15.7.2.

15.5.2 Fire based on turbulent flow function

Perlin (1985) has created a solar corona using his turbulence function described in Sect. 12.5.2. A corona is hottest near the emitting sphere and cools down with radial distance from the sphere center. At any value of radius, a particular spectral emission is visible, which is modeled using a COLOR_OF_EMISSION function.

The corona is simulated using the function CORONA(POINT-CENTER), where CORONA is implemented by adding turbulence to the radial flow:

$$CORONA(v) = COLOR\_OF\_EMISSION(\ |v| + TURBULENCE \ (v))$$

The MIRALab implementation of more general fire functions using the same approach is also described in Sect. 15.7.2.

15.6 Representation of trees, forests, and grass

15.6.1 Early tree models

One of the first impressive images of a tree was created by Brooks et al. (1974) using ray-tracing. A deciduous tree made up of several thousand leaves was produced using a combinatorial technique. The tree is made up of five parts: stems, primary branches, secondary branches, twigs, and leaves. The various elements are placed and repeated using statistical properties of different tree types. For each secondary branch, two parameters are stored—length and angle with the primary branches.

Marshall et al. (1980) propose a procedure model for a tree with many parameters:

- Number of leaves
- Size of each branch
- Leaf element description
- Color
- Position of tree
- Size of leaf element
- Distance between branches
- Distance between leaves

A tree based on this procedure model is shown in Fig.15.12.

Randomness is also used in combination with the parameters to produce unique trees of a given species. For example, leafs are organized on the branch using the parameters *number of leaves*, *length of the branch* , and *size of the leaf*. The positions are then slightly modified using a random number generator. Branches are positioned around the trunk according to the parameters *size of the branches* and *distance between branches*, then positions and rotations are randomly modified.

Mandelbrot (1977, 1978, 1982) and Kawaguchi (1982) used minimal recursive topologies and added simple geometric relationships to generate complex images of branching plants. Simple 2D trees may be also generated using the method described in Sect. 13.1.2. (see Fig. 15.13).

Magnenat-Thalmann and Thalmann (1983) also describe an implementation of trees based on a high-level graphic type declared as:

Fig.15.12. A procedural model of a tree. By Robert Marshall and Roger Wilson, © 1980 Computer Graphics Reseach Group, The Ohio State University

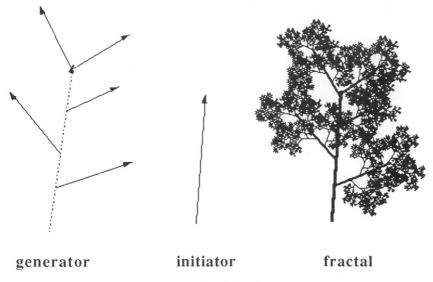

generator   **initiator**   **fractal**

Fig.15.13. A fractal-based tree

type TREE = **figure** (**var** BRANCHES:TFILE; NBRANCHES:INTEGER;
POSITION:VECTOR; HEIGHT, LENGTH:REAL);

where BRANCHES is a file of kinds of branches, NBRANCHES is the number of
branches, POSITION is the position of the trunk, and LENGTH the length of the
branches. The lower, primary branches are oriented in the four major directions. Other
branches are uniformly distributed in the vertical direction but are randomly distributed
around the trunk. The angle of the branch relative to the ground is dependent on the
height of the branch. This high-level graphical type was used in the computer-
generated film *Dream Flight* (Thalmann et al. 1982).

Trees were also included in images generated by Gardner (1984) using his
textured quadric surfaces (see Sect. 15.2.3). Irregularity and amorphousness of trees
are simulated using the texture function. This is accomplished by treating locally dark
texture regions on the tree's surface as though they were holes in the tree.

15.6.2 Botanical and rule-based trees

Lindenmayer (1968) showed that the branching patterns of primitive filamentous
organisms can be formalized using his extended L-systems (DOL systems). A
description of L-systems and DOL-systems has been summarized by Aono and Kunii
(1984). L-systems are similar to Chomsky (1957) grammars, except that rules are
applied in parallel to all symbols in the current state. The original DOL-system is
defined as a triplet <G,w,P> where G is a set of symbols, w the starting symbol, and
P a set of production rules. The rules are applied to give shapes to a set of generated
strings generated for either type of branching pattern. Each alphanumeric character of
the generated string denotes a filamentous cell (line segment) of different length, while
a pair of parentheses denotes a branch and its direction. Examples are shown in
Fig.15.14. L-systems are an interesting formal approach to tree modeling; however,
they have serious drawbacks because of their level of description is too low. In
particular, the patterns generated are inherently 1D linear arrays, expansion of cells
cannot be handled, and continuous quantities cannot be used. Moreover, the system
cannot generate 3D patterns.

Aono and Kunii (1984) propose four new geometric models (GMT1, GMT2,
GMT3, and GMT4) to generate botanical tree images.

GMT1 is an elementary bifurcation (branching) model capable of representing
simple tree shapes. The model consists of the following rules:

1. Two child branches are generated by one bifurcation
2. The length and diameter of the child branches become shorter at constant ratios and
   their branching angles are the same at any level of growth
3. Two child branches lie on the gradient plane of their mother branch
4. Branching occurs simultaneously at the tips of all branches

GMT1 cannot represent the effects of wind, sunlight and gravity nor cases in
which two child branches are generated from the same mother branch.

Because of these restrictions, Aono and Kunii introduce GMT2, which is a
modified model that can represent these effects. GMT2 is obtained by introducing
uniform and nonuniform deviations into the rule 3 of GMT1:

1. Child branch positions deviate uniformly by <dx,dy,dz>; the deviation depends on
   wind, sunlight, and gravity
2. Child branch positions also deviate in proportion to the controller's strength and in
   inverse proportion to the distance between the controllers and the original tip
   positions of the child branches. Controllers are either attractors or inhibitors
   (nonuniform deviation). An example is shown in Fig.15.15.

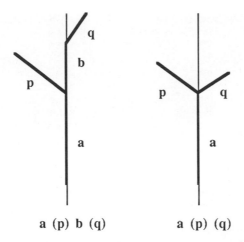

$$\textbf{a (p) b (q)} \qquad \textbf{a (p) (q)}$$

Fig.15.14. Examples of shapes produced using the L-system

For dealing with ternary ramifications, a third model GMT3 is introduced with the following new rules:

1. Three child branches are generated at one branching
2. A center branch contraction ratio is added to the two constant contraction ratios present in GMT1
3. The growth direction of the center branch is the same as its mother branch

By combining GMT3 with GMT2, more realistic images may be generated.

A fourth model, called GMT4, has been also introduced. It is a statistical branching model that can represent variations of the branching angles with growth level.

Aono and Kunii (1984) analyze and compare their models with the L-system approach. With the help of this approach, they propose the A-system, which produces tree images with leaves, shadows, and shades. Figure 15.16 shows a simulation of trees with tinted autumnal leaves.

Smith (1984) also describes a modeling technique called **graftals**, which represents plants using Lindenmeyer systems. Graftals are based on an extension of the formal languages of symbol strings to the formal languages of labeled graphs. The main difficulties of the technique are how the replacement rules work and how to define connectivity before and after. Smith does not propose a general solution but shows how to solve the problem for very simple graphs. The image shown in Fig.14.3 is based on several 3D renderings of the context-sensitive grammar 0.0.0.11.1[1].1.0 mixed with the particle system grass.

15.6.3 Particle-based trees and grass

Reeves and Blau (1985) describe an extension of the particle systems approach to produce sophisticated images of forests and trees. The trees are serially produced by the particle system program; each tree is modeled and rendered. The main trunk is first modeled as a truncated solid cone, then subbranches are generated using a recursive algorithm. Before starting the recursive process, a set of initial characteristics and dimensions is stochastically assigned: height, width, first branch height, mean branch

Fig.15.15. A nonuniform deviation model (strong inhibitor). Courtesy of Prof. T.L. Kunii, University of Tokyo

Fig.15.16. A simulation of trees with tinted autumnal leaves. Courtesy of Prof. T.L. Kunii, University of Tokyo

length, branching angle. For example, the height H of a tree is determined by the following equation:

$$H = \bar{H} + RANDOM \cdot \Delta H \qquad (15.57)$$

where $\bar{H}$ is the mean height, RANDOM is a pseudorandom number uniformly distributed between -1 and 1 and ΔH is a height variation. A relationship between parameters may also exist. For example, branch thickness T depends on the branch length L:

$$T = T_0 \sqrt{1 - \frac{D}{L}} \qquad (15.58)$$

where T_0 is the basic thickness and D is the distance from the base of the branch.

Subbranches are generated using a recursive algorithm. Each subbranch inherits many characteristics from its parent, but some dimensions like thickness are then adjusted.

Colors vary from tree to tree; two tables of colors are used—one for the trunk and main branches, and the other for the leaves. The trunk is rendered using a conventional texture-mapping technique. Effects of gravity, wind, and sunlight are added in a postprocessing phase.

Fire particles emit light, but tree particles reflect light, which requires the use of a shading model. Reeves and Blau use a probabilistic shading model, providing ambient, diffuse, and specular components and approximate forms of shadowing.

The diffuse component is defined as:

$$D = e^{-a\,d} \qquad (15.59)$$

where a is a coefficent and d the distance between the particle and the light source.

Highlights occur where the tree's branches or leaves are exposed directly to sunlight. Self-shadowing is simulated by controlling the ambient shading component. For shadows cast by other trees, an approximation is used. A plane is defined by the height of any trees positioned between a specified tree and the light source, as shown in Fig.15.17. If a particle is more than a specified distance below the plane, only the ambient shading component is used.

For a forest, it is not possible to generate particles for all trees and use a traditional visible surface algorithm because of the large number of particles. For this reason, a painter's algorithm (see Sect. 5.5.2) is used. However, as some branches of a tree obscure others, a special painter's algorithm depending on a bucket sort has been developed.

Figure 15.18 shows an image of the film *The Adventures of André and Wally B.* with particle-based trees.

Images of grass have also been generated using this approach. Clumps of grass are scattered randomly over the terrain. Each clump contains many separate blades of grass determined by stochastic processes. Stochastic bends and kinks are added to some blades of grass to improve realism. The grasses are shaded using a stochastic algorithm. The contribution of both the diffuse and ambient components depends on the distance from the top of the clump of grass to the particle. Using a kind of ray-tracing algorithm, tree shadows are cast onto the grass. As clumps of grass may intersect, a surface algorithm for grass has been developed based on a bucket sort. Stochastic processes also model the reaction of the blade of grass as it is hit by a gust of wind. In particular, the amount of bending is dependent on the gust of the wind and the distance from the ground.

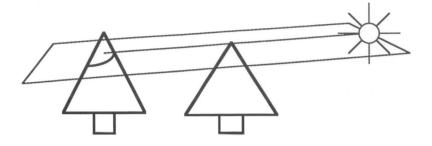

Fig.15.17. Shadow plane

Fig.15.18. *The Adventures of André and Wally B.* © 1986 Pixar; all rights reserved. *The Adventures of André and Wally B.* is a demonstration of several things. First it is a full classic character animation—as opposed to effects animation—the animation being fully 3D and designed by a professional animator (Disney-trained). Second, it has articulated motion blur. In particular, the two characters, André (the android) and Wally B. (the bee), are always motion-blurred. Third, there are very complex 3D background sets, realized here with particle systems. Fourth, it has laser input scanning, the background cards for the credits being some of the first input scans from the Pixar laser scanner. The sound track was partially produced using the ASP, the Lucasfilm digital audio system. Since this is a demo, it is rendered at only 500-line video resolution. Output of the completed piece on the laser scanner was planned, but the current version is filmed directly from a video monitor. The completed piece was premiered at the International Animation Festival in Toronto, August 17, 1984.

15.6.4 Other trees

Recently, three different approaches have been described for generating trees; although they cannot be considered really as new, they are interesting because they mix several other methods. The first method is from Bloomenthal (1985). It represents botanical trees, given a list of 3D points and a list of connections. Parameters such as the number of branches, branching angles and length, radius, and taper of a branch are stochastically assigned. The surface of the tree limb is considered as a generalized cylinder with a circular cross section of varying radii. Bloomenthal uses the tension of a spline (Barsky and Beatty 1983; Kochanek and Bartels 1984) to stiffen part or all of the tree skeleton or to increase the angularity of branching for smaller, non-supporting limbs. At branch points, the incoming and outgoing limbs are interpolated by a spline sequence. The surface at a point of bifurcation is described topologically as a triangular prism (called **ramiform**). Disks are created far enough along the outgoing limbs so as not to interpenetrate. A spline is then constructed between the points of proximity of the disks, providing the computed gradients at these points. Blobby techniques are used to model the tree trunk as a series of non-circular cross sections. Bark is simulated with a bump map digitized from real bark. Leaves are texture-mapped onto simple surfaces. The veins are emphasized for dramatic effect, using a paint program. Figure 15.19 shows an image of a maple.

The second method was introduced by Fournier and Grindal (1986). Trees are modeled as convex polyhedra for the description of the general shape, and 3D texture mapping is used for the detailed features. The volume of the tree is represented as the convex intersection of half spaces V:

$$V = \{ \langle x,y,z \rangle \in \mathbb{R}^3 \mid \bigvee i \ a_i x + b_i y + c_i z + d_i \geq 0 \} \quad (15.60)$$

Fig.15.19. The Mighty Maple. By J.Bloomenthal, NYIT Computer Graphics Laboratory

For the intersection of these half-spaces, a visible surface algorithm for convex intersection computes directly in the frame buffer (Fournier and Fussell 1986). A 3D texture mapping technique is then used to modulate the shape and color of the basic polyhedra. Small "chunks" of color are randomly placed in three-space. The colors are chosen by the user as well as the number of chunks and the percentage of each color; they can also be generated using 3D fractional Brownian motion. The trunk is shaded using a modified version of Blinn's wrinkled surface technique (Blinn 1978).

Oppenheimer (1986) proposes a recursive tree model based on fractals. In this model, a tree node is a branch with one or more attached tree nodes transformed by a 3x3 linear transformation. Branching stops when the branches become small enough and a leaf is drawn.

Numerical parameters control the tree's appearance:

- Angle between the main stem and the branches
- Size ratio of the main stem to the branches
- Rate at which the stem tapers
- Amount of helicoidal twist in the branches
- Number of branches per stem segment

Randomness is added to the model for generating a more natural-looking image and reflecting the diversity in nature. This randomness is performed by regenerating each parameter at each node. The regeneration is done by taking the mean value and adding a random perturbation, scaled by the standard deviation.

Stem shapes may be cylinders, spirals, helices, and squiggles.

For rendering the trees, Oppenheimer uses antialiased vectors for leaves and ferns and shaded 3D primitives for thicker branches. Bump-mapped polygonal prisms are used to flesh out the trees in 3D. Bark texture is simulated using Brownian fractal noise as follows:

$$bark(x,y) = s((x + R \ noise(x,y)) \ N) \qquad (15.61)$$

with:

$$s(t) = 2 \ fraction(t) \quad if \ fraction(t) < \frac{1}{2} \qquad (15.62)$$
$$2 \ (1\text{-}fraction(t)) \quad if \ fraction(t) \geq \frac{1}{2}$$

where N is the number of bark ridges, R is the roughness of the bark, and noise(x,y) a periodic noise function.

15.7 Water waves, fire, clouds and fog at MIRALab

15.7.1 Water surface based on analog cellular automata

One application of cellular automata to represent a natural system involves the modeling of a water surface. According to the traditional model of cellular automata, the plane is divided into a lattice of small regular cells.

The values of STATE correspond to a region of the surface and represent a displacement in the Y-axis from the XZ-plane. So, to model for instance the ripple made by a rock piercing the surface of water we build an initial configuration by modifying the position value of a few automata. Applying the state transition function will form a wave front in successive generations emerging from the disturbed automata and having the same shape as the perturbation. In this case, the

implementation was based on a velocity distribution as shown below which is a list of
the GENERATION procedure different from the version listed in Sect. 14.6.3.

```
procedure GENERATION (var STATE:MATRIX;
                          NU,NV,NTIMES:INTEGER;
                function TRANSITION(V1,V2,V3,V4:VECTOR): VECTOR);
var STATE2,VELOX,VELOX2:MATRIX;
    HORZ, HORZM, HORZP, VERT, VERTM, VERTP, U, V, K:INTEGER;
begin
  for K:=1 to NTIMES do
  begin
    for U:=1 to NU do
    begin
      HORZ:=NU;
      HORZM:=((U+NU-2) mod NU)+1;
      HORZP:=(U mod NU)+1;
      for V:=1 to NV do
      begin
        VERT=NV;
        VERTM:=((V+NV-2) mod NV)+1;
        VERTP:=(V mod NV)+1;
        STATE2 [U,V] := STATE[U,V] + VELOX[U,V];
        VELOX2[U,V]:= VELOX[U,V] - (STATE[U,V] -
                      TRANSITION(STATE[HORZP,VERT],
                      STATE[HORZ,VERTP],STATE[HORZ,VERTM],
                      STATE[HORZM,VERT]))
      end
    end;
    VELOX:=VELOX2;
    STATE:=STATE2
  end
end;
```

The operation STATESURF is applied to the planar lattice and the values of
STATE will build a "perturbed" surface. For example, to simulate the trail left by a
boat moving on water, we introduce one perturbation and apply 25 generations of the
state transition function, each time moving the center of the perturbation. The
corresponding code is as follows:

```
P:=5;
for U:=1 to 25 do
begin
  MODIFY(STATE,U+12,TRUNC(P),0.5);
  GENERATION(NU,NV,25,2400,TRANSIT);
  P:=P+U*0.05
end;
```

The animator may create a scene with several perturbations. For example, the
results shown in Fig.15.20 were obtained after 35 frames. At this frame, the center of
the perturbations has moved from <12,5> to <47,36.5>, where 36.5 is calculated as

$$5 + \sum_{i=1}^{35} 0.05\,i \qquad\qquad (15.63)$$

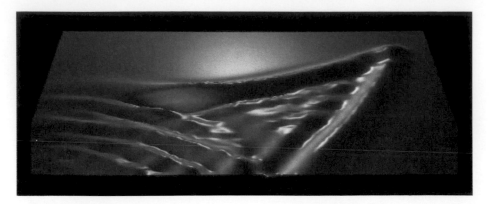

Fig.15.20. Simulation of the trail left by a boat moving on water. © 1986 MIRALab, H.E.C. and University of Montreal

15.7.2 Fire based on particle systems and solid textures

A short animated sequence has been produced at MIRALab, showing a pagoda destroyed by fire. The decor includes not only the pagoda, but also hills with snow and several trees, as shown in Fig.14.2.

Another approach has been used to model fire at MIRALab, it is based on the texture space described in Sect. 12.7.2. In fact, two different models have been implemented: a 2D model representing a turbulent flat fire and a 3D model representing the calm flame of a candle. Both models use transparency and color modifications.

The flat flame is obtained by concentric ellipses with gradation between the different ellipses. A perturbation is added using the TURBULENCE procedure described in Sect. 12.7.6.3. The importance of the Y-component was reduced in the turbulence in order to obtain shorter flames. Finally, the effect of turbulence increases with the Y-value in order to provide a calm basis and more turbulent flames. The user may control the global importance of the turbulence by giving the maximum value of this turbulence (between 0 and 1).

The 3D flame is based on a sinusoidal curve; the user may choose the amplitude of the sine function. As the texture is calculated for an observer located on the negative z-axis, a rotation of the texture space is performed around the Y-axis. The rotation angle is measured between the vector from the center of the flame to the camera eye and the Z-axis.

15.7.3 Clouds and fog

Two kinds of cloud model have been implemented using transparency and color spaces. The technique is something of a compromise between the Gardner approach (Gardner 1985; see Sect. 15.4.2) and the Perlin solid texture (1985; see Sect. 12.5).

The first cloud model is a flat model and the second model is really 3D and based on ellipsoids. Both models are based on a modification of the transparency and the color as in the Gardner approach, but a turbulent flow texture is added using the TURBULENCE procedure described in Sect. 12.7.6.3.

The principle is the same for both models: the color (gray value) is obtained from the TURBULENCE procedure. Then, if the color is less than a certain threshold, the pixel is completely transparent; otherwise, the transparency is calculated from the difference $\frac{\text{color-threshold}}{1\text{-threshold}}$. The threshold is not constant and varies from a minimum value T_{MIN} to a maximum value T_{MAX}. For the flat cloud, T_{MIN} is at the center and T_{MAX} at the distance DIST, specified by the user; in-between values are calculated by linear interpolation. For the 3D cloud model, the threshold is determined from the sine of the angle between the normal to the surface and the vector between the camera eye and the given point. If the angle is zero, the threshold is T_{MIN}; if the angle is 90^0 (corresponding to the ellipse boundaries), the threshold is T_{MAX}. In-between values are calculated using a sinusoidal interpolation. An example is shown in Fig.15.21.

As discussed in Sect. 15.4.3, fog is strongly related to the position of the object relative to the eye. For example, the fog may be defined by the following function:

```
procedure FOG (POINT,EYE:VECTOR; var CC:COLOR);
begin
  if POINT.Y < 10 then
    begin
    FRACT := POINT.Y/20 + 0.5;
    CC.R:=1-FRACT+FRACT*CC.R;
    CC.G:=1-FRACT+FRACT*CC.G;
    CC.B:=1-FRACT+FRACT*CC.B
  end
end;
```

Fog may also be simulated by combining an image with the background color. The fog is deeper when the distance between the point considered and the eye is longer. An example is shown in Fig.2.12.

Fig.15.21. Natural scene with 3D clouds. © 1986 MIRALab, H.E.C. and University of Montreal

16 Combination and composite images for complex 3D scenes

16.1 Integrated systems

16.1.1 Introduction

A complex 3D scene should probably be modeled and rendered using several different methods. For example, consider a scene with the sea, trees, a mountain, a ship, and clouds. Based on the preceding chapters, we would normally choose the following methods:

For the sea—free-form surfaces and particle systems (Sect. 15.3.2)
For the trees—particle systems (Sect. 15.6.3)
For the mountain—fractals (Sect. 15.2.2)
For the ship—a faceted model (Sect. 1.2.2)
For the clouds—textured quadric surfaces (Sect. 15.4.2)

Moreover, for refraction effects, ray-tracing is necessary, but some parts of the scene could be rendered by a less expensive method such as a z-buffer or scan-line algorithm.

One technique consists of processing small parts of an object description one at a time, accumulating the final image in frame-buffer memory. This technique has facilitated the development of hybrid systems which can process more than one type of object. Procedural models may control such processing (Newell 1975).

Csuri et al. (1979) describe a complex animation system, called ANTTS, which is based on the use of a run-length frame buffer that stores run-lengths or a sequence of pixels with the same value on a scan-line. The run-length buffer is a list of fixed memory arrays, one for each scan-line of the display. This is a unified approach to the display of data: polygons and solids modeled with polygons can be divided into triangles and then broken down into run-length segments. Lines can also be broken down into run-lengths of length 1 and points, and patch points are run-lengths of length 1. After the conversion of objects into run-lengths, the algorithm passes each run-length to the run-length buffer. When the frame has been completely processed, the run-lengths are decomposed into 3D pixel values. The z-values are compared with the same xy-values in the pixel buffer, effecting brute-force hidden-surface removal. The run-length buffer is stored in the main memory. The pixel buffers, in mass storage, contain the color and depth of each pixel and other information like image type, light information, and object identification.

Whitted and Weimer (1981) propose a system that reduces all objects to horizontal spans, which are composited using a list-priority algorithm. It allows scan converted

Fig.16.1. Foggy chessmen, created using a scan line algorithm and combining separate images of the chessmen, their reflections, and the chessboard. Courtesy of T. Whitted, University of North Carolina, Chapel Hill

descriptions of different surface types to be merged. Each object is described in terms of polygons, which are described by edges containing vertices. The display routines only recognize this structure and no higher hierarchical organization. Figure 16.1 shows an image generated using this approach.

Crow (1982) describes a system with a supervisory process that decides the order in which to combine images created by independent processes. The process of image generation is separated into two distinct phases—scene analysis and object rendering. In the first phase, interobject interactions are determined on the basis of crude estimations of the size and position of objects making up the scene. The generation phase uses information from scene analysis. Object priority is used to decide the order in which objects are to be rendered. Object overlap is also used to find those objects which may be rendered in parallel.

16.1.2 Shade trees

Cook (1984) proposes an interesting approach called **shade trees**. It is a flexible tree-structured shading model that can represent a wide range of shading characteristics. In a shade tree, all possible surfaces are not described by a single equation but as a set of basic operations such as dot products and vector normalization. Each operation is a node of the shade tree; the node has input and output parameters. For example, the input parameters to the diffuse node are a surface normal and a light vector, while the output parameter is the intensity value. The output parameter of a node is an input parameter for the next node in the hierarchy. The shader performs the calculations at the nodes in postorder. The output of the root of the tree is the final color. Basic geometric information such as the surface normal and the location of the object are the leaves of the tree. Cook similarly describes **light trees** and **atmosphere trees**. In a shade tree, main parameters are appearance parameters such as light source direction and color. These parameters are described by their own trees called light trees, which describe various types of lights including directional lights and spotlights. Shadows can be calculated or painted ahead of time and stored as textures that are accessed by the light tree. Atmosphere trees use the color obtained by the shade tree as input, but they may add effects like haze or rainbows.

16.1.3 Adaptive rendering systems

A few authors also propose systems with varying quality levels. The two most interesting approaches are a predefined number of quality levels proposed by Forrest (1985) and an adaptive refinement described by Bergman et al. (1986).

In the Forrest approach, a scene is rendered at the lowest quality level. If the scene parameters do not change, the scene is progressively rendered at higher levels. The levels described are:

1. What the hardware can draw
2. Antialiased lines without readback
3. Antialiased lines with readback

Bergman et al. extend this approach to allow automatically a continuum of quality levels without user definition, producing efficient image improvements by cutting down on the amount of data remaining for each successively higher level routing. The adaptive rendering system proceeds as follows:

1. **Vertex display**
   Transform the vertices
   Apply the Cohen-Sutherland algorithm
   Display the resulting visible points
2. **Edge display**
   Clip the edges of the visible polygons as line segments
   Display the visible edges with depth cueing
3. **Flat shading**
   Join the clipped edge segments
   Scan-convert the polygons using a z-buffer algorithm for hidden-surface removal
4. **Shadow display**
   if the data set contains precomputed shadow polygons
   then
      Scan-convert these shadow polygons
5. **Gouraud shading**
   Perform Gouraud shading on polygons where the range of intensity of a polygon's vertices exceeds a user-specified threshold
6. **Phong shading**
   Perform Phong shading on those polygons for which the direction of the specular reflectance vector at any vertex is within a user-specified tolerance of the direction of maximum highlight
7. **Antialiasing**
   Compute a threshold pixel map that designates which pixels need to be antialiased
   Build polygon fragments for the designated pixels
   Perform antialiasing with the A-buffer hidden surface algorithm (see Sect. 8.3.4)

16.2 Compositing

16.2.1 rgbα Representation

Porter and Duff (1984) discuss a process of compositing digital images. An image is separated into elements which are independently rendered. Each element has an associated matte, coverage information which designates the shape of the element. The compositing of these elements makes use of the mattes to accumulate the final image. Consider an element to be placed over an arbitrary background. Porter and Duff introduce the concept of α-channel; α is a mixing factor which controls the linear interpolation of foreground and background colors. This factor has to be of comparable resolution to the R, G, and B color channels for antialiasing purposes.

In this representation, called rgbα **representation**, the quadruple $<R,G,B,\alpha>$ indicates that the pixel is α covered by the color $<\frac{R}{\alpha},\frac{G}{\alpha},\frac{B}{\alpha}>$. Interesting cases are:

1. $\alpha=0$ $\Rightarrow$ R=0, G=0 and B=0
2. $\alpha=1$ $\Rightarrow$ true color $<R,G,B>$
3. $<0,0,0,1>$ $\Rightarrow$ the pixel is opaque black
4. $<0,0,0,0>$ $\Rightarrow$ the pixel is transparent

Porter and Duff introduce an algebra for compositing pictures at a pixel. Consider two pictures A and B. They divide the pixel into four subpixel areas:

1. The 0 subpixel area corresponding to $\neg A \cap \neg B$
   B=0 and A=0 and the contribution C to the composite is 0
2. The A subpixel area corresponding to $A \cap \neg B$
   B=0 and A=1 and the contribution C to the composite is either 0 or A
3. The B subpixel area corresponding to $\neg A \cap B$
   B=1 and A=0 and the contribution C to the composite is either 0 or B
4. The AB subpixel area corresponding to $A \cap B$
   B=1 and A=1 and the contribution C to the composite is 0, A, or B

Binary compositing operators are explained in Fig.16.2. We may now define the quadruple Q, indicating the input picture which contributes to the composite in each of the four subpixel areas 0, A, B, and AB.

For each of the operators in Fig.16.2, we give the name, the quadruple Q, F_A, and F_B, which represent the extent of the contribution of A and B; α_A and α_B represent the subpixel coverage of opaque objects:

1. Clear	$<0,0,0,0>$	$F_A=0$	$F_B=0$
2. A	$<0,A,0,A>$	$F_A=1$	$F_B=0$
3. B	$<0,0,B,B>$	$F_A=0$	$F_B=1$
4. A **over** B	$<0,A,B,A>$	$F_A=1$	$F_B=1-\alpha_A$
5. B **over** A	$<0,A,B,B>$	$F_A=1-\alpha_B$	$F_B=1$
6. A **in** B	$<0,0,0,A>$	$F_A=\alpha_B$	$F_B=0$

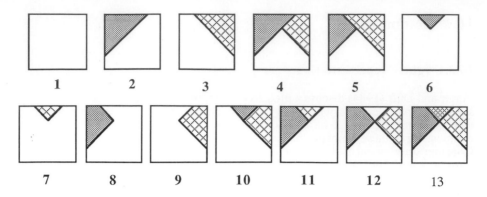

Fig.16.2. The binary operators of the rgbα representation

7. B **in** A	<0,0,0,B>	$F_A=0$	$F_B=\alpha_A$
8. A **out** B	<0,A,0,0>	$F_A=1-\alpha_B$	$F_B=0$
9. B **out** A	<0,0,B,0>	$F_A=0$	$F_B=1-\alpha_A$
10. A **atop** B	<0,0,B,A>	$F_A=\alpha_B$	$F_B=1-\alpha_A$
11. B **atop** A	<0,A,0,B>	$F_A=1-\alpha_B$	$F_B=\alpha_A$
12. A **xor** B	<0,A,B,0>	$F_A=1-\alpha_B$	$F_B=1-\alpha_A$
13. A **plus** B	<0,A,B,AB>	$F_A=1$	$F_B=1$

Porter and Duff (1984) show that the color of the composite c_C can be computed from the color c_A of A and the color c_B of B using the following equation:

$$c_C = c_A F_A + c_B F_B \tag{16.1}$$

For example, in the case of B **over** A, c_C is calculated as $c_A(1-\alpha_B)+c_B$.

Three unary operators are also defined for special effects: **dissolve, darken**, and **opaque**.

Figure 16.3 shows an image created as: Foreground **over** Hillside **over** Background.

16.2.2 rgbαz Representation

Duff (1985) introduces the **rgbαz representation**, which combine the rgbα representation and a z-buffer. The hidden-surface algorithms for these representations are based on binary operators that combine a pair of images A and B pixel-per-pixel to produce a composite image C=A **op** B.

Using the notation rgb_X for the color rgb of X, z_X for the depth of X and, α_X for the fraction of coverage of the pixel, the following operators are defined:

Fig.16.3. Composite image. By Thomas Porter, Tom Duff. © Lucasfilm 1984; all rights reserved

16.2.2.1 A zmin B
The composite image C at each pixel is defined by:

> **if** $z_A < z_B$ **then** $rgb_C := rgb_A$ **else** $rgb_C := rgb_B$
> $z_C := \min(z_A, z_B)$

16.2.2.2 A over B
The composite image at each pixel is defined by:

> $rgb_C := rgb_A + (1-\alpha_A)\, rgb_B$
> $\alpha_C := \alpha_A + (1-\alpha_A)\, \alpha_B$

16.2.2.3 A comp B
This operator combines the actions of zmin and over. A **comp** B is computed first by comparing z_A and z_B at each corner of the pixel. For each pixel edge for which $z_A \neq z_B$, the z's are linearly interpolated to find the point at which z_A and z_B are equal. If we designate by β the fraction by which A is in front of B, we may define the action of A **comp** B at each pixel as

> $rgb_C := \beta\,(A\ \textbf{over}\ B) + (1-\beta)\,(B\ \textbf{over}\ A)$
> $z_C := \min(z_A, z_B)$

According to Duff, the rgbαz representation is easily produced by almost any rendering program and has a simple, fast antialiased compositing operation output of sufficiently high quality for all but the most exacting applications.

16.2.3 Montage method

Nakamae et al. (1986) describe a montage method for overlaying computer generated images onto a background photograph. The method is analogous to the above compositing method and has two important characteristics:

1. Illuminance is calculated from information contained in the background picture.
2. Atmospheric effects (fog) are added using exponential functions as introduced by Schachter (see Sect. 15.4.3); these functions are also determined using information contained in the background picture

The montage method consists of five points:

1. Prepare the data for the computer-generated image
2. Photograph the land (background)
   Convert it from analog to digital
   Fit the photographic image onto a CRT screen
3. Match the computer-generated image and the photographed background scene from a geometric viewpoint
   Adjust the control parameters (camera position, view angle, ambient illuminance, fogginess)
4. Overlay the computer-generated image on the background scene
   Process hidden-surface removal, antialiasing, and fog effects
   Display the image
5. Display the foreground scene in front of the superimposed computer-generated image

17 MIRALab image synthesis software

17.1 Image synthesis and animation software at MIRALab

17.1.1 Introduction

MIRALab (Fig.17.1) is the image synthesis and computer animation laboratory of the University of Montreal.

As people working in the laboratory may come from either a computer science background or from the arts, two types of software have been produced and are still in production:

Fig. 17.1. MIRALab logo. © 1986 MIRALab, H.E.C. and University of Montreal

17.1.1.1 Research and development tools
This software has been developed mainly in two directions:

1. Programming languages for the synthesis and animation of realistic images, motion control and user interface control
2. Original algorithms and methods for animation and image synthesis; these algorithms and methods are also integrated into the languages

Typical languages developed at MIRALab are:

1. MIRA-SHADING, the main language for synthesis and animation of realistic images
2. CINEMIRA-2, an animation sublanguage
3. INTERMIRA, a specification language for interactive image synthesis and animation systems
4. EXPERTMIRA, an Artificial Intelligence language for the development of expert systems in image synthesis and animation (under development)

17.1.1.2 User-friendly systems
Several systems have been developed for end-users, in particular designers and animators:

1. The MIRANIM director-oriented system, an advanced actor-based animation system
2. The SABRINA image-synthesis system
3. The MUTAN multiple-track animator system for motion synchronization
4. The HUMAN FACTORY system, an animation system for articulated bodies

As the subject of this book is image synthesis, we shall emphasize the description of the SABRINA image synthesis system in Sect. 17.3. A brief introduction to the implementation language of SABRINA, called INTERMIRA, is given in Sect. 17.2. A summary of the MIRA-SHADING language and the animation software is presented in the Sects. 17.1.2 and 17.1.3. More information may be found in the following references:

MIRA-SHADING: Magnenat-Thalmann et al. (1985); Magnenat-Thalmann and
            Thalmann (1985b)
CINEMIRA-2: Magnenat-Thalmann and Thalmann (1985a)
MIRANIM: Magnenat-Thalmann et al. (1985a)
MUTAN: Fortin et al. (1983): Magnenat-Thalmann and Thalmann (1985b)
EXPERTMIRA: Thalmann and Magnenat-Thalmann(1986)
HUMAN FACTORY: Magnenat-Thalmann and Thalmann (1987)

17.1.2 MIRA-SHADING programming language

MIRA-SHADING (Magnenat-Thalmann et al. 1985) is a structured programming language for the synthesis and animation of realistic images. The most important concept of the language is the **3D-shaded high-level graphic type** (Magnenat-Thalmann and Thalmann 1983) as described in Sect. 1.4.2. In such a type, the user may define an abstraction of any complex object using a procedural model approach. For example, a transparent ß-spline surface may be defined by the following type header:

```
type SBETA = figure (CONTROL:FIG;  BIAS,TENSION,TMIN,TMAX:REAL);
              spec
                name;'BETA',
                shading PHONG,
                transparency TMIN, TMAX;
                ...
```

A ß-spline surface BETA is created from a control graph CONTR using the statement:

create BETA (CONTR, 1, 5, 0.4, 0.6)

where the bias is 1, the tension 5, and the transparency varies between 0.4 and 0.6, according to Equation (6.20).

For facet-based objects, statements to build edges and faces should be used in the body of the high-level types, as shown in Magnenat-Thalmann et al. (1985).

The MIRA-SHADING language also provides the following features:

- Over 100 predefined graphic types, including basic geometric primitives, free-form curves and surfaces, swept surfaces, ruled surfaces
- Over 200 image transformations, deformations, modifications applicable to any variable of graphic type
- Virtual camera control and manipulation
- Light, spot, shading primitives
- Over 50 texture primitives, including solid textures, fractal-based textures, image mapping
- Several color interfaces
- Antialiasing facilities
- Transparency, shadow control primitives
- Primitives for natural phenomena, including clouds, fire, fog, waves
- Primitives to control the generation and evolution of particle systems
- Over 100 3D computer animation primitives
- Display control for scan-line, z-buffer, and ray-tracing

17.1.3 Extensible director-oriented system MIRANIM and HUMAN-FACTORY system

MIRANIM (Magnenat-Thalmann et al. 1985a) is an advanced system which allows the creation, manipulation, and animation of realistic images. The most important features of MIRANIM are as follows:

- Basic geometric primitives
- Ruled and free-form surfaces
- 3D paths
- Multiple and stereoscopic cameras
- Actor motions
- Multiple lights and spots, shadows
- Transparency, 3D texture, fractals, particle systems
- Frame-by-frame control and real-time playback

Image rendering may be performed by a scan-line algorithm, a z-buffer, or a ray-tracing algorithm.

MIRANIM is a scripted system; the director designs a scene with decors, actors, cameras, and lights. Each of these entities is driven by state variables following evolution laws. The actor-based sublanguage CINEMIRA-2 allows the director to use programmers to extend the system. The great advantage of this is that the system is extended in a user-friendly way. This means that the director may immediately use the new possibilities. An entity programmed in CINEMIRA-2 is directly accessible in MIRANIM. This not only extends the system, but also enables specific environments to be created. For animation, CINEMIRA-2 allows the programming of five kinds of procedural entity: objects, laws of evolution, actor transformations, subactors, and animation blocks.

A CINEMIRA-2 subactor is dependent on an actor, which may be transformed in MIRANIM by a list of global transformations such as translation, rotation, shear, scale, color transformation, flexion, and traction. Several actors like these may participate in the same scene with other actors implemented using only algorithmic animation, cameras, lights, and decor.

The main purpose of the HUMAN FACTORY system is the direction of synthetic actors in their environment. In this system, which is typically a fourth generation language, synthetic actors are controlled by animators and designers without any programming knowledge. Not only the user has a high-level interface with menus and commands, but also he/she may add his/her own commands and menus to the system. The HUMAN FACTORY system is composed of several modules: skeleton control, body mapping, object grasping, and facial animation. This latter module has been specially developed to allow the synchronization of mouth motion with speech and emotion control.

Motions generated by HUMAN FACTORY may be completely integrated with MIRANIM animation scenes, which means that a character controlled by HUMAN-FACTORY may be present in a scene defined in MIRANIM, as shown in Fig.17.2.

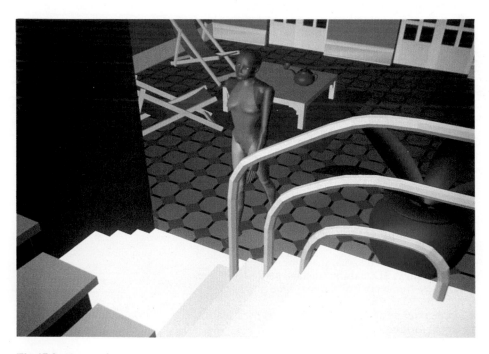

Fig.17.2. Frame of the film *Eglantine* © 1987 MIRALab, H.E.C. and University of Montreal

Fig. 17.3. Human characters. This is a frame of the computer-generated film "Rendez-vous à Montréal". © 1987 MIRALab, H.E.C. and University of Montreal

Fig. 17.4. Human characters. This is a frame of the computer-generated film "Rendez-vous à Montréal". © 1987 MIRALab, H.E.C. and University of Montreal

17.2 INTERMIRA specification language

17.2.1 Purposes of INTERMIRA

Our objectives in this project were to facilitate the design of graphics editors, object-modeling systems, image synthesis systems and animation editors by developing software to produce automatically graphic-based interactive systems. To build a specialized interactive graphics system, we need to provide a specification of the system to be produced.

The graphics editor generator has as data the formal specifications and a kernel editor, which is incomplete, or skeleton editor, which is invariant to the specifications. The graphics editor generator must analyze the formal specifications and extend the skeleton editor by adding new commands according to the specifications.

The graphics editor generator has two essential tasks:

1. To analyze the formal specifications written in the specification language INTERMIRA. The analysis is carried out by a preprocessor, which translates the specifications into the PASCAL language
2. To extend the skeleton editor, which is written in MIRA-SHADING, by adding the commands and the specific user interface resulting from the formal specifications

   Figure 17.5 shows the principles.

17.2.2 Skeleton editor

This is in fact the kernel of any computer-generated interactive system. It has seven main functions:

1. Link with the editor specifications
2. Interactive input and/or pop menus
3. Analysis of the user's response
4. Handling of error messages
5. Screen handling
6. Handling of user-defined graphic objects
7. Interface with the operating system, especially the file system

17.2.3 Specification language INTERMIRA

Any new interactive graphics system is described by a formal specification written in the INTERMIRA specification language. A typical specification is as follows:

```
specification <editor name>;
    <user interface specification>
    <local declarations>
    <sequence of command specifications>
begin
    <editor initialization>
end;
```

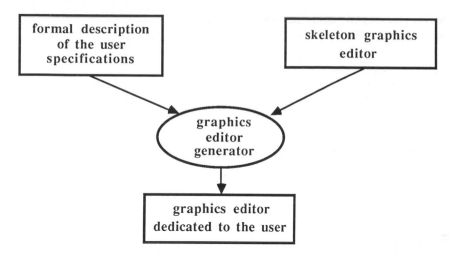

Fig.17.5. Principles of the graphics editor generator

17.2.4 User interface specification

The main purpose of a graphics editor is to manipulate graphics objects. The user determines these manipulations by the means of commands. A command may be very simple like 'END' or very complex because of a large number of parameters. In an INTERMIRA specification, several possibilities are provided:

- The interactive commands are typed by the user
- A pop menu of commands is displayed; the position of this menu may be decided in the specification, e.g.:

menu LEFT

Commands may be classified into a certain number of modes. These modes are declared in a list of names which corresponds to the command names to be entered in each mode, e.g.:

modes 'LIGHTS', 'CAMERAS', 'MOTIONS' **exit** 'QUIT'

A command name is also specified to quit a mode; in our example the name is 'QUIT'. This specification is also required in the main mode to terminate a session of the computer-generated interactive system.

A command is generally composed of a name and a sequence of parameters. There are three ways of entering parameters into such a command:

- By typing the parameters
- By entering them when required in an interactive dialogue
- By choosing a value in a pop menu

The three methods are possible with a computer-generated system and it is always possible to switch interactively to any kind of interface during a session of the computer-generated system.

17.2.5 Command specifications

The specification of a command requires three kinds of information:

1. The name of the command
2. Information about the parameters: number, names, types, default values
3. Information on what the command does and how it does it: this is the heart of the command

In INTERMIRA, these three parts are grouped together into a subprogram called a **command**. This may be described as:

command <command identifier> (<formal parameter list>)
param
    <parameters specifications>
end;
<local declarations>
begin
<statements>
end;

The formal parameter list is used to describe parameter types; the following types are available:

- INTEGER
- REAL
- VECTOR
- FIG (graphic object)
- LISTFIG (list of figure identifiers)
- STRING
- CHOICE (list of key words): e.g., RIGHT / LEFT or ON / OFF

Three transmission modes are available for parameters:

- Input parameter, e.g., F:FIG
- Output parameter, e.g., **var** F:FIG
- Input/output parameter, e.g., **mod** F:FIG

The purpose of the section on parameter specifications is to define the name of the parameter in the user interface of the computer-generated system, the list of keyword possibilities for CHOICE parameters, and the optional default values. For example:

command TEST(F:FIG; EPSI:REAL; SHADE:CHOICE);
param
    F: **name** 'INPUT FIGURE';
    EPSI: **name** 'THRESHOLD VALUE'
            default 0.001;
    SHADE: **name** 'SHADING TYPE'
            list 'CONSTANT', 'GOURAUD', 'PHONG'
            default 'CONSTANT'
end;

The body of a command subprogram really executes the action; it is in fact a sequence of MIRA-SHADING statements as described in Sect. 17.1.2. We now have to know how to process CHOICE parameters. These parameters may have as values a series of key words; however, they are considered in the INTERMIRA language as cardinal numbers. For example, consider a parameter defined as:

COLOR: 'COLOR NAME'
        list 'RED', 'GREEN', 'YELLOW', 'BLUE'
        default 'RED';

the red color may be tested by:

if COLOR = 1
then PUTCOLOR(F,<1,0,0>) {set color of object F to the rgb values 1,0,0}

We shall now give a complete example; suppose a command which allows the user to rotate an object around an axis passing through a point **C** and parallel to one of the main axes X, Y, or Z.
Such a command could be described by the following syntax:

ROTATE <object name> <point> <angle> <main axis>

Our three types of information are as follows:

1. The name of the command is ROTATE

2. There are four parameters, we may call them: OBJECT,CENTER,ANGLE,AXIS. Each one has a different data type. OBJECT is of figure type, POINT is a vector, ANGLE is a real number, and AXIS may be designated by one of the three values X_AXIS, Y_AXIS, and Z_AXIS. We may also decide default values, e.g.:

                CENTER=<0,0,0>
                ANGLE=90
                AXIS=X_AXIS

3. The active part of the command must describe how to rotate the object according to the current values of the parameters; this is typically a sequence of statements

In our example, we have:

command ROTATE(**mod** OBJ:FIG; CENT:VECTOR; ANG:REAL;
                     AXIS:CHOICE);

param
    OBJ: **name** 'OBJECT';
    CENT: **name** 'CENTER' **default** <<0,0,0>>;
    ANG: **name** 'ANGLE' **default** 90;
    AXIS: **name** 'AXIS' **list** 'X_AXIS', 'Y_AXIS', 'Z_AXIS';
end;
begin
case AXIS **of**
    1: ROTX(OBJ,CENT,ANG,OBJ);
    2: ROTY(OBJ,CENT,ANG,OBJ);
    3: ROTZ(OBJ,CENT,ANG,OBJ)
end;

17.3 SABRINA image-synthesis system

17.3.1 Overview of system

SABRINA is the MIRALab interactive object-modeling and image-synthesis system. The most important features of SABRINA are as follows:

- Object editing
- Color control
- Basic geometric primitives
- Ruled and free-form surfaces
- Curve and surface interpolations and approximations
- Spline editing
- 2D and 3D graphic input
- Three shading models: Lambert, Gouraud, and Phong
- Multiple cameras
- Multiple lights and spotlights
- Shadows
- Transparency
- Image mapping
- Solid texture
- Fractals
- Fog and stereoscopic effects

Figures 17.6 to 17.8 show decors produced using SABRINA.
SABRINA has a hierachical system of commands which are grouped into modes:

MAIN: supervision and general control, access to other modes
CAMERAS: definition, manipulation, and control of virtual cameras
COLOR: color interfaces, color definition, and manipulation
COMPOSE: object composition
CREATION: creation of basic objects
CURVES: creation and modification of curves
DRAWING: image display and selection of drawing style
EDIT_FIG: object edition
FILES: file control, save/restore of objects
LIGHTS: definition, manipulation, and control of light sources
MODIFY: modification of objects
REALISM: selection and control of realistic parameters: transparency, shading
SPLINES: definition and edition of interpolating splines
SURFACE: creation and modification of free-form and ruled surfaces
TEXTURE: creation of textures: image mapping, solid textures, fractals
TRANSFORMATION: object transformations

17.3.2 User interfaces

The system provides several kinds of interface which may be chosen by the user using the command INTERFACE:

- The COMMAND interface where each command has to be typed with its parameters. Parameters may be of several types:

Fig. 17.6. Frame of the computer-generated film *Rendez-vous à Montréal*. © 1987 MIRALab, H.E.C. and University of Montreal

Fig. 17.7. Decor © 1987 MIRALab, H.E.C. and University of Montreal

Fig. 17.8. Decor © 1987 MIRALab, H.E.C. and University of Montreal

Identifiers of figures, file names, integer numbers, real numbers, vectors (triples of integer or real numbers, separated by commas and enclosed by < and >), key words (e.g., YES / NO, RAY_TRACING)

The DIALOG interface where only the command name has to be typed; parameters will be requested from the user; when default values are defined, the user may select them by entering the "return" key

MENU interfaces which display a menu of commands to the user; menus may be on the left or on the right of the screen. Real, integer, vector, and string parameters are required using a dialogue mode; for figures and key words, menus are proposed; for lists of figures, the user may select ALL (all figures) or point to a series of figure names in the menu and then press ENTER

In this text, commands are described using the command interface.

17.3.3 SABRINA main mode

The role of the MAIN mode is to supervise the SABRINA system and to give access to the other modes. Two types of commands are available:

1. General-purpose commands
2. Commands to access other modes:

   CAMERAS COLOR COMPOSE CREATION CURVES DRAWING EDIT_FIG FILES LIGHTS MODIFY REALISM SPLINES SURFACE TEXTURE TRANSFORMATION

HELPC (<command name>)
Purpose: provides information on SABRINA commands

BACKUP <filename>
Purpose: creates a command file

DCL <dcl command string>
Purpose: executes a DCL command

DEFAULT <command name> <parameter values>
Purpose: changes the default values for parameters of a command

DISPLAY [YES/NO]
Purpose: selects whether a figure is automatically redrawn after it has been modified

EXECUTE <filename>
Purpose: executes a SABRINA command file

EXIT [YES/NO]
Purpose: terminates a SABRINA session

INTERFACE [COMMAND/DIALOG/MENU_RIGHT/MENU_LEFT]
Purpose: changes the editor's user-interface

LISTFIG <list of figures>
Purpose: displays the list of existing objects with their center, sizes, number of
          vertices, number of faces, and shading type.

SAVEPARAM [CAMERAS / LIGHTS / ALL] <filename>
Purpose: saves camera and/or light source definitions in a command file

17.3.4 Camera definition, control, and manipulation

The cameras mode allows the user to define, manipulate and control virtual cameras
(up to four cameras); the available commands are used to:

17.3.4.1 Define camera properties

PARCAMERA <camera number> <eye> <interest point>
                          <window width>
Purpose: defines a virtual camera with parallel projection

PERCAMERA <camera number> <eye> <interest point> <view angle>
Purpose: defines a virtual camera with perspective projection

VIEWPORT <camera number> <bottom left corner> <top right corner>
Purpose: defines a viewport for a camera

17.3.4.2 Turn cameras on or off

CAMERA <camera number> [YES / NO]
Purpose: turns a camera on or off

17.3.4.3 To define stereoscopic cameras

STEREO <distance between the eyes>
Purpose: selects stereoscopic views

17.3.4.4 To list camera properties

LISTCAM
Purpose: displays information concerning the cameras

17.3.5 Color selection, control, and manipulation

The color mode allows the user to select colors for the figures and the background using various interfaces; the available commands are used to:

17.3.5.1 Define the color system

COLORSYST [RGB/HLS]
Purpose: selects the RGB or the HLS color system

17.3.5.2 Color objects

COLOR <object to be colored> <color>
Purpose: colors a figure

DISTRICOLOR <object to be colored> <means> <std> <weights>
Purpose: distributes colors among the faces (or the vertices for Gouraud shading) of an object using means, standard deviations (std), and weights for each color

EXCHCOLOR <object to be modified> <original color> <new color>
Purpose: exchanges a color for another color in an object

FACECOLOR <object to be colored> <face number> <color>
Purpose: colors one face of an object

PAINT <palette number> <object to be colored>
Purpose: assigns a color to an object using a graphic color menu.

17.3.5.3 Control colors

PALETTE <palette number>
Purpose: generates colors using a graphics color menu.

17.3.5.4 Color background

BACKGROUND <color>
Purpose: defines the background color

17.3.6 Combination and assembly of several objects

This COMPOSE mode allows the user to create new figures by modifying and/or combining several figures in different ways; the available commands are used to:

17.3.6.1 Assemble objects

ASSEMBLE <fixed object> <movable object> <face_1> <face_2>
          [SYM / NOT-SYM]
Purpose: assembles two objects by a common face. The second figure is translated,
          rotated, and scaled in such a way that the selected face corresponds to the
          selected face of the first figure. It is possible to perform a symmetry (option
          SYM) on the movable object before assembling it

DIFFERENCE <original planar object> <planar object to subtract>
                    <result object>
Purpose: makes the difference (set theory operation) of two planar objects

UNION [<list of figures> / ALL] <result object>
Purpose: concatenates several figures into one

17.3.6.2 Divide objects

CUT <object to be cut> <point> <normal vector> [YES / NO]
       <result object>
Purpose: cuts an object using a plane given by a normal vector and a point. The holes
          created on the plane are closed by extra faces (YES) or not (NO)

REMOVE <original object> <subfigure to remove> <result object>
Purpose: removes a subfigure from a given figure

SECTION <object to be cut> <plane> <result object>
Purpose: performs a planar section of a 3D object; the plane is given by a normal
          vector and a point

SEPARATE <object to be separated> <plane> <part1> <part2>
Purpose: separates an object by a plane into two objects part1 and part2; the plane is
          given by a normal vector and a point.

17.3.6.3 Repeat objects

REPETITION <original object> <number of copies>
                <direction of translation><rotation axis>
                <rotation angle around the axis>
                <angles of self rotation> <scale factor> <result object>
Purpose: Generates a complex object as the concatenation of copies of a simple
          object; each copy may be simultaneously translated, rotated around an axis,
          rotated around its center and scaled.

17.3.6.4 Interpolate between two objects

INBETWEEN <first object> <last object> <interpolation method>
                <percentage between both objects> <result object>
Purpose: Interpolation between two objects. This command generates an interpolated
          object between two existing objects; a preprocessing step is performed to
          make a correspondence between both objects

17.3.7 Creation of basic objects

The CREATION mode is used to generate predefined types of figures; the available commands are used to create:

17.3.7.1 Nondisplayable objects

LINE <first point> <second point> <result object>
Purpose: creates a line between two points (cannot be displayed)

PLANE <first point> <second point> <third point> <result object>
Purpose: creates a plane from three points (cannot be displayed)

17.3.7.2 Planar objects

CIRCLE <circle center> <radius> <normal vector> <result object>
Purpose: creates a circle

ELLIPSE <first half axis> <second half axis>
                <normal vector to the ellipse> <result object>
Purpose: creates an ellipse

SEG <first point> <second point> <result object>
Purpose: creates a line segment from two points

SQUARE <square center> <one vertex> <normal vector>
                <result object>
Purpose: creates a square

TRIANGLE <vertex 1> <vertex 2> <vertex 3> <result object>
Purpose: creates a triangle given by three vertices

17.3.7.3 Regular polyhedra

CUBE <cube center> <face center>
        <direction of a vertex from the face center> <result object>
Purpose: creates a cube

DODECAHEDRON <dodecahedron center><face center>
                <direction of a vertex from the face center>
                <result object>
Purpose: creates a regular convex dodecahedron

ICOSAHEDRON <icosahedron center><face center>
                <direction of a vertex from the face center>
                <result object>
Purpose: creates a regular convex icosahedron

OCTAHEDRON <octahedron center><face center>
                <direction of a vertex from the face center>
                <result object>
Purpose: creates a regular convex octahedron

TETRAHEDRON <tetrahedron center><face center>
                              <direction of a vertex from the face center>
                              <result object>
Purpose: creates a regular convex tetrahedron

17.3.7.4 3D text

TEXT   <text origin> <character size> <character space>
             <character plane><result object> <string text to be represented>
Purpose: creates a 3D text

17.3.7.5 Parallelepiped and sphere

BOX <vertex 1> <vertex 2> <vertex 3> <vertex 4> <result object>
Purpose: creates a parallelepiped

SPHERE <center> <radius> <result object>
Purpose: creates a sphere

17.3.8 Creation, manipulation, and editing of free-form curves

The CURVES mode is used to create "curves," i.e. nonclosed 2D and 3D figures. The curves are usually drawn "freehand"; the available commands are used to:

17.3.8.1 Graphically input curves or polygons

ATTRACT [YES / NO]
Purpose: activates or deactivates the attraction grid for graphic input

DEFATTRACT <n>
Purpose: defines an n x n attraction grid for graphic input

DEFAXIS <axis>
Purpose: defines the plane for graphic input: XY, XZ or YZ

DEFDIRECT <figure>
Purpose: defines a reference figure for graphic input

DEFREFERENCE <n>
Purpose: defines an n x n reference grid for graphic input

DIRECT [YES / NO]
Purpose: activates or deactivates the reference figure for graphic input

READARC3D <3D arc name>
Purpose: reads a 3D circular arc by interactive graphic input
Method: when READARC3D is invoked, a grid appears; it corresponds to the XZ-
            plane; a Y-axis is also displayed

READGRAPH <output object>
Purpose: performs an interactive graphics input of a figure to read a polygon
Method: when READGRAPH is invoked, a grid appears. Figures must be entered
            using the graphics tablet

HEIGHT <object>
Purpose: adds a third dimension to a planar object
Method: when HEIGHT is invoked, the planar object appears; an axis is also
displayed on the right of the screen. The third dimension must be entered
using the graphics tablet

17.3.8.2 Close curves

CLOSE <curve to be closed>
Purpose: closes a curve by linking the last vertex to the first vertex

17.3.8.3 Edit curves

EDITCURVE <original polygon> <modified polygon>
Purpose: modifies the polygon by moving a vertex or an edge, splitting an edge or
killing an edge

17.3.8.4 Approximate or interpolate curves

AKIMA <original curve>
        <number of additional points between 2 existing points>
        <result object>
Purpose: applies an Akima local interpolation on a curve

BETACURVE <original curve> <bias> <tension> <resolution>
                <result object>
Purpose: creates a ß-spline curve from control points

17.3.9 Object display

This DRAWING mode is used to display any list of figures to the screen and to set
graphic display parameters; the available commands are as follows:

ANTIALIASING [1-TIME / 2-TIMES / 3-TIMES]
Purpose: performs shaded images with an antialiasing process; 1-TIME means no
antialiasing, 2-TIMES doubles the resolution and 3-TIMES uses the Bartlett
window for a three times resolution

DISPTYPE <div>
Purpose: selects an algorithm to fill the look-up table for colors when only 256 colors
are displayable at the same time; <div>is the number of colors used in the
images; the look-up table will be divided into <div> parts. If div=0, a
default algorithm is applied

REDRAW [WIRE_FRAME / SCAN_LINE / Z_BUFFER /
              RAY_TRACING] <list of objects>
Purpose: redraws one or several objects using the current cameras and lights; the
rendering algorithm may be chosen

SHADOW [YES/NO]
Purpose: selects whether shadows cast by figures should be calculated or not for all
figures; valid in scan-line and ray-tracing

SHOW <object>
Purpose: displays an object with viewing parameters corresponding to a good view

TRANSPAR [YES / NO]
Purpose: selects whether object transparency is activated or not for all figures

VISTEST <object> **[YES/NO]**
Purpose: selects a test of visibility at display time

WAIT <time>
Purpose: waits for a certain time or until an event

17.3.10 Editing of objects

The EDIT_FIG mode has been designed to allow the user to edit a 3D graphic object without reference to the vertex numbers or the coordinates of the vertices of the object. However, an experienced user may also perform low-level operations by specifying vertex numbers or coordinates. The editing is done in wire-frame mode in order to identify vertices graphically. EDIT_FIG has been mainly designed for limiting the problems due to the ambiguity of 3D wire-frame drawings. Because 3D wire-frame drawings are projected onto a 2D device (screen), it is difficult to tell when a vertex is in front of an object or not. One way to solve this problem of the missing dimension is to show the graphic objects viewed from several angles in order to be able to determine the third dimension without any ambiguity. Several concepts are essential for working with the EDIT_FIG mode:

17.3.10.1 Concept of active figure
An active figure is the current figure known by the EDIT_FIG mode. To make a figure active, use the command ACTIVATE. This command makes a local copy of the selected figure and identifies this figure as the figure used in all commands and operations of the EDIT_FIG mode. It also displays the active figure in each of the active cameras.

17.3.10.2 Concept of active camera
Four cameras are always defined in the EDIT_FIG modes. They are parallel cameras and they are called CAMERA_A, CAMERA_B, CAMERA_C, and CAMERA_D. They correspond to views from the front, above, left, and right. The user may, however activate, or deactivate cameras in order to accelerate the display process. During a display, the screen is divided into four viewports.

17.3.10.3 Concept of current vector
A 3D point or a vertex of a figure is defined by its three coordinates X, Y, and Z in three-space. A 3D point or a vertex is called a vector. Two vectors are always defined in the EDIT_FIG mode—A and B; each may be considered a box with two values—NUMBER and COORDINATES. NUMBER contains 0 for a 3D point and the vertex number for a vertex; COORDINATES contains the XYZ-coordinates of the vector.

17.3.10.4 Concept of current set
Some operations are defined by identifying a particular vertex of the figure and by specifying a radius limiting the vertices affected by the operation. However, it is sometimes difficult to specify such a radius, simply because it is better if some

vertices are not affected. For this reason, it is possible to select a set of vectors which will be affected by some operations. Once this set is defined, it is the current set until modified. New vectors may be added to the current set.

The EDIT_FIG mode contains many commands which allow the user to:

17.3.10.5 Activate and copy objects

ACTIVATE <object>
Purpose: makes an object current for the EDIT_FIG mode. The object is displayed in
the viewports corresponding to the active cameras

GIVE_BACK <object identifier> [YES / NO]
Purpose: makes a copy of the active figure for use in other SABRINA modes. The
user may continue to edit his/her figure.

17.3.10.6 Define and/or modify current vectors

COMBIN_A_B   <coefficient of vector A> <coefficient of vector B>
              [A / B]
Purpose: calculates a linear combination of vectors A and B and returns the result into
either A or B.
Result <-- (X * A) + (Y * B)

DIRECT_ID [A / B] <vertex number> <vector>
Purpose: defines one of the current vectors (A or B) without using graphic input.
The user has to provide the vertex number of the active figure or 0 if he/she
defines a three-space point. In this latter case

DIST_A_B
Purpose: returns the distance between the current vectors A and B

EXCHNG_A_B
Purpose: swaps A and B

GRAPHIC_ID [A / B] [ON_FIGURE / IN_SPACE]
Purpose: defines a current vector (A or B) using a graphic input; it is possible to
identify a vertex (option ON_FIGURE) or a 3D point (option IN_SPACE)

SHOW_A_B
Purpose: displays the contents of the current vectors A and B

17.3.10.7 Perform deformations of objects

BOXIC <first corner> <second corner > [A / B] <X severity>
      <Y severity> <Z severity>
Purpose: alters the active figure by limiting the affected vertices within the volume of
an imaginary box given by two opposite corners. The A or B vector
determines with the first corner the direction of the alteration; <X severity>
<Y severity><Z severity> are values controlling the intensity of the
alteration. The deformation is maximum at the first corner and minimum at
the second

CONIC <radius> <severity>
Purpose: deforms the active figure by moving vertices from a source vertex A to a

destination vertex B. Only vertices within a certain radius around A are affected and the effect is proportional to 1 / (distance from the vertex to A). The severity is a real number which controls the shape of the deformation.

Severity = 1 — cone
Severity < 1 — deformation like a bossel
Severity > 1 — deformation like a stalagmite

CONIC_SET   <severity>
Purpose: deforms the active figure by moving vertices from a source vertex A to a destination vertex B. Only vertices in the current set are affected and the effect is proportional to 1 / (distance from the vertex to A). The severity parameter has the same meaning as for CONIC

CYLINDRIC   <cylinder radius> <radial scale of the deformation>
<directional scale of the deformation>
<radial shape of the deformation>
<directional shape of the deformation>
Purpose: deforms the active figure by moving vertices contained in an imaginary cylinder. The shape of the deformation is defined by radial and directional radii and scale factors

STEP [A / B] [FORWARD / BACKWARD] <step>
Purpose: redefines the value of one of the current vectors (A or B) by the value of another vertex "step" forward or backward

UNDO
Purpose: suppresses the effects of the last operation

17.3.10.8 Modify a few vertices and/or faces

ADD_VERTEX [A / B]
Purpose: adds a vertex to the current figure; the vertex to be added must have been previously stored in A or B

CHANGEVERT
Purpose: changes the coordinates <X,Y,Z> of vertices of the current figure.

CLEANITUP
Purpose: deletes any vertex of the current figure that does not belong to any face

DUPLICVERT [A / B]
Purpose: doubles a vertex (contained in A or B) of the active figure; this operation is useful in Phong shading with figures having a large angle between faces

INVERTFACE <first vertex number> <last vertex number>
Purpose: inverts the list of vertices in one or several polygons

MOVEVERTEX <radius>
Purpose: moves vertices from a source vertex A to a destination vertex B. Only vertices within a certain radius around A are affected

REDEF_FACE <face number> <face color>
Purpose: redefines or adds a face to the active figure.

REMOVEFACE <first face number> <last face number>
Purpose: deletes faces of the active figure according to an interval of face numbers

VERTFUSION [A / B] <radius of the area>
Purpose: joins to a current vector (A or B) all vertices of the active figure located at a distance of the vector less than or equal to a given value (radius)

17.3.10.9 Define or modify the current set

ADD_IN_SET [A / B]
Purpose: adds one vector A or B to the current set

G_SET_ID
Purpose: defines the current set using a graphic input

MOVE_SET
Purpose: moves the vertices of the current set in the direction from A to B

17.3.10.10 Display of objects and camera definition

CAMERAS [YES / NO] [YES / NO] [YES / NO] [YES / NO]
Purpose: activates or deactivates parallel cameras for the EDIT_FIG mode

PERSPECTIV <camera number>
Purpose: displays the active figure using a perspective projection defined with the command PERCAMERA of the CAMERAS mode

REDRAW
Purpose: displays the active figure using the active cameras

ZOOM [IN / OUT] [A / B] <zoom value>
Purpose: allows zoom-in or zoom-out on one of the current vectors (A or B).

17.3.10.11 Display information about objects, current vectors, and current set

GETFACECOL <face number>
Purpose: returns the color of a face

HOLE_TEST
Purpose: checks the active figure in order to detect holes, inverted polygons

MARK [A / B / SET]
Purpose: draws a small square (mark) around the vertex contained in one of the current vectors (A or B) or around all vectors of the current set (SET)

MARKINTERV [YES / NO]
Purpose: draws a small square around all vertices specified by a range of vertex numbers

17.3.11 Store and retrieve objects

The FILES mode is used to load/save figures either in text or binary formats; the available commands are as follows:

READFILE <file name> <list of figures>
Purpose: reads one or several figures from a binary file

READTEXFIG <filename> <list of figures>
Purpose: reads one or many figures from a text file

SAVE <file name> <list of figures>
Purpose: saves one or several figures in a binary file

WRITEXFIG <filename> <list of figures>
Purpose: saves one or many figures in a text file

17.3.12 Definition, control, and manipulation of light sources

The LIGHT mode is used to define and manipulate light sources; the available commands are used to:

17.3.12.1 Define light sources

AMBIENT <intensity of the ambient light>
Purpose: defines an ambient light

DIRECT <light source> <intensity> <direction>
Purpose: defines a directional light source

PONCTUAL <light source> <intensity> <location>
Purpose: defines a ponctual light source

SPOT <light source><intensity><location> <direction><concentration>
Purpose: defines a spot light source

17.3.12.2 Modify and list properties of light sources

LIGHT <light source> [YES/NO]
Purpose: turns a light source on or off

LIMIT <light source> <cone axis or cylinder direction>
        <cone angle or cylinder radius>
Purpose: limits the scope of a light source by a cone (point light source) or a cylinder
        (directional light source)

LISTSOURCE
Purpose: displays the light source parameters for all sources

MOVESOURCE <light source> [LEFT / RIGHT / UNDER / ABOVE /
                BEFORE / BEHIND] <displacement value>
Purpose: moves a light source in one of the six main directions

17.3.13 Modification of object

The MODIFY mode is used to modify an object or to perform a special action on this object ; the available commands are as follows:

COMPACT **<original object> <limit angle between normals>**
                    <result object>
Purpose: concatenates adjacent faces when the angle of their normals is less than a
         given value

COPY **<original object> <copy name>**
Purpose: makes a copy of a figure

DELETEFIG **<objects to be deleted>**
Purpose: deletes one or several objects

DOUBLE **<original object> <limit angle between normals>**
                    <result object>
Purpose: doubles all vertices which are common to two faces with an angle greater
         than a specified value; this command is useful to remove parts of objects
         (see REMOVE) or to shade objects with the Phong algorithm when faces
         have an angle which is too large

FUSION **<original object> <minimal distance> <result object>**
Purpose: reduces vertices too near a single vertex

OPTIMIZE **<object to optimize>**
purpose: optimizes the memory space taken by a figure

POINT **<input object> <vertex number>**
                 <relative vector added to the vertex value>
Purpose: moves a vertex of a figure

PROJ_SPH **<input object> <sphere center> <sphere radius>**
                    <curvature factor> <result object>
Purpose: does a spherical projection of a figure.

ROUND **<original object> <sphere radius>**
                 <number of faces to generate a cylinder section>
                 <result object>
Purpose: rounds the edges and the corners of an object by creating sections of
         cylinders in the edges and sections of spheres at the corners

TRIANGULATE **<original object> <maximum edge length>**
                        <result object>
Purpose: triangulates an object by dividing each face into triangles

17.3.14 Controlling realism

The REALISM mode contains commands to improve realism in the display of figures
in shading; the available commands are as follows:

FOG **<distance from the camera eye to the point where the objects are**
              50% mixed with the background>
Purpose: creates a fog effect by mixing objects with the background

REFLECTANCE **<input object> <reflection factor> <highlight width>**
Purpose: defines the reflection factor and the width of the highlight for a figure

SHADE **<input object>** **[<CONSTANT>/<PHONG>/GOURAUD]**
Purpose: changes the type of shading; conversion from and to Gouraud shading
 involves averaging of colors and may be irreversible

TRANSPARENCY **<object to make transparent>** **<min. transparency
 factor>** **<max. transparency factor>** **<exponent>**
Purpose: defines transparency parameters for a figure

17.3.15 Creation, editing, and manipulation of interpolating splines

The SPLINE mode allows the creation and editing of Kochanek-Bartels interpolating
splines; the available commands are as follows:

BIAS **<vertex number>** **<bias value>**
Purpose: defines a bias value for a control point of the current spline

CONTINUITY **<vertex number>** **<continuity value>**
Purpose: defines a continuity value for a control point of the current spline

CURVE **<control polygon>**
Purpose: defines a set of control points for spline interpolation

DATA **<first control point number >** **<last control point number>**
Purpose: lists characteristics of the current spline: time, continuity, tension, and bias

SHOW **<spline curve identifier>** **<scale factor for the marks>**
Purpose: displays a spline figure with time marks

SPLINE **<spline curve identifier>**
Purpose: creates the spline

TENSION **<vertex number>** **<tension value>**
Purpose: defines a tension value for a control point of the current spline

TIME **<vertex number>** **<time value>**
Purpose: defines a time value for a control point of the current spline

17.3.16 Creation and manipulation of free-form and ruled surfaces

The SURFACES mode contains commands used to create free-form and ruled 3-D
surfaces; the available commands are used to:

17.3.16.1 Build ß-spline surfaces

BETA **<control graph>** **<first dimension of the control graph>**
 <second dimension of the control graph> **<u-resolution>**
 <v-resolution> **<bias>** **<tension>** **<result object>**
Purpose: creates a ß-spline surface from control polygons

FAT **<curve>** **<thickness>** **<tension>** **<result object>**
Purpose: creates a "fat" body around a given curve using propagation control graphs
 and ß-spline surfaces

MULTIBETA <curves> <polygon> <u-resolution> <v-resolution>
                    <bias> <tension> <result object>
Purpose: creates several ß-spline surfaces using multiple propagation control graphs

PBETA <propagation control graph> <u-resolution> <v-resolution>
                    <bias> <tension> <result object>
Purpose: creates a ß-spline surface from a propagation control graph

17.3.16.2 Build Bézier surfaces

BEZIER <control graph> <first dimension of the control graph>
                    <second dimension of the control graph> <u-resolution>
                    <v-resolution><result object>
Purpose: creates a Bézier surface from control polygons

PBEZIER <propagation control graph> <u-resolution> <v-resolution>
                    <result object>
Purpose: creates a Bézier surface from a propagation control graph

17.3.16.3 Generate surfaces by curve sweeping

CONE <director curve> <cone apex> <fraction of the cone>
                    <result object>
Purpose: creates a conic surface from a director curve and a given point (cone apex)

CONEP <director curve> <cone apex> <auxiliary vertex>
                    <parabolic cone resolution><result object>
Purpose: creates a parabolic cone from a director figure and two vertices

CYLINDER <director curve> <cylinder direction> <cylinder height>
                    <result object>
Purpose: creates a cylindrical surface

REVOLUTION <director curve> <revolution axis> <resolution>
                    <revolution angle>
                    <translation applied to the director curve>
                    <scale applied to the director curve> <torsion angle>
                    <initial scaling><final scaling>[CLOSE / NOT CLOSE]
                    <result object>
Purpose: creates a revolution surface; [CLOSE / NOT CLOSE] is a parameter
            indicating whether the revolution surface will be closed

TANGENT <generator curve> <director curve> <rotation angle>
                    <order> <result object>
Purpose: generates a surface by propagating a curve (generator) tangentially to
            another curve (director); <order> is an option for selecting the order of
            rotations: XYZ, XZY, YXZ, YZX, ZXY, ZYX

17.3.16.4 Generate propagation control graphs

PROPAGATE <path> <propagated polygon(s)> <interpol> <scale>
                    <size_1> <size_2> [YES / NO] <result object>
Purpose: creates a propagation control graph (PCG). A PCG is obtained by
            propagating a polygon along a path and applying evolution functions during

this propagation. <interpol> is an interpolation option; <scale> is an option allowing the size to vary between the values <size_1> and <size_2>. The law of variation may be: ACCELERATION, CONSTANT, DECELERAT, LINEAR, SQUARE, RANDOM, or NONE (no variation). It is possible to adjust automatically the polygon size dependent on the curvature of the path

17.3.17 Creation of textures and natural phenomena

The TEXTURE mode enables texture to be simulated on a figure; the available commands are used to:

17.3.17.1 Map 2D images

MAP <2D object> <3D object> <window bottom left corner>
    <window top right corner> <map orientation> <distance between
    the mapped image and the 3D surface> <result object>
Purpose: maps a 2D figure onto a 3D object

PATTERN <object to be filled> <pattern> <x-interdistance>
        <y-interdistance> <result object>
Purpose: fills a polygon with patterns

17.3.17.2 Simulate materials

BRICK <object to be textured>
Purpose: applies a brick texture to a figure. The texture is generated using a brick function defined by three parameters: a scale vector, the color of the brick, and the color of the cement.

MARBLE <object to be textured>
Purpose: applies a marble texture to a figure. The marble texture is a series of parallel bands of various colors perturbed using a turbulence function. The texture is generated using a marble function defined by seven parameters: three widths, a scale factor, and three colors. An example is shown in Fig. 17.9.

WOOD <object to be textured>
Purpose: applies a woody texture to a figure. The woody texture is based on a series of concentric cylinders with their axes parallel to Z and passing through the center of the object to be textured. Cylinders are alternatively colored using two colors. The texture is generated using a wood function defined by three parameters—the number of cylinders used in the object and the two colors.

17.3.17.3 Simulate natural phenomena

CLOUD_2D <basic shape>
Purpose: creates a flat cloud from a basic shape. The CLOUD_2D should be used with objects that are almost flat; it modifies color and transparency. The texture is generated using a cloud function defined by three parameters:

1. The probability that a pixel of the object center becomes totally transparent
2. The maximum threshold representing the probability that a pixel on the boundary of the object becomes totally transparent
3. The scale factor allowing longer clouds (cirrus) to be obtained

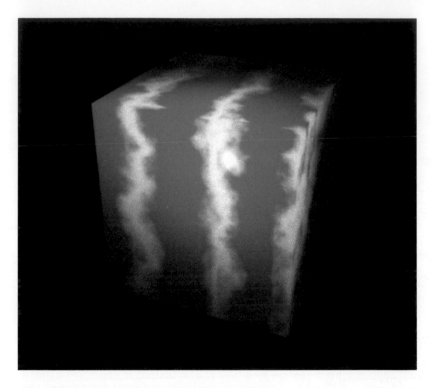

Fig. 17.9. Marble texture. © 1987 MIRALab, H.E.C. and University of Montreal

CLOUD_3D <basic shape> <camera position>
Purpose: creates a 3D cloud from a basic shape. The CLOUD_3D texture may be
    used with any 3D object; however, spheres or ellipsoids give the best
    results. The texture is generated using a cloud function defined by the same
    three parameters as for CLOUD_2D

FLAME_2D <basic shape>
Purpose: creates a flat flame from a basic shape. The FLAME_2D texture should be
    used with objects that are alomost flat; it modifies color and transparency

FLAME_3D <basic shape> <camera position> <flame center>
Purpose: creates a 3D flame from a basic shape. The FLAME_3D texture may be
    used with any 3D object. The texture modifies the color and the
    transparency

**WAVE <object to be textured> <number of random wave sources>
          <seed for random distribution>**
Purpose: creates waves on the surface of an object. The texture is generated using a
    wave function defined by three parameters: a damp factor, a scale of the first
    modification of the normal, and the wave amplitude. The damp factor may
    have three possible values: 0 for constant wave height, 1 when the wave
    height increases with the distance from the center, -1 when the wave height
    decreases with the distance from the center

17.3.17.4 Generate special solid textures:

BOSSELS <object to be textured>
Purpose: creates irregular bossels on the surface of an object. The BOSSELS texture creates this appearance by modifying the normals of the surface. The texture is generated using a function defined by three parameters: the detail level, the scale of the first modification of the normal, and the bossel amplitude. An example is shown in Fig.15.21.

COLORSPOT <object to be textured>
Purpose: creates color spots on the surface of an object. The texture is generated using a function defined by one parameter <scale>; the spot sizes are about proportional to 1 / <scale>

MERIDIAN <object to be textured>
Purpose: creates bossels on the surface of an object according to meridians. The MERIDIAN texture creates this appearance along meridians by modifying the normals of the surface. The texture should be applied to objects having a symmetry axis (revolution bodies). The texture is generated using a function defined by two parameters—the number of meridians and the bossel amplitude

PYRAMID <object to be textured>
Purpose: creates a texture by moving the normal. The texture is generated using a function defined by two parameters—a scale factor which controls the level of details and an amplitude which controls the displacement of the normal

17.3.17.5 Change and list function parameters in solid texture

INIT_PARAM <seed for the random generator>
Purpose: initializes the seed for random functions in textures

PARAM_COUL [MARBLE / WOOD / BRICK / CLOUD2D / CLOUD3D / COLORED]
Purpose: lists the current values of the function parameters for solid texture by color perturbation

PARAM_NORM [WAVE / BATTERED / PYRAMID / MERIDIAN]
Purpose: lists the current values of the function parameters for solid texture by normal perturbation

SETREALCOUL [MARBLE / WOOD / BRICK / CLOUD2D / CLOUD3D / COLORED]
Purpose: modifies the current real values of the function parameters for solid texture by color perturbation

SETREALNORM [WAVE / BATTERED / PYRAMID / MERIDIAN]
Purpose: modifies the current real values of the function parameters for solid texture by normal perturbation

SET_TEXTURE [COLOR / NORMAL] [YES / NO]
Purpose: selects the texture mode (normal or color perturbation) for particular use

SETVECCOUL [MARBLE / WOOD / BRICK / CLOUD2D / CLOUD3D / COLORED]
Purpose: modifies the current vector values of the function parameters for solid texture by color perturbation

17.3.17.6 Generate fractals

FRAC3 **<original object> <maximal edge length> <eccentricity of the revolution volume> <shape of the revolution volume> <pts_invol> <edg_kept> <result object>**
Purpose: generates a fractal surface from an existing figure using triangle recursive subdivision. If the original figure has nontriangular faces, they will be triangulated. The point which is calculated between two vertices is contained in a revolution volume. The shape of the revolution volume may be: 0 (circular cylinder), 1 (two circular cones), or larger (two disks). New points are generated either inside the revolution (<pts_invol> = YES) or only on the surface of the revolution volume (<pts_invol> = NO). Original edges are saved (<edg_kept> = YES) or not

FRAC4 **<original object> <maximal edge length> <displacement> <seed for the random generator> <result object>**
Purpose: generates a fractal surface from an existing figure using recursive quadrilateral subdivision

17.3.18 Point transformations

The TRANSFORMATION mode is used to transform a figure using matrix transformations; the available commands are used to:

17.3.18.1 Modify current location

ALIGN <object to be moved> <reference object (fixed)> <axes>
Purpose: moves an object in such a way that its center is aligned with the center of another object according to an axis.

MOVEFIG <object to be moved> [LEFT / RIGHT / BEFORE / BEHIND / ABOVE / UNDER] <displacement value>
Purpose: moves an object in one of the six main directions

POSITION <object to move> <new location of the object center>
Purpose: centers an object at a location

PUT <object to be moved> [LEFT / RIGHT / BEFORE / BEHIND / ABOVE / UNDER] <reference object (fixed)>
Purpose: places an object relative to another according to one of the six main directions

TRANSLATION <object to be translated> <translation vector>
Purpose: translates a figure

17.3.18.2 Modify current orientation

ROTATION <object to be rotated> [X_AXIS/Y_AXIS/Z_AXIS]
                    <rotation angle>
Purpose: rotates a figure around an axis passing through the current center of rotation

ROTAT_CENT [YES/NO]
Purpose: defines the center of rotation; YES indicates whether the user defines the
               center as the center of the object

SYMMETRY <object to be transformed by symmetry> [XY/YZ/XZ]
Purpose: performs a symmetric operation relative to a plane

17.3.18.3 Modify current size

SCALE <object to be scaled> <scale vector>
Purpose: changes the size of a figure

17.3.18.4 Combine operations

REFERENCE <original object> <RS$_1$ origin> <RS$_2$ origin>
                  <points determining axes> [SAME/DIFFERENT]
                  <result object>
Purpose: moves an object from a reference system RS$_1$ to a new reference system
               RS$_2$. The dimensions of both objects are the same (SAME) or may be
               different (DIFFERENT); in this latter case, new dimensions are dependent
               on the distance between the origins and the given points to determine axes

RELATIVE <fixed object> <movable object> <face specification of the
                  fixed object> <face specification of the movable object>
                  [INSIDE / OUTSIDE] <angle>
Purpose: positions an object in order to make the center of a face of this object
               coincident with the center of a face of another object. The face specification
               may be a face number or one of the following key words: LARGE (the
               largest face), HIGH (the highest face), LOW (the lowest face), LEFT (the
               leftmost face), RIGHT (the rightmost face), FRONT (the frontmost face),
               BACK (the backmost face).The center of both objects lies on the same
               (INSIDE) or the opposite side (OUTSIDE) of the plane of the two faces.
               The movable object will be rotated by an angle around an axis normal to the
               plane of the face and passing through the center

17.3.18.5 Cancels an operation

ALLOWS_UNDO [YES/NO]
Purpose: with this option, the effect of the last operation may be cancelled by
               selecting the command UNDO

UNDO
Purpose: cancels the effect of the last transformation

17.4 Particle systems

17.4.1 User-friendly control of particle systems

Interactive control of procedural models using the CINEMIRA-2 sublanguage has been introduced into the extensible director-oriented animation MIRANIM (Magnenat-Thalmann et al 1985a). With this approach, a user may define his own evolution laws in particle systems. As already discussed in Sect. 14.6, systems may be initialized by interactive commands and then updated by animation blocks, and the laws may return any state variables. With this approach, the possibility of defining any evolution law within an animation system may provide many new possibilities for motion. Systems are controlled using seven commands, which are responsible for locating the invariable fields of a system (particle shape, system shape, acceleration) and for initializing the variable fields (velocity, center position, generator point). These commands are described in the next section.

17.4.2 Main commands

17.4.2.1   CREATESYST <system identifier> <motion type>
<center of the system>

This command creates a new system or changes the center of an existing system. Motion may be either conventional or Brownian.

17.4.2.2 SHAPESYST <system identifier> <particle shape>
<system shape>

This command defines the particle shape and the system shape. In fact, 3D particle shapes do not really exist in the world space. Particle shapes on the viewplane may be circular or square. System shapes were chosen by a similar method to that of Reeves (1983): a sphere of radius r, a circle of radius r in the xy plane and a rectangle in the xy plane.

17.4.2.3 SHAPEVOL <system identifier> <volume shape>
<border action> <volume dimensions>
<volume center>

This command defines the initial center and the shape of the evolution volume; particles may only live in this volume. Available shapes are:

1. Unlimited volume
2. Parallelepiped of dimensions x,y, and z
3. Ellipsoid of half-axes a,b, and c
4. Elliptic cylinder of half-axes a and b and half-height h

When a particle reaches a volume border, two types of action are possible:
1. The particle dies
2. The velocity sign is changed

17.4.2.4 MOTIONSYST <system identifier> <system velocity>
<system acceleration> <particle acceleration>

This command allows the animator to specify the velocity and the acceleration of the system as well as the acceleration of the particles.

17.4.2.5 MOTIONVOL <system identifier> <system velocity>
<system acceleration>

This command allows the animator to specify the velocity and the acceleration of the evolution volume.

17.4.2.6 ORIENTATION <system identifier> <ejection angle>
<rotation angles>

This command defines the ejection angle and the three rotation angles of the system by a vector.

17.4.2.7 STATUS

This command provides the animator with a listing of the characteristics of particle systems

17.4.3 Evolution blocks and attributes

For each particle system, an animation block called EVOLUTIONx (where x is the system number) is activated. It controls the initial attributes of each new particle generated and global attributes like "rates of change." The blocks are activated by an interactive command as follows:

EVOLUTIONx <initial time><duration> <parameters>

There are 17 attributes which define the evolution of particle systems:

MPART:	average number of new particles at each frame
VPART:	standard deviation of the number of particles
MVIE:	average particle lifetime
VVIE:	standard deviation of particle lifetime
MSIZE:	average particle size at creation
VSIZE:	standard deviation of particle size
RSIZE:	particle size rate
MVELO:	average particle velocity at creation
VVELO:	standard deviation of particle velocity
RVELO:	particle velocity rate
MTRANS:	average particle translucency at creation
VTRANS:	standard deviation of particle translucency
RSIZE:	particle translucency rate
MCOL:	average particle color at creation
VCOL:	standard deviation of particle color
RCOL:	particle color rate
WIND:	wind velocity

References

Titles that are preceded by an asterisk are not referred to in the text

*Abram AG, Westover L, Whitted T (1985) Efficient alias-free rendering using bit-masks and look-up tables. Proc. SIGGRAPH '85, Computer Graphics 19(3):53-59

*Ahuja N, Schachter BJ (1981) Image models. Computing Surveys 13(4):373-397

Akima H (1970) A new method of interpolation and smooth curve fitting based on local procedures. Journal of the ACM 17(4):589 602

Amanatides J (1984) Ray tracing with cones. Proc. SIGGRAPH '84, Computer Graphics 18(3):129-135

*Amanatides J , Fournier A (1984) Ray casting using divide and conquer in screen space. Proc. Intern. Conf. Engineering and Computer Graphics, Beijing

*Aoki M, Levine MD (1978) Computer generation of realistic pictures. Computer and Graphics 3:149-161

Aono M, Kunii TL (1984) Botanical tree image generation. IEEE Computer Graphics and Applications 4(5):10-34

Appel A (1967) The notion of quantitative invisibility and the machine rendering of solids. Proc. ACM National Conf., pp387-393

Appel A (1968) Some techniques for shading machine rendering of solids. Proc. SJCC, AFIPS, Reston, Va. 32:37-45

*Appel A (1976) Hidden line elimination for complex surfaces. IBM Technical Disclosure Bulletin 18(11):3873-3876

Appel A, Rohlf FJ, Stein A (1979) The haloed line effect for hidden line elimination. Proc. SIGGRAPH '79, Computer Graphics 13(3):151-157

*Arnaldi B, Bouatouch K, Priol T (1985) LGRC:Un langage pour la synthèse d'images. IRISA Publ. No270, Rennes

Arnaldi B, Priol T, Bouatouch K (1987) A new space subdivision method for ray tracing CSG modelled scenes. The Visual Computer (to appear)

*Artzy E, Frieder G, Herman GT (1980) The theory, design, implementation and evaluation of a three-dimensional surface detection algorithm. Proc. SIGGRAPH '80, Computer Graphics 14(3):2-9

*Atherton P (1978) Polygon shadow generation with an application to solar rights, M.S. thesis, Cornell University

Atherton PR (1983) A scan-line hidden surface removal procedure for constructive Solid Geometry. Proc. SIGGRAPH'83, Computer Graphics 17(3):73-82

Atherton P, Weiler K, Greenberg D (1978) Polygon shadow generation. Proc. SIGGRAPH '78, Computer Graphics 12(3):275-281

*Badler NI, Bajcsy R (1978) Three-dimensional representations for computer graphics and computer vision. Proc. SIGGRAPH'78, Computer Graphics 17(3):153-161

Badler NI, O'Rourke J, Toltzis (1979) A spherical representation of the human body for visualizing movement. Proc. IEEE 67(10):1397-1403

Badler NI, Smoliar SW (1979) Digital representations of human movement. ACM Computing Surveys 11(1):19-38

Baecker R (1969) Picture-driven animation, Proc. Spring Joint Computer Conference. AFIPS Press, 34:273-288

*Baecker R (1979) Digital video display systems and dynamic graphics. Proc. SIGGRAPH'79, Computer Graphics 13(2):286-292

Baer A, Eastman C, Henrion M (1979) A survey of geometric modeling. Research report, 66. Institut of Physical Planning, Carnegie Mellon University

Ballard DH (1981) Strip trees:a hierarchical representation for curves. Comm.ACM 24(5):310-321

Barnhill RE, Riesenfeld RF (1974) Computer aided geometric design., Academic.

Barnhill RE (1983) A survey of the representation and design of surfaces. IEEE Computer Graphics and Applications 3(7):9-16

Barr AH (1981) Superquadrics and angle-preserving transformations. IEEE Computer Graphics and Applications 1(1):11-22

Barr AH (1984) Global and local deformations of solid primitives. Proc. SIGGRAPH '84, Computer Graphics 18(3):21-30

Barr AH (1984a) Decal projections. ACM SIGGRAPH '84 course notes on Mathematical of Computer Graphics

Barr AH (1986) Ray tracing deformed surfaces. Proc. SIGGRAPH '86, Computer Graphics 20(4):287-296

Barros J, Fuchs H (1979) Generating smooth 2D monocolor line drawings on video displays. Proc. SIGGRAPH'79, Computer Graphics 13(2):260-269

Barsky BA (1981) Computer-aided geometric design:a bibliography with keywords and classified index. IEEE Computer Graphics and Applications 1(3):67-109

Barsky BA (1984) A description and evaluation of various 3-D models. IEEE Computer Graphics and Applications 4(1):38-52

Barsky BA, Beatty JC (1983) Local control of bias and tension in beta-splines. ACM Transactions on Graphics 2(2):109-134

*Barsky BA, Beatty JC (1983) Controlling the shape of parametric B-spline and beta-spline curves. Proc. Graphics Interface '83. Edmonton, pp223-232

Barsky BA, DeRose T (1985) The beta2-spline:a special case of the beta-spline curve and surface representation. IEEE Computer Graphics and Applications 5(9):46-58

Barsky BA, Fournier A (1982) Computational techniques for parametric curves and surfaces. Proc. Graphics Interface '82. Toronto, pp57-71

Barsky BA, Fournier A, Schoeler P, Thalmann D (1985) Introduction to computer graphics. Tutorial Notes, Graphics Interface '85, Montreal

*Bass DH (1981) Using the video lookup table for reflectivity calculations. Computer Graphics and Image Processing 17:249-261

Batson RM, Edwards E, Eliason FM (1975) Computer generated shaded relief images. Journal Research U.S. Geol. Survey 3(4):401-408

Baumgart BG (1975) A polyhedron representation for computer vision. Proc. AFIPS Conf. 44:589-596

Beatty JC, Booth KS, Matthies LH (1981) Revisiting Watkins algorithm. Proc. Canadian Man-Computer Communications Society Conference '81, Waterloo, pp359-370

Beckmann P, Spizzichino A (1963) The Scattering of electromagnetic wave from rough surfaces. MacMillan, New York, pp1-33,123-129

*Beretta G, Nievergelt J (1981) Scan conversion algorithms revisited. Proc. Intern. Conf. Research and Trends in Document Preparation Systems, ETH, Lausanne, pp77-80

Bergeron P (1986) Une version générale de l'algorithme des ombres projetées de Crow basée sur le concept de volumes d'ombre, MSc thesis, University of Montreal, department of Computer Science

Bergman L, Fuchs H, Grant E, Spach S (1986) Image rendering by adaptive refinement. Proc. SIGGRAPH '86, Computer Graphics 20(4):29-38

Berk T, Browston L, Kaufman A (1982) A new color-naming system for graphics languages. IEEE Computer Graphics and Applications 2(3):37-44

Berk T, Browston L, Kaufman A (1982a) A human factors study of colour notation systems for computer graphics. Comm. ACM 25(8):547-550

*Beutler FJ (1970) Alias-free randomly timed sampling of stochastic processes. IEEE Trans. on Information Theory IT-16(2):147-152

Bézier P (1972) Numerical control-mathematics and applications. Wiley, London

Bier EA, Sloan KR (1986) Two-part texture mappings. IEEE Computer Graphics and Applications 6(9):40-53

Billingsey (1975) Noise considerations in digital image processing hardware. Springer-Verlag, New York

Bishop G, Weimer DM (1986) Fast Phong shading. Proc. SIGGRAPH '86, Computer Graphics 20(4):103-106

Blinn JF (1977) Models of light reflection for computer synthesized pictures. Proc. SIGGRAPH '77, Computer Graphics 11(2):192-198

Blinn JF (1978) Simulation of wrinkled surfaces. Proc. SIGGRAPH '78, Computer Graphics 12(3):286-292

*Blinn JF (1978a) Computer display of curved surfaces. PhD thesis, University Utah

Blinn J (1982) Light reflection functions for simulation of clouds and dusty surfaces. Proc. SIGGRAPH '82, Computer Graphics 16(3):21-29

Blinn J (1982a) A generalization of algebraic surface drawing. ACM Transactions on Graphics 1(3):235-256

*Blinn J (1982b) Systems aspects of computer image synthesis and animation. SIGGRAPH '82 Tutorial Notes, Boston

Blinn JF, Newell ME (1976) Texture and reflection in computer generated images. Comm. ACM 19(10):362-367

Bloomenthal J (1983) Edge inference with applications to antialiasing. Proc. SIGGRAPH'83, Computer Graphics 17(3):157-162

*Bloomenthal J (1984) A representation for botanical trees using density distributions. Proc. International Conf. on Engineering and Computer Graphics Beijing

Bloomenthal J (1985) Modeling the mighty maple. Proc. SIGGRAPH '85, Computer Graphics 19(3):305-311

*Bloomenthal J (1986) Nature at New York Tech. IEEE Computer Graphics and Applications 6(5):4-5

Blum R (1979) Representing three-dimensional objects in your computer. BYTE, May Issue, pp14-29

Böhm W, Farin G, Kahmann J (1984) A survey of curve and surface methods in CAGD. Computer-aided Geometric Design 1:1-60

*Booth KS, Forsey DR, Paeth AW (1986) Hardware assistance for z-buffer visible surface algorithms. IEEE Computer Graphics and Applications 6(11):31-39

Borto AG (1975) Modeling natural phenomena with cellular automata. PhD thesis, University of Michigan, Ann Arbour

Bouknight WJ (1970) A procedure for the generation of 3-D half-toned computer graphics presentations. Comm. ACM 13(9):527-536

Bouknight WJ, Kelley K (1970) An algorithm for producing half-tone computer graphics presentations with shadows and moveable light sources. Proc. SJCC, AFIPS 36:1-10

Bouville C (1985) Bounding ellipsoids for ray-fractal intersection. Proc. SIGGRAPH '85, Computer Graphics 19(3):45-52

Bouville C, Dubois JL, Marchal I (1984) Generating high quality pictures by ray-tracing. Proc. EUROGRAPHICS '84, Manchester, North Holland, pp161-177

Boyse JW, Gilchrist JE (1982) GMSolid:interactive modeling for design and analysis of solids. IEEE Computer Graphics and Applications 2(2):27-40

*Braid IC (1975) The synthesis of solids bounded by many faces. Comm.ACM 18(4):209-216

Braid IC, Hillyard RC, Stroud IA (1980) Stepwise construction of polyhedra in geometric modelling. In.Brodie KW (ed) Mathematical Methods in Computer Graphics and Design , Academic, London, pp123-141

Bresenham JE (1977) An incremental algorithm for digital display of circular arcs. Comm. ACM 20(2):100-106

*Bronsvoort WF, van Wijk JJ, Jansen FW (1984), Two methods for improving the efficiency of ray casting in solid modelling. Computer-aided Design 16(1)51-55

Bronsvoort WF, Klok F (1985) Ray tracing generalized cylinders. ACM Transactions on Graphics 4(4):291-303

Brossard A, Camarero R, Thalmann D (1985), Espaces de texture. MIRALab, University of Montreal

Brotman LS, Badler NI (1984) Generating soft shadows with a depth buffer algorithm. IEEE Computer Graphics and Applications 4(10):5-12

Brown CM (1982) PADL-2:a technical summary. IEEE Computer Graphics and Applications 2(2):69-84

Burgess M (1987) Introduction de la texture dans le langage MIRA-SHADING. MSc thesis, MIRALab, University of Montreal

Burk AW (1966) Editor's introduction in:Von Neumann. J Theory of self reproducing automata, University of Illinois Press

Burtnyk N, Wein M (1976) Interactive skeleton techniques for enhancing motion dynamics in key frame animation. Comm.ACM 19(10):564-569

Carey RJ, Greenberg DP (1985) Textures for realistic image synthesis, Computers and Graphics 9(2):125-138

Carlson WE (1982) An algorithm and data structure for 3D object synthesis using surface patch intersections. Proc. SIGGRAPH '82, Computer Graphics 16(3):255-263

Carpenter L (1984) The A-buffer, an antialiased hidden surface method. Proc. SIGGRAPH '84, Computer Graphics 18(3):103-108

Casciani T, Falcidieno B, Fasciolo G, Pienovi C (1984) An algorithm for constructing a quadtree from polygonal regions. Computer Graphics Forum 3:269-274

Catmull E (1974) Subdivision algorithm for computer display of curved surfaces. PhD thesis, University of Utah

Catmull E (1975) Computer display of curved surfaces. Proc. IEEE Conf. on Computer Graphics Pattern Recognition and Data Structures, pp11-17

Catmull E (1978) A hidden-Surface algorithm with anti-aliasing. Proc. SIGGRAPH'78, Computer Graphics 12(3):6-10

Catmull E (1984) An analytic visible surface algorithm for independent pixel processing. Proc. SIGGRAPH '84, Computer Graphics 18(3):109-115

Catmull E, Smith AR (1980) 3-D transformations of images in scanline orders. Proc. SIGGRAPH'80, Computer Graphics 14(3):279-285

Chellappa R, Kashyiap RL (1981) On the correlation structure of random field models of images. Proc. Pattern Recognition and Image Processing (PRIP) '81, pp574-576

Chellappa R, Kashyiap RL (1981a) Synthetic generation and estimation in random field models of images. Proc. Pattern Recognition and Image Processing (PRIP) '81, pp577-582

Chiyokura H, Kimura F (1984) A new surface interpolation method for irregular curve models. Computer Graphics Forum 3:209-218

Chiyokura H, Kimura F (1985) A method of representing the solid design process. IEEE Computer Graphics and Applications 5(4):32-41

Chomsky N (1957) Syntactic structures. Mouton, The Hague

Christiansen HN, Sederberg TW (1978) Conversion of complex contour line definitions into polygonal element mosaics. Proc. SIGGRAPH'79, Computer Graphics 12(3):187-195

Clark DR (1981) Computers for imagemaking , Pergamon, Elmsford, N.Y.

Clark JH (1976) Hierarchical seometric models for visible surface algorithms. Comm.ACM 19(10):547-554

*Clark JH (1976a) Designing surfaces in 3-D. Comm. ACM 19(8):454-460

*Clark JH (1979) A fast algorithm for rendering parametric surfaces. Proc. SIGGRAPH '79, Computer Graphics (supplement) 13(2):289-299

*Clark TL (1979a) Numerical simulations with a three-dimensional cloud model. J. of Atmospheric Sciences 36:2191

Cleary J, Wyvill BM, Birtwistle GM, Vatti R (1986) Multiprocessor ray tracing. Computer Graphics Forum 5(1):3-12

Cline A (1974) Curve fitting in one and two dimensions using splines under tension. Comm.ACM 17:218-223

Cohen E, Lyche T, Riesenfeld RF (1980) Discrete B-splines, subdivision techniques in computer-aided geometric design and computer graphics. Computer Graphics and Image Processing 14(2):87-111

Cohen MF, Greenberg DP (1985) The hemi-Cube:a radiosity solution for complex environments. Proc. SIGGRAPH '85, Computer Graphics 19(3):31-40

Cohen MF, Greenberg DP (1986) An efficient radiosity approach for realistic image synthesis. IEEE Computer Graphics and Applications 6(3):26-35

Cook RL (1981) A Reflection Model for Realistic Image Synthesis. MSc thesis, Cornell University

Cook RL (1984) Shade trees. Proc. SIGGRAPH '84, Computer Graphics 18(3).223-231

Cook RL (1986) Stochastic sampling in Computer Graphics. ACM Transactions on Computer Graphics 5(1):51-72

Cook RL, Porter T, Carpenter L (1984) Distributed ray tracing. Proc. SIGGRAPH '84, Computer Graphics 18(3):137-145

Cook RL, Torrance KE (1981) A reflectance model for computer graphics. Proc. SIGGRAPH '81,Computer Graphics 15(3):307-316 (also published in:ACM Transactions on Graphics 1(1):7-24)

Coons SA (1964) Surfaces for computer aided design. Techn. Report, Design Division, MIT, Cambridge

Coquillart S (1985) An improvement of the ray tracing algorithm. Proc. EUROGRAPHICS '85, Nice, pp77-88

*Coquillart S, Gangnet M (1984) Shaded display of digital maps. IEEE Computer Graphics and Applications 4(7):35-42

Courter SM, Brewer JA (1986) Automated conversion of curvilinear wire-frame models to surface boundary models:a topological approach, Proc. SIGGRAPH '86, Computer Graphics 20(4):171-178

Crocker GA (1984) Invisibility Coherence for faster scan-line hidden surface algorithms. Proc. SIGGRAPH '84, Computer Graphics 18(3):95-102

Cross GR, Jain AK (1981) Markov random field texture models. Proc. Pattern Recognition and Image Processing (PRIP) '81, pp597-602

*Crow FC (1976) The aliasing problem in computer synthetized shaded images. Ph.D thesis, University of Utah

Crow FC (1977) The aliasing problem in computer-generated shaded images. Comm. ACM 20(11):799-805

Crow FC (1977a) Shadow algorithms for computer graphics. Proc. SIGGRAPH '77, Computer Graphics 13(2):242-248

Crow FC (1978) Shaded computer graphics in the entertainment industry. Computer, 11(3):11

Crow FC (1978a) The use of grayscale for improved raster display of vectors and characters. Proc. SIGGRAPH '78, Computer Graphics 12(3):1-5

Crow FC (1981) A comparison of antialiasing techniques. IEEE Computer Graphics and Applications 1(1):40-48

Crow FC (1982) A more flexible image generation environment. Proc.SIGGRAPH '82, Computer Graphics 16(3):9-18

Crow FC (1984) Summed-area Tables for texture mapping. Proc. SIGGRAPH '84, Computer Graphics 18(3):207-212

Crow FC (1986) Advanced image synthesis. In:Enderle G, Grave M and Lillehagen F (eds) Advances in computer graphics I, Springer

Csuri C, Hackathorn R, Parent R, Carlson W, Howard M (1979) Towards an interactive high visual complexity animation system. Proc. SIGGRAPH '79, Computer Graphics 13(2):289-299

Dadoun N, Kirkpatrick DG, Walsh JP (1982) Hierarchical approaches to hidden surface intersection testing. Proc. Graphics Interface '82, Toronto, pp49-56

*Deguchi H, Nishimura H, Yoshimura H, Kawata T, Shirakawa I, Omura K (1984) A parallel processing scheme for three-dimensional image creation. Proc. Intern.Symp.on Circuits and Systems, pp1285-1288

Deken J (1983) Computer images, Stewart, Tabori and Chang Publ., New York

Demongeot J, Goles E, Tchuente M (1985) Introduction dynamic behaviour of automata. In:Dynamical Systems and Cellular Automata, Academic

*Dill JC (1981) An application of color graphics to the display of surface curvature. Proc. SIGGRAPH '81, Computer Graphics 15(3):153-161

*Dippé MAZ, Swensen J (1984) An adaptive subdivision algorithm and parallel architecture for realistic image synthesis. Proc. SIGGRAPH '84, Computer Graphics 18(3):149-158

Dippé MAZ, Wold EH (1985) Antialiasing through stochastic sampling. Proc. SIGGRAPH '85, Computer Graphics 19(3):69-78

Doctor LJ, Torborg JG (1981) Display techniques for octree-encoded objects. IEEE Computer Graphics and Applications 1(3):29-38

Duff T (1979) Smoothly shaded renderings of polyhedral objects on raster displays. Proc. SIGGRAPH '79, Computer Graphics 13(2):270-275

Duff T (1985) Compositing 3-D rendered images. Proc. SIGGRAPH '85, Computer Graphics 19(3):41-44

*Dungan W, Stenger A, Sutty G (1978) Texture tile considerations for raster graphics. Proc . SIGGRAPH'78, Computer Graphics 12(3):130-134

Dungan W (1979) A terrain and cloud model image generation model. Proc. SIGGRAPH'79, Computer Graphics 13(2):143-150

Dutton RD, Brigham RC (1983) Efficiently identifying the faces of a solid. Computers and Graphics in Mechanical Engineering 7(2):143-147

Eastman CM, Weiler K (1979) Geometric modeling using the Euler operators. Proc. First Annual Conf. Computer Graphics CAD/CAM Systems, MIT, Cambridge, pp248-254

Encarnacao J (1970) Survey of and new solutions for the hidden-line problem. Proc. GC Symp. Delft, pp26-28

Faux ID, Pratt MJ (1979) Computational geometry for design and manufacture. Ellis-Horwood

*Feibush EA, Greenberg DP (1980) Texture rendering system for architectural design. Computer-aided Design 12(2):67-71

Feibush EA, Levoy M, Cook RL (1980) Synthetic texturing using digital filters. Proc. SIGGRAPH'80, Computer Graphics 14(3):294-301

Field D (1984) Two algorithms for drawing anti-aliased lines. Proc. Graphics Interface '84, Ottawa, pp87-95

*Fishman B, Schachter B (1980) Computer display of height fields. Computers and Graphics 5:53-60

Fiume E, Fournier A, Rudolph L (1983) A parallel scan conversion algorithm with anti-aliasing for a general-purpose ultracomputer. Proc. SIGGRAPH'83, Computer Graphics 17(3):141-150

Foley, J, Van Dam A (1981), Fundamentals of interactive Computer Graphics Addisson-Wesley

*Forrest AR (1972) On Coons and other methods for representation of curved surfaces. Computer Graphics and Image Processing 1(4):341-359

Forrest AR (1985) Antialiasing in practice. In:Earnshaw RA (ed) Fundamental algorithms for Computer Graphics Springer, pp113-134

Fortin D, Lamy JF, Thalmann D (1983) A multiple track animator system for motion synchronisation. Proc. SIGGRAPH/SIGART Interdisciplinary Workshop on Motion:Representation and Perception, Toronto, pp180-186

Fortin M, Léonard N, Magnenat-Thalmann N, Thalmann D (1985) Animating Lights and Shadows. In:Magnenat-Thalmann N, Thalmann D (eds) Computer-generated Images, Springer, pp.45-55

*Fournier A (1980) Stochastic modeling in computer graphics. Ph.D thesis, University of Texas at Dallas

Fournier A, Fussell D, Carpenter L (1982) Computer rendering of stochastic models. Comm. ACM 25(6):371-384

Fournier A, Grindal DA (1986) The stochastic modeling of trees. Proc. Graphics Interface '86, Vancouver, pp164-172

Fournier A, Milligan T (1985) Frame buffer algorithms for stochastic models. IEEE Computer Graphics and Applications 5(10):40-46; also in:Magnenat-Thalmann N, Thalmann D (eds) Computer-generated Images, Springer, pp35-44

Fournier A, Reeves WT (1986) A simple model of ocean waves. Proc. SIGGRAPH '86, Computer Graphics 20(4):75-84

Franklin WR (1980) A linear time exact hidden surface algorithm. Proc. SIGGRAPH '80, Computer Graphics 14(3):117-123

Franklin WR, Barr AH (1981) Faster calculation of superquadric shapes. IEEE Computer Graphics and Applications 1(3):41-47

*Fu KS (1980) Syntactic image modeling using stochastic tree grammars. Computer Graphics and Image Processing 12:136-152

Fu KS, Lu SY (1978) Computer generation of texture using a syntactic approach. Proc. SIGGRAPH '80, Computer Graphics 12(3):147-152

Fu KS, Lu SY (1979) Stochastic tree grammar for texture synthesis and discrimination. Computer Graphics and Image Processing 9:234-245

*Fuchs H, Goldfeather J, Hultquist JP, Spach S, Austin JD, Brooks FP, Eyles JG, Poulton J (1985) Fast spheres, shadows, textures, transparencies and image enhancements in pixel-planes. Proc. SIGGRAPH'85, Computer Graphics 19(3):111-120

Fuchs H, Kedem ZM, Naylor BF (1980) Optimal surface reconstruction from planar contours. Comm.ACM 20(10):693-702

*Fuchs H, Kedem ZM, Uselton SP (1977) On visible surface generation by a priori tree structures. Proc. SIGGRAPH'80, Computer Graphics 14(3):124-133

Fujimoto A, Iwata K (1983) Jag-free images on raster displays. IEEE Computer Graphics and Applications 3(9):26-34

*Fujimoto A, Perrott CG, Iwata K (1984) A 3-D graphics display system with depth buffer and pipe-line processor. IEEE Computer Graphics and Applications 4(6):1123

Fujimoto A, Tanaka T, Iwata K (1986) ARTS:accelerated ray-tracing system. IEEE Computer Graphics and Applications 6(4):16-26

*Gagalowicz A (1981) A new method for texture fields synthesis:some applications to the study of human vision. IEEE Trans. Pattern Analysis and Machine Intelligence 3(5):520-533

*Gagalowicz A, Pratt A, Fangeras OD (1981) Application of stochastic texture field models to image processing. Proc. IEEE 69(5):796-804

Galimberti R, Montanari U (1969) An algorithm for hidden-line elimination. Comm. ACM 12(4):206-211

*Gangnet M, Perny D, Coueignoux P (1982) Perspective mapping of planar textures. Proc. EUROGRAPHICS'82, Manchester, pp57-71

Ganter MA, Uicker JJ (1983) From wire-frame to solid geometric: automated conversion of data representations. Computers in Mechanical Engineering 2(2):40-45

Garber DD (1979) Models for texture analysis and synthesis. Technical report, USCIPI, N0910

Garber DD, Sawchuk AA (1981) Texture simulation using a best-fit model. Proc. Pattern Recognition and Image Processing (PRIP) ' 81, pp603-608

*Gardner GY (1979) Computer-generated texturing to model real-world features. Proc. 1st Interservice/Industry Training Equipment Conf., pp239-245

Gardner GY (1984) Simulation of natural scenes using textured quadric surfaces. Proc. SIGGRAPH '84, Computer Graphics 18(3):11-20

Gardner GY (1985) Visual simulation of clouds. Proc. SIGGRAPH '85, Computer Graphics 19(3):297-303

*Gardner GY, Berlin Jr EP, Gelman B (1981) A real-time computer image generation system using textured curved surfaces. Proc. 1981 Image Generation/Display Conf., pp60-76

Gardner M (1971) Mathematical puzzles and diversions. Penguin

Gargantini I (1982) Linear octrees for fast processing of three-dimensional objects. Computer Graphics and Image Processing 20(4):265-274

Gasson PC (1983) Geometry of spatial forms. Ellis Horwood

Giloi W (1978) Interactive Computer Graphics data structures, algorithms, languages. Prentice-Hall, Englewood Cliffs

Glassner AS (1984) Space subdivision for fast ray tracing. IEEE Computer Graphics and Applications 4(10):15-22

*Glassner AS (1984a) Computer graphics user's guide. Sams, Indianapolis

Glassner A (1986) Adaptive precision in texture mapping. Proc. SIGGRAPH '86, Computer Graphics 20(4):297-306

Goldman RN (1986) Urn models and beta-splines. IEEE Computer Graphics and Applications 6(2):57-64

Goodman TNT, Unsworth K (1986) Manipulating shape and producing geometric continuity in b-spline curves. IEEE Computer Graphics and Applications 6(2):50-56

Goldstein E, Nagel R (1971) 3D visual simulation. Simulation, 16(1):25-31

*Goldstein RA, Malin L (1979) 3D modeling with the syntha vision system. Proc. First Annual Conf. on Computer Graphics in CAD/CAM Systems, MIT, Cambridge, pp244-247

Goral CM, Torrance KE, Greenberg DP, Battaile B (1984) Modeling the interaction of light between diffuse surfaces. Proc. SIGGRAPH '84, Computer Graphics 18(3):213-222

Gouraud H (1971) Continuous shading of curved surfaces. IEEE Transactions on Computers C-20(6):623-629

*Gouraud H (1971a) Computer display of curved surfaces. PhD thesis, University of Utah

Grant C (1985) Integrated analytic spatial and temporal anti-aliasing for polyhedra in 4-space. Proc. SIGGRAPH '85, Computer Graphics 19(3):79-84

*Greenberg DP (1977) An interdisciplinary laboratory for graphics research and applications. Proc. SIGGRAPH '77, Computer Graphics 11(2):90-97

Greenberg DP, Marcus A, Schmidt AH, Gorter V (1982) The computer image. Addison-Wesley

*Greene N (1984) A method of modeling sky for computer animation. Proc. Intern. Conf. Engineering and Computer Graphics Beijing, pp297-300

*Greene N (1986) Environment mapping and other applications of world projections. IEEE Computer Graphics and Applications 6(11):21-29

*Greene N, Heckbert PS (1986) Creating raster omnimax images from multiple perspective views using the elliptical weighted average filter. IEEE Computer Graphics and Applications 6(6):21-27

Griffiths JG (1978) Bibliography of hidden-Line and hidden surface algorithms. Computer-aided Design 10(3):203-206

Guangnan N, Tanner P, Wein M, Bechtold G (1983) An algorithm for generating anti-aliased polygons for 3-D applications. Proc. Graphics Interface '83, Edmonton, pp23-32

Gupta S, Sproull R (1981) Filtering edges for gray-scale displays, Proc. SIGGRAPH'81, Computer Graphics 15(3):1-5

Haines EA, Greenberg DP (1986) The light buffer: a shadow-testing accelerator. IEEE Computer Graphics and Applications 6(9):6-16

Hall RA, Greenberg DP (1983) A testbed for realistic image synthesis. IEEE Computer Graphics and Applications 3(8):10-19

Hamlin G, Gear C (1977) Raster-scan hidden-surface algorithm techniques. Proc. SIGGRAPH'77, Computer Graphics 11(2):206-213

Hanrahan P (1982) Creating volume from edge-vertex graphs. Proc. SIGGRAPH'82, Computer Graphics 16(3):77-84

Hanrahan P (1983) Ray tracing algebraic surfaces. Proc. SIGGRAPH '83, Computer Graphics 17(3):83-90

Hanrahan P (1986) Using caching and breadth-first search to speed up ray-tracing. Proc. Graphics Interface '86, Vancouver, pp56-61

Haralick RM (1979) Statistical and structural approaches to texture. Proc.IEEE 67(5):786-804

Harrington S (1983) Computer graphics:a programming approach. McGraw-Hill

Haruyama S, Barsky BA (1984) Using stochastic modeling for texture generation. IEEE Computer Graphics and Applications 4(3):7-19

Hassner M, Sklansky J (1980) The use of Markov random fields as models of texture. Computer Graphics and Image Processing 12:357-370

Hearn D, Baker MP (1986) Computer graphics. Prentice Hall, Englewood Cliffs

*Heckbert PS (1983) Texture mapping polygons in perspective. NYIT Computer Graphics Lab Tech memo #13

*Heckbert PS (1986) Survey of texture mapping. IEEE Computer Graphics and Applications 6(11):56-67

*Heckbert PS (1986a) Filtering by repeated integration. Proc. SIGGRAPH'86, Computer Graphics 20(4):315-321

Heckbert PS, Hanrahan P (1984) Beam tracing polygonal objects. Proc. SIGGRAPH '84, Computer Graphics 18(3):119-127

Hedelman H (1984) A data flow approach to procedural modeling. IEEE Computer Graphics and Applications 4(1):16-26

*Hégron G (1985) Synthèse d'images:algorithmes élémentaires. Dunod, Paris

Herbison-Evans D (1978) NUDES-2:a numeric utility displaying ellipsoids solids. Proc. SIGGRAPH '78, Computer Graphics 12(3):354-356

Herbison-Evans D (1980) Rapid raster ellipsoid shading. Computer Graphics 13(4):355-361

Hillyard R (1982) The build group of solid modelers. IEEE Computer Graphics and Applications 2(2):43-52

Hodges LF, McAllister DF (1985) Stereo and alternative-pair techniques for display of computer-generated images. Proc. Trends and Applications, Washington DC, IEEE Computer Society, pp107-115

Hodges LF, McAllister DF (1985a) Technology and techniques for stereoscopic display of computer generated images. IEEE Computer Graphics and Applications 5(9):38-45

*Horn BKP (1981) Hill shading and the reflectance map. Proc. IEEE 69(1):14-47

*Hourcade JC, Nicolas A (1983) Inverse perspective mapping in scanline order onto non-planar quadrilaterals. Proc. EUROGRAPHICS '83, pp309-319

*Hourcade JC, Nicolas A (1985) Algorithms for antialiased cast shadows. Computers and Graphics 9(3):259-265

*Hubschmann H, Zucker S (1981) Frame-to-frame coherence and the hidden surface computation:constraints for a convex world. Proc. SIGGRAPH '81, Computer Graphics 15(3):45-54

Huitric H, Nahas M (1985) B-Spline surfaces:a tool for computer painting. IEEE Computer Graphics and Applications 5(3):39-47

*Hutchinson J (1981) Fractals and self-similarity. Indiana Univeristy Journal of Mathematics 30:713-747

Idesawa M (1973) A system to generate a solid figure from a three view. Bull. JMSE, 16:216-225

Immel DS, Cohen MF, Greenberg DP (1986) A radiosity method for non-diffuse environments. Proc. SIGGRAPH '86, Computer Graphics 20(4):133-142

*Jacklins CL, Tanimoto SL (1980) Octrees and their use in representing three-dimensional objects. Computer Graphics and Image Processing 14(3):249-270

*Jackson JH (1980) Dynamic scan-converted images with a frame buffer display device. Proc. SIGGRAPH '80, Computer Graphics 14(3):163-169

Jansen FW (1984) Data structures for ray tracing. Computer-aided Design and Geometry, pp57-73

*Jansen FW, van Wijk JJ (1984) Previewing techniques in raster graphics. Computers and Graphics 8(2):149-161

*Jarvis JF, Judice CN, Ninke WH (1976) A survey of techniques for the display of continuous tone pictures on bilevel displays. Computer Graphics and Image Processing 5:13-40

*Jones CB (1971) A new approach to the hidden line problem. The Computer Journal 14(3):232-237

Joy KI, Bhetanabhotla MN (1986) Ray tracing parametric surface patches utilizing numerical techniques and ray coherence. Proc. SIGGRAPH '86, Computer Graphics 20(4):279-284

Kajiya JT (1982) Ray tracing parametric patches. Proc. SIGGRAPH '82, Computer Graphics 16(3):245-254

Kajiya JT (1983) Tutorial notes on ray tracing, SIGGRAPH'83, Detroit

Kajiya JT (1983a) New techniques for ray tracing procedurally defined objects. Proc. SIGGRAPH '83, Computer Graphics 17(3):91-102; also in:ACM Transactions on Graphics 2(3):161-181

Kajiya J (1984) Ray tracing volume density. Proc. SIGGRAPH '84, Computer Graphics 18(3):165-173

Kajiya JT (1985) Anisotropic reflection models. Proc. SIGGRAPH '85, Computer Graphics 19(3):15-21

Kajiya JT (1986) The rendering equation. Proc. SIGGRAPH '86, Computer Graphics 20(4):143-150

Kaplan MR (1985) Space tracing:a constant time ray tracer. Tutorial on State of the Art in Image Synthesis, SIGGRAPH '85, San Francisco

Kaplan M, Greenberg DP (1979) Parallel processing techniques for hidden surfaces removal. Proc. SIGGRAPH '79, Computer Graphics 13(3):300-307

Kaufman A (1986) Computer artist's color naming systems. The Visual Computer 2(4):255-260

*Kaufman A, Azaria S (1984) Texture synthesis languages for computer-generated images. Proc. 4th Jerusalem Conf. on Information Technology, pp174-179

Kaufman A, Azaria S (1985) Texture Synthesis techniques for computer graphics. Computers and Graphics 9(2):139-145

Kawaguchi, Y (1982) A morphological study of the form of nature. Proc. SIGGRAPH '82, Computer Graphics 16(3):223-232

Kay DS, Greenberg D (1979) Transparency for computer synthetized images. Proc. SIGGRAPH '79, Computer Graphics 13(2):158-164

Kay TL, Kajiya JT (1986) Ray-tracing complex scenes, Proc. SIGGRAPH '86, Computer Graphics 20(4):269-278

*Kelley KC (1970) A computer graphics program for the generation of half-toned images with shadows. MSc thesis, University of Illinois

Kirk DB (1986) The simulation of natural features using cone tracing. In:Kunii TL (ed) Advanced Computer Graphics Springer, Tokyo, pp129-143

*Klinger A, Dyer CR (1976) Experiments on picture representation using regular decomposition. Computer Graphics and Image Processing 5

Knowlton K (1981) Computer-aided definition, manipulation and depicture of objects composed of spheres. Computer Graphics 15(1):48-71

Knowlton K, Cherry L (1977) ATOMS, a three-D opaque molecule system. Computers and Chemistry 1(3):161-166

Kochanek DHU, Bartels RH (1984) Interpolating splines with local tension, continuity and bias control,.Proc. SIGGRAPH '84, Computer Graphics 18(3):33-41

Korein J, Badler N (1983) Temporal anti-aliasing in computer generated animation. Proc. SIGGRAPH'83, Computer Graphics 17(3):377-388

Kunii TL, Satoh T, Yamaguchi K (1985) Generation of topological boundary representations from octree encoding. IEEE Computer Graphics and Applications 5(3):29-38

Lafue G (1976) Recognition of three-dimensional objects from orthogonal views. Proc. SIGGRAPH'76, Computer Graphics 6(3):103-108

Laidlau DH, Trumbore WB, Hughes JF (1986) Constructive solid geometry for polyhedral objects. Proc. SIGGRAPH '86, Computer Graphics 20(4):161-170

Lane JM, Carpenter LC (1979) A generalized scan line algorithm for the computer display of parametrically defined surfaces. Computer Graphics and Image Processing 11, pp290-297

Lane JM, Carpenter LC, Whitted T, Blinn JF (1980) Scan line methods for displaying parametrically defined surfaces. Comm. ACM 23(1):23-34.

*Lane JM, Riesenfeld RF (1980) A theoretical development for the computer generation of piecewise polynomial surfaces. IEEE Trans Pattern Analysis and Machine Intelligence, PAMI-2(1):35-46

Lee ME, Redner RA, Uselton SP (1985) Statistically optimized sampling for distributed ray tracing. Proc. SIGGRAPH '85, Computer Graphics 19(3):61-67

*Levin JZ (1976) A parametric algorithm for drawing pictures of solid objects composed of quadric surfaces. Comm.ACM 19(10):555-563

Lindenmayer A (1968) Mathematical models for cellular interactions in development I and II. Journal of Theoretical Biology, 18:280-315

Liskov B, Zilles S (1974) Programming with abstract data types. Proc. SIGPLAN Symposium on Very High Level Languages, pp50-59

*Lispcomb J (1981) Reversed apparent movement and erratic motion with many refreshes per minute. Computer Graphics 14(4):113-118

Liu MC, Burton R, Campbell D (1984) A shadow algorithm for hyperspace. Computer Graphics World, July , pp51-59

Lobry C, Reder C (1985) Concerning the support of the solutions of certain automata. In:Dynamical Systems and Cellular Automata, Academic

Lossing DL, Eshleman AL (1974) Planning a common data base for engineering and manufacturing. Proc.SHARE XLIII

Magnenat-Thalmann N, Burgess M, Forest L and Thalmann D (1987) A Geometric Study of Parameters for the Recursive Midpoint Subdivision, Proc. Computer Graphics International '87, Karuizawa, Japan, pp.45-56

Magnenat-Thalmann N, Thalmann D (1981) A graphical extension of PASCAL based on graphical types. Software-Practice and Experience, 11:55-62

Magnenat-Thalmann N, Thalmann D (1983) The use of high level graphical types in the MIRA animation system, IEEE Computer Graphics and Applications 3(9)1983:9-16

Magnenat-Thalmann N, Thalmann D (1983a), Actor and camera data types in computer animation. Proc. Graphics Interface '83, Edmonton, pp203-210

Magnenat-Thalmann N, Thalmann D (1985) Area, spline-based and structural models for generating and animating 3D characters and logos. The Visual Computer 1(1):15-23

Magnenat-Thalmann N, Thalmann D (1985a) 3D computer animation:more an evolution problem than a motion problem. IEEE Computer Graphics and Applications 5(10):47-57

Magnenat-Thalmann N, Thalmann D (1985b) Computer animation: theory and practice. Springer, Tokyo

Magnenat-Thalmann N, Thalmann D (1985c) Subactor data types as hierarchical procedural models for computer animation, Proc. EUROGRAPHICS '85, Nice, pp121-128

Magnenat-Thalmann N, Thalmann D (1986) Building complex bodies:combining computer animation with CAD. Computers in Mechanical Engineering (CIME) 4(6):26-33

Magnenat-Thalmann, N, Thalmann, D (1986a) Three-dimensional computer animation based on simultaneous differential equations. Proc. Conf. Continuous Simulation Languages, San Diego, Society for Computer Simulation, pp.73-77

Magnenat-Thalmann N, Thalmann D (1986b) Special cinematographic effects using multiple virtual movie cameras. IEEE Computer Graphics and Applications 6(4):43-50

Magnenat-Thalmann N, Thalmann D (1987) The direction of synthetic actors in the film Rendez-vous à Montréal. IEEE Computer Graphics and Applications 7(12)

Magnenat-Thalmann N, Thalmann D, Béland S (1986), The integration of particle and polygon rendering using an A-buffer algorithm. Proc. EUROGRAPHICS '86, Lisboa, pp.161-169

Magnenat-Thalmann N, Thalmann D, Fortin M, Langlois L (1985) MIRA-SHADING:A language for the synthesis and the animation of realistic images. In: Kunii TL (ed) Frontiers in Computer Graphics Springer, Tokyo, pp.101-113

Magnenat-Thalmann N, Thalmann D, Fortin M (1985a) MIRANIM:an extensible director-oriented system for the animation of realistic images. IEEE Computer Graphics and Applications 5(3):61-73

*Mahl R (1972) Visible surface algorithm for quadric patches. IEEE Trans. Computers, C-21(1):1-4

Mandelbrot B (1971) A fast fractional gaussian noise generator. Water Resources Research, 7(3):543-553

Mandelbrot B (1975) Stochastic models for the earth's relief, the shape and fractal dimension of coastlines, and the number area rule for islands. Proc. National Acad.-Sc USA 72(10):2825-2828

Mandelbrot B (1977) Fractals:form, chance and dimension. WH Freeman, San Francisco

Mandelbrot B (1978) The fractal geometry of trees and other natural phenomena. In:Geometrical probability and biological structures:Bufon's 200th anniversary, Lecture Notes in Biomathematics 23, Springer, New York, pp235-249

Mandelbrot B (1982) The fractal geometry of nature. WH Freeman, San Francisco

Mandelbrot B (1982a) Comment on computer rendering of fractal stochastic models. Comm. ACM 25(3):581-582

Mandelbrot B, van Ness J (1968) Fractional brownian motions, fractional noises and applications. SIAM Review 10(4):422-437

Mantyla M (1983) Set operations of GWB. Computer Graphics Forum 2(2):122-134

Mantyla M (1984) Solid modeling:theory and applications. In:ten Hagen PJW (ed) EUROGRAPHICS Tutorials '83, Springer, pp391-425

Mantyla M, Sulonen R (1982) GWB:a solid modeler with Euler operators. IEEE Computer Graphics and Applications 2(7):17-30

Mantyla M, Takala T (1981) The geometric workbench (GWB) - an experimental geometric modeling system. Proc. EUROGRAPHICS '81, Darmstadt, North Holland, pp205-215

Markowski G, Wesley MA (1980) Fleshing out wire frames, IBM Journal of Research and Development, 24(5):582-597

Marshall R, Wilson R, Carlson W (1980) Procedure models for generating three-dimensional terrain. Proc. SIGGRAPH '80, Computer Graphics 14(4):154-159

*Maver TW, Purdie C, Stearn D (1985) Visual impact analysis -- modelling and viewing the natural and built environment. Computers and Graphics 9(2):117-124

Max NL (1979) ATOMLLL:- ATOMS with shading and highlights. Proc.SIGGRAPH '79, Computer Graphics 13(2):165-173

Max NL (1981) Vectorized procedural models for natural terrain:waves and islands in the sunset. Proc.SIGGRAPH '81, Computer Graphics 15(3):317-324

Max NL (1983) Computer representation of molecular surfaces. IEEE Computer Graphics 3(5):21-29

*Max NL (1983a) Computer graphics distortion for IMAX and OMNIMAX projection. Proc. Nicograph '83, pp137-159

Max NL (1986) Shadows for bump-mapped surfaces. In:Kunii TL (ed) Advanced Computer Graphics Springer, Tokyo, pp145-156

Max NL (1986a) Light diffusion through clouds and haze. Computer Vision Graphics and Image Processing 33:280-292

Max NL (1986b) Atmospheric illumination and shadows. Proc. SIGGRAPH '86, Computer Graphics 20(4):117-124

Max NL, Lerner DM (1985) A two-and-a-Half-D motion-Blur algorithm. Proc. SIGGRAPH '85, Computer Graphics 19(3):85-93

*Meagher D (1982) Geometric modeling using octree encoding. Computer Graphics and Image Processing 19:129-147

*Meyer GW, Greenberg DP (1980) Perceptual color spaces for computer graphics. Proc. SIGGRAPH'80, Computer Graphics 14(3):254-261

Mezei L, Puzin M, Conroy P (1974) Simulation of patterns of nature by computer graphics. Information Processing 74, pp52-56

*Miller GS, Hoffman CR (1984) Illumination and reflection maps:simulated objects in simulated and real environments. SIGGRAPH '84 :Advanced Computer Graphics Animation Seminar Notes

Miller GSP (1986) The definition and rendering of terrain maps. Proc. SIGGRAPH '86, Computer Graphics 20(4):39-48

*Modestino JW, Fries RW, Vickers AL (1980) Stochastic image models generated by random tessellations in the plane. Computer Graphics and Image Processing 12:74-98

Monne J, Schmitt F, Massaloux D (1981) Bidimensional texture synthesis by Markov chains. Computer Graphics and Image Processing 17:1-23

*Moravec HP (1981) 3D graphics and the wave theory. Proc. SIGGRAPH'81, Computer Graphics 15(3):289-296

Mortenson ME (1985) Geometric modeling. Wyley, New York

Mudur SP (1985) Mathematical elements for computer graphics. In: Enderle G, Grave M, Lillehagen F (eds) Advances in computer graphics I, Springer, Heidelberg

Murch GM (1986) Human factors of color displays. In: Hopgood FRA, Hubbold RJ, Duce DA (eds)Advanced computer graphics II, Springer, Heidelberg, pp1-27

*Myers AJ (1975) An efficient visible surface algorithm. Report to the National Science Foundation, Grant Number DCR 74-00768A01

Nakamae E, Harada K, Ishizaki T, Nishita T (1986) A montage method:the overlaying of the computer generated images onto a background photograph. Proc. SIGGRAPH '86, Computer Graphics 20(4):207-214

Nemoto K, Omachi T (1986) An adaptive subdivision by sliding boundary Surfaces for fast ray tracing. Proc. Graphics Interface '86, Vancouver, pp43-48

Newell ME (1975) The utilization of procedure models in computer synthetized images. PhD dissertation, University of Utah

Newell ME, Blinn JF (1977) The progression of realism in computer generated images. Proc. ACM National Conf., pp444-449

Newell ME, Newell RG, Sancha TL (1972) A new approach to the shaded picture problem. Proc. ACM National Conf., p443-450

Newman WM, Sproull RF (1973) Principles of interactive computer graphics. McGraw-Hill

Nielson GM (1974) Some piecewise polynomial alternatives to splines under tension. In: Barnhill RE, Riesenfeld RF (eds) Computer aided Geometric Design Academic, pp209-236

Nielson GM (1984) A locally controllable spline with tension for interactive curve design. Computer Aided Geometric Design 1:199-205

Nielson GM (1986) Rectangular v-splines. IEEE Computer Graphics and Applications 6(2):35-40

Nishimura H, Ohno H, Kawata T, Shirakawa I, Omuira K (1983) LINKS-1:A parallel pipelined multimicrocomputer system for image creation. Proc. 10th Symp. on Computer Architecture, SIGARCH '83, pp387-394

*Nishita T, Nakamae E (1974) An algorithm for half-Tone representation of three-dimensional objects. Proc. Information Processing Society of Japan 14:93-99

Nishita T, Nakamae E (1983a) Half-tone representation of three-dimensional objects illuminated by area sources or polyhedron sources. Proc. IEEE Compsac, Chicago, pp237-242

*Nishita T, Nakamae E (1983) A perspective depiction of shaded time. Proc. I4th Intern. Symp. on the use of Comp. for Env. Eng. Related to Build, p565

Nishita T, Nakamae E (1985) Continuous tone representation of three-dimensional objects taking account of shadows and interreflection. Proc. SIGGRAPH '85, Computer Graphics 19(3):23-30

Nishita T, Nakamae E (1986) Continuous tone representation of three-dimensional objects illuminated by sky light. Proc. SIGGRAPH '86, Computer Graphics 20(4):125-132

Nishita T, Okamura I, Nakamae E (1985) Shading models for point and linear sources. ACM Transactions on Graphics 4(2):124-146

Norton A (1982) Generation and display of geometric fractals in 3-D. Proc. SIGGRAPH'82, Computer Graphics 16(3):61-67

Norton A, Rockwood AP, Skolmoski PT (1982) Clamping:a method of antialiasing textured surfaces by bandwidth limiting in object space. Proc. SIGGRAPH '82, Computer Graphics 16(3):1-8

Nowacki H (1979) Curve and surface generation and fairing. In: Computer aided design modelling, systems engineering, CAD-systems, Springer, Berlin, pp137-176

Okino N, Kakazu Y, Morimoto M (1984) Extended depth-buffer algorithms for hidden-surface visualization. IEEE Computer Graphics and Applications 4(5):79-88

Oppenheim AV, Shafer RW (1975) Digital signal processing. Prentice Hall, Englewood Cliffs

Oppenheimer PE (1986) Real time design and animation of fractal plants and trees. Proc. SIGGRAPH '86, Computer Graphics 20(4):55-64

O'Rourke J, Badler NI (1979) Decomposition of three-dimensional objects into spheres. IEEE Transactions on Pattern Analysis and Machine Intelligence 1:295-306

Overhauser AW (1968) Analytic definition of curves and surfaces by parabolic blending, Techn. Report No SL 68-40, Ford Motor Co. Scient. Lab.

Parent RE (1977) A system for sculpting 3-D data. Proc. SIGGRAPH'77, Computer Graphics 11(2):138-147

*Parke FI (1980) Simulation and expected performance of multiple processor z-buffer systems. Proc. SIGGRAPH'80, Computer Graphics 14(3):48-56

Peachey DR (1985) Solid texturing of complex surfaces. Proc. SIGGRAPH '85, Computer Graphics 19(3):279-286

Peachey DR (1986) Modeling waves and surf. Proc. SIGGRAPH '86, Computer Graphics 20(4):65-74

*Peachey DR (1986a) PORTRAY - an image synthesis system. Proc. GRAPHICS Interface '86, Vancouver, pp.37-42

*Peitgen HO, Richter PH (1986) The beauty of fractals. Springer, Berlin

*Perlin K (1984) A Unified texture/reflectance model. SIGGRAPH '84 :Advanced Image Synthesis Seminar Notes

Perlin K (1985) An image synthesizer. Proc. SIGGRAPH '85, Computer Graphics 19(3):287-296

Phong Bui-Tuong (1973) Illumination for computer-generated images. Ph.D thesis, University of Utah

Phong Bui-Tuong (1975) Illumination for computer-generated Pictures. Comm.ACM 18(6):311-317

*Phong Bui Tuong, Crow FC (1975) Improved rendition of polygonal models of curved surfaces. Proc. 2nd USA-Japan Computer Conf

Piller E (1980) Real-time raster scan unit with improved picture quality. Computer Graphics 14(1-2):35-38

*Piper T, Fournier A (1984) A hardware stochastic interpolator for raster displays. Proc. SIGGRAPH '84, Computer Graphics 18(3):83-91

Pitteway M, Watkinson D (1980) Bresenham's algorithm with gray scale. Comm. ACM 23(11):625-626

Plunkett DJ, Bailey MJ (1985) The vectorization of a ray-tracing algorithm for improved execution speed. IEEE Computer Graphics and Applications 5(8):52-60

Porter TK (1978) Spherical shading. Proc. SIGGRAPH ' 78, Computer Graphics 12(3):282-285

Porter TK (1979) The shaded surface display of large molecules. Proc. SIGGRAPH'79, Computer Graphics 13(2):234-236

Porter T, Duff T (1984) Compositing digital images. Proc. SIGGRAPH '84, Computer Graphics 18(3):253-259

Potmesil M, Chakravarty I (1981) A lens and aperture camera model for synthetic image generation. Proc. SIGGRAPH'81,Computer Graphics 15(3):297-305

Potmesil M, Chakravarty I (1982) Synthetic image generation with a lens and aperture camera model. ACM Transactions on Graphics 1(2):85-108

Potmesil M, Chakravarty I (1983) Modeling motion blur in computer-generated images. Proc. SIGGRAPH'83, Computer Graphics 17(3):389-399

Potter TE, Wilmert KD (1975) Three-dimensional human display model. Computer Graphics 9(1):102-110

Purgathofer W (1986) A statistical method for adaptive stochastic sampling. Proc. EUROGRAPHICS '86, Lisboa, North Holland, pp145-152

Reeves WT (1981) Inbetweening for computer animation utilizing moving point constraints. Proc. SIGGRAPH'81, Computer Graphics 15(3):263-269

Reeves WT (1983) Particle systems—a technique for modeling a class of fuzzy objects. Proc. SIGGRAPH '83, Computer Graphics 17(3):359-376

Reeves WT, Blau R (1985) Approximate and probabilistic algorithms for shading and rendering structured particle systems. Proc. SIGGRAPH '85, Computer Graphics 19(3):313-322

Renner G (1984) Conventional elements of engineering drawings - free form curves. Proc. EUROGRAPHICS '84, North Holland, pp59-72

Requicha AAG (1977) Mathematical models of rigid solid objects. Tech.Memo, No28, Production Automation Project, University of Rochester

Requicha AAG (1980) Representations for rigid solid. Computing Surveys 12(4):437-464

Requicha AAG, Voelcker HB (1977) Boolean operations in solid modeling. Tech. Memo No26, Production Automation Project, University of Rochester

Requicha AAG, Voelcker HB (1982) Solid modeling:a historical summary and contemporary assessment. IEEE Computer Graphics and Applications 2(2):9-24

Requicha AAG, Voelcker HB (1983) Solid modeling:current status and research directions. IEEE Computer Graphics and Applications 3(7):25-37

Riesenfeld RF, Cohen E, Fish RD, Thomas SW, Cobb ES, Barsky BA, Schweizer DL, Lane JF (1981) Using the Oslo algorithm as a basis for CAD/CAM geometric modelling. Proc. National Computer Graphics Association (NCGA) 81, pp345-356

Roberts LG (1964) Machine perception of three dimensional solids. In:Tippet JT (ed) Optical and Electro-optical Information Processing, MIT, Cambridge, pp159-197

*Robertson PK, O'Callaghan JF (1985) The applications of scene synthesis techniques to the display of multidimensional image data. ACM Transactions on Graphics 4(4):247-275

Rogers D, Adams JA (1976) Mathematical elements for computer graphics. McGraw-Hill

Rogers D (1985) Procedural elements for computer graphics. McGraw-Hill

Romney GW (1970) Computer assisted assembly and rendering of solids. Computer Science Department, University of Utah, TR-4-20

Rossignac JR, Requicha AAG (1986) Depth buffering display techniques for constructive solid geometry. IEEE Computer Graphics and Applications 6(9):29-29

Roth SD (1982) Ray casting for modeling solids. Computer Graphics and Image Processing 18(2):109-144

Rubin SM, Whitted T (1980) A 3-dimensional representation for fast rendering of complex scenes. Proc. SIGGRAPH '80, Computer Graphics 14(3):110-116

Sabella P, Wozny MJ (1983) Toward fast color-shaped images of CAD/CAM geometry. IEEE Computer Graphics and Applications 3(8):65

Sarraga RF (1982) Computation of surface areas in GMSolid. IEEE Computer Graphics and Applications 2(7):65-70

Schachter BJ, Ahuja N (1979) Random pattern generation process. Computer Graphics and Image Processing 10:95-114

Schachter BJ (1980) Long crested wave models. Computer Graphics and Image Processing 12:187-201

Schachter BJ (1983) Generation of special effects. In: Computer Image Generation. John Wiley, New York, pp155-172

*Schmitt A (1981) Time and space bounds for hidden line and surface algorithms. Proc. EUROGRAPHICS '81, Darmstadt, North Holland, pp43-56

Schmitt FJM, Barsky BA, Du W (1986) An adaptative subdivision method for surface-fitting from sampled data. Proc. SIGGRAPH '86, Computer Graphics 20(4):179-188

Schmitt F, Maitre H, Clainchard A, Lopez-Kram J (1985), Acquisition and representation of real object surface data. SPIE Proc. Biostereometrics '85 Conf, 602

Schmitt F, Massaloux D (1981) Texture synthesis using a bidimensional Markov model. Proc. Pattern Recognition and Image Processing (PRIP) '81, pp593-596

Schoeler P, Fournier A (1986) Profiling graphic display systems. Proc. Graphics Interface '86, Vancouver, pp49-55

Schoenberg IJ (1946) Contributions to the problem of approximation of equidistant data by analytic functions. Quaterly Applied Mathematics 4(1):45-99 and 112-141

Schumacker RA, Brand B, Gilliland M, Sharp W (1969) Study for applying computer-generated images to visual simulation. AFHRL-TR-69-14, US Air Force Human Resources Lab

Schweikert D (1966) An interpolation curve using splines in tension. J. Math. and Phys. 45:312-317

Schweitzer D (1983) Artificial texturing:an aid to surface visualisation. Proc. SIGGRAPH'83, Computer Graphics 17(3):23-29

Schweitzer D, Cobb ES (1982) Scanline rendering of parametric surfaces. Proc. SIGGRAPH'82, Computer Graphics 16(3):265-271

Sears KH, Middleditch AE (1984) Set-theoretic volume model evaluation and picture-plane coherence. IEEE Computer Graphics and Applications 4(3):41-46

Sechrest S, Greenberg DP (1982) A visible polygon reconstruction algorithm. ACM Transactions on Graphics 1(1):25-42

Sederberg TW, Anderson DC (1984) Ray tracing of Steiner patches, Proc. SIGGRAPH '84, Computer Graphics 18(3):159-164

Sederberg TW, Parry SR (1986) Free-form deformation of solid geometric models. Proc. SIGGRAPH '86, Computer Graphics 20(4):151-160

*Shelley KL, Greenberg DP (1982) Path specification and path coherence. Proc. SIGGRAPH'82, Computer Graphics 16(3):157-166

Shoup RG (1973) Some quantization effects in digitally generated pictures. Proc. Society for Information Display Intern. Symposium, p58

*Smith AR (1980) Incremental rendering of textures in perspective. SIGGRAPH'80:Animation Graphics Seminar Notes

Smith AR (1983) Digital filmmaking. Abacus 1(1):28-45

*Smith AR (1983a) Digital filtering tutorial for computer graphics. Introduction to Computer Animation Seminar Notes, SIGGRAPH '83, Detroit

Smith AR (1984) Plants, fractals and formal languages. Proc. SIGGRAPH '84, Computer Graphics 18(3):1-10

Sparrow EM, Cess RD (1978) Radiation heat transfer. Hemisphere

Speer LR, DeRose TD, Barsky BA (1985) A theoretical and empirical analysis of coherent ray-tracing. In: Magnenat-Thalmann N, Thalmann D (eds)Computer-generated Images, Springer, Tokyo, pp11-25

Steinberg HA (1984) A smooth surface based on biquadratic patches. IEEE Computer Graphics and Applications 4(9):20-23

Sutherland IE, Hodgman GW (1974) Reentrant polygon clipping. Comm.ACM 17, p43

Sutherland IE, Sproull RF, Schumacker RA (1974) A characterization of ten hidden-surface algorithms. Computing Surveys 6(1):1-55

Sweeney MAJ, Bartels RH (1986) Ray tracing free-form B-spline surfaces. IEEE Computer Graphics and Applications 6(2):41-49

Szabo NS (1978) Digital image anomalies:static and dynamic. Proc. Symposium Society of Photo-Optical Instrumentation Engineers, 162:Visual Simulation and Realism, pp11-15

*Tamminen M, Karonen O, Mantyla M (1984) Ray casting and block model conversion using a spatial index. CAD 16(4):203-208

Tamminen M, Sulonen R (1982) The EXCELL method for efficient geometric access to data. Proc. 19th Design Automation Conference, IEEE Computer Society, pp345-350

Tezenas du Montcel B, Nicolas A (1985) An illumination model for ray-tracing. Proc. EUROGRAPHICS '85, Nice, North Holland, pp63-75

Thalmann D (1986), A lifegame approach to surface modeling and rendering. The Visual Computer 2(6):384-390

Thalmann D, Magnenat-Thalmann N (1979) Design and implementation of abstract graphical data Types. Proc. Compsac '79, Chicago, IEEE Computer Society, pp519-524

Thalmann D, Magnenat-Thalmann N (1986) Artificial Intelligence in Three-Dimensional Computer Animation. Computer Graphics Forum 5(4):341-348

Thalmann D, Magnenat-Thalmann N, Bergeron P (1982) Dream Flight:a fictional film produced by 3D computer animation. Proc. Computer Graphics '82, Online Conf., London, pp353-368

*Torrance KE, Sparrow EM (1966) Polarization, directional distribution and off-specular peak phenomena in light reflected from roughened surfaces. Journal Opt. Soc. Am. 56(7):916-925

Torrance KE, Sparrow EM (1967) Theory for off-specular reflection from roughened surfaces. Journal Opt. Soc. Am. 57(9):1105-1114

Toriya H, Satoh T, Ueda K, Chiyokura H (1986) UNDO and REDO operations for solid modeling. IEEE Computer Graphics and Applications 6(4):35-42

Toth DL (1985) On ray tracing parametric surfaces. Proc. SIGGRAPH '85, Computer Graphics 19(3):171-179

Trowbridge TS, Reitz KP (1975) Average irregularity representation of a roughened surface for ray reflection. Journal Opt. Soc. Am. 65(5)5:531-536

Turkowski K (1982) Anti-aliasing through the use of coordinate transformations. ACM Transactions on Graphics 1(3):215-234

*Turkowski K (1986) Anti-aliasing in topological color spaces. Proc. SIGGRAPH'86, Computer Graphics 20(4):307-314

Van Wijk JJ (1984) Ray tracing objects defined by sweeping a sphere. Proc. EUROGRAPHICS '84, North Holland, pp73-82

Van Wijk JJ (1984a) Ray tracing objects defined by sweeping planar cubic splines. ACM Transactions on Graphics 3(3):223-237

Varady T, Pratt MJ (1984) Design techniques for the definition of solid objects. Computer Aided Geometric Design pp207-225

Verbeck CP, Greenberg DP (1984) A comprehensive light-source description for computer graphics. IEEE Computer Graphics and Applications 4(7):66-75

Von Neumann J (1966) Theory of self reproducing automata, University of Illinois Press

*Voss RF (1983) Fourier synthesis of Gaussian fractals:1/f noises, landscapes and flakes. Tutorial on State of the Art Image Synthesis, 10, SIGGRAPH'83, Detroit

Voss RF (1985) Random fractal forgeries. In:Earnshaw RA (ed) Fundamental Algorithms for Computer Graphics Springer, pp805-836

Vossler DL (1985) Sweep-to-CSG conversion using pattern recognition techniques. IEEE Computer Graphics and Applications 5(2):9-24

Walker RJ (1950) Algebraic curves. Springer, Berlin Heidelberg New York (reprint 1980)

Warn DR (1983) Lighting controls for synthetic images. Proc. SIGGRAPH'83, Computer Graphics 17(8):13-21

Warnock JA (1969) Hidden-surface algorithm for computer generated half-tone pictures. Univ of Utah Comp. Sc. Dept. ,TR 4-15, NTIS AD-753 671

*Warnock J, Wyatt D (1982) A device independent graphics imaging model for use with raster devices. Proc. SIGGRAPH'82, Computer Graphics 16(3):313-319

Watkins GS (1970) A real-time visible surface algorithm. University of Utah Comp. Sc. Dept., UTEC-CSc-70-101, NTIS AD-762 00

Weghorst H, Hooper G, Greenberg DP (1984) Improved computational methods for ray tracing. ACM Transactions on Graphics 3(1):52-69

Weil J (1986) The synthesis of cloth objects. Proc. SIGGRAPH '86, Computer Graphics 20(4):49-54

*Weiler K (1978) Hidden surface removal using polygon area sorting. MSc thesis, Cornell University

Weiler K, Atherton P (1977) Hidden surface removal using polygon area sorting. Proc. SIGGRAPH '77, Computer Graphics 11(2):214-222

*Weiman CFR (1980) Continuous anti-aliased rotation and zoom of raster images. Proc. SIGGRAPH'80, Computer Graphics 14(3):286-293

*Weinberg R (1981) Parallel processing image synthesis and anti-aliasing. Proc.SIGGRAPH'81, Computer Graphics 15(3):53-62

Whitted T (1980) An improved illumination model for shaded display. Comm. ACM 23(6):343-349

*Whitted T (1981) The causes of aliasing in computer generated images. SIGGRAPH'81:Advanced Image Synthesis Seminar Notes

*Whitted T (1981a) Hardware enhanced 3D raster display systems. Proc. Canadian Man-Computer Communication Conf., Waterloo, pp349-356

Whitted T (1983) Anti-aliased line drawing using brush extrusion. Proc. SIGGRAPH'83, Computer Graphics 17(3):151-156

*Whitted T (1985) The Hacker's guide to making pretty pictures. Course Notes:Image Rendering Tricks, SIGGRAPH'85 , San Francisco

Whitted T, DM Weimer (1981) A software test-bed for the development of 3-D raster graphics systems. Proc. SIGGRAPH'81, Computer Graphics 15(3):271-277, also in published in:ACM Transactions on Graphics 1(1):43-58

Williams L (1978) Casting curved shadows on curved surfaces. Proc. SIGGRAPH '78, Computer Graphics 12(3):270-274

Williams L (1983) Pyramidal parametrics. Proc. SIGGRAPH '83, Computer Graphics 17(3):1-11

Wolfram, S (1984) Cellular automata as models of complexity. Nature 311(4):419-424

*Woon P, Freeman H (1971) A procedure for generating visible line projections of solids bounded by quadric surfaces. Proc. IFIP Congress Information Processing, North Holland, pp1120-1125

Wordenweber B (1983) Surface triangulation for picture production. IEEE Computer Graphics and Applications 3(8):45-51

*Wylie C, Romney GW, Evans DC and Erdahl A (1967) Halftone perspective drawings by computer. Proc. AFIPS, Fall Joint Computer Conf. 31:49-58

*Wyvill B, Liblong B, Hutchinson N (1984) Using recursion to describe polygonal surfaces. Proc. Graphics Interface '84, Ottawa, pp167-171

Wyvill B, McPheeters C, Novacek M (1985) High level descriptions for 3D stochastic models. In:Magnenat-Thalmann N, Thalmann D (eds) Computer-generated Images, Springer, Tokyo, pp26-34

Wyvill B, McPheeters C, Wyvill G (1986) Animating soft objects. The Visual Computer 2(4):235-242

Wyvill G, Kunii TL (1985) A functional model for constructive solid geometry. The Visual Computer 1(1):3-14

Wyvill G, Kunii TL, Shirai Y (1986a) Space division for ray tracing in CSG. IEEE Computer Graphics and Applications 6(4):28-34

Wyvill G, McPheeters C, Wyvill B (1986b) Soft objects. In: Kunii TL (ed) Advanced Computer Graphics Springer, Tokyo, pp113-127

Wyvill G, McPheeters C, Wyvill B (1986c) Data structure for soft objects. The Visual Computer 2(4):227-234

Wyvill G, Pearce A, Wyvill B (1986d) The representation of water. Proc. Graphics Interface '86, Vancouver, pp217-222

Yamaguchi K, Kunii TL, Fujimura K (1984) Octree-related data structures and algorithms. IEEE Computer Graphics and Applications 4(1):53-59

*Yao FF (1980) On the priority approach to hidden-surface algorithms. Proc. 21st Annual Symp. on Foundations of Computer Science, pp301-307

Yaeger L, Upson C, Myers R (1986) Combining physical and visual simulation - creation of the planet Jupiter for the film "2010". Proc. SIGGRAPH '86, Computer Graphics 20(4):85-94

Yessios CI (1979) Computer drafting of stones, wood, plant and ground materials. Proc. SIGGRAPH'79, Computer Graphics 13(2):190-198

*Yokoi S, Yasuda T, Toriwaki J (1984) Simplified ray tracing algorithms for rendering transparent objects. Technical report, Dep. of Information Engineering, Nagoya University, Japan

Yokoyama R, Haralick RM (1978) Texture synthesis using a growth model. Computer Graphics and Image Processing 8:369-381

Youssef S (1986) A new algorithm for object oriented ray tracing. Computer Vision, Graphics and Image Processing 34:125-137

Subject index